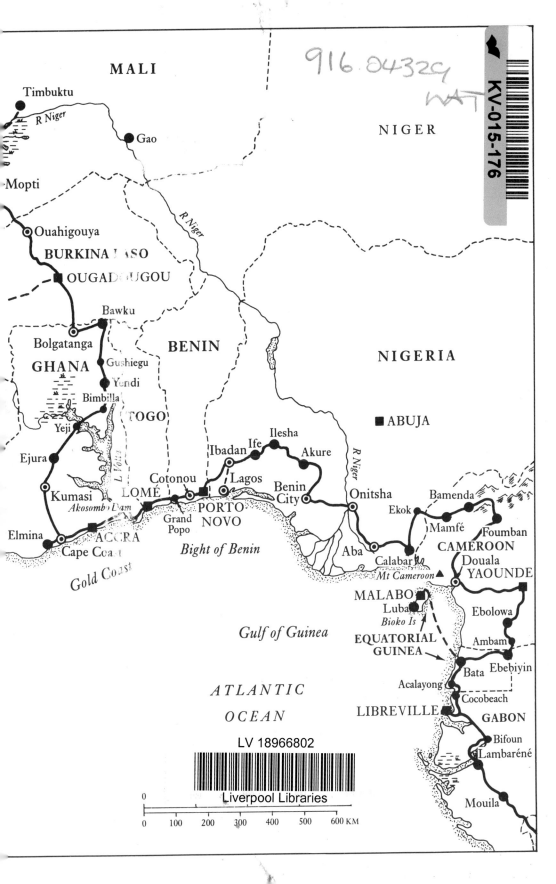

MALI

Timbuktu

R Niger

Gao

Mopti

NIGER

Ouahigouya

BURKINA FASO

OUAGADOUGOU

Bawku

Bolgatanga

GHANA

Gushiegu

Yendi

Bimbilla

BENIN

NIGERIA

ABUJA

TOGO

Yeji

Ejura

Ilesha

Ife

Ibadan

Akure

Cotonou

Kumasi

L Volta

LOMÉ

Lagos

Benin
City

Onitsha

Bamenda

Akosombo Dam

Grand
Popo

PORTO
NOVO

Ekok

Mamfé

Foumban

Elmina

ACCRA

Aba

Calabar

CAMEROON

Cape Coast

Bight of Benin

Mt Cameroon

Douala

YAOUNDE

Gold Coast

MALABO

Luba

Ebolowa

Bioko Is

Gulf of Guinea

EQUATORIAL
GUINEA

Ambam

Bata

Ebebiyin

ATLANTIC

Acalayong

OCEAN

Cocobeach

LIBREVILLE

GABON

Bifoun

Lambaréné

Mouila

0

0   100   200   300   400   500   600 KM

Esprit de Battuta

Esprit de Battuta

Alone Across Africa on a Bicycle

PAMELA WATSON

AURUM PRESS

First published in Great Britain 1999
by Aurum Press Ltd, 25 Bedford Avenue, London WC1B 3AT

A catalogue record for this book is available from the British Library.

ISBN 1 85410 629 5

Design by Roger Lightfoot
Typeset in 10/12 Ehrhardt by
Action Publishing Technology, Northgate Street, Gloucester
Printed and bound in Great Britain by MPG Books Ltd, Bodmin

For
Mum and Dad

Gwen and Frank Watson

For accompanying me all of the way

Contents

Acknowledgements

'I believe we are destined to meet the people who will support, guide and nurture us on our life's journey, each of them appearing at the appropriate time, accompanying us at least part of the way.'
ALICE WALKER

There are many people who helped me on my journey in Africa and to bring this book into reality, each of whom appeared at the appropriate time and supported me part, or all, of the way.

My deepest and heartfelt thanks go to the Africans of the villages and cities who welcomed me into their homes and lives, and who generously provided hospitality, security, friendship and fun. There are so many men and women and their families who remain unnamed, yet who I remember with great fondness, gratitude and respect. Truly, it was their open, warm welcomes and terrific smiles – even when I was crabby with their children! – which kept me going through the toughest parts of the journey. Their stories, and especially those of the hardworking, responsible women of Africa, provided the inspiration and passion to write this book. These people will travel with me, inspiring me, always.

There were many Europeans who also helped me before and during my journey, including, of course, my sponsors. Thanks to Gerry Bridge at Bridge The World Travel Centre for being the first businessperson to believe enough in me as an Adventurer to provide me with the flight to Dakar; to the principals of GEMINI Consulting for their financial support; to the late Professor Dean Berry, also of GEMINI, for his mentorship and practical help; to Michael Hirst of Hilton Hotels for some comfortable hotel nights; and also to Barbara Cassani at British Airways for the flight back from Dar Es Salaam and for the distracting crime novels along the way! Huge thanks also to Andy Booth of DHL and to the staff at DHL offices in Africa, who were friendly supporters of the journey and got all my goodie parcels and necessary spares to me.

Of course, I am especially grateful to all the folk at Shell who supported me and gave me their friendship. Without Catherine Shovlin energetically jumping to my aid in enlisting Shell and DHL's support at the eleventh hour before departure, my journey would have had a very different flavour and maybe a different outcome. Her ability to convince sceptical Shell country managers and DHL to lend their support to my 'dangerous' journey was amazing, and her willingness to spend eighteen months with my family and friends pestering her for news was incredible! Thank you very much, Catherine. Also a special thank you to all the people at the Shell marketing companies in Africa. At the outset, I had hoped for a poste restante address and a phone call home. Instead, I got very warm welcomes, bubbling enthusiasm to raise my flagging, tired spirit and fantastic insights into your countries.

Thanks to Kate Young and all the staff and volunteers at WOMANKIND Worldwide for your support and interest in my journey and book; to Hallam Murray for the initial inspiration; and to Ninon Asuni and Tom Bord of the Bicycle Workshop for a great bicycle and their friendship. And thanks again to my friend William, for accompanying me at least part of the way.

Many friends and ex-colleagues provided fabulous support and understanding not only during the bicycle journey but also during my other adventure – writing this book. Special thanks to Lorna Ness, Julie and John Frearson, Anne Kordic, Earl Foran, Doug Tigert, Bronwyn Scheuerer, Mary Ann McCabe, Tony Annis, Al Paul, Susannah Talbot, Adam Baines, Andrew Jamieson, Des Mouratides, Kate Rowley, Charles Morgan, David Parish and Ibrahim Seushi. Also, thanks to Christine Bielby and my brother, Andrew Watson for your encouragement and use of your flat! And thanks to everyone else who, through their words and deeds, has helped me pursue my wildest dreams.

Of course, the book may have never happened without the initial support and ongoing help from Sandy Grant and Fiona Hardie of Hardie Grant Books, nor without the clearly expressed ideas, professional help and enthusiasm of Anica Alvarez, my editor at Aurum Press. Thanks to all the staff at Aurum and Hardie Grant for your hard work and help. It's been exciting and fun!

Unexpectedly, given my lack of contact or knowledge with the firm or its people before my journey and the peripheral way in which I was involved with the company during my journey, in late 1997, I ended up working at Shell. I am indebted to my current boss Mac McDonald for allowing me, a new employee, to suspend my contract only months after starting work, and to take the unpaid leave to rewrite this book (again)! Thanks are also deserved for his ongoing flexibility as the book continues to demand my attention. I am grateful to Michael Megarry, again Catherine Shovlin, Déti Amegee and other friends and colleagues at Shell who have supported me and become involved in promoting the book and fund-raising for WOMANKIND Worldwide.

Last but not least, a massive thank you to my parents, Gwen and Frank Watson. Even though they may have wondered at my choice of dreams to follow, they have always unconditionally supported me – emotionally and practically – in everything I've done. Amongst so much else – like looking after my flat and cat, coming to Africa to meet me at the end of the journey and providing a home to retreat to afterwards – they have always had confidence in my ability to finish what I've begun, even when I've started doubting myself! Thank you for supporting, guiding and nurturing me on all my life's journeys.

PART ONE

Facing the Unknown

'She would tell herself that she was free, in face of the unknown, and she would recognise herself for what she was.'

– CECILY MACKWORTH describing Isabelle Eberhardt in
The Destiny of Isabelle Eberhardt

'Of the gladdest moments in human life, methinks, is the departure upon a distance journey into unknown lands. Shaking off with one mighty effort the fetters of Habit, the leaden weight of Routine, the cloak of many Cares and the slavery of Home, man feels once more happy. The blood flows with the fast circulation of childhood ... Afresh dawns the morn of life'

– RICHARD BURTON, journal entry, 2 December 1856,
quoted in Fawn M. Brodie's *The Devil Drives*

One

Travel with Prudence

Dakar, Senegal – Kounkané, Senegal

It is a common enough dilemma for travellers, but in Africa, finding a decent toilet is so unlikely that there is immense psychic pressure to put the moment off. However, bladder pressure always wins out. Eventually. Will I wait till I get to the bush, or will I see if there's a latrine here? I pushed the thought to the back of my mind. Again.

I looked around at the men sharing my breakfast table in the dusty market-place by the *gare routiére* – the bush-taxi station – of the remote border town of Kounkané.

This October morning, I was cycling for the Senegalese border, to enter the Republic of Guinea, an isolated country reputed not to have any serious postal service, or telecommunications, or paved roads. The next place with a post office would be Bamako in Mali, at least 1000 kilometres and one month away.

There was no need to catch the eyes of my breakfast companions – they were, as they had been doing throughout my reflections, staring at me.

'*Toubab!*' a newcomer called, setting off a new round of identification cries. '*Toubab*', I had learnt in Dakar, the capital of Senegal, three weeks ago, meant White. It was shouted as a statement rather than a query, sometimes as a greeting but more often as an amazed exclamation. To see a hot, rather unkempt, female, white cyclist, by herself, was a source of curiosity. It was reasonable and logical for people to be curious, I told myself. However, the labelling of me by my colour, the stir I caused by my presence and the constant staring were extremely disconcerting. I had this impact everywhere I had been so far in village Africa, and perhaps it should have been flattering to be the focus of attention, but I felt their relentless gazes as piercing probes examining my soul.

How imaginative I had become. Twenty-four days from Dakar, twenty-three nights in itinerant accommodation, 1000 kilometres of potholed but paved roads in Senegal and The Gambia. I was not finding adjustment from London Armchair Traveller to African Adventurer easy. Funny the things I missed most – clean flush toilets, refrigerated diet soft drinks, electricity to run a fan, bathroom shelves to hold my clothing and shampoo. Anonymity. Privacy. Solitude.

I took in the nearby cluster of children, neat in their school uniforms of blue shorts and white shirts, but also staring, giggling and pointing. Oh, no. Go away. As soon as the thoughts surfaced, I tried to squash them back, horrified by my impatience and inability to reach out. I managed a brief smile. There was not much action in this remote border town, and for now I was it.

My breakfast table, one of several, was located under the solid shade of a massive mango tree whose arthritically twisted branches reached out across the taxi park. Even the dark green of its thick, oily leaves was muted by the ubiquitous red dust. Flies buzzed around the patches of sticky wetness on the faded plastic tablecloth. It was so very hot, surely already in the high 20s, and only 8 a.m. Late again. I had intended to start by 7 a.m., then rest in the shade during the worst heat. No such luck. I had an upset stomach.

As my companions dunked their dry bread into coffee sweetened with condensed milk, my habit of pouring condensed milk on my bread and drinking my coffee black drew intrigued smiles. But my entertainment value was about to improve. My bowels were squelching like a washing machine in rinse cycle. I needed to ask for a loo. Now.

My hesitant, quiet request in French to the woman who served the break-

fast coffee and bread was relayed rapidly around the assembled men, and urgent discussions in Wolof broke out, opinions accompanied by hands pointing in entirely different directions. One of my breakfast companions took charge and summoned a young girl who immediately ran toward the taxi park. Was I to follow? The man raised his long-fingered, pale-brown palm. I took that to mean: wait. I stood, shuffled around, bent over, then crossed my legs. Tactics to lessen the pressure. Minutes passed, the men continued to talk in quiet Wolof, the main tribal and trading language of Senegal and The Gambia, and other tables picked up on the news. I felt hot and bothered. With each mention of the word '*toubab*', I knew the news of my request was spreading. Finally, the child returned with a key attached to a thin, twisted wire, and the man indicated that I should follow her. It was not so far – along the dusty road to the rear of what seemed to be an administrative building. In the far corner of the allotment stood a mud-brick building with the unmistakable dimensions of a toilet. A lock held the wooden door shut and there was some delay in opening it, allowing time for the following throngs of children to catch up and gather around. The *toubab* was going to the toilet.

I wondered how other Adventurers responded to this attention.

The smell in the toilet was appalling. In Africa, one is always assaulted by smells, not only by the invasive reek of rotting fish or shit, but also by the intense wafts of bougainvillea or frangipani. The smell in this latrine, not uncommonly, was so strong that I could taste it. So I held my breath. Looking down I could see white, crawling maggots at work in the cesspool. I looked away and concentrated on undressing with one hand, while keeping the door shut and clutching my precious roll of toilet paper with the other. I removed my bum bag and gripped it between my teeth. T-shirt and money belt were pulled up and held in place by a tensed upper arm. My shorts and undies stuck to perspiring skin as I tugged them down. It seemed to help if I stepped outside the situation and viewed it more dispassionately as someone else's problem. But it was hard to sustain the charade. Please don't let me drop my bum bag, I thought unhappily as I squatted over the hole. As I started breathing again and felt relief down below, my mind went back to London, to when it all began, to how I had come to be here in this horrible toilet.

The beginning was a rainy Monday night in London when I was at the Royal Geographical Society (RGS) in Kensington Gore. I loved the RGS. It was a musty world of explorers and adventure, my escapist bolthole from my more mundane world of management consulting. That night, I had left work early to come to listen to an eccentric Englishman who had made a bicycle journey from the northern- to southern-most tips of South America. He had clearly suffered, yet he was so intensely alive, and, during his talk, something – a latent masochistic gene, or perhaps my suppressed spirit – jerked free like a butterfly from its cocoon.

'That's what I'll do,' I thought suddenly, as a slide showed him staggering up a frosty Andes mountain slope, bicycle over his shoulders. 'I will cycle across Africa!'

I had backpacked and travelled by various means along the length of the White Nile from Alexandria in Egypt to Jinja in Uganda, and then on to Dar Es Salaam in Tanzania, at the age of twenty-three. In Alexandria, I had woken up to an Egyptian trying to force himself inside my sleeping bag; I had crossed a desert on the roof of a railway car under a hot Sudanese sun; I had been badly beaten in an attack in a remote village in southern Sudan; I had been arrested and questioned, forcefully, in the Uganda recovering from Idi Amin; and I had unwittingly walked with drug smugglers into Tanzania. Surely I had already lived a wild enough life and, at thirty-three, should have been more settled and concerned about career and children. Instead, for years, and more intensely in recent months, I had felt a strong and growing obsession to go back to Africa. To experience real life, to test my limits, to feel the world again – to be a Real Adventurer. I had considered driving a Land Rover from one end to the other, but discarded the idea as too expensive and impractical – I was not a mechanic, and nobody I knew wanted to come with me. 'Maybe, when I'd been younger,' they would explain. Or, 'Before the promotion ...' Or before my marriage, or the children, or the mortgage, or ...

That was their problem; I did not need them. Now, I knew I had the right idea, something I could do alone, and I felt a rush of blood and optimism. The fact that I had not actually done any cycle touring before was merely a small detail to overcome.

At least, while listening to the talk at the RGS, in my fog of enthusiasm and optimism, that is how it felt.

I liked cycling to work, I was sure I could learn to fix a bike, cycling would let me meet people and have more intimate experiences, I knew my body and mind had relatively high endurance levels, but mostly, deep in my soul, I just wanted to do it.

As I started announcing my plans, tentatively at first, to test people's reactions, friends were disbelieving. After all, as they explained quite accurately, 'You've been talking of travelling in Africa for years.' I realised then that, in telling friends, I was actually testing my own reaction and their disbelief confirmed how strongly I felt: this time I knew it was not just talk.

I was very impatient with the need of people to know why, possibly because there was no simple answer to be offered, probably because I did not want to probe, then, into my own motivations. Anyway, they seemed to get bored with my relating the story of my life, my passions and my neuroses as I searched for answers during conversations with them. After my *nth* waffling explanation and a friend's blank look, I settled for the shorter: 'Mid-life crisis.' It had the virtue of giving folks something concrete and quick, and a laugh, and possibly, just possibly, an element of truth.

Resigning from my job, however, was a major test of commitment. 'Oh, you are so courageous!' people said. I mainly dismissed it, but resigning was, and is, the real act of courage I admit to. I was a project manager, a senior corporate strategy consultant in London with an international firm, and I had a big investment in my career. After completing my Master of Business Administration in Canada, I had worked for ten years for global corporate clients on major issues of acquisition and divestiture, growth strategies, downsizing and change management. In fact, all the jargon business issues of the eighties and nineties. 'What do you do?' people would ask at parties. My reply, 'I'm a corporate strategy consultant,' brought blank stares from those outside the consulting world, but it didn't really matter – my friends of the time tended to be in the same business, and anyway, like so many of us, I defined myself by my work. After all, it was all I had time for.

But over the years, I increasingly felt I had lost sight of who I was behind the corporate façade. It made me wonder and it made me restless.

As the day approached when I planned to resign, I became extremely nervous, like I was about to do a bungee jump from a cliff – without the bungee cord. It felt like I was saying goodbye to a way of life, with the hope – but by no means the guarantee – of finding a new, more fulfilling life. I felt very anxious about whether or not I was doing the right thing.

My boss, who had married a childhood sweetheart, took clients to Ascot, drove a Bentley and had a country home, had always expressed dismay that others did not seek and find satisfaction in his kind of life – that prospect made me shudder! I did not have a problem with the luxury and comfort of his life; it was the entrapment to a particular, predictable lifestyle and narrow-mindedness that I found horrifying. I guess I should have expected his response to my resignation.

'Will you be joining a competitor or going into industry, Pamela?'

Life for this conservative and unimaginative man held few options.

But I was following a dream, and after I finished explaining that I was going to cycle from one side of Africa to the other, there was a long, long silence. Clearly, he had not expected my answer.

Then he said, 'But will this be good for your career, Pamela?'

I found his incomprehension soothing. For some reason, it was a balm to my own uncertainties about whether this was a good idea. I may not have known why I was doing this (as opposed to having a baby, buying an Alfa Romeo or climbing a mountain), but I did know there were more things in life than a career, and more to being me than living the associated life like my boss's. I was willing to take the risk to explore.

After resigning, I spent four months in London in practical preparation for the journey – I still had the mind-set of a project manager. My greatest enthusiasm was for route planning, and I spent many hours seeking out and talking to experienced adventure cyclists and pouring over the original maps of Victorian explorers in the RGS map room. I did not romanticise Africa (or so I thought at the time) – I had been there, after all. But I idealised Exploration and Adventure, and had the stories of Mungo Park, Sir Richard Burton, Mary Kingsley, Sir Samuel and Florence Baker, Henry Morton Stanley, Isabelle Eberhardt and, especially, Ibn Battuta etched in my yearning psyche. I did not want to follow in their actual footsteps – after all, they were only a short blip in African history. And I certainly did not want a 'fastest' or 'longest', Guinness Book of Records type of journey. I wanted to find reality, the reality of modern-day Africa, and hopefully, in doing so, I would find adventure and, maybe, even find myself.

My 15,000-kilometre cycling route would be a west to east crossing, start-ing in Dakar, Senegal, on the northern Atlantic coast of Africa, meandering through West, Central and East Africa, before finishing in Dar Es Salaam, the main Indian Ocean port in Tanzania, and the city where my first backpacking journey had ended successfully. A good portent, I thought; plus, discussions with other cyclists revealed that the best cycle journeys started and finished in place names starting with the same letter! You know, Birmingham to Belgrade, Manchester to Melbourne. So, I would cycle Dakar to Dar.

The route would wander where I wanted but generally take in the courses of two of the great African rivers, the Niger and the Zaire (now again known as the Congo, but for both the country and river, I shall use the names I knew them by). During my first journey in Africa, I had followed the course of the White Nile, and for years I had wanted to see and follow these other great African rivers. In fact, in Zaire I would even be forced to put the bicycle on a boat for an additional 1750 kilometres, as there weren't any roads from Kinshasa to Kisangani. (There was an alternative road route to Kisangani through the Central African Republic, but then I would barely experience Zaire. Even then, I knew Zaire would be a highlight not to be missed.)

Ibn Battuta, a fourteenth-century Moroccan from Fez, had travelled curi-ously for twenty-eight years throughout the known world, excluding Europe, of his era. He travelled as far eastwards as China, as well as venturing into West and East Africa. I wanted to travel like him, keen to encounter the people whose paths I crossed, willing to let Fate look after me as she willed. I would travel, I hoped, in his spirit, and I called my journey 'Esprit de Battuta'. In my mind, soaring on the stories from the books of the RGS library, I saw myself as having a grand expedition, a Real Adventure. Cycle forth Sir Richard Burton, a.k.a. Pamela Watson.

'What will you do when you get your period?' asked one friend. The RGS had no answers to that, and anyway, that was practicality gone mad; better not to think about some things, I reasoned, or I might never leave.

'How will you get fit?' asked my boyfriend William. I embarked on a regimen of going to the gym and cycling several times around Hyde Park daily, as well as cycling at weekends to his home in Reading. However, as I later discovered, this was a tame effort – I only became strong once I arrived in Africa and had to cope with pushing my heavy load on appalling roads.

'What will you do at night?' Also William. He only arrived on the scene after I had resigned from work. Part of my new life, I guess, although he too was a management consultant. It was a relationship entered casually because it was only temporary. I don't think he ever really believed I would leave him. Poor, dear, conservative, handsome William. I was still obsessed with my journey even when the relationship became more important to both of us than we had expected. And so I left him behind, hoping he might either follow or wait.

'I'll stay in villages!' I answered bravely. (In previous journeys to Africa, I had stayed in towns, but an African cyclist I met in London had suggested villages would be more appropriate.)

Really, I had not the faintest idea how I would be received.

'How will you repair the bike?' That was a very good question, as mechanics and repairs were definitely not my thing. I hated getting grease embedded in my skin and under my nails – mentally, at least, I was still in my career woman's world of facials at Fenwicks and designer clothing from Harvey Nichols. I was seemingly made with a nomadic spirit but fussy about dirt and grease! Although these were contradictions in my personality I wasn't ready to confront, I could face practical issues – so I tackled learning repairs by doing a bicycle-maintenance course at Tower Hamlets.

'What kind of bicycle will you use?' Everyone asked about this. Prior to this journey, I had a woman's touring bicycle, lightweight, good for wheeling through London traffic and accelerating around Marble Arch, but I definitely needed something else for Africa. Fortunately, I met Ninon Asuni, the owner of The Bicycle Workshop in Westbourne Grove, London, near my flat. She had grown up in Nigeria and gave lots of common-sense advice as I puzzled over which latest technological gizmos to design into my custom-built bicycle – a hybrid with a touring frame and a mountain-bike drive mechanism, handlebars and wheels.

'You need a strong bike,' she said. 'And a simple one – you want to be able to fix it with the kinds of materials and spares available in Africa.'

Luckily, I had the sense to listen. The Bicycle Workshop's Tom Bord built the frame using Reynolds 503 lightweight tubing. I decided against suspension for simplicity and to save weight. I chose a Suntour Microdrive system which had a low gear-ring profile and therefore, I hoped, less chance of getting tangled in branches or other vegetation on the back roads. I chose thumbshifters, the Suntour Accushift, and had twenty-one gears. This was not the popular brand at the time, but Ninon had the repair experience and said their systems had given her customers fewer problems. The real strength went into the wheels: Michelin tyres, with Kevlar lining to limit punctures, and double-walled Alesa wheel rims with eleven gauge spokes – so thick and tough that, despite most of my pannier load being over the rear wheel, I would only have one broken spoke the entire journey.

'What will you do when you get sick?' That was my parents, of course. Gwen and Frank. Still ready to send out Interpol if I went missing on one of my journeys. I had gone off the radar in Mexico once and they had indeed had Interpol – *and* the Red Cross *and* the Australian High Commission *and* the Canadian Mounties – all looking for me. Not that they found me. Besides, I was quite safe that time. Well, sort of – I had fallen down a well and broken my arm – but that's another story! What I did know was that my folks would worry no matter what I answered now.

'Mum, Dad …' even at thirty-three a kind of childish whine entered my voice. 'Don't worry … I'll carry medicines. I'll be injected, and anyhow, there's doctors everywhere. And I won't get sick.'

They weren't convinced.

As my plans began to take shape, I did start to have some inkling of the enormity of the undertaking. I wasn't letting on to anyone else I was worried, but well, this could be something big I had bitten off here. It was going to take a long time and a lot of effort and I started feeling that I wanted – and needed – a more serious purpose than Adventure or soft stuff like 'finding myself'.

As I searched for a relevant cause, I heard about WOMANKIND Worldwide, a charity based in London that helps women in developing countries to be empowered to help themselves. It focuses on providing grassroots assistance, that is, direct support relevant to the women's lives in rural or urban situations. They might help women with a health centre or literacy training or a credit fund or a grinding mill. But it is up to the women to identify their own needs – what will best help them.

I had once worked at the opposite end of the aid spectrum, leading a team evaluating public enterprises for privatisation in Madagascar, and had seen first hand the problems of bilateral and institutional large-scale aid; the aid that helps donor countries and not the recipients, the aid that goes into big men's pockets and bank accounts. I had nearly become an aid consultant, specialising in privatisation and commercialisation of public enterprises, but had seen the kind of cynical Africa specialist that bred. When there needed to be a choice between continuing in aid and economic development versus strategy consulting, I had been forced to recognise my own impatience. I decided to stick with the business culture I knew and instead support charities providing tangible outcomes at the grassroots level.

Thus, I liked WOMANKIND's approach and, at an intellectual level, it seemed appropriate that if I was crossing Africa, staying in villages, witnessing women's daily lives, I should be helping a charity that helped them. Initiatives to provide poor rural women with credit to fund their own businesses particularly intrigued me. But frankly, at this time, I had only a superficial understanding of and empathy for rural women's lives – I had seen the posters and read the literature. I hoped this would change.

The decision to raise money and generate publicity for WOMANKIND made the preparation and the journey far more complex. Where would I find sponsors? How would I get messages out of Africa? How would I get publicity?

But it became another kind of consulting assignment. I had an *Esprit de Battuta* logo designed, stickers and T-shirts made, ran a market stall to raise money for WOMANKIND, did research into companies that might be interested in supporting me and WOMANKIND, wrote letters and received many rejections.

'What's it like to be a lady of leisure?' asked one friend. I was insulted.

I wrote more letters – and received more rejections. British-based companies like supporting charities that help British people, especially children, I discovered. Hence, the popularity of supporting the Great Ormond Street Children's Hospital. It's a great cause, but how about donating to other causes, especially helping others outside Britain? I was becoming cynical even before I got to Africa. Once I got desperate – and on the telephone – I had better success at generating offers for access to services. Gerry Bridge, at Bridge The World Travel Centre in Camden Town, kindly gave me an air ticket to Dakar, and my friend Barbara Cassani at British Airways arranged for that airline to fly me back to London from Dar Es Salaam – if and when I eventually arrived. DHL agreed to let me send air express parcels into and out of Africa free of charge – crucial for getting spare parts. I even convinced my sceptical ex-boss to pay for the bicycle! However, I was still missing crucial ground support in Africa.

Then, luck, or fate, or the spirits I later came to know, helped me out.

I met Catherine Shovlin, a trustee of WOMANKIND, and a senior manager at Shell, just four weeks before my departure. It turned out that Shell had marketing offices in each of the seventeen countries I intended to visit except Equatorial Guinea, and even there, Shell had an agent. I don't think any other company had such a widespread network.

Did being associated with an oil company give me any qualms? Well, this was before the environmental criticisms of Shell's operating company in Nigeria were first raised publicly, and before the Ogoni people of Rivers State in Nigeria started using Shell to highlight their political oppression; and anyway, my whole career had been with big international companies. While there continues to be scope for most companies to improve their social responsibility, I don't think of companies as great or even sinister entities. They are just groups of people with money to spend – and my job had always been to influence those people and how and where they spend their money. Right then, I wanted them to spend their money on me. So, I didn't make any value judgements about Shell, the company. Primarily, I was interested in helping my cause and if these people were willing to assist, great. I certainly had no inkling of how our futures might eventually entwine.

Catherine was enthusiastic and asked me what help I wanted. Not wanting to scare the people in the operating companies, I kept my requests limited. I asked that when I arrived in the capital cities of each African country, I could go to the Shell office and make telephone calls to Catherine, who was to be my 'communications hub' for worried relatives and friends. Given my parent's track record, this was essential! I also asked to have access to a computer to write a newsletter for WOMANKIND, to be introduced to local businesswomen and women's groups where possible, to use the offices as a poste restante for advance parcels of money, spare parts and clothing – goodie parcels I sent out to myself ahead of time, and to be helped with getting onward visas. Within days, all the Shell marketing companies of Africa were lined up to provide the assistance I had requested. It was remarkable, but there was a catch.

'You can say we are supporting you, not sponsoring you,' said one office minion (okay, a manager) in London. 'Sponsorship implies too much responsibility, and we're not sure you'll survive.'

At least he was honest – I wasn't that certain I'd survive myself. It was a sign of the guardedness with which Shell and I entered our relationship, and of the limited expectations on both sides.

Then, suddenly, there were only three weeks to go until my flight to Dakar in mid-September. The countdown pressure was really on, but I was still spending my time planning, still a bloody project manager!

I had not, I now realised, actually accumulated a lot of practical touring cycling experience.

There was always some other task to do, some other task that seemed more important. What could be more important than pedalling practice?! It finally struck me that I better discover the gruelling nature of the long task I had ahead *before* I actually landed in Africa, so I used my Air Miles to fly to Nice in the south of France.

My 'gruelling' practice trip in late August was two weeks cycling around Provence.

Well, at least my bum was in the saddle.

I met some sexy Frenchmen who cried '*Bon courage!*' – have courage – as I cycled swiftly by on smooth tarmac surfaces, and at nights I pitched my tent in comfortable campgrounds and visited nearby restaurants to sample extremely good cheeses and wines. I had a wonderful time. No doubt, the last pleasures of a condemned woman. Even in my naïvety, I knew Africa would not be so easy

Then, even more suddenly, it was time to write a will, make tearful farewells to William and friends, get on a plane and just do it.

Africa. Senegal. Dakar.

Even once I was there, once *Esprit de Battuta* was actually starting, the journey still was not real to me. It was only a fun game that was, perhaps, starting to go a trifle too far.

To give myself an easy start to build my confidence, I had decided to do another practice trip, one where I could get a bit more African road-wise while still close to phones and cities, where I could get progressively fitter, could make up my mind about what equipment to carry and what to leave behind, and where I could still abort if it was really too awful. Dakar to St Louis return: 268 kilometres each way along the coast. I guessed it would be reasonably flat and the map indicated that it was sealed all the way. (Little did I know what a luxury tarmac would become.)

Shell helped by arranging for me to stay with the *gérant* – managers – of Shell service stations at intervals that stretched my existing endurance but which were in fact not too great. It actually turned out to be a very easy start: tarmac, electricity, fine cheese and sexy men calling '*Bon courage!*' Not that different from Provence!

The practice trip also had an unexpected consequence. It allowed time for the Shell staff to get to know about my journey and for me to get to know them. Everybody showed remarkable enthusiasm for what I was setting out to do. On the fateful day of my real departure, 2 October, I planned a quiet goodbye, but while inside the main office building – a fifties, stone-and-glass monument – the fire alarm sounded.

'What's that?!' I exclaimed to one of my friends, Balla Lo, the always effervescent commercial manager, who I had got to know well.

'That's for you!' he cried, and hurried me out the back entrance and then around to the front.

What a surprise! At least a hundred cheerful staff were assembled on the front steps. Men and women were dressed in rich and colourful traditional robes. On most days they wore dull western suits and dresses, but it was a Friday, the Moslem holy day, so traditional robes were worn. It seemed to add vibrancy and the first hints of authenticity to the occasion.

In retrospect, I realise I was dressed like a great white hunter ready for a safari: in white leather sneakers, khaki shorts, white T-shirt, and a wide-brimmed, rabbit-fur hat – an authentic Australian Akubra! No bicycle helmet – my logic was that if I was hit by African traffic, no helmet would save me, while a wide-brimmed hat would protect me from a more subtle enemy – the sun. My bicycle, still shining with the factory gleam, a handsome steed, was fully laden with two front panniers, a handlebar bag, two rear panniers and a top sack containing my camping gear – a staggering 40 kilograms. I had learned the perils of weight from my practice trips but the lesson had not yet sunk in; I still found many things to be utterly essential. I would learn. Slowly.

The *directeur général* (managing director) of Shell in Senegal, Roel van Zummeren, made a formal farewell speech in French. He was a tall Dutch man in a grey business suit, but despite his conservative appearance, his voice conveyed real enthusiasm and support for my journey.

'We all wish that you receive the *teranga* [welcome] of Senegal throughout your travels.'

They're treating me like a hero before I've done anything, I thought.

'May you always travel with prudence,' continued the *directeur général*. I appreciated his wise words and was comforted that he must believe I was going to survive. Suddenly, he offered me the microphone.

'*Merci*,' I stumbled along in Australian-accented French. My French had once let me work in Madagascar – I had been semi-fluent with poor grammar. Now it was rusty. 'Thank you for your wishes, and I promise to travel with prudence.'

There was a lot of good-natured laughter. I didn't think my French was *that* bad.

But I didn't have time to brood on that. It was time to mount my bicycle and cycle away to cries of '*Au revoir!*' and '*Bonne chance!*' – goodbye and good luck! People took photos and waved and cheered. It was sad, exciting and scary – a very addictive cocktail of emotions.

However, for the next hour, I was more focused on staying alive. To leave Dakar was an adventure in itself. I cycled past 8 kilometres of closely packed factories and shanty houses, through swarms of traffic and crowds of strolling folk. I coped with well-intentioned toots of greeting and shouts of '*Bonjour*', and breathtaking clouds of carbon monoxide. Vehicles ranged from well-maintained, air-conditioned, dark-windowed Mercedes, to trucks with loads of sacked produce teetering 5 metres above their flat beds, to Peugeot taxis stuffed with twelve or more people. Women selling watermelons, baskets, clay pots and tomatoes by the side of the road created busy pools of colour and, upon spying me, they also cried out.

'*Ça va?*' – How's it going?

'*Ça va bien!*' – It's going well! – I replied enthusiastically, as I waved, and wobbled, in return.

I was exhilarated! After four months of planning and of safe 'practice trips', I was finally on my way. I had committed to letting go, to the real journey, to the road across Africa.

A truck whooshed passed. Too close.

Whooah, Pamela, I thought. You don't want to be pet food. Take care. Remember, travel with prudence.

Within an hour, the people and traffic ebbed away.

I had a narrower stretch of tarmac, and although some of my adrenalin had subsided, sweat rivulets ran distractingly into my eyes, down my calves, and my back ached a little from the strain. My outstretched forearms were turning a beetroot pink. Nonetheless, with the waning traffic, I was once again content and in a lyrical frame of mind. The resurgence of nature was invigo-rating: the lush green grass blew in the silent wind, pregnant-looking baobabs promised a fertile land, even a burning sun in an empty blue sky was welcome. I was alone on the road, me and my heavily laden bike, setting off on our adventure.

Adventure, I meditated, as I settled into the slow tempo of cycling with 40 kilograms of baggage; surely I would find adventure on my planned route. Fifteen thousand kilometres through seventeen countries over twelve months.

'Oh my God,' I thought abruptly, a shiver running down my back. Finally, the journey seemed brutally real. 'What have I done?!'

I left the toilet to return to my audience, which now consisted of not only the children but also some fascinated young women. I tried to maintain a smile, easier now my bowels were empty and calm, but really, I thought prudishly, did they have no sense of letting someone have peace?

If I was such an adventurer, why was I so disturbed by staring kids and eating fish stew and rice and having to use a smelly latrine? Real adventurers would not think like this. I was very hung up that I was not behaving – and feeling – like a *Real* Adventurer. It will change, I told myself, just wait. But would it? And what was *real* adventure anyway?

In the twenty-four days and twenty-three nights since leaving Dakar, I had travelled according to my route and timetable, meeting my target of an average of 50 kilometres a day, five days a week (still a time-driven consultant). That was easy on the good roads of Senegal and even on the not-so-good roads of The Gambia. The Gambia was a tiny ex-British colony that stretched inland from the Atlantic Ocean for 400 kilometres in a narrow band between 24 and 48 kilometres wide, either side of the westward-flowing Gambia River. Surrounded by Senegal, cartographically, it seemed like a tampon! After entering The Gambia about 300 kilometres south of Dakar, via the small town of Kaolack and the border village of Karang, I travelled from Banjul, the laid-back and friendly capital on the Atlantic, eastward for nine slowly paced days alongside the river to the large regional centre of Basse-Santa-Su. From there, I had crossed back into southern Senegal at the remote and quiet town of Velingara. In both of these verdant and heavily populated countries I had briefly met some interesting people in the villages when I stopped for cooling drinks, I had been pursued relentlessly by children calling '*Toubab!*' and I had been consistently offered *teranga* – that warm 'welcome' I had been wished on my departure from Dakar. At nights, I had retreated into hotels, stayed with whites I'd met, or even, on a few occasions in Senegal, taken refuge in a Shell service station. In some ways, I was still clinging to Provence.

'Are you Pamela?' a Gambian voice asked in English, breaking my reflections as I returned to the breakfast table and my untouched bike. My French was already improving, but it was good to hear English in Senegal, a Francophone country.

Uncertainly, a little warily, I said 'Yes' to the young, vigorous-looking man. He was cleanly dressed in civvies and didn't look like a policeman, but how did he know my name?

'You are *the* Pamela? On the bicycle tour of Africa? I saw your picture in the *Observer*.' I understood now – a photo and article about my journey had been in a daily Gambian newspaper, and I burst into my first real smile of the day. 'I am very pleased to meet you,' said the man, offering me a huge grin and a guava. He had a wonderful smile and brilliant white teeth, and was quite short and muscular, like many Gambians.

Despite their obvious charms, I was generally being guarded with men I was meeting. Not much different from being in London. Still, in many encounters I was finding the first question was 'Are you married?' which, after I answered 'No', was followed by 'Will you marry me?' 'You don't even know my name!' I would exclaim. 'But I love you,' they answered, quite hurt.

Men. Exasperating creatures. Just the same everywhere, I guess. But some here in Africa were very handsome.

'My name is Seth,' said my new friend. As I looked harder, I decided Seth was very handsome indeed, with soft, curling eyelashes and deep, dark-brown eyes. For the moment, William was forgotten.

Seth was travelling to Guinea, too, and rummaged in his overstuffed totebag for a camera, then asked another man to take a photo of us. We laughed together and the spell of being an alien in an alien world was rapidly broken. Then, Seth spoke excitedly in Wolof, his common language with these villagers, to tell the others about my journey. My breakfast companions changed their intimidating silence to a rush of noisy questions.

An overloaded vehicle passed along the dusty street leaving a red cloud to descend on me and my smiling Gambian friend. We did not mind, but it acted as a reminder – it was time for me to leave. My irritability and pensiveness were forgotten and I was ready for another day of encounters with Africa and Africans.

I stood up from the breakfast table, reloaded my toilet paper in my handlebar bag and resolved to shed some of my load. Again. My cycling life was full of resolutions and I had been making this one since leaving Dakar. I started wheeling the bike towards the junction with the main road and the children came running behind.

'Goodbye, Pamela,' said Seth.

'Bon courage!' called the men from my breakfast table and those sitting on shady verandahs.

With a contented sigh, my stomach forgotten, handsome Seth waving at me, and adrenalin and caffeine once more surging through my veins, I lifted my bum onto the cycle seat and slid my foot into the pedal. Africa was great again and I was pleased I was here.

Then I saw the sign, a small, faded billboard on a corner store. A smiling couple, holding hands, were gazing into each others eyes, above a barely legible slogan. 'Love with Prudence', it said.

Prudence, I only now discovered, was a Senegalese brand of condoms.

Two

A Spirit Acts

Missara, Republic of Guinea – Labé, Republic of Guinea

From my breakfast (and toilet) stop at Kounkané, I cycled about 60 kilometres to the Senegalese border post. The rough, ochre laterite track edged by scrubby trees and rustling green grass proved lonely going. The previous day, a Senegalese man had recommended this back road to the border.

'On the main road to Medina Gounas there are too many lions, *madame*,' he had said. 'Take the road to Kounkané, and then to Missara, where you will enter Guinea. There, the chance of meeting lions is not so high.' But, on this back road, I could imagine lions slinking after me, and the track was as badly maintained as I had feared.

The border post was not even a village. It was just a collection of wooden shacks in a shady clearing, some selling coffee and bread, others selling enamel pots, clothing and plastic goods – things I was later to discover were hard to find in Guinea. It was quite a lively place for one so small, with women in traditional dress looking for bargains in the stalls. Most had babies strapped to their backs by fabric tightly wrapped around their middles and also had loads wrapped in cloths on their heads. Several battered bush taxis were parked opposite the stalls; their young drivers, in jeans and brightly coloured, local fabric shirts or faded T-shirts, drank coffee or touted for business. I let myself be led by youngsters to the immigration hut, but completing Senegalese departure formalities took some time. Despite my timetable, I was happy to pause; I only had a short stretch of no man's land before reaching the Guinean border at Missara. I was confident Missara would be a sizeable place – after all, I had been hearing about it for two days now.

'Are you *madame* or *mademoiselle?*' enquired the gaunt Immigration Officer. He had rather a cheeky grin and a manner of turning his head to one side when asking questions.

'Ah, *mademoiselle!*' he exclaimed, on hearing my reply. He turned his head again. 'Will you marry me?'

Men were indeed proving reassuringly predictable on this journey. I accepted tea instead.

When I did leave, it soon became clear that covering the 10 kilometres to Guinea would be very slow going, an unfortunate miscalculation with the sun

already low in the sky and temperatures cooling.

The meandering, narrow track required concentration, low gears and slow speed. As I reached my first junction, a scattering of tracks, like the fingers of a river near its mouth, spread before me. I paused, lost, unable to choose my way. Bicycle bells tinkled behind, and in a flash of pedal power, two men passed me. Quickly, I remounted and decided to use them as my pathfinders to the Republic of Guinea.

Once out in the tangled bush with them, alone, they seemed less trustworthy. Were they bandits leading me to their remote den? The bush was dense, and the track too muddied and potholed to allow for a fast exit. The men must have known I was following, but they showed no sign of greeting – no 'Ça va', no smile, no nod. Stares and a call of 'Toubab!' would have been quite welcome now.

I remembered a long time ago, on the other side of the African continent in Sudan, when I had been beaten up by a man who followed me out of a village to a remote spot. Cowering with my arms protecting my head, blows from a cattle-stunning stick striking my back, I bit at the hand of my lanky, glazed-eyed Shilluk attacker, screaming, running …

I shook myself to lose the memory, but on this dim afternoon, following these scruffy men, it wouldn't budge.

This memory and the thought of enduring another experience like that had been the recurring nightmare in London, too, but I had convinced myself that on the roads in Africa, there would always be villages around the next bend, and people in the fields, and I would be able to cycle faster than any would-be attackers. But this was a track in no man's land, not a main road. We had passed no houses or people for an hour, and the strength of these men and their unloaded bicycles made them faster. Much faster. Where were they taking me?!

The Guinean border post, it turned out. Not only were they *not* bandits, they were Guinean border officials!

Missara, the destination I had pictured as a comfortable village, was merely a dimly lit clearing in the tangled, vine-covered forest. I was to find that many of the border crossings I made were at remote places like this, and would learn that roads through no man's land were always awful. In future, I would allow more time, but now I was just grateful for reaching a refuge before dark – it was sunset, and night falls rapidly in Africa. Missara was even smaller and felt more isolated than the post I had passed through on the Senegalese side. Four women selling tiny piles of overripe tomatoes, desiccated oranges and scrawny chili peppers sat in a tiny market, with ramrod backs and legs straight out in front, wearing faded T-shirts and traditional wraps. There was none of the vibrancy or noise of the Senegalese side, and none of the same bright goods. A few men sat in the shadows of a large, waxy-leaved mango tree; a few others were gathered, talking and playing cards, near a row of small wood-and-thatch huts. They looked up, startled, as I entered the clearing. I paused, whipped back my hat – my still pristine Akubra – wiped my brow with grease- and dust-coated bicycle mitts and looked around.

Grubby children ran towards me, and in the compound behind one of the huts, a woman was rhythmically pounding away with her giant, wooden pestle, grinding millet. I listened to her regular beat and the barking of the mangy dogs, watched hens pecking at the ground and tried to ignore the children's stares and cries. I knew if I waited, the border entry officials would find me in this small place. My guides had gone to some nearby huts to chat with their mates, all sprawled on mats outside and apparently off-duty. Wearing jungle-fatigue trousers, T-shirts and thongs, Kalashnikovs casually looped over their shoulders, none looked inclined to move, all looked like bandits. And everybody looked so poor, much poorer than the Senegalese.

Soon, two men approached, regarding me with what seemed a mixture of awe and suspicion. The formalities started. My passport was handed over. One of the men regarded it intently, then handed it on to the other, who solemnly rifled through each page. I knew they would be looking for some reason to get a little extra cash, so I assumed an innocent air and chatted about my trip to disarm them, to get a laugh, a sign of humanity. It was my strategy for avoiding paying bribes or antagonising officials.

But these guys were having none of that. They remained serious and rather intimidating.

I produced my canny back-up strategy: a letter on a WOMANKIND letterhead that I had composed myself and had translated into French, telling people about my journey and requesting they give me every assistance.

Magic. They smiled – not my most friendly encounter, but at least they stamped me in.

'*Attendez le douanier*' – Wait for the customs officer, I was commanded sternly, so I retreated with my bike to a nearby shady, thatched cabana and played peekaboo with the assembled children.

Now that I knew I was safe, I could relax.

Le douanier did not cut a dashing figure. He was a middle-aged man, as dishevelled as the rest, but with a big belly over which his red-and-white-striped T-shirt constantly rode up. He too wore jungle-patterned trousers, and thongs that were repaired with string. He tried to look stern, but the effect was ruined by huge, kind, brown eyes. He made a thorough search of my panniers and asked questions about my marital status, but at least my spate of inane chatter broke through his official barriers.

Too well.

'My name is Otis, *mademoiselle*,' he volunteered, as he stamped my passport, yet another page used. I was alarmed at the consumption of pages by visas and stamps. How many countries could I cover before my passport would be filled? Could I make it to Nigeria where there was an Australian Embassy, the only one in West Africa? What if I couldn't? My worries were interrupted by Otis. 'You can put your tent up in my compound.' Very generous. Then he added, 'Or you could rest with me.'

We sat in the dark of Otis's compound. It was still humid, and I slapped at the mosquitoes biting around my ankles. However, being able to stretch my legs and knee joints, stiff after a day in the saddle, to support my sore back on a wooden-slat chair, which was angled like a deck chair, to enjoy occasional wafts of breeze over my newly washed, dry skin, and to feel the flapping of soft, cotton trousers, clean and dry against my badly scratched legs, was enough to make me feel that this was five-star accommodation. Perhaps it was not the Hilton, but already I luxuriated in small pleasures, and particularly after the afternoon's bumpy ride I needed softness. While rearranging my buttocks on the slats, I sought Otis's attention.

'Will all the roads in Guinea be like that one today?' I asked.

Otis was seated opposite me, just a dark shadow, his large body marked by a flickering candle on the table between us. He was plying me with fish stew and rice. We both had spoons for eating from a communal bowl, but he motioned me to eat more and shoved morsels of fish – a treat – towards my side of the bowl.

'Eat this, it is good for you,' I heard, mumbled through a mouthful.

He was clearly enjoying his food and did not seem to have heard my question. I leant forward and played at filling my fork with a ball of rice and then stabbing at the dried fish. I detested the strong taste and bone-filled texture of the fish, but it seemed to be the main source of protein in these parts. And, as a guest, I was often offered the best bits, like the head. It seemed rude not to eat what was considered an expensive delicacy. Looking at the fish on my fork, my stomach already heaving at the thought of having to swallow, I repeated my question, with plaintive emphasis. Cycling across Africa was not meant to be like an off-road experience, was it?

'Really, Otis, are all the roads in Guinea so awful?'

'Oh, more of the same,' said Otis, completely oblivious to my concern.

I cringed.

'Of course, when the French left, they took everything,' he said deeply, his face an unreadable, ghostly shadow in the candlelight. 'We got freedom in poverty,' he added without a trace of the irony or bitterness that I thought should be there but could not detect.

Guinea had suffered an appalling path from colonialism to freedom, and the consequences were still with Guineans. Sekou Touré, a Malinké who had risen to be head of the trade union movement, demanded independence from Charles de Gaulle in September 1958. France had offered its colonies, including Guinea, independence or membership of a Franco-African community, but in reality, the pressure to choose allegiance with France was immense.

Sekou Touré stood on a dais in Conakry and, famously, had declared to de Gaulle, 'We, for our part, have a first and indispensable need, that of dignity. Now, there is no dignity without freedom ... We prefer freedom in poverty to riches in slavery.'

De Gaulle was embittered. He immediately stopped all technical, economic and financial aid, and withdrew all French administrative personnel from Guinea; I was told stories of the French ripping out all equipment and spares, of them stripping all the administrative records, and of French private investors closing operations and quitting the country. Together, these acts ensured Guinea's total economic collapse.

Ultimately, Sekou Touré was also responsible for the inability of Guinea to pull itself up by its bootstraps. Understandably, after the French departure, he allied his government with Soviet Communists, but soon fell out with them, fearing their interference. I met a remarkable Frenchman in Guinea, M. Berçan, an old trade unionist who had stayed in the country during the Marxist years of closed borders – he had a Malinké wife and settled in Kankan. He spoke fondly of the Touré he knew as a young man, but admitted Touré eventually became paranoid and ill.

'He became obsessed with plots,' he told me as we ate *bifteck frites* – steak and chips, a real treat – at his shady, empty restaurant, 'and many Guineans fled his persecution into exile, mainly people from the other major tribes, the Fula of the Fouta Djalon and the Susu of the coast and south.'

In 1967, Touré adopted the Chinese path of cultural revolution and communal, state-run farming. It proved ruinous, and the country became dependent on food aid. Then, using the threat of foreign plots, he imposed terrible internal oppression. There were 'economy police' and spies everywhere, bloody purges of suspected opponents, a huge prison population and a mass exodus of refugees. In 1977, when Touré announced that all agricultural trade must pass through the state-run cooperatives, the market women, who survived on trading food, rebelled. On 27 August, now a revered public holiday, the women revolted, first in the capital, Conakry, then in provincial towns. Three governors were murdered in the general riots that followed, and Touré had to listen. He re-legalised petty trade and started making some overtures to restore a relationship with France. In 1984, after twenty-six years in power, Touré died from a heart attack. There was a spectacular funeral honouring him, yet only the next day there was a coup d'état, followed by celebration and dancing in the streets.

Guineans hate and love France, but they also have mixed feelings toward their hero and tormentor, Touré, particularly if they are not Malinké. One cannot go far in Guinea without knowing about Sekou Touré and the French past. For me, it explained a lot of the malaise.

'Now we are an open country with lots of tourists, and things will improve.' Otis had finished eating, and talked as he washed his hand in a bowl.

'We are a democracy now,' he said proudly, although I knew they were still planning their first presidential elections. He was keen to understand how Australia's democracy worked. All Guineans, I found, were hungry for information about 'outside', although many had no conception of the world, its geography and politics. Soon, I was explaining why Australia was not yet a republic (very hard to explain, particularly to a Guinean whose country had given up everything for freedom), and discussing the Westminster system of government, an intriguing thing to be doing in a clearing in a forgotten corner of Africa. It was to happen often, finding forest intellectuals, especially amongst the military – they were educated, then sent to some distant border post or checkpoint, and were eager for news and to talk about their favourite issues. These contacts provided a much-needed break from the endless repetition of 'the marriage question'.

However, it was difficult to speak in French through an incessant cough – I had caught my first dust cold. My lungs burnt and I had a harsh, rib-wrenching cough. During the day, my hands were busy holding the handlebars – to stay upright on the ruts – so I blew my nose not only without a tissue or but also without a hand to my nose. I just made a gutteral explosion of phlegm and let it fly to the road. Or wherever it landed. Yuk!

Otis called to an underling to bring me a cucumber to ease my bark, and the pause let my mind wander back to where it wanted to be: the issue of roads.

Could I really manage these tough conditions?

I had travelled African roads before, in vehicles, and knew they were rough, but they seemed worse on a bicycle. Why was I surprised?

Then another thought. What creatures were lurking in the scrub? My practice trip had been in Provence – no wild animals there. Nervously, I remembered again, 'There are too many lions, *madame*.' Why hadn't I thought of all this in London?

Having accepted an enormous cucumber, cut into chunks by Otis, I asked once more about the roads.

'You will be fine,' Otis said, perhaps a little impatiently, then in a different tone added: 'But you must beware of the spirits in the *brousse* – the bush.'

There was an interruption as a shadow moved closer to Otis and saluted. Orders were exchanged in the local language, and I drifted to an earlier warning I had received.

'Beware of the spirits, particularly in Guinea – in the bush, in the mountains, in the forests,' Balla Lo, my friend, the commercial manager at Shell in Senegal, had said before I had even left Dakar. 'They have many spirits in Guinea.' He was in his modern, air-conditioned office. A computer sat on his desk. 'Especially, beware of snakes and people without shadows – they are spirits, and people with turned-back feet – they are the devil.' I must have looked sceptical, which I was, for he added, 'We believe in these things …'

He told me of a time when he was a boy and had been coming home late through the dark streets of Dakar when he stopped for a piss. An old lady, white-skinned – 'All spirits are white-skinned,' he had said, as an aside – with hair to her waist and crouched over, her arms outstretched, came creeping towards him. He knew she would grab him and he was frozen with fear; it was only at the last minute that he was able to run away. I had listened incredulously, but now, here from a local intellectual, was another warning about spirits.

'The spirits are of our dead ancestors,' continued Otis. 'Some spirits are good, but many are evil and will try to harm you. You must be careful.' But how to tell a good spirit? 'Ah, that is hard, but avoid the lonely roads.' Useful advice when all the roads seemed lonely.

I lurched forward, coughing harshly, uncontrollably again; it was probably as annoying to Otis as the cockadoodledoos of roosters were to me – they always crowed in the middle of the night, never at dawn, always skulking up to my tent wall to give me an awakening blast. I wanted to throttle them and have a roast-chicken dinner, instead of awful dried fish. I wondered what Otis wanted to do to me.

'Drink this,' said Otis from his dark corner. 'It is *café militaire*,' and he passed a filled plastic cup toward me. I took a deep swig, and something warm, milky and alcoholic slipped down my raw throat. I coughed again in surprise, and Otis guffawed.

'It is made from Gloria and *whiskey africain*' – evaporated milk and a potent home-made brew. He added, 'It is good for sore throats.'

As the warm mixture soothed my limbs as well as my cough, I reflected on another conversation.

'In Guinea, there are many strange things that happen,' a Frenchman, a tough man who ran a trucking business, had told me. 'In the south in the forest, something strange happened one night. I never knew what it was about, but I heard shuffling and looked out my window. The whole village was passing with candlelight. They walked out of the clearing into the forest and I stayed awake to watch for their return. It was not until several hours later.'

He had paused, sweat glistening on his brow, and taken another swig of beer. 'I will tell you the strangest thing. It was that during the time they were gone ... you know how the dogs are always barking in the forest?'

I did.

'Not a single dog barked. They all remained quiet.'

He had also told me to beware of drinking strange potions.

'There are love philtres made by healers and medicine men – once you drink them you cannot resist the man who gave it to you. You will be pulled by a force to his side in the middle of the night.'

I looked at my *café militaire* and across at Otis, but I thought of William.

Another cool breeze wafted through the compound and rustled the leaves of a long-limbed tree. Otis was smoking a cigarette, and the red butt glowed cheerfully. I stretched in my chair and sighed contentedly.

'You must always stay in a village – never stay out in the *brousse* at night,' Otis said suddenly, gravely, breaking the spell. He brought the candle closer to his side of the table. 'In Koundara you must go to a marabout to get a *juju* to protect you.'

He spoke in a serious, slightly drunk tone, but there was no hint of mysticism. This was everyday conversation.

He looked down to replace the batteries in his massive cassette player. I wanted to ask him about his experiences with the spirits, but he finished replacing his batteries and began playing some African high-life music very loudly. The fast beat filled the compound, alarmed a goat that had been nibbling our leftovers and made further talk impossible. Already his voice was slurring from the *whiskey Africain* and when he offered to top up my cup, I let him.

I was content now to be lulled by the pulsing rhythms of the music and to watch the beauty of the velvet-black night sky pierced by the bright lights of the Milky Way. I wondered what mysteries of Guinea I might encounter and discover.

I thought a lot about Otis and our conversations as I cycled away the next day and for days afterwards as I climbed into the rugged Fouta Djalon highlands heading for the provincial town of Labé. Certainly he was right about the road, and soon my ability to keep going became my overriding concern.

I really must reduce my load, I thought. Again. Various items like clothing and jars of jam and peanut paste had made good gifts, but truly savage cuts meant choices about which tools and spares, camping and food preparation gear, medicines and cosmetics were still necessary. I was starting to see many of these things, which had seemed so precious, as 'toubab toys'. That is, I saw them as ridiculous.

My next target, I decided, would be my toiletries bag. When I left Dakar, the bulging bag had contained cleansing, moisturising and make-up essentials. Now it seemed to contain an amazingly irrelevant range of cosmetics. Did I really need hair conditioner? Or a sunscreen as well as a body moisturiser? A bulging bag just meant I dropped things on muddy floors as I struggled to get to the soap. Tonight, I promised myself. Tonight.

Before the first burst of invigorating endorphins had worn off and while sero-tonin was still buzzing in my brain, a wide, muddy stream cut through the track. I was amused, and wandered about looking for a crossing, but just kept finding slushy ground. Finally, a little miffed, I took my shoes off, and waded gingerly through. Mud oozed between my toes, and, on the other side, I paused to clean my feet with precious drinking water before carefully replacing my shoes.

I laughed at myself – still not much of an adventurer – then set off again, only to be brought up short at the next turn.

The road disappeared under a swamp.

With serotonin rapidly evaporating, I sighed and realised that this was going to be habitual.

I pushed the bike and paddled through, letting my bicycle's carefully main-tained chain and gears turn a muddy brown, my panniers and their load skim the water and my shoes fill with slime. I tried to laugh again.

Koundara, my first Guinean town, was about 60 wet and muddy kilometres through the dense forest from the Missara border post. It was marked on my bible – the Michelin 953 map of North and West Africa – in bold black, suggest-ing to me from previous experience that it was a big regional town, hinting of nice things like hotels and running water. When I finally arrived, having passed through several police checkpoints, accumulating even more stamps in my pass-port, I was disappointed. It was indeed a major provincial town for Guinea, yet it had no electricity, no water supply, no sewerage, no telephones, no radio, no bus service. Nothing. Otis's optimism that 'things would improve now' was necessary. At least, things could not get much worse.

Late in the afternoon, after leaving my bicycle and belongings in my rundown room in the majestically named but thoroughly decrepit Grand Hotel Boiro (the only hotel in town – a cavernous and empty wreck), I walked into the subdued market square nearby. Koundara was a colonial town about the size of a small English town like Glastonbury – comparing dimensions of the commercial area that is, nothing else. It is very hard to estimate popula-tions of African towns, as families are so large and populations can be densely packed in shanty houses. However, it was clear that not many people lived in Koundara – there was no reason to. Koundara was stuck in a time warp and was now covered by red dust, awaiting resurrection. Surrounding the square were single-storey, porticoed colonial buildings made from once white stone. Attractive, except that their now dust-covered façades were ripped by bullet holes – from the French exit or from Touré's reign of terror? Sometimes trading must be brisk as, in the centre, there were massive, rotting piles of vegetable matter and the stench was high. Now, there was little activity to occupy people, and bored traders were scattered around the perimeter, under the porticoes, or at trestle tables nestling in the dirt. I wondered why they did not at least clear the rubbish.

The traders of the same items tended to cluster together. Women sat in front of mats selling a few, unappetising tomatoes, onions and chilies, or guavas and tough, dry oranges. They had glazed looks on their faces. Probably they knew that only outsiders would buy these products – all local families grew the same food – and at that time of day there were no trucks or taxis passing through. In fact, I realised I hadn't heard a vehicle at all during my few hours in Koundara.

Some elderly men sat behind similarly aged, black iron, pedal-operated sewing machines. They seemed to have grown old together. Nearby, brightly coloured *pagnes* of material – *pagne* is the term used interchangeably for the patterned cotton fabric sold in three-yard lengths and the portion used as a skirt wrap – were neatly folded on a cloth on the ground, waiting for someone to want some tailoring. But today, there were no customers. The tailors looked at me with interest, but it seemed to be curiosity, not opportunity, that drove their regard; these people were not aggressive traders.

I had forgotten about Otis's suggestion to buy a protective *juju* until I saw the stall of a traditional healer. He was located between a weary-looking tomato seller – her tiny, red balls grouped in pyramids of five on her mat – and a young boy selling small tubes of Colgate, some tiny locks, sewing needles, and single cigarettes. In all African markets, products are sold *au détail* – singly. People cannot afford bulk purchases.

The healer's dirty mat was spread with all kinds of herbs, bark and dried animal parts which did not really tell any story alone, but an illustrative placard leaning against a nearby tree trunk revealed the ailments that could be cured. A crudely painted male figure squatted with excrement squirting from his rear end – diarrhoea; a female figure holding her back – back pain and rheumatism; a figure holding its forehead – headache; a pregnant woman – pregnancy problems; a silhouette sneezing – colds. Nothing for malevolent spirits, and no sign of protective *juju*s. Otis had told me the *juju*s were tiny leather parcels to be worn around the neck or waist on a leather thong. They contained herbs and paper with quotes from the Koran, and the soothsayer would have said an incantation to provide protection for the wearer.

Perhaps this man was only a medical healer. Apparently, only some traditional healers were diviners – the traditional soothsayers – who could invoke the spirits and provide these powerful *juju*s. Similarly, not all marabout – itinerant Moslem holy men – were diviners, but it was hard to tell. As I later discovered, one should always assume a marabout has supernatural powers and avoid antagonising him.

This elderly, rag-covered healer was busy with a talkative woman. I felt embarrassed to butt in to ask the healer if he had *juju*s for the forest spirits, and anyway he did not seem to speak French. Also, the woman's children were surrounding me like park-bred swans aggressively demanding bread. At least, now that I was in the country of the Peul people – I had been told this proudly several times – their children did not call me '*toubab*', but they still stared. I turned away.

That night, I sat in the dark, cave-like dining room of the Grand Hotel Boiro, and ate dinner with the manager, M. Keita. His face was ghostly in the light of the only kerosene lamp, but his depression was clear. He was a young university graduate from Conakry, another informed, well-educated person in a remote place. I really needed to let my preconceptions go. He hated being cut off in Koundara and I asked him why it was so decrepit.

'You must understand the mentality here. In Africa, one's own pocket comes first. If you sent out money for a project in Koundara, say for a water supply and a generator, and came back in three years, I would say: what project?' He gave me the example of the school in Koundara – the children have no desks, yet the director of the school has been given a four-wheel-drive vehicle. 'The president gets a percentage on each four-wheel-drive landed, you see – so there is an incentive.'

'Why doesn't it change?' I asked, in the eerily quiet room.

'In Africa, things go slowly. The villagers are not educated, and here in the provinces they get no news – no television, no radio, no newspapers, no alternative views. And whether they hear something about Conakry or France or Australia, it is all the same – it is about outside.' I listened and chewed slowly on tough chicken – poor thing, it must have led a hard life. 'At its most basic, justice is not available here,' he said. 'In the provinces any of the magistrates, judges, police, when they are presented with a problem, they just think of how much money they can make. That's why things don't change.'

The next morning, I was torn between taking a couple of days off – I was very weary – and my eagerness to leave dirty, depressing Koundara. But there was a timetable to adhere to if I was to get to Dar inside twelve months. People, including myself, had expectations, and already I was a few days behind schedule. Fifty kilometres a day, five days a week had not sounded a daunting objective in London, but some days now, and not on a sixth or seventh day, I just wanted to rest.

Well, I bargained, how about one day off?

Labé was 244 kilometres away according to my Michelin – three days' travel if conditions improved, four or five days if conditions remained poor. It was not only marked in big, black letters on my map, it also had a blue underline! Surely, there would be better times to be had in Labé, and five days wasn't too long to keep going. If necessary, I could keep myself going by dreaming of running water and electricity, and that way, I'd still be on schedule and have a rest in a real town.

I was just a little time-obsessed and deluded.

I felt a bite on my hand. It was a fly, a huge creature, more than a centimetre long, grey and ugly. I swiped at it, but the fly stayed, drinking my blood. I pulled my other hand from the handlebars, took my eyes from the road, and slapped hard at the fly and my steering hand. The bicycle wobbled dangerously.

I was only 30 kilometres from Koundara, cycling on a red gravel road through parched, fire-blackened bushland, and the sun weighed heavily, like a gold bar on my head. The road was deeply rutted, requiring care to stay on narrow ridges. I had left a few more items in Koundara, including some souvenirs I had bought in The Gambia. Strangely, despite the frustration of parting with things I had just bought, I found it easier to shed myself of new things than the original, carefully chosen items. However, the bike was still overloaded, particularly at the front which made fine steering adjustments difficult. I now recovered my balance as the fly fell satisfyingly away, squashed and dead. That will teach him to bite me, I thought vindictively and without any animal-liberationist compassion, but then there was a twinge on my shoulder. Another bite?

Trying to maintain control, I slapped wildly at my back. Then, I felt a stab of pain on my eyebrow. My muscles flexed instinctively in retreat from the attacks. Two more flies settled on my left hand, and as I squashed them two more attacked my right hand. They were impossible to ignore – stabs of pain came on my back, my ankles, my bum, my ear.

I jumped off the bike, letting it fall to the ground – and did an aggressive jig, stamping my feet, pulling off my hat, flailing uselessly at the air. No good. Still the flies landed, in swarms. They were biting with probosci the size of hypodermic needles, and my skin writhed in horror and pain.

There was nothing to be done except scream and swear, and even that provided only fleeting satisfaction.

'Why the fuck are you doing this to me?!' This I yelled at myself for having brought me to Africa.

I had no coherent response to that.

The attacks continued, so I tried dousing myself with drinking water. But, there was no escape, no respite in return for regaining composure. Only distance would save me.

As this horrific morning progressed on the flatlands of red laterite, I lurched from stopping place to stopping place. At each, I desperately pulled more clothing from my panniers and layered myself in it, like some reverse dance of the seven veils. I was cycling toward the base of the Fouta Djalon highlands across an intensely hot, still plain that was wreathed in heat haze, but I wore trousers, socks, several T-shirts, my Gortex rainjacket, and a scarf around my face. My eyes were enclosed in sunglasses, my head was covered by my Akubra and wrapped by my scarf, and yet still the flies bit me.

In some ways the clothing made it worse. I was overheating, but also the flies became entrapped and enraged between the layers. My brain screamed for release. I stopped even being able to swear at myself. By the time I arrived at a tiny village at nearly noon, I was just making queer whimpering noises, breathing shallowly and going mad.

'These are tsetse flies,' said the gentle man who greeted me calmly. He was standing outside his grass circular hut, the last of six or seven I had passed. Not intending to stop – children had been chasing me – I had cycled relentlessly forward, but now, as this doe-eyed, middle-aged man greeted me and I saw the dry bush about to start again, I lurched to a halt.

'There are many more in the bush ahead – there are many wherever the bush is very dry and undisturbed,' he told me, and I shook my head in dismay. No words would yet come, but I sensed this was a kind man, and at least I was no longer being mobbed by children.

He shook his head too, possibly in bewilderment at why a white woman should arrive so unexpectedly outside his hut, possibly in sympathy. He told me his name was Mohammed, and he suggested I stop awhile.

At least in human habitation, the flies abated, and I stripped off my excess clothes in an effort to get cool. I was still panting hard, either from the heat or panic, and Mohammed called to his wife to bring me water, then sat me in the shade of a nearby mango tree. I wiped vigorously at my skin with a damp cloth like a young chimp intent on ridding itself of fleas, but I was futilely trying to wipe away the pain and itchiness of the bites.

'Do not worry,' he added. 'They will not give disease. It is only tsetse flies in wetlands that carry the sleeping sickness.' I had not even thought of this.

'We Africans are habituated, but your skin is too soft.' He laughed, but I could not smile.

Mohammed was a small, wiry man, perhaps fifty or more, who had a mischievous, lively face. He was wearing a brown Moslem tunic, but he was bareheaded. Suddenly, he rushed inside his hut and returned with a notebook, his diary.

'There was another cyclist who passed by our village, a German.'

I had visions of catching him up for company, but Mohammed was looking for his diary entry. Success! He grinned as he passed me the relevant page.

It was dated 1962.

Mohammed insisted his young, smiling, but shy wife bring me some groundnut (peanut) paste. Embarrassed to take food from such poor folk, I offered to pay, but was rebuffed. Soon, Mohammed's wife came with an enormous pile on a chipped enamel plate, then immediately returned to her chores behind the hut.

We started chatting about Australia. 'Is it farther than Conakry?' he asked.

I gave Mohammed an Australian sticker and pin. I had brought these specifically to hand out as gifts, but now they seemed a totally inadequate present for his hospitality. As I prepared to depart, temporarily cooled and recovered, Mohammed also had a warning for me.

'Beware of the spirits in the Fouta Djalon ... take care in the forest.'

I was more worried about the tsetse flies, and for two excruciating days, I had to endure blistering heat, exaggerated by my layers of clothing, and the abominable bites of those bloody flies. At each bend on the lonely road through the yellow, scanty scrub, I searched eagerly for signs of human habitation. I listened intently for the sounds of trucks going my way. If one had come, I would have thrown the bike and myself aboard. Nothing but the buzzing of flies.

The only reason I kept going was because there was no choice – and because my timetable demanded progress. Each day I covered only short distances, about 60 kilometres the first day, only 35 the second, until I could endure no more. My skin was punctured and badly bruised from my own vicious swipes. Several times, as I swiped at flies, I dropped the bike and had its fully laden weight land on my leg.

'I can't take this!' I would cry to no one in particular.

When I did arrive in villages – just small collections of circular mud-walled huts with grass-thatch roofs, stretched along the roadside at about 5-kilometre intervals – I was surrounded by amazed and alarmed children and adults. They could not tell my sex, covered as I was in so many layers, and I was wild-eyed, too hot and distressed to say soothing words. They probably thought I was a crazed and dangerous spirit, but often a woman, clearly impoverished and dressed in a holey *pagne* and paper-thin T-shirt, would arrive with a basin of cold water and a precious cake of soap so that I could soothe my wounds. People with so little were being so kind. But I never stayed long. Once I could manage a smile and a few words, I knew I was sufficiently recovered to tackle the flies again.

I was still determined to make Labé before I would rest.

Outside Kounsitel, a police checkpoint village, on the second day of this torture, a local caught up with me on his old, wobbly Chinese bike.

'*Ça va?*' he called.

I was miserable and must have looked it.

Wordlessly, he took my heavy bike from me, and pushed it up the hill while I pushed his light one the last 5 kilometres into the small roadside stop. It was just a collection of wooden huts selling the usual items for travellers – fish stew and rice, fried beignets and hot Cokes in chipped bottles. The man refused any payment or even a Coke; we just exchanged bicycles and he cycled off to see friends.

I passed on to the police checkpoint, where there was a bar across the road, and was taken to see the police commissioner, Jackie. He was expecting me – somehow news had reached him from his friend Otis.

Jackie was another bear of a man, with a huge beer belly and a friendly nature. He had good news.

'The flies will end soon – the road starts to go up.'

I knew I had to rise over the 780-metre Col de Sita to reach the high plains of the Fouta Djalon and trek toward Labé. But I wondered why the flies would stop.

'It will be cold on the mountain,' Jackie explained, surprising me; I looked forward to cold.

The evening with Jackie was as comforting as the one with Otis, except that, this time, to avoid being given any love philtres or receiving any unwanted offers of night-time company, I turned William into a husband.

Then, I was alarmed at having to create a history for us to answer Jackie's inquisitive questions.

Where did you get married? What was it like? Why did you choose not to have children? Why has William let you go?

I resolved to make William a fiancé, a status that would be easier to explain but still conveying to my companions that I was already claimed.

'Can I rest with you?' asked Jackie quite directly, as I went to bed. I guess my stories didn't make much difference anyway.

Despite avoiding Jackie's charms, that night was a restless one. Was I already claimed? William was often in my thoughts. Too often really. We had parted with him saying it was over and me asking him to come and join me for sections of the journey. No resolution at all, just confusion. Was I free or not? Emotionally, I was certainly still very attached and missing him very much. Yet, it would be at least a month before I could phone him from Bamako in Mali, to see if he had changed his mind. It was proving hard to leave an old life behind, particularly when my replacement life was so strange and difficult.

The next morning, I wished Jackie well and gave him my mascara and red nail polish for his absent wife. Yes. For four weeks, I had thought these were essentials for life on the road! I was a slow learner, and it was still only a small dent in the enormous toiletries bag.

As I prepared to cycle away, I felt sad to be always moving on when I had briefly met someone with whom I could connect – if only I had more time. I wanted to explain how I felt, but it was too hard, particularly in French. Anyway, Jackie had pressing advice for me.

'Beware of the spirits in the Fouta Djalon,' he warned solemnly.

Climbing into the Fouta Djalon without a rest break was not a good idea.

Jackie was right: the tsetse flies finally stopped. Heaven. And I still had on all my clothes, but for a different reason. Now, I was freezing!

At the outset, I was content – struggling up a cold mountain side was preferable to being bitten by flies. As I began the ascent, spectacular views emerged, glimpses through the thick, tall trees to the yellow, shimmering plains, far below. I was at peace again and knew that slowly, slowly, I would cross the Col de Sita. Soon, though, there was no time for gazing at scenery, as I found I needed to focus my energy on pedalling. Cycling on any hill with that load would have been hard, but at each zag, the nearside of the road was washed away, which forced me to detour and find a precarious route along any remnant ridge on the cliff side of the road. Still, the air was refreshing and there was no traffic to worry about. My mood remained buoyant.

Then, I realised I had seen no sign of humans since leaving the plain. Did nobody farm the mountain side? It seemed very lonely here. Was anyone home?

I also started to realise it was going to be hard to make Tianguel Bory, the next town, before nightfall. My Michelin, folded inside a clear plastic wallet attached to the top of my handlebar bag, showed my route, and I estimated it was still about 80 kilometres from Kountsitel – a longish day on rough roads. My cycle computer showed I had already come about 40 kilometres before the rise, but my speed was slowing to about 10 kilometres per hour on this muddy, curving mountain road. There were a good four hours of daylight left. Just take it easy, I soothed myself. Now, I was a little less buoyant.

Then, the sun disappeared under high, black cumulonimbus clouds. It was the end of the wet season, and I had escaped any rain, so far. The day got darker. I could see rain sweeping in sheets towards me across the plain, blocking out any view to the horizon with its arrival. Shit.

'Not now!' I yelled at the sky. Why did the gods or the spirits have to give me rain on the day I was crossing the col? Just bad luck, I guessed. Then, thinking about the past few days, I yelled at the sky again. 'Is this a bloody test?!' Who did I think was listening?

I cycled a little harder.

Lightning lit up the dull air, for an instant draining the scene of colour like some bizarre X-ray. Thunder belched loudly and was followed by the long rumble of ongoing indigestion. The first rain did not take long to arrive, large drops, pellets from a shotgun in the sky. At first, it felt cleansing and refreshing, but soon, new gullies and ridges appeared, and the road turned from laterite to mud swept crosswise by fast-flowing streams. The water seemed to pour off the mountain side, gathering momentum as it reached the road, carving a deep channel, then tumbling into the vegetation on the other, downward side. Terrific evidence of the power of nature, but not much fun when trying to find reserves of power to take the bike, its load and myself ever upwards. My speed was touching just 5 kilometres per hour.

'One, two, three, four, five,' I panted softly, over and over, trying to maintain rhythm in my legs. I tipped the brim of my hat and let water gush forward – at least it wouldn't look so pristine from now on, I thought. Is this adventure? Is this the time to think about that?! The proximity of the rapidly moving storm gave me more immediate worries – the thunder and lightning spectacular was intensifying. I switched to counting the time between blinding flash and resounding crack.

Ten seconds. Eight seconds. Six seconds.

This storm was not going to veer away. There was a silent, pupil-searing flash above my head, and the startling crack came just four seconds later. Otis had told me a story about a villager who had been killed when he came out of his hut during a storm and was struck by lightning.

Dear Otis.

By now, I was seriously worried – not about whether I was going to get to Tianguel Bory, but about how to avoid being fried alive! Should I stay on the road, or take cover under a tree? Something in my memory banks said the latter was not a good idea, but I didn't like just rolling along with a metal object. I saw a rocky ridge by the side of the road. Aha! I laid the bike against the ledge, a fair distance away from me, and sat down, soaked and cold, but quite pleased I had outsmarted the storm.

Eventually, the storm passed. Rain was down to a steady pour, and the gap between lightning and thunder had widened. Time to move on, no time to lose, I thought.

I pulled my bike to the road, but quickly realised it was handling awkwardly.

The rear tyre was punctured and completely flat.

Double shit.

At this point, I locked up my emotions, held my breath, gritted my teeth and decided I could swear and throw a tantrum tonight.

'But *not now*, Pamela.' It was like scolding someone else. 'No one is going to fix this if you don't.'

It was my first flat in Africa. In London, I had always got punctures on wet days too. However, there, I just locked the bicycle to a lamp post, hailed a taxi and went home.

Half an hour later, the inner tube was changed and the bike reloaded, and I was feeling reasonably chuffed. I had done a good job and had won the battle with the storm, or with these spirits I did not believe in.

Or had I?

I started doing mental calculations. It was already 4 p.m., a maximum of three hours of light left, and probably 30 kilometres to Tianguel Bory. I would only make it if a long downhill emerged.

I soon left the forests behind, and the ground opened out into marshes with foggy vistas out to far rolling hills, but still the road went up.

It was quiet, with a cloying smell of dampness and an eerie lack of villages and people.

Suddenly, the sounds of a flute, a sweet, high-pitched melody, came from somewhere across the marshes to my right. I was going to call out, it would be good to see people again, but then the sound shifted. It was coming from my left.

During the next hour the music seemed to always remain the same distance away. Sometimes it stopped, then I cycled around another bend and the flute's sound would be there to greet me. It was not normal.

Spirits?

Probably a shepherd, I thought brusquely, rounding up his goats. But still I did not call out.

I remembered too, Otis's warning about camping in the *brousse* at night, but as the road kept mounting in the waning light, it seemed a real possibility.

Near dusk, a number of bush taxis and overloaded trucks passed, going toward Koundara. Each paused to greet me, undoubtedly surprised by my appearance. I was surprised by their presence – I had not seen so many vehicles in Guinea before! The drivers told me they travelled at night so their headlights would pick up the potholes, but I was only interested in the distance and terrain to Tianguel Bory.

'*Ça mont encore?*' – Does it keep going up? Up and down, was always the reply, but ever hopeful of hearing, '*Non, c'est la descente!*' – No, it goes down – I kept asking. Stubborn, optimistic me. I also started scanning for places to camp – optimism tempered by realism – but either the ground fell away sharply, or it was marshy on the flats.

It began raining again, and the light seemed to seep away. Soon, the road was completely silent. I cycled with new energy, frantic to make it to a village before nightfall. Inexorably, the blackness descended, until it was a solid, impenetrable curtain. There was no moon and no stars. I kept pushing – cycling was impossible now – but a small pearl of light from my headlamp was not enough to show the way. I tripped through streams and over unseen rocks and could feel that the forest had closed in again. I ran through the dark trying to escape the bush. I was crying.

'Cut it out!' I told myself sternly – I recognised my mother's voice and tone talking to me. Then, I got angry and started yelling at the spirits who had done this to me, who were out there waiting for me to give in. But finally, even the anger ebbed, and again, numbed of emotion, I scanned with my headlamp for a suitable place to camp. Spying a tiny piece of flat ground near the road, I pushed the bike over and laid it flat in the wet grass. I would have to be brave and camp out.

Then, hearing the rumble of an approaching truck, a loner, separate from the dusk convoys, I laid myself flat in the grass, too. Very brave.

Erecting the tent in the total close blackness was done by feel – I did not use my headlamp as I did not want to risk being observed. I stripped in the rain and crawled inside, for once pleased to be carrying a sleeping bag – this was its first use. The wind tugged at my tent flaps and I snuggled into my sheet, anxious to obliterate the outside world. I would be all right now.

Then, notes soared above the wind, an eerie musical accompaniment to the wild night. It was the flute again. I realised no shepherd would be out in this wild weather. Could it be a spirit? My skin tingled.

Fortunately, I fell almost immediately into a heavy and dreamless sleep, and awoke only with the heat of the sun.

So much for spirits, I thought, and was amused by what rot I could believe in, alone in the dark.

The two remaining days in the Fouta Djalon, cycling the mere 75 kilometres towards Labé, provided very different scenery to either the plain or the wild mountain side. It was a much friendlier landscape, with rolling hills and culti- vated fields. In the morning, the sky was a soft, hazy blue, dotted with white clouds like cotton wool, and the air was fresh and cool. These high plains were at an altitude of about 1000 metres, and generally, I was still climbing. The land was clearly very fertile and therefore more densely populated. After the small, storm-dampened town of Tianguel Bory – it turned out I had camped just 5 kilometres short of my target – there were few long hauls without a village or a field. Cries of '*Bonjour!*', '*Ça va?*' and '*Bon courage!*' peppered each day. The road, still quite muddy and rutted after the heavy storms, allowed slow pedalling at best, giving everyone time to see and talk to the stranger. An old lady staggering under a heavy load of straw might call out with clear amazement, a man passing on his bicycle would always give me a friendly greeting and cycle with me for a time, and women and children, looking up from the streams where they were washing clothes or themselves, would shout or scramble after me.

Simple, rectangular houses, made of clay-fired brick with tin roofs, nestled alongside the road. They had separate allotments and were surrounded by brush fences. Often, from my high vantage point on the road, I could see goats nibbling at the bark and remaining leaves of almost denuded trees and chickens pecking at seemingly spotless, swept clay floors. A woman might be there pounding grain, but if she sensed my presence, she would look up from her labours, grin and shout '*Djarama!*', the equivalent of '*Bonjour*' in Fulbé, the language of the Peul, or '*Tanalatum?*', the equivalent of '*Ça va?*'. Few women spoke French, making my contacts with them frustratingly limited.

It should have been pleasant, but the days with the tsetse flies and the night on the Col de Sita had taken their toll, and my spirit and body were weary. My tent was damp, all my clothes were wet, and the bites of the flies were starting to become infected. The day I passed through Tianguel Bory, I spent five hours pushing the bicycle over medium- and large-sized laterite boul- ders; and when an early afternoon storm shortened the day, I took refuge for the night having covered just 30 kilometres. I was very concerned that I was slipping further behind on my schedule.

However, as is the way of these things, at last, I was a mere 30 kilometres outside Labé and could start dreaming of what I might find. Surely, it would not be as isolated and decrepit as Koundara. Surely, there would be electricity and running water. Things would be all right soon.

Early that last morning, the road broke through into a large, flaxen meadow of swaying grass, which was surrounded by gentle, low, golden hills. A small brook meandered through one way, the red road meandered through the other. It was a magical, silent place and as I crossed the brook, waving to some women washing their clothes, I decided to rest and absorb the beauty of this Garden of Eden. There was a single, shady tree with time- rounded granite rocks scattered under it; perfect for a quiet meditation, I thought. I propped the bike against the tree, and went to sit on a rock.

A snake slithered out from underneath.

I yelped, and shivered despite the heat. It was a small, black snake, but I didn't stop to consider it further, and neither did it stay to contemplate me. I leapt back toward the bike.

There is a very special book about Guinea: *The African Child* by Camara Laye, which I had read in London. There, the opening chapter had seemed mystical rather than instructive. Now that I was in the heart of Guinea, where people daily warned me about spirits and the form they might take, I wondered.

During the time of French colonisation, Camara Laye had grown up in Kouroussa, further east, on the Niger River, a town I would eventually pass through on my way into Mali. He wrote of how, as he played in his family's compound one day, he had spied a small, black snake with striped markings. He called to warn his mother, expecting her to kill it as she usually did.

'My son, this one must not be killed,' she said gravely as soon as she saw the black snake. 'He is not as other snakes, and he will not harm you; you must never interfere with him.' His mother added, 'This snake is your father's guiding spirit.'

Camara Laye was dumbfounded. He wrote that he was familiar with the supernatural but still did not understand these guiding spirits that he encountered almost everywhere, spirits that forbade one thing, and commanded another to be done. There were good spirits, and there were evil ones; and it seemed to him, more evil than good ones. And how was he to know this snake was harmless?

He waited until nightfall to ask his father.

'That snake,' his father said, 'has always been with us; he has always made himself known to one of us. In our time, it is to me that he has made himself known ... It is to this snake that I owe everything, and it is he likewise who gives me warning of all that is to happen. Thus I am never surprised, when I awake, to see this or that person outside my workshop: I already know that he or she will be there ... But all this – let it never be forgotten – I owe it to the snake, I owe it to the guiding spirit of our race.'

Could the snake I saw have been a guiding spirit arriving to warn me of something about to happen? Or was it one the women would have thrashed to death?

My corporate clients would have been bemused if I had advised them to follow their guiding spirits. I wondered at how fanciful I was becoming out here on the lonely roads.

I made it the few kilometres on to Popodara, still a little shaken from the close encounter with the snake, and decided on a break with people, rather than nature, this time.

It was two days since the night camping in the rain, and I had seen Popodara labelled enticingly on the map, the only other town before Labé. Often, I had two or even three days between towns marked on the Michelin, so even small ones developed an aura of being a special place, with possible refrigeration and cold Cokes for sale.

Popodara let me down.

It was fly-ridden and very dirty, with piles of decaying vegetable matter and rusting car bodies on the far side of the dusty road. On the other side were wooden buildings, weathered to a gunmetal grey, in a single, 100-metre-long row straight from the American West. I searched for cowboys and horses, but got only staring eyes instead. People in this town were silent, there were no welcoming cries, just hungry, resentful, disconcerting stares.

I sat on the verandah of one of the shops to drink a warm Coke, and to avoid the onlookers' stares, I searched the sores on my legs for signs of infection. For some days now, I had been keeping going by just focusing on getting to Labé and resting.

Now, being tired, I was not in a good mood. Well, I guess I was a volcano ready to blow.

Someone approached me, but I focused on my Coke.

'*Cadeau.*' And then louder, '*Cadeau.*'

Expecting to see a child, I looked up and saw an elderly marabout.

'*Cadeau,*' he repeated, demanding a gift and shoving his tin plate toward me. He was hunched over and dressed in a once white, ragged robe, but there was no smile, just heavily wrinkled, dark-brown skin and pale, menacing eyes.

I snapped. My only excuse was that it had been a hard week.

'*Allez!*' – Go away! – I called gruffly, and looked around to the others watching, waiting. What were they waiting for?

'All of you go away!' I yelled, in English now, and stood and waved my hands at them. 'Why can't you leave me alone?!'

The marabout came even closer to me, still holding out the plate, and I glanced at the contents – there was no money, just metal objects, screws, and bolt and springs, and some shells. The marabout was ragged and thin, but I felt an evil presence and was frightened by his blank, pale, demanding eyes. I felt threatened, and so once more rushed to my bike seeking escape. I mounted and rode for Labé; I would stop for nothing now.

All I wanted was a room with a door where I could shut out Africa and its hardships, where I could take myself home in private dreams, and where I could rest.

It was quite a while, on the road to Labé, before I had coherent thoughts again, and then was astonished and embarrassed at my behaviour.

You're overwrought, girl, I muttered to myself, it's definitely time for a rest.

Labé rose before me on softly rounded, pine-clad hills. The light seemed crystal clear, and the air was filled with pinewood scents, very cool against my skin. I had gained even higher altitude. People I passed seemed so happy, filled with energy.

'*Bonjour!*' I cried to the startled men and women walking on the roadside, before they had a chance to spy me. '*Djarama!*' I added for good measure.

Soon, there was heavenly tar and sedans – not just the heavily laden trucks moving like nocturnal slugs. My mood was lightened by the thought of the coming rest.

A white missionary stopped her car to greet me. White strangers were rare, I guessed, a source of potential interest. I asked her for advice on a hotel.

'You could try the Hotel Salaah,' she said. 'It's very simple, but I think it's clean.'

Arriving at a high fence that was reassuringly painted with 'Hotel Salaah', I went through the driveway leading to a cluster of decrepit, mud-brick buildings surrounding a central dirt courtyard. I left my bike outside and called for assistance. A surly young man arrived and beckoned me to follow him through the courtyard to see a room. I thought hopefully of running water and electric light.

Suddenly, I heard a low, ravaging growl and felt the clamp of teeth behind my left knee. I gasped at the sharp spasm of pain and looked down to see my assailant. It was an angry, female Alsatian, fat, teats hanging from a distended stomach, teeth bared as it was restrained from moving forward for a second attack. I had been badly bitten by a dog.

That night I stared at the amber liquid in my glass. My legs were propped on a chair in front of me, my right elbow leant on the table by my side, my hand cradling my head. I was quite drunk, and quite depressed. I kept seeing the wound in my left leg, the pink flesh spattered with red blood and the white, squashy mess of fat hanging out, and I again felt the heave of my stomach. The vision would not be erased by alcohol.

How can I keep going? How can I do anything but stay here? Labé is just another town in the middle of nowhere. Running water and electricity? Huh! Every second or third day only, but no telephone, no transport, no way out. I felt rage. How could it have happened?

I took another gulp of my beer. It was my second 600 ml bottle, but already I was shaking again at the memory of my arrival, and wanted to forget. The Chinese doctors I had been taken to that afternoon had said no cycling for one month to allow the deep wound to heal. Apparently, the wound from a dog bite cannot be stitched as the risk of infection is too high. One month! After just four and a half weeks of travel from Dakar, with fourteen countries still to traverse and 13,000 more kilometres to travel, I was stuck for at least a month. And I needed a full week's course of anti-rabies injections. It was too much to take in. Maybe it was time to give in and go home. I felt imprisoned in this horrible town – imprisoned by a bloody spirit.

'Definitely, it was a spirit,' said Françoise, a cheery young woman who worked in the Hotel Salaah bar.

There were no other customers, so Françoise was sitting on the other side of my table, concentrating on her game of patience to see if the cards would come out. Already I knew she would cheat if necessary, moving a card to get herself out of being stuck, but I liked her positive attitude and friendly nature. She was a chunky, independent woman dressed in jeans and a checked cotton shirt – very unusual. Françoise was chatting about spirits as she played and I gloomed at my glass and thought of all the might have beens. I wondered at what I should've done to the snake: welcomed him properly? Or, perhaps if I'd been generous and respectful to the marabout, this wouldn't have happened?

But aloud, while thinking evil thoughts about the menacing marabout, I agreed with Françoise, 'Yes, the work of a bad spirit.'

'No,' said Françoise, and she looked up from her cards. 'It was clearly a good spirit – there must have been an evil spirit waiting further down the road to do something worse to you.'

I shook my head, struggling to agree, to see her point of view. With barely controlled rage, I thought that if it was the work of a good spirit, it had miscalculated. I hate this country, this continent, I just want to shoot the dog and get the hell out of here! I am going home.

This journey felt too hard. I had spent a week in soul-destroying tsetse-fly country, climbing over a wild, storm-battered mountain pass, cycling through lonely hills on impossible tracks. This was adventure, but had it brought any satisfaction, some glimmer of insight into my true self? I still distrusted men, then felt fear, then guilt, about my reactions to them. I wasn't reaching out to the women, I didn't know how – we didn't even share a common language. It was just a journey of endless kilometres. Now, I couldn't even make friends with strange dogs. What was the point of keeping going? Surely, my guiding spirit – that snake? – was telling me to go home.

Then, I despaired. How could I give up so easily?

I was glum and disheartened, and watched Françoise as she rapidly moved the cards; her game had come out, but I hadn't noticed if she had cheated. She seemed oblivious to my mood. My mind was picturing home comforts, William, my parents, my brother and even my cat, Jesse – I was lonely – and an insistent voice was telling me to give up.

But my heart wanted to keep going; there were things to discover. I could feel it even in my drunken despair.

'Yes, it was a good spirit who wants you to stay with us.'

Françoise said it cheerfully, as if there had been no break in her words, no time for my brooding misery, my internal debate on whether to stay or go.

'It is good to stay, and then you can go forward again.' She spoke slowly, precisely, so I would hear and listen. 'But you will travel more slowly. Be kinder to yourself and take more time to rest. It will go better like that.'

They were wise words, if I could follow them.

Three

Esprit de Battuta

Labé, Republic of Guinea – Kouroussa, Republic of Guinea

'There must have been an evil spirit waiting further down the road to do something worse to you.' It was comforting the way people's words stayed with me, would be played over and over in my mind, and often created sentimentality, a smile, a sense of companionship, as I travelled the quietest roads. However, four weeks after my injury, the memory of Françoise's words made me uneasy.

I was negotiating a slippery, loose gravel-strewn, heavily gullied road taking me down out of the Fouta Djalon mountains, back onto the lower-altitude hot plains. This time, the road travelled eastwards into Haute Guinée (Upper Guinea, the easternmost province) that would eventually – in about 350 kilometres – lead to my first sighting of the Niger River at Kouroussa (a bold, black Michelin town) and, ultimately – in another 300 kilometres – to a new country, Mali.

'*Doucement, doucement!*' I said to myself. Softly, softly. Take it easy.

Come on, calm down. I had already dropped the bike four times. The dry, thick bush that edged the road was silent, except for my own panting and the occasional crackle of leaves and twigs as some small animal scuttered away. I felt bewitched, watched, and wanted to be out of the Fouta Djalon, but perhaps I was spooking myself into taking the road too fast for the conditions.

The conditions were awful. The road was red laterite, which clearly had not been graded since the last rains. It had a steep camber towards the open cliff side, offering the possibility of a sideways fall into oblivion. Where vehicles had passed during the wet, they had gouged deep tracks, which were plaited, separate then entwined, along the road. Trying to find a continuous ridge to cycle along was impossible, and often I had to let the wheel thud into a gully. These gullies were littered with sharp rocks, 20 or so centimetres in diameter, providing a very unstable surface for cycling, so I was forced to pull the bicycle up onto another ridge to continue. With so much weight from the front handlebar bag and two front panniers, it was difficult to steer, much less correct for these slides. So far, I had managed to avoid toppling the weight onto me, but I knew that, with a misjudged fall, I could easily break a leg. Perhaps I should have been walking, but my muscles were weak, and when I stopped, they shook, jelly-like, from the previous effort. It had taken four weeks for the dog bite to heal, four weeks without much cycling, and I had lost a lot of strength.

There were good reasons then for me to sense I was at risk, but was it the work of an evil spirit?

Françoise had told me another story. 'Just three weeks ago,' she said as she dealt her cards on another slowly passing night in Labé, 'a woodcutter near here took no notice of the warnings from a spirit. Three times he ignored an old woman who appeared when he went to chop a large tree down. Three times the old woman pleaded with him: "The tree is my home, leave it alone!" On the third time, she swore revenge: "If you chop the tree down, my children will die and you will have a slow and painful death." The dog-bite wound and the tsetse-fly bites had become badly infected, and for several days I had lain in bed with a high fever. Now, I was apathetic about time passing and content to sip my beer, bandaged leg propped on a chair, and listen. 'I think you do not believe, Pamela,' said Françoise, with the perceptiveness and sparkling eye so characteristic of her. 'But I tell you. He chopped the tree down and was struck down with paralysis. He lay in a ditch for a whole day before he was found and taken home to his wife. And he has been unable to move since! You must look for the warnings and take heed.'

As I remembered her story, and again felt an evil presence in this still, dry air, I wondered whether the skids were warnings; scepticism was easy in the cities and towns, but alone on a mountain side, with so many stories about spirits spinning in my head, I was feeling more susceptible to these ideas. I looked up toward the exposed granite hillside, a black, weather-rounded, looming presence which I had been following for about an hour, scanning it for signs of life. It was bad timing.

The ridge I was cycling along narrowed to less than a hand's width. As the front wheel of the bike slid sideways, I thrust a leg down to stop the fall. No joy. My foot slipped on the loose gravel, and the bike and I started skating down the hill: me on my bum, the bike on my leg, my hands scrabbling for a hold.

'Shit!'

I was all right. Only grazed. And there was a long rip in my

trousers, exposing my backside and lacerated leg to the world, if there had been anyone there to look. The rear panniers had come off and had slid further down the hill. For the moment, I just sat, a little dazed, pulled off my dusty Akubra and used my bicycle-mitted hand to wipe my sweaty, dirty brow. What was the warning in this?

'Be kinder to yourself,' Wasn't that what Françoise had said too? Shit. That was hard out here in the wilds, but recently I had been kind to myself. For eight days I had let myself be cared for by Shell in Conakry and, as I picked myself up and started gathering my scattered belongings, I tried to recapture the sense of security and comfort I had felt while I was there.

One afternoon, about ten days after the dog bite, there had been commotion in the courtyard of the Hotel Salaah. Françoise and I were settled comfortably in the shade, chatting and drinking coffee I had just made on my stove, when a perspiring man in trousers, shirt and peaked cap rushed into the yard, glanced around a few times, then came straight to me and said in French: 'You must be Pamela. I have a message for you from M. Calloway.' I noticed the Shell logo on his cap, but was still very surprised. M. Calloway was the *directeur général* of Shell's new marketing operations in Guinea. I had been given his name by Catherine Shovlin – it was on a fax I had received in London of all my contacts and their contact numbers in each country. Knowing my parents would be expecting a call from Bamako in Mali – I had estimated a mid-November arrival into Bamako, yet now, with the month's delay, it was likely I would only get to Bamako for Christmas – soon after the dog bite, I had sent M. Calloway a note via a traveller *en route* to Conakry. I had told him about the dog bite and asked him to telex Catherine, though I did suggest he just mention a delay – no point worrying folks too much! Now I read his response.

'Come to Conakry and stay with us while you recuperate. Mark Calloway.'

The flustered message carrier was a tanker driver. He told me he was making a delivery of fuel to Labé, and would return in one hour to pick me up and take me back. Then he was gone.

Well, I had no intention of going anywhere. I did not want to be rescued. That was before Françoise's words had sunk in. Silly me.

Within the hour, I had changed my mind – the prospect of real comfort was irresistible! But even so, I was still my headstrong self: rather than being rescued, I would come *my way* – so that I did not incur any gaps in my cycling. I figured that with one more week's rest, I could then cycle in short stages the 150 kilometres to Mamou, the major crossroads town on the southern edge of the Fouta Djalon. From Mamou, I was willing to take a bus westwards to Conakry on the Atlantic coast. That was a deviation from the original plan, but I could return to Mamou after the bite was fully healed and pick up cycling where I had left off – on an eastward road to Dabola and

Kouroussa. Thus, when the driver returned, I had a note ready thanking M. Calloway for his offer and explaining my alternative plans.

The final days of my incarceration in Labé passed slowly. My Chinese doctors were not keen on my cycling idea, but agreed that on the sealed road to Mamou, the risk of further infection in the still open wound should be low. The hardest part of following my plan was saying goodbye to Françoise, the doctors and other friends I had made. And that, when I was cycling to Mamou, I could feel the pressure of the fat still trying to ooze through the gash. Bleah! Once in Mamou, I was fortunate in befriending a local Lebanese shopkeeper. I left my bicycle and most of my belongings with him, and took a bus the 230 kilometres westwards to Conakry.

On arrival at the bus station on the outskirts of Conakry, I discovered the Shell depot was fortuitously located nearby. It was a Sunday, but a security guard there gave me directions to the Calloways' home and I took a clattering taxi to their bizarre luxury palace with Arab and Asian influences. Coming off the road, I was shocked to find myself outside a three-storey pyramid with an elevated pagoda-temple-style roof over the top terrace and decorative lamps hanging from the overhang of each balcony. The house was surrounded by a high concrete wall topped by jagged glass. Later, Mark told me why he chose to live in the *Cité des Nations* – city of the nations – a rich, waterfront quarter. 'In case of emergencies, we can always escape by water,' he said. For now, only servants were at home, and they told me that M. *et* Mme Calloway were out and not expected back until evening.

'However, you can wait inside.' Initially, I felt that going inside their home was too presumptuous, and left to walk around town. Conakry was small and very quiet and looked like it had been cut off from the outside for thirty years. Army tanks and gun placements still guarded the waterfront, and the squalid streets smelt of urine. People lived in multi-storeyed, dilapidated tenements, with washing hanging outside windows and noisy children playing in the surrounding gutters, or they lived in tin shanties. None seemed to have a water supply – the only crowds I saw were at the corner water pumps. Once night fell, my qualms about my manners became secondary and I returned to the Calloways' house – I decided the safest place to be was their living room.

I hated it.

The interior of the living room was covered in white carpet, long, beige satin curtains hung at the floor-to-ceiling windows, while most other walls were covered in mirrors, and a ghastly gold-and-crystal chandelier was matched by a set of gold-legged and glass-topped side tables and a carved-wood and plushly upholstered lounge suite. I figured, I hoped, the decor and furniture came with the house and was not the choice of my hosts.

Regardless, I did not want to be there; I did not belong. Despite wearing my tidiest town clothes – jeans and a T-shirt, they were dusty from the bus trip and I just felt dishevelled. I went to look in the mirror.

Horror! I was so fat!

For the first time in two months, I saw myself in a full-length mirror and it confirmed what I suspected – I was more round than ever! Why do most people come to Africa and lose weight, I wailed inwardly, and here I am doing a bicycle expedition and I've put it on? Incredible. Deciding it was the heavy carbohydrate loading in my diet, I resolved not to eat any bread or peanuts again.

Very upset by this revelation, I sat in one of the armchairs to wait and my eyes settled on a copy of British *Good Housekeeping*. I picked it up, discovered it was the Christmas edition, filled with ideas for gifts, decorations and recipes, and initially I was enthralled by its glossiness and photos of tempting items and the other world it showed, the world where I used to live. Then, I started seeing waste and extravagance – at best, most items were of transient beauty or offered amusement, but most were useless and expensive. I was travelling Africa with 35 kilograms of worldly goods which included just two pairs of trousers and two pairs of shorts, and still I felt I had too much. What would I want with a pair of tartan booties for decorating the Christmas tree, costing £18.95?

And how the money could be used instead – I lived in a world of poverty now, where people who generously gave me board and lodgings each night would be lucky if they earned that much in one month. I shut the magazine in horror and looked around the decorative salon, with its artworks and coffee-table books and felt revolted and grubby and uncomfortable.

I belong to the bush now, I thought sanctimoniously, just as Mark and Francis Calloway bustled in and made their introductions, and *their* apologies for being late!

'Like a gin and tonic?' asked Mark, unfazed by finding an unexpected guest sitting in his lounge.

'Thanks, that would be great,' I replied.

I was soon utterly seduced by the food, the company and the conversation.

I liked Francis a lot, although I found her rather overwhelming after the peaceful days in Labé. Funnily enough, another strong Françoise, except this Francis came from a wealthy background and spelt her name the masculine way. A tall whirlwind of energy, one of those incredibly efficient English women who get things done, she took me in hand, helping me get my visa for Mali, arranging meetings, taking me to the market to buy essential supplies – all the while getting her own chores and charitable activities done. In particular, it being near Christmas, she was heavily involved in organising the Christmas bazaar for the English Speaking Women's Association (ESWA) – a kind of African Rotary for expatriate women, I gathered. The house was filled with felt and half-finished sewing – stockings, Christmas-tree skirts, tree decorations and boxes of things for sale at the bazaar; things kept arriving at the house taking over even more space. It was all another world, again, to me, but I wished I'd had her help getting sponsorship!

Mark was a short, stocky man (well, neither shorter nor stockier than me in my current state!), with a distracting, bushy, grey moustache – and a total preoccupation with things Shell. Mark was struggling to establish the company's new operations in Guinea. Recently, different assets of the state oil operations had been privatised – separately – to Shell, Total and Elf, and I didn't see much of him, only hearing the stories over gin and tonics and at dinner. Nonetheless, he had interesting stories to tell, and was great fun and good company once he could be extracted from work.

Mark and Francis took me on a whirlwind of social engagements during my stay.

We drove in the air-conditioned, dark-blue and silver Nissan patrol to a Thanksgiving party at the home of a Columbian and Cuban couple.

'It's quite a fiery mix,' commented Francis as we arrived, 'but it seems to work.'

Large, exuberant Philippe, the Cuban part of the couple, made me feel extremely welcome. His wife, a diminutive but volatile Colombian, was preoccupied with cooking the turkey, but called out for a drink on hearing ours being poured.

'What would you like, love of my life?' called Philippe.

Love of my life! That upset me. I had received a telex from Catherine mentioning that William had called her and sent me his regards. His regards! What kind of message was that? Not that he was missing me madly, that he was pleased I was safe, that he was going to jump on the next plane to see me. No, his bloody regards. I brooded over my gin and tonic as Mark started telling his stories, again, and contemplated why I had ever got involved with a bloody Englishman. However, I still lived in hope of a passionate letter. Perhaps one would be waiting in Bamako.

Another day, Francis took me to the central market, on a visit arranged for the ESWA women. Apparently, some of the expatriate women had been in Conakry for two years and had never visited the market! They were too scared. The wife of the US Ambassador had come up with the idea of giving unemployed young boys jobs – in exchange for tips and literacy lessons – as Guardian Angels. We were on the test visit, and all the women (except Francis, who was sensibly low key) were dressed to kill – jewellery, gold belts, handbags, high heels. No wonder they were nervous. Being with them made me nervous!

Afterwards, we had drinks at an air-conditioned coffee shop, and finally only Francis, myself and Francis's friend, Zulrika, were left. Good. Now we could dissect and diagnose the others!

'Did you hear the woman speaking French?' asked Francis, addressing me. I nodded. 'That's the French ambassador's wife – she's a thorough nuisance at ESWA and the bridge club.'

Zulrika agreed. 'She will only speak English at ESWA,' she commented in her sexy voice. Zulrika was serene and statuesque, a real exotic. She was tall and thin, and her blond hair was pulled tightly back to show off her high Slavic cheekbones. Her thick orange lipstick would have been grotesque on some – on her it looked striking against her olive complexion. She was wearing a tight mini-skirt in beige calf, a silk shirt with a gold belt and gold sandals, and had antique rings on each finger – gold and silver and bronze. Totally inappropriate for a market visit, but she would have drawn attention in anything. I was extremely envious.

'She has now taken over the printing of the leaflets for the Christmas bazaar so she can get her way,' said Francis. 'She wants it called the Embassies and ESWA Christmas Bazaar even though the embassies are only contributing a few stalls!'

'And at the bridge club, she is so fierce in telling her partners off,' laughed Zulrika huskily again. 'People are not coming any more!'

One evening, Francis and Mark hosted a dinner party. The menu was incredible. Crab mousse, roast pork with mandarin sauce, Parmesan potatoes and cauliflower cheese, followed by cheeses (cheddar, soft Brie, Danish blue, havarti) and pavlova. All washed down with a 1986 Burgundy. The dining-room table was set with flowers and the good silver. Jean, the houseboy, was dressed up in white trousers and black jacket, and did all the serving. I was rather stylishly dressed in my new Africa outfit, made from wax fabric purchased during the market visit and designed and made by Francis's tailor. It consisted of drawstring trousers and a long-sleeved, V-necked shirt, all in an interesting, blue psychedelic pattern. I felt quite dashing until Zulrika arrived.

Conversation over the delicious crab mousse was about democratisation – the word used to discuss the transition process to democracy that most countries in Africa were undergoing during this time. Democratisation was the hot topic because the first presidential elections were edging closer, with attendant risks of violence. Each tribe wanted their own candidate to win, yet the Susu, the smallest tribe, was apparently the one with current military and political strength. It was thought they would not let go of power easily. I didn't know what a common story this was to become in the countries I was later to visit. At this stage, I mainly listened. The sentiments expressed were similar to those I had heard from M. Keita, the young manager of the Grand Hotel Boiro in Koundara.

I told the guests of how touchingly hopeful Otis, and so many others I had met, had been about the elections. I repeated Otis's words: 'Democracy will help – now that the people can speak out.'

'We will see,' said Mark cautiously, probably realistically.

Over the roast pork and mandarin sauce we discussed Shell, business and consulting – happiness – I was in my element! Then over cheese and pavlova we discussed aid projects for women – I could contribute only a little. (Later in the journey, I would have more to say.)

'Ah, projects these days,' said one of the guests, who worked for USAID, the United States Agency for International Development. 'It is always necessary they help women. So many funding agencies look for that when they decide whether to fund a project.' I thought he was being cynical. Certainly I had passed many buildings in small villages or signs in fields that said: *Projet Pour l'Assistance des Femmes Rurales* – Project for the Assistance of Rural Women, or *Fonds de Credit Pour les Femmes* – Credit Fund for Women. Helping women seemed somewhat flavour of the month, although from what I had observed of women's lives in the villages, the need was huge.

'Women do the most of the work here in Africa,' commented Francis dryly. 'Why shouldn't they participate in the funding?' Then she continued in her energetic way. 'I must take you to the *Concession des Femmes* tomorrow, Pamela.' Another visit, I thought, slightly exhausted. As a feminist career woman who believed in equal opportunity, I had knowledge and views about women's issues like how to juggle a career and personal life, how to overcome the glass ceiling, and the need for gender quotas and protection against sexual harassment in the workplace. However, I had little understanding of, or connection with, other important women's issues in my own society, like single motherhood, wife bashing, rape, going back after a career break for children, child care, prostitution or surviving on a minimum wage. Now, through Francis's introductions, which included a government administrator and founder of a group helping unemployed women gain new skills, and a mission doctor who had a clinic for poor families, I was learning about a whole new range of issues facing disadvantaged women in both traditional and urban African societies – and how they were being helped. It was stimulating, but I wouldn't have minded some time just to explore Conakry, to be a tourist. It was not to be. 'They provide women with sewing machines,' she explained. 'You see, it is not common for women to be tailors, either, and there is a shop where they sell their clothes. Yes, we will go there tomorrow.'

I smiled resignedly, and tucked into my meringue pavlova with strawberries and cream.

I would not have minded some more pavlova with strawberries and cream now I was out on the road again! Having reloaded the panniers on the bicycle after my spectacular slide, I started scrabbling in the food bag – for a banana. It was squashed. I pulled out the hot, soft mess and cleaned my fingers on the ripped trousers of my 'dashing' Africa outfit. Instead of 1986 Burgundy, I swigged warm water from my bottle and chuckled at the memories of Conakry. But I didn't want to be back there – I loved my sense of freedom from being back on the road, being my own boss. Africa here might be worrying, but it felt more real. For now, I was pleased to think that at least

I was more of an Adventurer than Zulrika.

'She wouldn't be out here doing this,' I thought smugly.

Of course, she wouldn't *want* to be doing this.

I squirted water over my head to cool myself down, and thought I should be getting on my way. I was headed for Dabola that night, a reasonably big town, if the Michelin was to be relied upon.

'Take things more slowly.' Again, Françoise's words echoed in my mind.

There was a rustle of leaves and a snake slithered across the road.

Bugger taking things slowly, I thought. I'm out of here!

Elephant grass, yellow, thick and tall, lined the well-graded gravel road as I cycled swiftly out from Dabola the next day on the flat landscape of Haute Guinée. I had budgeted on taking three days to ride the 164 kilometres to Kouroussa, given my snail's pace in the mountains, but now I realised I could do it in two – I had forgotten how fast I could go when the road was good and how fantastic cycling could feel!

Dabola had been a good stop. It was a sizable town, as big as Koundara, but with electricity, and what a difference that made. When I walked out looking for a beer, people were on the streets, standing laughing in groups, walking hand in hand, seated at open-air stalls eating beans or dried fish with rice or millet dishes. There was energy and noise, with people selling things and others walking around doing nothing in particular. It was like a village *place* in Provence on a hot summer's night after market day, and I loved it. Of course, the energy came from a hydropower scheme that had resulted in the damming of the Chutes du Tinkisso. I had seen the remnants of the waterfall during my descent from the Fouta Djalon. Then, it had seemed a shame, but the liveliness and laughter of this town, so much in contrast to misery-bound Koundara, now made me think it was worth it.

My start from Dabola had been delayed while I repacked the bearings of my pedals with grease – they had stopped turning easily, and on opening them, I found the bearings were dry – but I had not contemplated staying on another night; once again, I was enjoying the rhythm of being on the road and wanted to get many kilometres between me and the Fouta Djalon.

Clearly, I was planning to travel more slowly, but not today.

The scenery was beautiful – on each side of the road above the shimmering grass were the proudly raised heads of grey-green, drought-resistant acacias and shea butter trees, and, higher still, the rolling outlines of grey-blue, misty mountains. My smiles to infrequent passers-by, my energy and my sense of exhilaration were hard to contain. Africa was wonderful!

In London, sometimes I felt pointlessness in the daily grind because I could exactly predict the likely outcomes of my life. I was a cog in a well-known system. Now, sometimes, the adrenalin rush of my life was so exhilarating! I had days of sustained highs (when the roads, like today, were good) and felt like Sir Richard Burton or Mary Kingsley. Sometimes, I hit such lows (when the roads were bad, or the mental gulf between myself and the Africans I was meeting seemed insurmountable). On bad days, or portions of bad days, it troubled me to be viewed like an alien with bewildering ways and the open-eyed amazement of others made me feel lonely and isolated. Yet, it was the emotional roller coaster, and the unexpected good and bad, which were so bloody addictive! I might die, I might not, or more prosaically, I might have a good stretch of road, or a bad stretch, I might meet interesting people for a chat – at least I couldn't predict any of it!

After about an hour's ride, I began to pass villagers coming toward me on bicycles or walking with a purposeful stride. Their numbers increased until I had to weave my way through the crowds. Some women wore wrap skirts and matching frilled-sleeve shirts made from waxed-cotton cloth, with a headscarf – a *fula* – tied with flair, the ends perkily standing up at the side or down the back. Others were dressed in similar outfits but made with indigo-dyed and patterned damask, a traditional product of the Fouta Djalon and prized by women throughout West Africa. However, most women wore a *pagne* around their middle with a T-shirt depicting some unlikely image – like Jean-Claude van Damme – and a different length of fabric to tie their baby to their back. The women walked with an erect posture and most were laden with produce they were carrying on their heads – perhaps folded piles of indigo cloth or an enamel basin half filled with fried dough balls, groundnuts or bananas. Men were dressed in greys or whites or blues – plain fabric tailored in a traditional Moslem robe, a *boubou* – and all wore a skull cap – a *tarboosh* – on their heads. Few carried anything.

I smiled happily at people, but although all eyes followed me, not many smiled back – they looked uncertain about my presence and possibly were worried that I was a spirit.

Soon, around a bend I arrived in a small village, and the crowds were denser still. Conversations ceased and eyes stared as I cycled deeper into the busy market square. I could see the brushed clay ground surrounded by shelters made using straight tree branches as uprights and thatch for a flat roof shade. Tables were made of machine-sawed but well-weathered grey planks. Often I passed through quiet villages and deserted marketplaces, but here there were treasure-laden stores and I decided to stop.

'*Toubab!*'

'*Toubab-oo!*'

The cry went out – I had been spotted by the children and they came running toward me from all sides. Some faces had the same worried or awed look as their parents, but most were smiling and laughing, and they pointed fingers at me, clearly finding my strange appearance highly amusing. Shy youngsters hid behind the skirts of their sisters, while the cheekiest came up and touched me or the bike then, squealing, ran away.

The normal welcome I received in villages, then.

I whisked off my hat and scarf and let down my sun-lightened hair to really give them something to talk about. Young men and women smiled shyly at the outer edges of the crowd, but nobody made any attempt to talk to me and, once again, I started feeling a little intimidated by the staring eyes and silent crowd.

Pushing the bicycle towards the stalls, the children parted to let me through and I scanned the tables and mats on the ground for their wares. I wanted some oranges. Except for bananas, it was very hard to find fruit during this season but tiny, tough oranges were sometimes available. I came to the place where several women were seated together – selling oranges.

I smiled and pointed to a pyramid of six orange bullets and, in French, asked the price. The woman seller looked at another trader and they smiled. Her neighbour did not speak French either but sensing my question, undid a knot she had made in the corner of the *pagne* she had around her shoulders, unwrapped the tightly folded but small bundle of notes and coins, extracted the right amount and showed me.

The price was 200 Franc Guinean, then less than 10 pence.

I pulled out coins from my waist bag, handed them to her, bent down to pick up the oranges, undid a rear-side pannier on my bicycle and tossed them in. The crowd watched my pantomime transaction with awe. Their staring was beginning to irritate me; one inner voice was telling me to stay calm – remember, their curiosity is reasonable – but I knew I needed to find someone who could speak French so I could break the spell of silence that my presence had cast over them, so that I could feel I had made contact, make them realise I was human, too!

Walking deeper into the market did not help. With my bike and following crowd, my arrival began to interrupt market transactions and some upset traders started waving their arms and shouting to my entourage. Enough, I thought. I turned the bicycle and picked up my pace. I wanted to get out, to get back onto the road where I could just shout '*Bonjour!*' and escape the relentless stares of any people I passed.

At the road, mounting the bicycle and waving goodbye to my silent watchers seemed to unleash a lot of pent-up excitement; the children started running after me.

'*Toubab-oo!*' they screamed in a frenzy, and literally chased me out of the village.

The next couple of hours grew steadily hotter, and the road became hilly and rutted; it was not the easy day I had expected earlier.

A man came up beside me on a black, unladen Chinese bicycle, the only kind I saw in Guinea (and, in fact, the main bicycle used throughout Africa). I jumped in fright; it was quiet by myself in the bush. I was a little suspicious – what did he want?

'*Bonjour,*' he said calmly. '*Est-ce que vous êtes madame ou mademoiselle?*'

The conversation unfolded predictably, including the request for marriage and for a present. My refusals were taken lightly and were lightly given, for he was a middle-aged man wearing a brown Moslem *boubou* and an old and squashed, embroidered *tarboosh*, and I felt his questions were out of politeness, not with serious intent. It was the younger men, who kept the barrage of marriage questions and requests for gifts going, who really irritated me.

'*Est-ce que vous avez peur?*' he asked. Aren't you afraid?

'*Non,*' I replied. I was cautious about injury, kept my antennae sensitive to risky situations and threatening people, but was not really afraid – that would be an impossible way to live. I continued, as honestly as I could, '*On prend chaque jour par chaque jour*' – I take one day at a time. There was no point in worrying about the possibility of illness, attack or being run over.

'*Vous êtes courageuse,*' he said. You are courageous.

I started warming to him now, feeling content again, and asked him about the next village. I often got recommendations from passers-by for villages where I should stop for lunch or pass the night.

'Kourokoro,' he said. 'About one hour.' My informants were generally better at estimating times than distances. Getting bored with me, he picked up his pace and cycled ahead; I was left to hear my own breathing, to watch the shimmering heat haze again, and to long for female company. I still found African men either handsome, irritating or threatening. What I really wanted was a good gossip. With an African woman. Like I'd gossiped with Françoise.

I remembered Madame Fall, whom I met during the practice journey to St Louis from Dakar. That seemed a lifetime ago, though it was just over two months. Madame Fall was in her early thirties, very pretty and dressed in folds of expensive, cream embroidered cotton. She wore leaf-shaped gold earrings, a gold medallion on a fine chain around her neck and a thick gold bracelet. She was a widow, she told me, and had taken over the running of the service station when her husband had died. After an evening meal, we sat outside under a dark and starry night and gossiped about the 'problem of men' as Madame Fall described it. She told me she would like to marry a rich *blanc*.

'Ah, but men change,' she said.

I nodded in agreement. This was a profound statement.

'At the beginning it is like this …' she crossed two fingers knowingly. 'But afterwards, they do what they want …' She shook her head, a little bitterly, a little disappointed, a little sadly. Like me.

That night, I had been optimistic that the cultural differences were not insurmountable; some things were going to stay the same. But finding African women like Madame Fall or Françoise, or finding any village women, with whom I could gossip was proving rare indeed. Even at night, the women hung back, so even if, unknown to me, a woman could speak French, I was soon monopolised by the men. Despite living an itinerant life for over two months, village women were still strangers.

These reflections took me to the village of Kourokoro. It seemed empty when I arrived. The white turret of a minaret on a small mosque was the main feature of the village; the few small houses I could see were tucked away in compounds behind mud-brick and white stucco-covered walls. There was a dusty marketplace, but it was deserted, and the only likely-looking place for a *sucré* – a soft drink, a small, whitewashed building with a verandah and '*Alimentation Générale*' painted below the roof, was locked.

'*Bonjour!*' It was a child, a small boy of about ten in a grubby white T-shirt and shorts, with a cute, round-faced, younger boy, in a huge shirt dangling to his knees, shyly hiding behind him.

'*Bonjour,*' I replied, and gave them what I hoped was a reassuring smile. I really did not know how to relate to children – they had not been a part of my previous life, but they were a big part of this one! '*C'est fermé?*' – Is it closed? – I asked, pointing at the store. Without a reply, the eldest boy ran away with the younger one running, scared, after him. It made me sad to have this frightening effect on the younger children. Other children started appearing, watching me silently. I greeted another young boy. Even at this age, the girls seemed shyer, but perhaps, given the inequalities of education, they simply had not been taught French. Asking where everybody was only brought a sharp '*Attendez!*' – Wait! – so I concentrated on bringing out my food bag. I pulled out my kitchen knife, a triangle of Laughing Cow cheese, an onion, a squashed piece of baguette and my enamel plate – and made a sandwich.

'*Bonjour!*' I looked up, expecting another child but it was a neat, energetic man, dressed in a brown-and-white-striped cotton robe. He had a black moustache, a short goatee beard and a wicked grin. To my chagrin, I discovered he had been called away from Friday prayers at the mosque to open his store for the *toubab*. I apologised, but he would not hear of it, and as he opened the padlock to his store, he told me his name was M. Kounkaye and that he had been a driver of bush taxis for many years and had travelled all over West Africa. Like taxi drivers everywhere, he loved to talk.

'I have even been to Cameroon!' he exclaimed. On my map that was at least six folds away – too far for me to contemplate, yet. He had painted on one wall of his store the names of Guinean towns and their distances from Kourokoro. 'They are accurate,' he said proudly, 'not like when you ask these villagers.'

We spent a happy two hours together, poring over my maps, me sipping on a warm tonic, M. Kounkaye relating tales from his driving days and providing a guide to the conditions and levels of friendliness I would find in different countries. Children surrounded us, watching intently, but with good conversation I found their company amusing, not intimidating.

'You will like the roads in Burkina Faso and along the coast,' he said. 'But be wary of the traffic in Nigeria!' He reminded me of the cyclists I had met early in the journey who told me they chose their route by looking on the Michelin map for the red lines – the sealed roads. I chose my route by where I wanted to go – and got rutted gravel. I wondered where roads could be worse than in Guinea.

'Make sure you are in Cameroon before the rainy season,' continued M. Kounkaye. 'The roads there are very bad!' (Then, I did not realise the accuracy of his advice.)

I considered stopping for the night – he was an amusing man, a proud Malinké, another cosmopolitan found in a small village – but M. Kounkaye, ever the taxi driver, did not seem to even consider I might not press on today.

'Do not go to Sanguiana. It is too far tonight, and it is only a small village.' That was useful news as it was marked on my Michelin as a big place, like Cisséla. But Cisséla seemed off the road, and I had not thought of going there. 'Stay at Cisséla. It is a prefecture and they will have somewhere for you to stay.' I heeded his practical advice but, as I cycled away, the track through the elephant grass still misty with afternoon heat haze, I still felt that I would have rather stayed in the company of a friendly person rather than in an anonymous prefecture.

Arriving at Cisséla near dusk, I discovered it was just a village, and the prefecture office, a thatch-fenced compound behind which there was a substantial, mud-brick, French colonial-style building, was easy to spot. A group of about ten men, all dressed in traditional and richly embroidered Moslem *boubou*s and *tarboosh*, were seated around a wooden table on the verandah. A meeting? Fierce discussion stopped, it seemed reluctantly, as they saw me. I was given a perfunctory welcome, then, after telling another man to find me a room in the prefecture building, they resumed their meeting.

As I wheeled my bicycle into the allocated bedroom, I was a little put out – I didn't like to be the centre of attention, but now I expected it! Although I was aware of being contradictory and rather self-centred, in this thought I was close to the spirit of Ibn Battuta.

Ibn Battuta, the source of the name of my journey, was born in Tangier in 1304, made his first pilgrimage to Mecca at the age of twenty-one and continued into East Africa and Asia, including China. After returning to Fez in 1349, he crossed the Sahara and travelled extensively in West Africa from 1352 to 1354. On his final return in 1354, Ibn Battuta was allocated a scribe by the Sultan of Fez so that he could record an account of his travels. In fact, the document became one of the major sources of European information about Africa until as late as the eighteenth century, and it remains one of the few written accounts of West African customs and practices at that time.

Battuta's chronicles are filled with value judgments about societies, mostly based on the kind of welcome he received. If he was given gifts and provided luxurious accommodation, he was full of praise for the civility and culture of the welcoming chief or village. If, on the other hand, he was not happy with the hospitality and gifts, whole cities and kingdoms were denigrated.

As I started unpacking my clothes bag and my still large toiletries bag in my room, I thought that I must beware of developing this trait, too.

This was a good stop and these people were generous.

Hell, I had been given a bucket of water for a shower, hadn't I?!

A little later, while closing my eyes on the lumpy bed, letting my muscles start to stretch and listening to a crackling BBC World Service on my small shortwave radio, there was a knock at my door.

'*Madame! Madame!*' called an urgent voice. The president wanted to see me.

I greeted him, but the president, a tall, well-built man in a yellow embroidered *boubou* and white silk *tarboosh*, merely stretched out his arm and pointed.

'*Madame*, thank you. Do you know how to make this work?'

There, next to an empty carton stamped with the words 'Philips' and '*Medécins sans Frontières*', was a video monitor and player.

'It was delivered to us today by a doctor from *Medécins sans Frontières* and we would like to watch a video tonight.'

No wonder no one was interested in my arrival!

The monitor and player were connected to a generator that was operating noisily at the rear of the building – a special supply of diesel fuel must have accompanied the monitor – but no picture appeared when the trial video was pushed in.

'*Je suis desolée,*' I explained, embarrassed, having flipped through the instruction manual and fiddled with a few dials. 'I am sorry. I have never used a video.' In London, I barely watched television. No time. 'I don't know how they work.'

Bewilderment showed on his face: how could a white not know how to operate the video? I was perfunctorily dismissed; again, understandably, of no interest.

I prepared an awful dinner – spaghetti and a tomato paste and onion sauce, no tomatoes (my tomatoes were squashed and fermented) and no spices except salt – on my temperamental petrol stove (its fuel nozzle kept blocking) in the rear of the compound near the noisy generator. As I ate it alone (no children after dark), I reflected on the potential power of this new medium to convey information. In Senegal, I had met a woman who spoke passionately on this subject – she was a film maker – and she had been involved in making educational videos to show in remote villages like this, particularly to help educate the women in their own language.

Around 8 p.m., a boy was sent to fetch me. '*Madame, madame*, would you like to watch the video?' I returned to the front compound to find the whole village was arriving.

The atmosphere was electric, and I was excited to witness what was clearly to be this village's first chance to watch a video. Men, women and children were crowded onto benches, but they fell silent when a man pushed in the cassette. The screen flickered to life. A green channel indicator rested stubbornly on the screen and there were advertisements for forthcoming video releases seen in snowy black and white.

The credits started to roll, and my curiosity turned to horror as I realised these villagers' first encounter with video culture was to be *Rambo II*.

More shattering of preconceptions on my part, and really, I pondered, why should these villagers have their viewing censored or be more restricted, more serious than ours? How much of Sky TV is filled with educational content? *Rambo II* may not have been my choice of a first taste of western culture (or at any time!), but now there would be no denying the arrival of western culture, whatever its form, in Cisséla.

The Niger River was very tranquil at Kouroussa.

I leant over the handrail of the red metal span bridge that carried the tracks of the abandoned Conakry to Kankan railway line and gazed down to the languid green waters below. The river's source was no more than 300 kilometres away in the southern mountains of Guinea, yet here it was already lazy and broad, perhaps 100 metres wide. The dry season had arrived and the water level had already dropped, revealing sandbanks of rich orange loam on either side. Further downstream, dark-green vines entangling bushes and short trees grew densely to the water's edge. The sky was a misty white and the outlines of distant low hills were soft. This haze was formed by sand blown into the air by the harmattan, the strong wind that sweeps continuously across the Sahara into the Sahel, the semi-arid region south of the Sahara, from December until February.

For me, being at the Niger was exciting, a realisation of part of my dream, yet, looking back down to the gentle waters, I wondered, again, why I was here. Why had I left a home and a career to come to Africa? For Adventure? But what was that anyway? A dog bite? Bad roads? Or simply living an emotionally turbulent life that was continually delivering the unexpected?

As I continued to watch the river's languid progress at the start of its journey to the Nigerian delta and to the Atlantic Ocean, I thought of Mungo Park, a late-eighteenth-century Scottish explorer who came in search of the Niger and its course. While 250 years earlier, Ibn Battuta had described the region as peaceful and wealthy, by 1795, huge European demand for slaves had caused tremendous instability and inter-tribal warfare (not unlike the early effects of democratisation). Exhausted by illness and disheartened after many robberies and demands for tribute, Park could only report savagery and greed, thereby shaping emerging European perceptions of the continent. When he returned in 1805 he became even more isolated from hostile tribes and, when under attack, committed suicide by jumping into some dangerous rapids. Poor Mungo.

I dropped a stick over the side of the bridge and watched it catch an eddy then start to be pulled by the current. What *was* I discovering – learning – on this journey? Was I travelling like Mungo Park, remote from those I was meeting, mystified by their ways and, often, suspicious of their motives in helping me? Was I travelling like Ibn Battuta, with an eye for good hospitality? A bit of both, I suspected, yet I could relate to these very human, if not very attractive, reactions to travel in remote, strange lands.

Esprit de Battuta. What was it? About curiosity and discovery? Then, I must not let my bewilderment and suspicion cut me off from others. If I wanted more of it in my voyage, it was up to me, I knew now. Reaching out to women might still be difficult unless the language gap closed in other countries, but certainly, if I wanted to know more about people and their lives I needed to be more open, to ask more questions, to be more trusting, to be the one to make the first move.

Simple, I thought.

Four

Three's Company

Bamako, Mali – Mopti, Mali

Arriving in Bamako, the capital of Mali, marked an achievement: 2300 kilometres completed, three and a half months without getting killed and it was nearly Christmas! Most importantly, it marked a return to bitumen, *le goudron*, the first since leaving Mamou nearly three weeks before. It was better than – well, I won't exaggerate, as good as – an orgasm, so I stopped the bicycle and kissed it, much to the bemusement of the young girls walking past with buckets of water on their heads. They ran squealing away from the mad white woman, but I did not care, I was nearly back to a city.

Conakry had been a Rip Van Winkle town waking up from a thirty-year snooze; Bamako was different.

Vehicles crammed the roads – there were overloaded trucks lumbering their way to some unknown destination, packed bush taxis, an occasional, immaculate four-wheel-drive vehicle, and of course, rickety carts charged with people and produce being pulled by one or two skinny, white oxen. Throughout the chaos weaved noisy motorbikes, all heavily laden with several passengers. Sometimes, an entire family – the man in Moslem *boubou* hitched up to reveal skinny legs, driving, a toddler hanging to his stomach, another child straddling the petrol tank, at the rear a woman in traditional *pagnes* sitting side saddle with a baby secured to her back *and* a large basket of tomatoes held tightly in her arms. Then there were the motorbikes that passed with a goat as passenger, its two back legs tied together, its two front legs tied together, loaded on its back over the rear carrier and understandably bleating loudly about its awful last trip. I weaved my way in and out, too, nerves jangling at the increased noise and pace in my life, hoping it wasn't *my* last trip.

The power lines and shops started, small wooden stalls open to the street so I could see their trestle tables of goodies, their refrigerators and posters advertising Castel beer and ice creams! It was exciting to be back in the world of goodies, but I had to stay calm to cope with the increasing traffic, to spot the signs for *Centreville*. I spied an *alimentation générale* with a telephone symbol and cycled over so I could call my Shell contact – M. Adebunu, the *directeur général*.

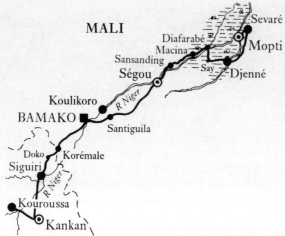

'You're late! We were expecting you a month ago!' I was also back in a world of timetables. 'Where are you now?'

'On the outskirts of Bamako.'

'*Aye!*' There was a surprised pause, followed by, 'Why didn't you call us sooner?'

'There were no phones in Guinea, and I've just come in on the road from Kourémalé.'

Phones were not plentiful in the villages, but this seemed a hard concept for the business world to comprehend.

Quickly he gave directions to the office, becoming more excited as he spoke. 'You must stay with my wife and family, and I will get someone to start working on your programme!' I welcomed the offer of accommodation and admired his enthusiasm for this unexpected stray from the bush, but cringed at the thought of another packed programme – it was Christmas, after all.

In fact, I ended up having a great time with charming Tevi Adebunu, his friendly wife Cherita and their three children. My programme was light and I did chores like changing money, writing a newsletter for WOMANKIND and getting a visa for Burkina Faso, my next country.

Soon, I became aware of Bamako's poverty. As I walked its noisy, hot streets, hazy from dust blown up by the harmattan, it was impossible not to see the beggars – the ragged, gaunt cripples, their legs wasted and twisted – who scurried about on their hands, the lepers on crutches with bandaged hands and feet, sufferers of oncho (river blindness), and orphans looking like hungry *Oliver Twist* urchins. The poverty here seemed more evident than in other West African cities I had visited so far. Perhaps I had been too insulated in other capitals, but perhaps, with per capita incomes in Mali amongst the lowest in the world, it was simply because people here were poorer.

After independence in 1960, the country became Marxist, with nationalised industries, fixed agricultural prices and isolation from the French and other African neighbours leading to economic stagnation, huge foreign debts and bloated bureacracies. Even as the economy weakened, Mali continued down a socialist path until the early eighties. Reforms eventually started, but the terrible droughts of the seventies and eighties and the accompanying famine contributed to worsening poverty. As a landlocked country with few natural resources, accelerating desertification of land in previously semi-arid but arable areas due to poor land management and rapid population growth, Mali's prospects were not great.

By Christmas Day, I was ready for a retreat from confrontation with human suffering and poverty.

While not Moslems, Tevi and Cherita did not celebrate Christmas, so I spent the day with Connie, an American Peace Corps Volunteer (PCV) I had first met about a week before my arrival in Bamako. For her two-year PCV commitment, she was living in the remote village of Doko in eastern Guinea near the Malian border.

'There is a white here, we will show you,' said children when I arrived in Doko's market. Intrigued, I followed them willingly to her hut – to meet a tall, blonde twenty-six year old from the Midwest. However, she was thoughtful, lonely and nearly as dishevelled as me, so we got on immediately! She invited me to stay in her hut, I had another dust cold – no argument. For three days we talked in her hut, happy to seal out Africa, to be nostalgic about 'home' and, especially, to reminisce about Christmas foods – turkey, stuffing, pudding and wine. She was heading to Bamako for her leave, and we decided to meet there.

We spent Christmas Day together at the lavish, art-filled home of the influential director of USAid who was away in the US for the holidays. He entrusted his home to a Peace Corps administrator, Trent, who invited Connie, who invited me – complicated, but camaraderie was high in Africa amongst European folk who were living a spartan village life. It was definitely a retreat from impoverished Bamako.

'Let's look at the art!' said Trent, our host, an insipid and rather shallow man, of about thirty-five, with thinning hair and a compensatory bushy beard. I was not impressed by him, but as I said, camaraderie was high – particularly when there was a pool on offer.

Connie and I followed him into the air-conditioned house to tour the glass cases filled with Bambara goldwork, Tuareg silverware, Nigerian bronze sculptures, Ghanaian Ashanti stools and many different kinds of masks. It was a private, tiny museum of the artwork of West Africa's glorious past – especially rich in artwork of the gold wealthy Mali empire, founded in 1234 by Sundiata Keita, and visited by Ibn Battuta in 1350. Fabulous!

Clearly, the old Mali empire was not to be confused with today's Mali.

Afterwards, outside on the terrace, overlooking the pool and garden – a lush riot of different types and maturities of palms – we ate our midday Christmas dinner. It was not quite turkey.

We sourced our meal from goodie parcels Connie and I had both received. I had a huge one from William – no passionate letter, but maybe actions from an Englishman were meant to speak louder than words. For main course, Connie had a peanut butter and jelly sandwich, I had a Vegemite sandwich.

Then, we shared some of my mother's Christmas cake, William's mince pies and Connie's father's M&Ms. Mmm. More orgasmic pleasure.

During the afternoon, we discussed a lot of topics, including the abhorrent practice of female genital mutilation.

'I want to find out more,' said Connie, 'but the women in my village avoid talking about it.' Connie was learning the local language, one up on me in the challenge to talk with African women. We knew little other than that the practice was very prevalent in West Africa and ranged from clitoridectomy to excision of the inner labia to excision of most of the outer labia as well. The reasons it was performed varied – from ensuring women did not enjoy sex and remained faithful to their husbands, to a more vague but insidious belief in it as a necessary tradition.

'Apparently, educated women are less likely to adopt the practice for their daughters, but older women in the villages want it continued,' explained Connie. 'In fact, one woman in Conakry told me that she wouldn't let her daughters see their grandmother by themselves – she knew the grandmother would immediately arrange the girls' operations.' (Connie not only went on to make an educational video about this practice for Guinean village women, on her return to the US she studied video making for traditional societies and now works in the field.)

Late in the sleepy, hot afternoon, as Connie and Trent dozed, I sipped at my beer and felt very lucky to be behind the high compound wall. This retreat was definitely helping to recharge my emotional batteries, and I was again looking forward to the relative solitude of the road.

'Swim, anyone?' asked Connie, suddenly waking up. She was a more energetic and enthusiastic Connie than the one I first met in Doko; her batteries, like mine, had been recharged by this break.

'Sure,' I called. 'Beat you in!'

'Aye, it's a white!' cried a woman, mimicking the usual amazement of children at seeing me in their midst. Two Europeans, the woman and a man, were standing drinking the ubiquitous Miranda orange sodas, under the awning of a mud-brick shop in the road-stop village of Santiguila, 60 kilometres outside Bamako. Their laden bicycles were propped against the wall of the shop.

My original plan – to take a boat from Koulikoro, near Bamako, along the Niger River to mysterious Timbuktu – had been scuttled by the dog bite and the month's delay. Now, the water levels had dropped and no boats were running. So my revised plan was to cycle to Mopti – about 800 kilometres north-east of Bamako, leave my bicycle in Mopti, then take a boat to Timbuktu return – *if* the water levels there were still high enough for shallow boats to pass.

'Aye, it's two whites!' I called in return.

They were Susanna and Alistair from Glasgow. They had cycled from Banjul in The Gambia and, like me, were headed for Mopti, but they were not intending to travel to Timbuktu. Instead, they were going to immediately travel south by the same route I had planned into Burkina Faso and Ghana, finishing their journey in Accra, the capital of Ghana, on the Atlantic coast.

Susanna had long red hair, was deeply tanned and wore an outfit of loose-fitting trousers and sleeveless shirt, clearly locally made, like my own tattered Africa outfit made in Conakry. Susanna was the more exuberant of the two, and while we excitedly exchanged our tales, Alistair, her lanky, blond partner, remained more reserved. I soon learnt that was just Al's pleasant way.

We exchanged tales about our routes – bad roads figured highly! It felt comforting to talk with people who knew this region of Africa and who had shared similar experiences.

I tried to draw Al into the conversation. 'What do you do, Al?'

'I'm a graphic designer.'

'What do you design?'

'Och, various things,' he said slowly, enigmatically. 'I had my own graphic design firm in Glasgow.'

This was evidently a lot of words from Al.

Suze took over – our stories were still bubbling out – but it was getting dark.

'We've already put up our tent in the grounds of the *commandant*, want to join us?' I did. There were no hotels in town and camping required permission from the police chief, so half an hour passed arranging permission and putting up my tent near Al and Suze's; then we decided it was time for food. How energised I suddenly felt with company!

Using torches to guide our way, we walked back to the main road where we found a long line of tables, kerosene lamps now burning and women cooking on charcoal stoves.

'I'm having *brochettes*!' I exclaimed, seeing beef kebabs cooking as I shone my torch at a stove. After so much rice and fish stew, I found kebabs a fantastic new addition to my diet in Mali.

'We're vegetarian,' said Al. Oops.

'We've started eating fish, but we're always looking for beans,' said Suze, then chuckled. 'We're so fed up with omelettes!' I could imagine – being a vegetarian in Africa would not be easy and, unthinkingly, I related the story I knew of a vegetarian couple who had died in the Sudan because they wouldn't eat meat.

'Why do you have a '*J'aime Shell*' T-shirt?' asked Al suddenly. My 'I love Shell' T-shirt was a gift from M. Adebunu. I explained about Shell's logistical support and also about the connection to WOMANKIND, but I sensed Al didn't approve of Shell. My having been a business consultant didn't seem to cut much ice either.

'I worked for Oxfam, and now we volunteer,' said Suze. 'We're active in the Glasgow campaign group.' Oops, again.

Two vegetarian, Oxfam-supporting Scots from Glasgow and an oil company-supported, big-business Australian from London. Could we really get along? We decided to cycle together to Ségou, the next major town two days' cycle away, but made no commitments beyond that. We needed to get beyond our mutual stereotyping to discover any real compatibility. Fortunately, as all travellers experience, once you travel with someone, you get to know them very quickly.

'STOP following us!!' yelled a hot and bothered Susanna the next day, turning her bicycle to chase the hordes of screaming children who had been running after us beyond their village. The alarmed children retreated, their aggravating calls of '*Toubab! Toubab-oo!*' subsiding in the face of this assault from the angry redhead.

I grinned and could have kissed and hugged her. Yes!! I was not the only white female in West Africa who didn't like these kids chasing me, who didn't like their yelling, screaming and touching. I was not, therefore, the defective, uncaring and horrible person I feared; someone else found their screams insupportable, too. Yippee!

'How do you feel about their staring?' I asked Suze as she wheeled the bicycle around and came back to cycle beside me, somewhat calmed down, but now embarrassed. I liked that, too, because that was how I always felt once I had lost my temper with the little brats.

'I hate it. Isn't it awful? It's like you're really weird, and you're trying to stay calm, but they just keep staring and it is soooo annoying.' Hallelujah!

On the road to Ségou, we had to ride single file much of the time – it was extremely busy with fast vehicles – but Suze and I found time to chat. She was not an African woman but I had found a gossiping partner! We seemed to have the same cycling pace – at least, Suze and I would cycle together far ahead, with Al trailing behind.

'The more you two talk,' commented Al at one water stop, 'the faster you cycle – and the more you talk!'

We arrived in handsome, large Ségou desperate for a beer – we had that in common, too.

'I feel like a desert survivor from *Ice Cold in Alex*!' exclaimed a parched Suze.

It was New Year's Eve, and we were determined to have fun. Our drunken renditions of an off-key 'Auld Lang Syne' and 'Waltzing Matilda' seemed to astonish local African, Lebanese and French patrons at a Ségou restaurant, as did loud shouts of '*Bonne Année!*' to Malians as we weaved our way back to our hotel through the dark, quiet, tree-lined streets of Ségou in the early hours of the New Year.

We spent three days in Ségou, not having made any conscious decision to stick together – we just liked its pace and style after the noise and dirt of

Bamako. Despite being the second largest town in Mali after Bamako, it was more like a big, sprawling village than a mini-city. Having obtained information from some locals, we stayed at the *Office du Niger Campement*, a fairly plain building in the quiet administrative quarter of Ségou, a little out of town but nestled amongst some magnificent sandstone buildings, relics of the French colonial period when Ségou was the headquarters for an irrigation scheme planned for the growing cotton. The buildings were in a very graceful, neo-Sudanic architectural style, which meant two-storey (generally) box-like buildings with 360-degree balconies on both floors, each balcony enclosed by stone arches shaped like the prow of a boat, and the entire building surrounded by external turrets, looking like multiple Cleopatra's needles, reaching from the ground to above the flat rooftop. I spent hours drawing one building, enchanted by the detail of its turrets and shuttered windows surrounded by palms and mango trees.

The streets of Ségou were generally dirt but well-shaded by mango and neem trees, important, for as we got further into the dry season, temperatures were soaring. Inhabitants walked the streets in a slow shuffle, barely lifting their legs, seemingly to preserve their energy in the sometimes suffocating heat.

'*Bonjour.*'

'*Bonjour.*'

'*Ça va?*'

'*Ça va bien, merci, et vous? Ça va?*'

'*Ça va bien, merci, et les femmes? Ça va?*'

'*Ça va, merci.*'

'*Ça va.*'

Greetings in Mali go on forever! These exchanges would be made with any casual passer-by, and were essential before you could get down to the business of asking them for directions to the market or the post office or the river. If we had been locals, the greetings would continue, enquiring after our health, the health of our father, our mother, the brothers, the sisters, and so on. At least a benefit of being a threesome with a male was that Al got most of the greetings, Suze and I were only his appendages in Moslem male eyes; I didn't mind, as it took away some of the pressure of always being the centre of attention.

We adopted the Mali shuffle and were content to see the traditional houses of the Bambara people and to walk by the wide Niger River. The houses had a different architectural style to the Malinké of Guinea, even though the two tribes were closely related. Compounds were enclosed by red-painted, stucco-covered, mud-brick walls. Inevitably, the small dwelling made from the same material was in one corner, the hen and goat house in the opposite corner. Bamako, also built alongside the Niger, had its town centre far back from the river, and its banks were not as accessible as in Ségou. We particularly enjoyed watching the women washing clothes in the river, children soaped up, playing and shouting at each other as they cleaned themselves, and the black cigar shapes of the traditional wooden dugout canoes far out in the stream where the fish were biting.

During our three days in Ségou we talked – while walking, while eating at the *Snack Golfe*, our favourite cheap restaurant where we could get chips (with chicken, meat or fish, but usually everything was off, except fish and chips), and while drinking beer, passing away stifling afternoons at the *campement*. Again, Suze and I were garrulous, Al added comments intermittently.

We shared our histories, discovering we were each at watershed periods in our lives. In some ways, we were both using our journeys to take time to reflect on future directions. We also had pet topics – typical African conversation fodder about aid and development.

'Women spend so much time on chores!' declared Suze. 'They go to fields, they come back, they gather wood for fuel, get water from pumps, prepare food, clean the compound, wash the clothes, the children, themselves. They have such long days. Projects help women if they just get villagers to allocate nearby land to grow trees for fuel or to put pumps closer to their homes.'

'Projects implementing new agricultural techniques or an irrigation system need to involve women to be effective,' said Al quietly. 'Sometimes, when they've only involved the men, they've later found it's the women who do most of the farming – but by then they've taken poor advice!'

Suze smiled wryly. 'Mm,' she agreed. 'Then agricultural experts at aid agencies comes up with a great idea like getting the women to grow lettuce!' She was referring to the fact that in Mali, on our nightly food forages, we were occasionally able to buy a salad of lettuce greens, a few cut-up radishes and tomatoes, no dressing. Aid agencies had introduced the new vegetables to the women to help them increase their sources of income. Although undoubtedly suggested with good intentions, the experts seemed to have neglected the fact that Malians were not very familiar with salad ingredients or recipes. 'They haven't thought whether the women can sell what they produce!'

My pet topic, drawing on my Madagascar consulting experience and general knowledge of big aid from my previous life, was the International Monetary Fund (IMF)'s Structural Adjustment Programmes (SAPs). These were the tough economic policies demanded by the IMF for rescheduling African nations' huge foreign exchange debts. Debt forgiveness was not on the table, and the policy blueprints were almost identical in every country, encompassing privatisations, sacking bureaucrats, devaluations of local currency and other market reforms, plus political reform toward democratisation. Terrible pain was being experienced by the country's poorest people as they implemented the SAPs.

'If corrupt bankers and aid donors hadn't given that money without adequately monitoring where it was going, maybe the debt wouldn't be so high and a country like Mali wouldn't have to follow the IMF's rigid policies,' I said to Al and Suze, up on my soap box. Until recently, lenders in the World Bank – the IMF's sister infrastructure funding agency – were not evaluated on the performance of their loan books, only on their size, so of course, their incentive was to make big loans for big schemes. They had no vested interest in whether the road, dam or bridge was ever built and the loan repaid.

'Did you hear the story about the bridge in Bamako?' asked Al.

'That it had been funded three times before it was built?' I queried, and he nodded. These kinds of 'jokes' were everywhere in aid circles. 'Yes, I heard it – but I bet the corruption wouldn't have been one-sided.' During the Cold War, many so-called 'loans' were made with the full knowledge of the donors that the money would be diverted into official pockets, but this was the price of a friendly government being kept in power. These 'loans' supplied the Swiss bank holdings of Africa's old dictators and, to me, it seemed unfair that their country's people should have to repay.

'The lenders got the services they paid for,' I suggested. 'The debts on the books should be written off.'

Clearly, there was, and is, a lot of economic mismanagement in Africa; in Mali, during socialist times, people found employment as state-paid *functionnaires* – administrators, public servants – even when the productivity of those enterprises was in sharp decline and there was nothing for them to do. However, sacking *functionnaires* and taking away the social safety net, and devaluing the currency, making imports like pharmaceuticals beyond the reach of ordinary Africans, had not delivered any replacement investment or employment. The pain was meant to be short term, leading to a new era of efficiency and international competitiveness, the ability to export more and earn foreign exchange income. But this was not happening.

'Did you hear the French have been accused of dumping beef in Bamako?' asked Suze. Shit. 'I heard they're selling it at lower prices than the Peul farmers can produce it.' This was typical – the developed nations tell poorer countries to become internationally competitive, then put up their trade barriers to agricultural imports – the principal exports of the developing world. As a final insult, they then dump their own subsidised surplus – taking away even the local markets of poor farmers! In my opinion, there needed to be some serious rethinking of the SAPs and debt forgiveness to help big aid deliver its stated objectives and become more humane.

(Later, especially in Asia, the IMF's policies would be called into serious question. Debt write-off for African nations continues to be only tentatively explored.)

Through our quiet, talkative and fun days in Ségou, we had discovered we were compatible, and so we decided to continue cycling together. I was very happy to have the company.

Rather than follow the main road to Mopti that we had both initially planned to take, we identified a quieter road alongside the Niger – although unsealed, it would be better for Suze and I to talk! We would cross to the northern bank, travel to Sansanding, Macina and Diafarabé, then cross to the south bank and travel to Say, Djebbé and Djenné. After this, having covered about 300 kilometres from Ségou, we would rejoin the main road for the final 130-kilometre stretch to Mopti. All in all, a short hop.

Our route along the Niger River to Djenné was very beautiful. The golden-yellow stubble of the cotton or millet was scattered over ochre, sandy, furrowed fields. Thorn-filled, scrubby acacias marked the road edge and the boundaries between fields; these left Al and Suze with several punctures each day, while my kevlar-lined tyres proved their worth. Bozo fishermen in *pirogues* – long wooden canoes carved from tree trunks – poled their way along the Niger, or used small, white cotton sails, dragging nets and their catch behind them; Peul herdsmen with sometimes fifty, sometimes ten, head of hump-backed, hollow-sided cattle crossed our path, or we encountered the bones and wide, curving horns of an unlucky bull.

In fact, we were cycling through the inland delta of the Niger River. Once a lake, this huge, elevated region where the Niger meanders is still flooded between June and October. It is a perfect place to grow cereals, and the pasture that grows following the wet is good cattlefood for the livestock of the Peul nomads. Near Kolongotomo the land became marshy, and we cycled across dykes. At dusk, Al pulled up sharply. We stopped and listened as cracks sounded.

'Are those rifle shots?'

'Is it hunters? Perhaps we need to wear brighter clothes so they know we're not cows,' I said flippantly.

'Perhaps it's bandits,' said cheerful Al – the road was pretty quiet.

Suze had kept cycling, but further ahead, we could see she'd stopped. As we caught up with her, she pointed into the field. A large number of men stood in the fields cracking long whips and yelling to scare off birds.

That night at the remote village of Kolongotomo, we stayed at the *campement*, a two-storey structure with a flat roof. The evening was hot and still, so we decided to set up our tents – both self-standing – on the roof. We stayed dirty and dusty, didn't bother to find a shower that night, content to chat and let the evening descend upon us. Soon, it was dark and stars densely studded the sky.

'Look, I have found a new use!' cried Suze with glee, after she had been looking for somewhere to settle her burning candle. She had emptied her large, purple plastic bucket, upturned it, let a few drops of grease drop on its base and then secured the candle. '*Voilà!*' she said with a satisfied flourish and flip of her long red hair. 'It's a table!'

The bucket had been bought in Ségou, much to Al's disgust. However, we had found many uses for it: for washing clothes, washing dishes, and washing ourselves; during the day, attached to the carrier, it could be used for holding the dirty charcoal stove and charcoal; and in the markets, it was a grocery bag for buying fruit and vegetables. A bucket was a Very Useful Thing.

Cycling to Macina, our destination for the next day, Suze discovered a Less Than Useful Thing.

'I'm fed up with you!' yelled Suze, not at Al, but at her poor bicycle helmet. In Africa, it was just dead weight tied to the back of the bicycle, where it kept slipping and hitting the rear wheel – and making an irritating clunking noise. She stopped – Al and I also halted in awe of another spectacular Suze explosion – then, she grabbed the helmet and threw it into the bush. 'Just go, then!'

Al and I exchanged an amused glance, and Suze huffed onwards.

Later in the afternoon, Suze and I chuckled, once again, about the extreme emotions Africa drew from us.

'Don't you think that's an essential part of the African experience?' she asked, now calm. 'Those intense ups and downs, and those contradictory emotions – sometimes, even in the same day, hating Africa, and sometimes loving it so much!' I certainly did.

That evening, we arrived in Macina, a fairly ordinary, although pleasant, small administrative town, with a wide, main avenue shaded by a long line of ancient, giant neem trees.

Suze and I wandered out into the dark streets looking for food. I wanted meat, not beans, so we went to a small, deserted restaurant and called out to find the cook.

'Yes, you may have chicken, *madame*,' said the young man, looking like he had been asleep. 'But it will take one hour.'

'One hour?' I queried. That seemed a long time. In response, the man pointed out into the compound – towards chickens scratching in the dirt. I gulped – one of those poor creatures would be my dinner?

Susanna chuckled. 'Not so keen now, eh? Ready to be a vegetarian, eh?'

'Let's go get some beans,' I said, laughing at my own squeamishness.

A few days later, travelling to Diafarabé, the track was particularly close to the Niger river and, in a deep waterhole, we saw a herd of grey hippopotami.

'Ibn Battuta wrote about those,' I told Suze – Al was far behind by this time, and we had been chatting for some time. 'He was pretty impressed, but could only describe them by what they were not – neither horses nor elephants.'

'Well, he probably couldn't see much of them,' answered Suze, quite accurately; they were impressive but elusive creatures, just raising their eye ridges above the waterline to give us a haughty glance.

We cycled through small villages that seemed little changed from Mungo Park's time, or even from that of Ibn Battuta. They were mud walled, always quiet, with a cleared marketplace filled with simple, shaded structures, and always a dominating, turreted mosque. We became used to the loud, mournful calls of the imam to the faithful to come to prayer – five times a day! In even the tiniest village, the calls are made over loudspeakers – not like in Ibn Battuta's time – and we saw the faithful, usually men, unrolling their mats in the dirt, and bowing down to their God. The mosques in each village were different – sometimes they were built with regular, manufactured bricks, covered in stucco and painted white or rosy pink, mostly they were made from irregular, locally formed mud bricks and covered in a hand-smoothed mud surface, left in the colour of the earth. Each had original features – turrets, protruding wooden stakes, arched windows or small openings in the mud walls. These handcrafted mosques seemed sensitive and sensual structures in a land that demanded practicality and will to survive.

Later, on the dry road to Say, the track merely a series of tyre marks weaving across the dusty plain dotted by thorn trees, Al and I spent a long afternoon cycling, talking about our dreams for the future.

'Suze and I want to move out of Glasgow, buy a house on Arran, and run a cycle touring business.' Having established that Arran was an island off the coast of Scotland, I felt my consultant's hat come on.

'Surely Scotland's too wet for tours, and it will be a short season. Why don't you do cycle tours to Africa in the winter?'

'No,' said Al thoughtfully, 'I think bringing a lot of people on tours would be too disruptive to the local culture.'

I mulled on that for a while. 'But it's a hard business to be in – anybody can come and do the same thing. It means you'll find it hard to make a profit.' Shut up, Pamela, I told myself, this is the man's dream!

'What are you going to do, then?' he asked, 'Go back to consulting?'

'No, I want a business in Africa – something that is worthwhile, probably in food processing, so that I can employ people, maybe buy the raw materials from women and give them a market, or maybe something that is useful for them. Then, I'd like to use some of the profits back in the local community, maybe with a credit scheme for local women to help them with their businesses.'

'What would you produce?' asked Al. It all sounded a bit vague, even to me.

'I've always wanted a sweet factory ...'

Al snorted good-humouredly. 'Och, rot little children's teeth, then?' He was right.

'Well, I might grow apples in Madagascar ...' and I told him about that dream. 'Except the climate is too cold for me!' I was easily turned off. 'Okay, I'll produce Vegemite for Africa – that's healthy and good for the kids. And it's made from dead yeast – they make so much beer here in Africa, and I bet all the waste yeast is just dumped.' Later, I discovered in several places that brewery yeast is dumped in waterways, creating an environmental problem –

at a minimum, it could be used for cattle food or fertiliser. It was my favourite idea, uneasily disclosed, but Al thought it was very funny.

(Of course, I'm still dreaming, and as Al foretold, back in the world of consulting, while Al and Suze now live on Arran and run a cycle touring business.)

The villages were often quiet – and we seemed to be always missing market day. Were the people at markets somewhere else? The mud-walled houses sat closely together and had closed wooden doors, tiny openings for windows and mud stairs leading to flat roofs where prayer, or chores, or conversation in the cool of the evening and morning, could occur. But there were few people and, particularly, few women in these villages; perhaps they had gone to distant markets to sell the produce from their harvests. A common sight was a few cattle wandering through the sandy streets, encouraged on by a young boy with a stick who trailed behind, and bullocks towing carts laden with sacks of rice, and donkeys being coaxed into carrying heavy loads of millet.

However, it was not completely quiet. After a brief lull of clear weather and quiet days, the harmattan came up strongly and the scene turned milky white. The wind shrieked continuously, and we pulled scarves around our faces to protect our eyes from the whirling sand and the glare-filled landscape. We looked like bandits. It was cold without the sun, and we even had to wear our fleeces during the day. With the January sun low in the southern sky, the misty veil of air over the river was backlit and iridescent. The Niger River glittered steel-grey. Distant trees, boats and villages had soft outlines, while nearby scenes jumped intensely from their milky, obscure backdrop. It was exquisite, although often our mood did not let us appreciate it. The wind coming from the north-east across the Sahara made cycling, even breathing, very difficult, and our track became sandier – sometimes we had to push for hours.

'You bloody bike!' I yelled as I threw my bicycle down into the sand in a fit of anger. I had become bogged – yet could see Al and Suze cycling onwards through the deep drifts, a common sight. Despite continued shedding of my load (no water filter now, tape recorder or second camera), Al and Suze each had a lighter load. I thought couples had weight advantages – many of a bicycle expedition's essential items don't directly multiply with the number of people. Suze thought I did too much shopping.

'Take that!' I shouted as I kicked the poor bicycle. Oops. My kick snapped the front handlebar bag carrier.

Emotional ups and downs – an essential part of the Africa experience!

We left early from our night stop at Djebbé, a small village, to travel the 15 kilometres to Djenné. It was now a week since we had left Ségou, and a Monday – Djenné's famous market day. We wanted to arrive in good time. The harmattan was still blowing, and we muffled our faces with scarves, but the sun was not blocked out by the sand in the air, so the day seemed brighter. We passed a boy pulling a stubborn goat by a string around its neck, and two Peul men expertly leading a herd of cattle. Then there was a group of talkative, excited women, colourfully dressed, each with a baby attached to her back by a cloth wrap and an enamel basin containing dried fish on her head. We progressed further and passed a sack-laden donkey, its nimble-footed young owner and several bullock carts. Some seemed to be carrying just one couple and their produce, others seemed to be public transport, the carts filled with sacks, basins, pots and basketware, and passengers arranged over the top. Soon, the trickle of encounters turned into a traffic jam of people walking, animals and carts. Everybody was headed for Djenné's market.

Suddenly, unmistakably, above the muddy plain, the misty outline of a great city rose magically before us – the high turrets of a massive, mud-brick mosque, far larger than any we had encountered before, enclosed by a long, mud-brick wall. The whole city was surrounded by lush, green vegetation and elevated high upon an island. It was magnificent, a place from a distant time.

In fact, Djenné has long been one of the greatest of the Sahelian trading cities and a centre of religious scholarship. It was founded in the ninth century, became Moslem in the late twelfth or early thirteenth century and rapidly grew to be the most famous Moslem city in the western Sudan. It was an entrepôt for salt coming from the desert, which was in great demand from traders going further south, and became (and still is) a major centre for Islamic missionaries. Timbuktu was only a later rival as a trading and religious centre.

We entered the city across a dyke, joining a throng of others. It was extremely busy: the market was underway even in the narrow streets, and in the main square, we were confronted by an incredible sight – tangles of sellers, produce, animals, customers, beggars, dust, and overshadowing it all, the wood-staked turrets of the magnificent mosque. People were unloading and jostling for position and new arrivals were still trying to squeeze their way through the square.

'These children look like they're starving!' cried Suze, as disturbed as I was by the children who surrounded us. These were not the usual curious kids, but hungry-eyed, grasping beggars, their heads shaven, their skin white from dust and their clothes just holey rags. They were orphans and children put into the care of marabouts who were meant to educate and feed them. We heard during our stay in Djenné that they were made to recite the Koran until word perfect and kept in near-starvation conditions so that they had to beg to survive; it was all a part of their training. We felt distressed for them and could not understand how this was educational or humane, but their clutching presence and almost mad eyes made our walks into Djenné very disturbing. We could not give to them all, yet how could we buy or eat anything with such an audience?

Seeing such dense crowds before us in the market and knowing we would probably soon get separated, we decided to split up.

'Meet you at the *campement*,' called Suze to me. 'Don't buy too much!'

The market itself was extraordinarily colourful and multi-ethnic, with an immense variety of produce for sale. It was clearly still an international entrepôt, and there were products I recognised: indigo cloth from Guinea and garments from Senegal. Roughly ground salt, heaped on hessian and watched over by a keen seller, was still available. Usually, African markets are dominated by food, the necessities – rice, beans, dried fish and the seasonal items like tomatoes, and by the manufactured goods, like waxed fabrics and plastic buckets. But this market was remarkable for the range of traditional products, hand crafts and the work of artisans, even broader, I thought, than that available at the *grande marché* in Bamako. There were hand-woven rugs, patchwork cloth, calabashes (from the fruit of the baobab), large clay cooking pots, decorated clay water urns, locally made mud cloth, Tuareg silverware, handcrafted ceramic beads, elaborate woodcarvings, clay ovens, basketware and hand-cast gold jewellery. Artisans were not only selling finished products, but also making them to order. Goldsmiths were at work, so were the makers of mud cloth. I even found a blacksmith – *un forgeron* – who made me a new handlebar carrier for my bicycle. I watched in awe as he used the bellows to heat his coal fire and softened a scrap of thick wire. He removed it from the fire with forceps and used a hammer to beat the wire into shape; it worked perfectly for the rest of my journey.

Despite Suze's warning, I shopped! I bought cloth – lightweight cloth, better for the heat – found a tailor, drew my designs on a piece of paper and left him to make up my new Africa outfits. Having also bargained intensely for mud cloth, beads, Ashanti cloth from Ghana, some silverware *and* a basket, I decided I better go to the post office – before Suze saw my purchases!

'It must be sewn,' said the postal worker.

Huh? Then, I realised that, for better security, the post office asked that parcels be wrapped in cotton fabric and sewn up. Another visit to the tailor!

By dusk, people were going home and, dropping on my feet, I headed back to the *campement*. The imam called the faithful to prayer, his haunting cries, loud over the speakers, reverberating in the emptying marketplace and down the alleyways of this ancient town.

We stayed in Djenné several days, before continuing cycling, now back on bitumen and away from the Niger River, for the final, hot 130 kilometres to Sevaré, the small crossroads town 12 kilometres outside Mopti. Rather than cycling into Mopti, an ancient, but dirty and crowded, trading town on three islands in the Niger, we decided to stay together in Sevaré, where there was a clean hotel, real beds and running water, and to visit Mopti on day trips. It was as well we did, because Al became very ill with fever.

Al had had a few bouts along the way, the first in Ségou, another in Macina, another in Djenné. Suspecting malaria, he had been dosing himself with chloroquine, and we had rested, always a day or so beyond the fever, always hoping that now it was cured. In Macina, he had even tried to have his blood tested, but the solar-powered microscope used to examine the blood for the malaria parasite was not working – the sand lifted by the harmattan had blocked out the sun.

Now, in Sevaré, the fever took hold again, fiercely, and Al, who had never been robust looking to start with, became paler, thinner and more listless daily. While I went in to Mopti to research boats to Timbuktu, Suze took Al to the medical centre, where they confirmed that he had malaria.

This disease, the major child killer in Africa, is dreadful. Al took a succession of Halfen and Fansidar, two of the modern 'cures'. It seemed that, despite taking prophylactics as we all did, poor Al had picked up a strain resistant to these drugs, probably from a mosquito in The Gambia, where these tougher strains were common. His fever was returning every three or four days, and he was very weak. It was alarming to see his health evaporate, his eyes become sunken and pale, the little stored fat there had been on his lanky body melted away by the fever and by not eating.

I stayed five days with Al and Suze in Sevaré and during that time cycled in to Mopti: I discovered there were small boats still travelling on the river. During our misty days beside the Niger, Al and Suze had talked of joining me on the boat, but with Al's illness, going to Timbuktu seemed increasingly out of the question. They even started talking about having to catch a bus southwards.

Travelling with Al and Suze, I had become aware of how lonely I had been feeling when by myself – like a wild, weary wolf encircled by strangers, causing me to snarl and snap, even when at another level, I felt deep wells of gratitude for the hospitality I was being shown. As a threesome, when we had been mobbed by children, it had not felt as intimidating to me personally – their attention was diffused – and the kilometres had passed in laughter and chatter.

However, with water levels dropping all the time and the boat's passage threatened, I knew that it was time for me to move on. I had cycled 3000 kilometres and there was a long way to go, so much more to be seen, felt and experienced. While feeling fortunate to be so well, I was also melancholy to be leaving such good friends – we had only spent three weeks together but it felt much longer. I would take my own path, hope my guiding spirit knew what she was doing and hope my health stayed good. Being alone again was going to be very hard.

Five

Trading Places

Mopti, Mali – Tonka, Mali

'I've got to buy some oranges ... and a bucket!' I called hurriedly to the four or five young men, skinny youths wearing jeans, grubby T-shirts and baseball caps who were trying to bustle me to the harbour in Mopti in the late afternoon. I was running through the Mopti market, panting down the crowded, hot alleys between the rows of stalls, blue sack of possessions over my shoulder, clutching my Akubra. The ever present young men, ostensible guides, hangers on, had attached themselves to me as I arrived near the marketplace and harbour of Mopti. They now knew that I was travelling this afternoon on the boat to Timbuktu and the apparent leader of the group, a youth in dark sunglasses, very baggy jeans and a black T-shirt (hustler cool style) was pulling at my arm. He was anxious that I get to the harbour, as he claimed the boat was leaving.

Panic merchant, I thought. I was not going to be pulled anywhere while I needed to make these important purchases.

I guess I should have considered that nobody seemed ever in a hurry in Mali ...

My enquiries in Mopti had revealed that the only boats making the 500-kilometre voyage along the Niger River to Timbuktu at this time of year were *pinasse*. These were small, wooden cargo boats with shallow draughts, powered by engines, not sails. Sacks of rice and other produce were laid deep in their hulls and passengers were required to find a place on top under a protective canopy. I had seen the captain of my *pinasse*, a reliable-looking man in a huge turban that matched his huge girth, negotiated my ticket and been informed the boat was leaving late in the afternoon. It was a bit vague, but surely 3.30 p.m., the time now, was too early.

'*Ça va aller!*' – it's going! – called the youths again.

Hey, be cool, I thought as I ran.

Somehow, despite waiting days for this boat, I had left the task of buying provisions to the last minute. Nothing unusual for me. I wanted oranges because my expectation of the cleanliness and tastiness of foods available in the remote villages *en route* to Timbuktu was low. The bucket was so that I could wash myself or purify river water for drinking – as Suze and I had discovered, it

would be a Very Useful Thing.

I figured I had at least an hour, well, maybe a half hour given the anxiety levels in the youths.

Separating from Al and Suze was one wrench – I had left them that morning in Sevaré – but after these months together, leaving my bicycle behind was hard, too. I had developed a strong attachment to this heavy contraption.

Yet, as this would be a journey there and back, and feeling my bicycle would be more hindrance than help in the sands of Timbuktu, I had arranged to leave him (my bicycle that is) in Mopti. It seemed normal to think of the bicycle as a male: he carried heavy loads without a murmur (not an African male, then), and he was an obstinate devil who relished attention – daily, to keep him sweet, he was lubricated and had his nuts tightened. I would miss him.

'Where can I buy a bucket?' I abruptly asked a man selling fabric, and was directed with an extended arm and pointed finger toward another maze of stalls. Then, I was running again.

At last, out of breath, I saw the section where plastics of all shapes and sizes were on sale. There was no time for bargaining: selecting a blue, 10-litre version, with lid, I paid the exorbitant price asked by the opportunistic seller and ran off in search of oranges.

'*Vites, vites!*' – Quickly, quickly! – called the youth in the dark sunglasses. Yes, I had heard that before. 'The boat is leaving, *madame!*'

The youth did seem very agitated, so I let the seller fill my bucket with oranges, again without bargaining on price. I passed the heavy load and my blue sack of possessions to the youth and he and his friends started running for the harbour; I ran after them.

'*Vites, vites!!*' The urgency was increasing and I was being bustled towards two motorbikes by my companions.

Why to a motorbike? I was going to a *pinasse* and the harbour wasn't that far away. It was very confusing.

My sack and bucket were being thrust in front of the rider of the second bike, and I was lifted into the pillion position behind the other.

'What's going on?!' I yelled.

The most familiar youth in the dark sunglasses pointed toward the river's glistening strip of silver water, and I turned to see. I looked through the milky haze, across the vibrant marketplace where heavy trading occurred all day, across the busy harbour on the river where hundreds of *pinasses* were moored like Chinese junks in Kowloon, out to the open channel and squinted against the glare off the water.

There was my *pinasse* – it had left!

I was sheepish now. What had happened to my decision to be more open and less suspicious? Not so simple, eh? I was being helped and needed it, so I paid my guide, clutched at my driver as the engines were started and our bike lurched forward. We raced through the back streets of Mopti and then towards open country. The other bike carrying my possessions had vanished, but I was more concerned about where I was being taken. I didn't think I was being kidnapped, or that they were going to drive me to Timbuktu, so I hoped they knew what they were doing. Holding on to my driver tightly, telling myself to be cool now, closing my eyes against the dust, I waited for our destination to be revealed.

After about five minutes, when we were perhaps 5 kilometres from the town, we subsided to a halt, the noisy engine was switched off and I opened my eyes.

We were at a point where the riverbank was sheltered by a promontory and other people had gathered, trouser legs rolled up, possessions at their side. I saw the *pinasse* rounding the point. People started picking up their sacks and wading into the water. Evidently, this was a latecomers' pick-up point.

I looked around and saw that the other motorbike was there and my sack and bucket were brought to me. It was really all very efficient and I thanked the two drivers effusively and gave them some more money, nearly the equivalent of the ticket to Timbuktu! Oh, well, my fault, and I had to be quick as the loaded *pinasse* was approaching fast. Bending down to roll up my own trouser legs, I grabbed my sack and bucket of oranges and waited on the sand as the low-lying boat, heavy with passengers and produce, was manoeuvred into the calm water about 30 metres from the shore. A bare-chested crewman leapt over the side and the water came to his waist – so much for rolling my trouser legs up, I thought resignedly. Oh well, I would dry.

Other passengers were already in deep water, and some had reached the *pinasse* and were being helped aboard. The crewman was coming towards me and I decided to wait, as I didn't think I could manage my load alone and with his strength he might be able to keep my possessions out of the water. I held out my sack and bucket toward him – if he could take those, I didn't mind getting wet.

He stretched out his arms and I went to pass my possessions. Then, swiftly, unexpectedly, he bent low, grabbed me behind the knees and lifted me over his shoulders!

I shrieked!

He was quite unperturbed and started wading back toward the boat with his new load – a white female.

Seeing only water, I had to concentrate on holding my sack and bucket out of it. I could hear laughter from the other passengers as we approached the *pinasse*. The crewman dumped me, flour sack-like on the edge, someone took my possessions, as another man grabbed my arms and pulled me aboard. I was the last arrival, the engines were already re-started and we were moving off.

'*Bonjour,*' said the captain calmly, his features undetectable behind the turban wrapped around his face.

I was mortified! And I had to travel with these people for several days. I wasn't sure whether I was more embarrassed by my undignified mode of entry or by receiving special loading treatment.

Other passengers encouraged me to find a spot behind the captain and helmsman, in the first section of the boat on top of layers of sacks. I also accepted this privilege – I was too flustered to do other than I was told – and settled myself down by squashing my blue sack into shape as a backrest against the wooden crossbar that defined our section, and put my bucket between my extended legs. Phew. I paused to take a breath and regain my composure.

I took in my section companions – I had one man to my right between me and the rail and two others to my left. They were each dashingly dressed in *boubou*s, their faces covered by turbans (protection against the sand still stirred up by the harmattan). Only their deep, dark eyes were visible. I started feeling less mortified and more excited by the adventure – this was like being Kathleen Turner in *Romancing The Stone*.

But where was Michael Douglas? (At home in Reading, darn it.)

I was headed for Timbuktu for romantic reasons – not the male kind but rather the historic kind. To travel along the Niger River, like Ibn Battuta, like Mungo Park, was part of why I was here, but famous Timbuktu, a Sahelian trading and religious centre fabled for its wealth and learning since the early Middle Ages, had its own mysterious aura.

I had been warned against going to Timbuktu. Few tourists went there since the Tuareg rebellion in Algeria had forced the closure of the cross-Saharan routes. I knew little about this situation except that it had ruled out cycling, or rather pushing, my way across the Sahara – in my mind, no great loss. In Mopti, stories were circulating that there had been Tuareg attacks close to Timbuktu. However, it seemed that travelling by boat was safe enough, and I wanted to see romantic Timbuktu for myself.

I didn't know what I was letting myself in for ... nor how it would affect me.

The captain had said it would take 'five or six, or perhaps seven days' to reach Timbuktu, so I must get used to the new rhythm of this voyage and to my new companions.

I looked at my solitary neighbour to my right – he was a large, handsome, superior-looking man with a green turban on his head, the loose end wrapped over his mouth and nose and I could feel his penetrating gaze.

'*Bonjour,*' I said, trying to start a conversation.

'*Bonjour,*' he said with minimum courtesy. He didn't seem very friendly and he continued to stare, unblinking.

'My name is Pamela,' I continued, somewhat abruptly, trying again.

'My name is Mohammed.' Then, nothing.

Mohammed seemed to think very highly of himself, and seemed disdainful of me, so I looked to my left, searching for friendlier companions. My neighbours were playing cards, but when they felt my gaze, they stopped their game and stared at me. I smiled.

'*Bonjour,*' I said.

'*Bonjour.*'

'*Ça va?*'

'*Ça va bien, merci.*'

They watched, but didn't ask me any questions; I felt a little shy.

The captain, seated in front of me, seemed to be looking beyond the long, pointed prow of the *pinasse*, watching the river ahead intently. The helmsman was the muscular, bare-chested, bronze-skinned man who had lifted me so effectively. He now had charge of the 1-metre diameter wheel, and he turned it, sometimes under instruction from the captain, mostly of his own accord, effortlessly. Both men were serious and gazed at the river, presumably looking for eddies and telltale signs of low water. The captain's head was ensconced in metres of white cotton wrapped into an enormous turban, and his long, massive arms stretched out along the back of his bench, nearly reaching the bow width of the boat.

He turned briefly toward me.

'*Vous êtes madame ou mademoiselle?*' he asked. I was fed up with the charade and answered, '*Mademoiselle.*'

'*Est-ce que vous avez des enfants?*' – have you any children? No, I answered.

'I am a family man,' he said, and added with a broad grin, 'I have three wives and many children, so you should not be concerned.' Then, he turned back to watching the river.

The harmattan was blowing strongly and sand whipped around our faces, even out here in the middle of the river, and I pulled my own scarf across my face. The air was misty with the blown-up sand and turned the scenery to a milky watercolour of indeterminate edges and shades. On each bank, scrubby vegetation and low acacias grew to the high-water mark and the scrub land continued flatly before disappearing into the haze. There were no settlements, and I imagined the scenery would become drier and sandier as we followed the northward and westward swing of the Niger River during the days to come. The sun was setting, but there was no colourful sky, just an intense sphere of bright light glowing through the mist over the glistening river ahead.

I turned and looked behind into the main section of the *pinasse*. There were well over a hundred people crammed into this tiny boat, about 5 metres wide and 30 metres long, ending in a rounded stern. Thick wooden poles, roughly hewn by hand, ran across the boat at 4-metre intervals, creating sections for produce and people. Other poles were erected vertically down the centre of the boat to hold the roof up. The roof frame was formed by clusters of long willows lashed together, arched from one side of the boat to the other, and attached firmly on the centre poles. The canopy was thatched matting, also firmly lashed in place. The smoking engine was at the stern. It sent a soothing rumble and vibration through the boat.

Millet sacks were piled high above the boat's hull, and in each section bodies were stretched out haphazardly, overlapping, curled into foetal positions, confined by other bodies and by other cargo they were travelling with – there were plastics tied together in massive bundles of basins, buckets and kettles, there were towers of enamel basins, hens in wicker cages and many calico sacks with who knows what inside. From the latticework of the overhead canopy hung more items – hats, clothing and food; it maximised the space available for people and prevented valuable belongings getting lost underneath the sacks. Now that the sun had started setting and the day cooling, people were talking more energetically or listening to their radios.

Interestingly, all the Malian women were seated farther towards the back of the boat, in a section empty of cargo where smoke was rising, charcoal stoves were burning, cooking was going on and their children were crying. This was the kitchen section of the boat and, I later discovered, a very hot and unpleasant place to be. Lucky women, always enduring, always serving.

I guessed I was an honorary man, although not quite a man, not a normal, everyday, run-of-the-mill man. Not at all, because as I looked backwards, everybody on the boat paused in their conversations, put down their radios, stopped their cooking and looked at me.

I smiled at them, but got no smiles back. None of the men seemed interested in talking to me, only gazing with those intractable stares which seemed to strip me. (I hadn't been alone with such a vast number of Moslem males before.) It felt worse than the stares of children in villages, because here I could not ride away. And they were adults. There was no escape. I felt devalued by these lust-filled men into an object. A white female object. I sighed and realised that again I would need to become used to being the sole focus of attention. I missed the insulation of travelling as a threesome.

As the last glimmers of light were gone from the sky, canvas canopies were rolled down from the roof to enclose the sides.

'It will be cold tonight,' observed the captain. Conversation throughout the boat eased off, and the heartbeat throb of the engine became more noticeable.

At least in the dark, I could not see the intense eyes of my companions and I curled up, trying to flatten out some lumps, trying to achieve some comfort, and some sleep.

As the hours passed, my companions also sleeping (or trying to) and touching me on both sides, I wondered at my sense of loneliness. In London, I had problems with too many people and not enough time to myself – I was always trying to carve out time to be alone. Yet, here, on this boat, with more than a hundred people, sleeping body to body with strangers, I felt alone and lonely.

Was it the different language that increased my sense of isolation? With Al and Suze I had been cocooned in a comfortable, English-speaking social group, and maybe if these people spoke English, I could crack jokes and find a commonality more easily.

Was it that we were strangers from such different cultures with so little in common? With Al and Suze we did not really need others outside our self-contained unit. We could talk together, observing and commenting on the strangeness we saw and using our beliefs and ideas to draw conclusions and to argue about them, all while moving through the different culture. Here, I knew I needed to enter their world on their terms, not as an observer, and it was hard to find reference points for conversation.

Was it that, no matter what the environment, I was shy in crowds and hated being stared at? Probably, I thought, as I watched the silhouettes of the captain and helmsman and the glints of light off the river ahead, but maybe the greater truth is that, alone, I was discovering a need for people and companionship that I hadn't been so intensely aware of before. I was not the self-contained unit I had liked to think.

My stomach rumbled; it must be getting on for morning, I thought, and I shone my torch at my watch. Two a.m. The hours were passing slowly. I had only eaten an orange for dinner, and I was hungry.

However, I was not going to eat because I was desperate, bursting, to go to the loo. Yet again, I was facing the dilemma of finding a decent toilet.

On this *pinasse*, there was no toilet at all.

And I had already needed a trip to the loo when I boarded the *pinasse*, now ten hours ago!

We were supposed to be having regular stops at villages where we could 'go', yet there had been no stops so far and there was no sign of one coming. I strained to see lights of a forthcoming village, concentrated on crossing my legs and holding my tight bladder.

A man in the next section moved himself to the edge of the boat and lifted the awning. By moonlight I could see his raised *boubou*. Then, there was the unmistakeable sound of trickling water. Seeing the arc of falling water and hearing the trickle was excruciatingly painful, and I was envious of his anatomy and dress.

Then, following his lead, another man shifted to the edge, and another.

I tried to think of anything but relief, even sang a little tune to myself, and rocked myself about, probably to the annoyance of my companions.

However, the boat continued.

Around dawn, the engine throb changed, and I could feel the nose of the boat being edged toward shore.

At last, relief was coming!

'Find your shoes if you want to go ashore,' said Mohammed gruffly as he awoke from his light doze. 'We will not stop here long.'

The boat was coming alive with activity, and as soon as the boat stopped, the exodus of people began. Light arrived swiftly, and I saw we were anchored 20 metres offshore in a stagnant and dirty-looking stretch of water. The only way to get to shore was to wade, and I was beyond caring about getting wet. It was also too bad if I got bilharzia – all African guidebooks warn travellers not to wade or swim in African rivers due to the danger of catching this worm-carried disease. Evidently the travel book writers had not travelled all night on a *pinasse* and had such an urgent need to go to the toilet as me.

Holding my shoes and toilet paper above my head, I leapt overboard into the waist-deep, murky water.

My fellow passengers arrived at the water's edge before me, and it became clear that most people's need was urgent too. Each person was carrying a small plastic kettle – water from the spout was the Islamic alternative to toilet paper – and immediately sprinted from the water into the sand dunes that edged the shore.

I followed suit.

There was little cover in the sand dunes, as the low vegetation and trees of the landscape of the previous afternoon had vanished.

I saw lots of bare bums as I ran past, but I was anxious to find privacy, and ran over another sand dune, and another, until I was at least 500 metres from the shore, before squatting down and I remained nervously alert for the sounds of others arriving.

Relief was blissful.

The next night, after a day of slow travel and few stops, my bladder was again bursting, and I decided to try going over the side like the men. I crept to the side of the *pinasse*, hung my behind over the edge and wrapped my arms tightly around a roof pole to avoid becoming fish food. There were some men chatting quietly nearby, but it was dark and I figured they could not see me, as I could barely make out their shadowy forms. I edged down my trousers and undies and let fly with my own trickle.

Too late, I realised that white skin reflects moonlight!

I yanked up my undies and trousers and, knowing eyes could be watching, flushed red hot with embarrassment.

It was remarkable how stressed I became over the lack of privacy and the staring during the journey along the Niger River to Timbuktu. I scolded myself that I would have to get used to it, but how could I change ingrained sensibilities?

On the third day, we stopped for nearly a whole day at one small village. The village itself seemed located a long way from the river, at least a kilometre back across what was now a dry, barren plain. That was probably because the area was subject to flooding during the wet. The few houses were built of grey mud brick: just boxes, with flat roofs and small windows, no glass or netting. A small, mud-brick mosque stood near the market square. There were no trees, just a few bushes, and some goats who, typically, were having a go at eliminating these, too. The village was dirty; sand was blowing in squalls, and although only around 10 a.m., it was already fiendishly hot. I rapidly tired of being the centre of attention and of looking at the tiny market where only a meagre range of rotten tomatoes, salted fish, soaps and plastic bowls were on sale, stock mainly provided by my *pinasse* companions. Walking back to the river, I boarded the *pinasse* to retrieve my swimsuit, towel and toiletries bag. I had seen other passengers going to bathe – the men soaped up naked – and I felt extremely dirty from two harsh, hot days and three sweaty nights. Now, I was determined to find a quiet spot for a swim. Still obsessed with privacy, and knowing that a white female splashing around in the water, even in a swimsuit, would be potentially offensive to Moslems and would definitely fetch lots of stares, I was willing to walk a long way along the sandy shore to find a private place.

For my daring escapade, having considered various locations, I chose a place around a bend in the river where the beach was narrow, a sand dune rose behind, and which I hoped wasn't a stretch of the river used as a crocodile feeding place. After changing rapidly, clandestinely, into my swimsuit – one-piece and very modest – I then lay in the dune watching for a clear shot at the water. It seemed quiet, yet whenever I gathered courage to run forward, a villager would pass, and I sank back into cover.

Even I had to laugh at my pathetic behaviour, but I didn't want to offend and I knew I couldn't face any more strip-searching stares. An hour went by, people kept passing and it was nearly as frustrating as waiting for toilet stops.

The morning grew hotter, the sun shifted high overhead, and a heat haze shimmered above the land. It was even hotter than at the village earlier. Trickles of sweat ran down my neck; my swimsuit was clammy against my skin. The water was clearly deep and fast-flowing in this narrow channel – it looked very inviting.

I wondered where the hell did all these people come from?!

Finally, exasperated with waiting, I took courage and ran into the water.

It was cool and cleansing. I soaped myself rapidly, then turned to check that no one was there.

Three robed and turbaned men on camels had pulled their animals to a halt. From high on their saddles the men were watching me; even at 50 metres, I could see their wide eyes and hungry looks.

Like three wise men, I thought, amazed that they of all people should have arrived. I felt sorry to be shocking three middle-aged gents, so I turned my back on them and dunked myself below the water, concealing my white and, to them, scantily clad body. I hoped they would get bored, leave me in peace and continue on their way.

After a few minutes, I risked another glance toward shore, and there they were, unmoved, still staring, no facial movement, no greetings, just burning eyes.

I felt my ire rising.

Allez! – Go away! I said silently, as I gritted my teeth and tried to stay calm. I did not want to offend them. I had walked a long way and waited a long time. No one was asking them to stay and be shocked, and I felt I had done enough to find privacy. Why couldn't they leave me alone?

I wasn't being very successful at staying calm.

Trying to ignore them, I swam a bit and kept my body below the water, but their stripping eyes, like so many others from the boat, were inescapable and penetrated my awareness; I waved them off.

'*Au revoir!*' I called cheerfully, hoping they might take a hint.

No response, just the shocked stares. I tried to think of what else I could do, but they seemed set to sit and watch me for as long as I remained.

After a couple more minutes, my calmness totally evaporated. I waded, then ran from the water, arms waving. An uncontrolled, Susanna-like rage had taken hold of me.

'*Allez! Allez!* Leave me alone! I've had enough. Take a good look, then! You buggers! Don't you understand privacy? Just go! *Allez! ALLEZ!!*'

I might as well have been naked – their gaping looks grew more wide-eyed – and their silence and unblinking stares fuelled my rage. I had started in French but now, hysterically, I was shrieking in English and 'Franglais'.

'*Vous avez* no right to stare like that!' I might have even stamped my foot.

Finally, thankfully, one of the men, elderly, his facial skin wrinkled and sagging into heavy folds, responded. I wasn't just shouting at a stare, but I had someone shouting back at me – in Arabic, I supposed. He was wearing a brown *boubou*, and only now I noticed his rifle in a holster on the elaborate leather saddle, a rope of ammunition looped over his shoulder, and a curved dagger sheathed at the belt around his waist. I didn't understand his shouting, and yet I did.

'You white hussy! You loose woman! If you bathe like that and swear like that, what can you expect? We have a right to be here. You are the stranger. You ask us to stare by how you behave.' Something like that, and even through my hysteria, I knew he was right. I was the stranger, always would be, and everything I did was either culturally fascinating or culturally insensitive and offensive.

His arms were waving and he was very angry. So was I, and I kept up my side of the argument while standing my ground in a dripping swimsuit.

However, these men, who did not speak French, who were probably from a remote village, who were being confronted by this bizarre and probably shocking sight, were not moving. I rushed for the sand dune in distraught tears. The encounter lasted only a few minutes but it left me feeling stripped naked and assaulted.

It took a long while in the sand dune for me to calm down, to consider how they felt, to feel sorry for offending them. I had forgotten that being alone was this hard.

Around 4 p.m., as we prepared to depart after our day at the village market, I found I had a new companion next to me in the bow. Mohammed had left the boat and, still feeling a bit sensitive about men and stares following my farcical swim, I was looking forward to more space and not having to speak to anybody. A short, stocky man of about thirty-five or forty years of age came to squeeze in.

The fellow seemed totally insensitive to my introspective mood, and immediately on settling down started a conversation.

'Hallo, my name is Gaby,' he said in English. I was surprised, but my interest was only marginally sparked. He quickly informed me that he was a Ghanaian from Kumasi (a big regional city in Ghana and one I would later visit). He followed by telling me that he was a trader in second-hand children's clothes, that he was travelling Mali to sell his wares with his Malian assistant, Amita, and that Amita was sitting with the other women in the kitchen section. Gaby talked rapidly and kept squirming around. He seemed hyperactive and I wished he would settle.

Like everyone else, as protection from the pervasive sand, Gaby wore a turban, a large blue one. He was wearing very baggy jeans and, despite the stifling heat, a thick, denim bomber jacket. I realised later that he probably had his money concealed in the jacket, as he never took it off.

'I am the Best Trader In West Africa,' he eventually declared, with a twinkle in his eyes and a grin.

Who is this man? I wondered, as he made this outrageous pronouncement. Companionship was one thing, but not with a preposterous, self-involved trader. Wrapping my scarf tightly around my face, I wished he would leave me alone.

However, without offering much encouragement to his monologue by way of interest or questions, I learnt about his trade routes.

'When the Niger River is high, I travel from Mopti to Timbuktu and Gao, selling at the villages along the way, but now the water level is getting Too low.' He emphasised his 'Too's with clear capital letters; I was later to learn that this is a distinctively Ghanaian and Nigerian way of speaking. 'And this will be my last journey to Timbuktu this season. On my next journey I will travel upriver to Bamako ...' He seemed to want to educate me about the things I was seeing, what I was experiencing.

He paused and asked about what I was doing in Africa.

'You try,' said Gaby, having heard about where I had come from and where I was going. 'You try.' He was shaking his head and his bright, round eyes were alight with life. 'You are trying.' It was my first encounter with this pleasant and useful Ghanaian expression that conveys admiration or support, but I thought that was a good way of describing what I was doing. Who knew what the outcome would be, but I was trying.

Perhaps he was not such a preposterous, self-involved trader. Well, perhaps he was, but then I was pretty preposterous and self-involved, too. Come to think of it, aren't we all? What counts, I figured, is how much someone can make others laugh and be happy, and Gaby's excitement about life was infectious. My bad mood started melting before his vivacious charm and openly offered friendship.

That evening, as the sun went down, or at least disappeared behind a milky curtain of sand, and as the night grew cooler, we talked – at least, Gaby talked, mainly about himself and the relative advantages of Ghana over Mali.

'These people ...' he began, with laughter in his voice, 'these people ... they are Too poor.' He shook his head and added that in Ghana things were very different. 'These people have no roads – it is not like that in Ghana. Our roads are Very Fine.' Another Ghanaian expression. He added that he thought Malians were very uncivilised in how many people they squashed into a bush taxi. 'In Ghana, everyone has a seat. The buses are Very Fine.' Gaby retold his comments to Malian neighbours in Malinké, as they had not understood our English and, fortunately, his smile seemed to allow him to get away with many things for, most times, our neighbours would break into laughter or excited, but not angry, rebuttals.

He paused, thinking of another advantage of Ghana.

'These people,' he tutted and shook his head, 'these people do not eat good foods. Not like in Ghana where we have yams. These people eat Too much rice!'

After three days on the *pinasse*, it was very refreshing to be with someone who did not focus solely on my journey or my marital status, who had things to say for himself and could keep the conversation going, who seemed to enjoy life so much and could make me laugh, and who, most importantly, did not undress me with his eyes. Having found some companionship again, I started feeling insulated from the continuing stares of the other men.

The sun sank lower in the western sky. The iridescent glow behind the white haze was now to our right as we were travelling on a northward-flowing stretch of the river. It was also a shallow stretch and the helmsmen or two boatmen frequently had to take it in turns using long poles to heave our way through shallow stretches. They reached out along the long poles, pushed, then released. They were shirtless, and their sleek, dark, muscular torsos made wonderful sculptures.

I was staring now.

In fact, the previous day, around noon, we had been unexpectedly trapped in shallows mid-river. The men had been called upon to leap over the side into the waist-deep water and to pull us through to the channel. I had taken refuge in being a woman in a Moslem society to gain the benefit of staying dry. As the men had taken their shirts off I had seen another advantage of not participating – I could watch. What a collection of taut stomachs and rippling biceps and fine, shiny skin, I had thought admiringly. I had tried to imagine a group of blokes jumping off the Number 7 bus, trying to push it along Oxford Street in London. The thought of all those pale white bodies, soft flesh and beer bellies – better not to see or even imagine some things! Here, not a slither of fat was to be seen. And such wonderful skin – its oiliness had repelled the water and in the direct sunlight the silky deep-brown and ebony torsos had glowed. I had been happy to stare then.

Now, as I continued to watch the helmsman push the pole rhythmically against the river's bed, I figured this staring business was not so complex. It was fine as long as people were not staring at me!

Dusk was turning into night on this third day. Most people were engaged in quiet conversation as they finished their meals and started stretching out for the night. Gaby was still hyperactively loud and maintaining two conversations, one with the captain and my neighbours in Malinké, one with myself in English. His topic had been navigation on the Niger, but he suddenly he turned to religion.

'These people ...' he commented to me, with his usual generalisation, and head shaking, 'these people know nothing. They are Moslem.'

He said that Malians did not believe in Jesus Christ as Our Saviour, and they would be Damned. Being an atheist, religion was a subject I stayed away from. In the north, people were Moslem, elsewhere strong, often fundamentalist Christians. A few times I had stated my belief, or lack of it, and had found villagers totally bewildered by my view: 'You do not believe in God?!' With Gaby, I let his comments rest, although I suggested that to repeat them to this boatful of people might be risking a jihad. He was not deterred and swiftly turned to my companions and presumably offered his views in Malinké.

Soon, fierce discussion broke out and then erupted like a volcano along the length of the boat – people became animated and found lost energy. Arms waved and men stood, screaming their points, or insults. All the arguing was in Malinké; comments were yelled to Gaby from the back of the boat, just as he retorted to someone in the middle. He had the whole boat against him. Gaby clearly loved it.

It took nearly an hour, until complete darkness, for the arguing, and the boat, to calm down.

'Gaby ... that was courageous,' I said, when he finally turned to me again. He was more courageous than I was in provoking controversial discussions. I also thought he was completely mad, particularly when he had to travel with this boat for several more days and wanted Malian Moslems as customers.

'Ah ... these people,' and he shrugged with a self-righteous flush, 'these people know nothing.'

'*Oui, s'il vous plaît,*' – yes, please, I said to the helmsman, when he offered to carry me ashore at another village the fourth morning. The water looked especially fouled, so being carried in over his shoulder seemed quite sensible. I even passed it off with some dignity, I imagined. At least this time, I did not shriek.

The market day had not yet commenced, and many of our boat's traders, including Gaby, immediately rushed to set up their stalls. I did a circuit of the shabby market area which was about 500 metres from the river, but there seemed little of interest so I returned to the shore. There was a small wooden hut that seemed open – tables and a few chairs were clustered outside and some men were seated eating food from plastic dishes. I approached, got some looks, said some '*Bonjours*' to break through the distance between us, and went inside. A woman was cooking over a charcoal fire, and several cauldrons were bubbling.

'*Qu'est-ce que les plats du jour?*' I asked. What are today's dishes?

As usual, she did not understand my French, but a man eating inside answered for her.

'Fish stew and rice.'

Oranges had not been very filling, so I bought a bowl and joined some men at the table outside.

They didn't have much to say to me, but nearby I spotted Gaby's assistant, Amita. Amita was a quiet Malian girl who only spoke Malinké, so I had not got to know her well. She was very pretty and daintily featured with a long, swan-like neck, and I thought she looked a little like Audrey Hepburn. She was tressing the hair of another girl. She smiled when she saw me, and I moved to a table closer to her to watch her work. I was intrigued by the process of plaiting in false tresses, tightly plaiting the extension, and finally tieing it off with black cotton. As the tresses were tiny, a headful could take a half day to tie, or longer. In Senegal, tresses had been available in reds and blondes, and styles were far more complex, but Malian women seemed more conservative – they used only black.

Amita laughed at me as I started feeding a skinny stray cat some of my fish stew and signalled to ask if I would like my hair tressed.

Why not? I thought and went over to sit on a low stool.

Amita giggled with the other girl and she handed me a small piece of broken mirror. Local children started gathering now, amused to see the *toubab* having her hair plaited. Of course, with my long, thick hair I needed no extensions, and the first few minutes just contained lots of laughter as everyone reached over to touch my hair. Amita worked at my hair for at least half an hour but she only put in three plaits on each side and the back, so I still had some hair free. Using the piece of mirror to look, I said, as Gaby would say in Ghanaian English, that it was Very Fine. I received lots of approving nods from the locals.

Really, I thought it looked not Too good but I was happy.

Again, Amita signalled to me. She bent her elegant head and delved into her small bag of possessions to pull out a piece of green Rexona soap, and her scrubber – the tearings of a nylon sack which were used commonly throughout Mali to scrub black skin to a shiny finish. Would I like to bathe with her?

I nodded and followed her, and was in turn followed by a large procession of kids. I started to feel a little nervous about a repeat of the swimming episode, but Amita shooed them away, and after a time, as we walked downriver along the shore, they let us go. The river was narrow here and the flat, hard muddy banks were wide. We had walked about 500 metres, still within long sight of the town, when she indicated that we had reached the place for bathing. It looked cleaner than where we had moored, and the water was more swiftly flowing. Other women were already soaped and did not look up as we arrived. I glanced around, checking for watchers. For once, nobody was taking any notice. Men walked by further up the shore, perhaps 50 metres away, but kept their eyes straight ahead; this was the women's bathing area and no intrusive stares were allowed.

I felt amazed.

Amita bared her breasts, but kept her *pagne* around her waist. She never took her undies off and washed that area in a squat. I followed her lead, taking my T-shirt, bra and shorts off but leaving on my undies. We used stones from the shore to scrub the rough skin on our soles, and I was impressed by how much effort she made to scrub her skin, and clean her teeth; I was finished long before her.

I was most impressed by men passing and *not* looking in our direction.

What relief, what bliss! By joining with the women, by following the local way, my colour didn't matter and I was freed from stares.

Finally, early on the fifth day, we motored into Tonka. It was supposed to be our last stop before Timbuktu, but we were going to be there the entire day, for market day.

'I must get there early to set up a good spot,' Gaby had said a few times, clearly agitated at my slowness to get my things together on the boat once we had moored, and I had told him to go on ahead.

I wandered around the village, which was bigger than others where we had stopped – there were even shops. They were small, wood-framed, mud-walled, straw-roofed buildings, dark on the inside, their wares spread over an old glass or wooden counter. They surrounded the perimeter of the large market area. I walked in and out of these shops, keen to see what western goodies were available. There was some chocolate, but I ended up again buying some rice and fish stew. As with so many other things, I was getting used to it.

Then, seeing a faded sign for Coca-Cola on one shop's wall, I entered to find if it was available. I had been purifying some cloudy, warm pump water by adding tablets I carried, but it was not very appetising. On the *pinasse* I had been getting most of my moisture from my oranges. They were desiccated, but as that meant going to the loo less often, that was Very Fine by me. Now, I fancied a Coke. Packaged drinks had an appealing image of cleanliness. I bought a warm bottle, flicked at flies buzzing around my nose and sat on a sack of rice by the doorway to drink it. A group of robed and turbaned men were sitting outside the shop's entrance, chatting, drinking tea, listening intently to the radio. This was common during my sojourn in Mali, as each day the compelling trial of Moussa Traoré, the former president of Mali, for murder and treason, was being broadcast live. (Traoré was accused of order-ing troops against pro-democracy demonstrators in Bamako in 1991, resulting in 150 deaths and nearly a thousand injured. Ultimately, he was found guilty and sentenced to death, but remains in prison.)

One distinguished-looking, tall and straight-postured old man turned toward me and started talking to me in French. He had gentle, wise eyes, a very wizened face and an aura of calm.

'Omar; Hadji Omar,' he said. If he carried the respected title of El Hadj, he must have made a pilgrimage to Mecca. He was from Goundam, a village to the north, some 60 kilometres away, and had come to Tonka for market day.

'We have problems in Goundam – instability, killings – from the Tuareg and from the military,' he started telling me. 'It is bad in my town now, but I am an old man. I must return.'

He told me about some relatives who had been killed, and I asked him about the Tuareg rebellion. He was non-judgmental and philosophical.

'The Tuaregs suffered badly during the droughts, like we all did, but they have not been able to go back to their old ways. They feel badly treated and want a separate state. But it is not all the Tuaregs. There are talks now with the government so the situation should improve.'

He asked about my travels and I started telling him about my journey. Suddenly, his grey eyes lit up.

'*Esprit de Battuta*? Is that the name of your journey? Does it have anything to do with Ibn Battuta?'

'Yes,' I said, with growing interest of my own, and told him of how much I admired Ibn Battuta and how I was trying to travel like him. I did not say I was wondering about my success.

'As a young man,' he began, putting his glass of tea down by his side, 'I also was intrigued by Ibn Battuta. When I had finished my studies at an agricultural college in Bamako, I decided to set off to follow in his footsteps.'

I was tantalised by this coincidence. Here, at the edge of the Sahara, was someone else who travelled in the spirit of explorers. He went on to tell me that he went to Mecca, and on into Egypt and Israel, but not into Turkey. It must have been in the fifties, and he did not look a wealthy man.

'I came home, but I could not settle – so I left to continue travelling through West Africa and down into Central Africa.' He searched his memory for the names of countries. 'There was Gabon, and the Central African Republic, but I did not like it there.'

We discovered that we had both decided not to follow exactly in Ibn Battuta's footsteps, but rather to wander in his spirit. Hadji Omar paused to tell his elderly friends of our common idea and travels in their language. They smiled and sounded surprised. I was dumbfounded.

'But eventually, after five years, I came home,' he said, flicking at some flies, picking up his glass and turning to me once more, 'to work my father's land. I have never travelled since.' He may not have travelled again, but I felt this man had a nomadic soul. Hadji Omar seemed a kind and very wise man. We exchanged addresses, and I felt a warm glow from this chance meeting. Surely it was arranged by the spirits and offered a message.

'*Esprit de Battuta* is a good name for your journey,' Hadji Omar added as I was leaving. 'In our language, *battuta* means good luck.'

By now, the Tonka market was very busy and, as it was extremely large, I wondered how I would find Gaby. I pushed my way through the crowds, trying to look at the tables and mats of produce of the sellers. As in most markets, people selling the same produce were sitting together. I passed rows of dried fish, rows of thongs, rows of onions, rows of miscellaneous stalls selling batteries and elastic and nail polish. Sellers were silent, waiting for prospective buyers to take an interest in their wares. Seeing tomatoes for sale, I stopped at the mat of one woman seller and bent down to squeeze one of her small pyramids of four ripe tomatoes. I was checking their firmness with a view to buying them, but the serious woman pointed me toward the tomatoes of her neighbour. There did not seem to be much competitive commercial spirit here.

The market was a maze of sections. There was not just one market square, but several, each separated by rows of wooden shops. The sun was strong and there were no shadows, except from the umbrellas held overhead by a few savvy traders. Flies were thick and smells were strong, particularly from the dried fish and fermenting millet beer, the rotten vegetables and the ditches draining dirty, stinking water. Buyers seemed frantic, much more than the sellers, and had no patience for anyone else when they paused to look. I was elbowed, my feet were stood on and I was ready to retreat to a shop again.

However, I was attracted by the ringing of a bell. It was a series of sharp rings that pierced the noise of the crowd. The noise seemed to be coming from the centre of the market, and wondering what was going on, I moved toward the sound, pushing my way through an even thicker crowd, perhaps also attracted by the noise.

Then, I recognised Gaby at the centre of the throng. Of course, the Best Trader In West Africa.

'These people,' he said, as he greeted me with his wide, white-toothed grin. He had a woman's vinyl handbag looped over his shoulder – his cashbox. 'Oh, they like clothes for their children Too much!'

I could see his pile of second-hand children's clothes spread out on a cloth at his feet. Women were frantically grabbing at the clothes, and holding them up to check for style, or quality, or size. There were tiny T-shirts and faded lacy dresses, but children's underwear seemed especially popular.

'It is nearly Ramadan,' Gaby explained patiently to me. Amita wasn't there – she had relatives in Tonka and had gone to see them – so while Gaby spoke to me, he continued to eye the women's choices and tell them the price. He seemed to be an even more vivid and animated character; trading was his drug. 'When it is over, there is a holiday, like Christmas. These people give Too many presents to their children.'

He was also holding a black-velvet-lined tray of gold-plated earrings. Gaby told me they were 50 CFA and 100 CFA, set price. At 20 US cents and 40 US cents, they were cheap, and the women seemed to love them. Having bargained for some undies, the women spied the earrings, and bought a pair of those as well. There was a great deal of giggling around Gaby.

Suddenly, he thrust the bell toward me. It was an old school bell with a wooden handle.

'Here you sell, I must go ...' and, inexplicably, he was gone.

'*Aye!*'

For a moment I stood startled, then began ringing the bell, experimentally, a few times. One woman smiled shyly at me, while another waved a pair of undies at me. She was dressed in traditional *pagnes* and had a baby attached to her back. Her hair was plaited into tiny tresses that stood up vertically like needles and made her look quite mischievous.

'Er, 100 CFA,' I said in French, with no idea of the price. My customer shook her head vigorously.

'Er, 50 CFA.' I cut my price to make the sale, then, realising she didn't speak French, I showed her the coins. Another woman, older and with a young boy in tow in one hand, grabbed at my arm.

'50 CFA,' I said, again showing the coins. She smiled enthusiastically, and handed me the money.

I am an African trader, I thought, and liked the idea. I rang the bell again. No longer was I fussed about being looked at; I had a role. The throng of women, enthusiastic for bargains, were disinterested in the skin colour of the seller, and moved in around me. I was probably going to give them some cheap deals, and not earn much foreign currency for Ghana. However, I was trying! Bending down to help a woman find some underpants, I pulled out a sweater. A young mother grabbed it from me and started checking the seams. A hand shook my shoulder – another woman wanted my attention for a price. I showed her the coins, she nodded and passed me the same. Another transaction completed

My African business, like my African life, was slowly getting underway.

Six

Not a Noble Nomad Experience

Timbuktu, Mali – Tintahaten, Mali

I had arrived in Timbuktu nearly two weeks before – the *pinasse* had landed at Korioumé, about 30 kilometres south and, like many of my fellow passengers, I had used local transport, an old Land Rover, to travel the potholed road to Timbuktu. Gaby had unexpectedly left the boat in Tonka – knowing Gaby, some deal that was Too good to pass up – so I had been on my own again. Initial views of Timbuktu had been disappointing.

It had been bigger than I expected, had paved roads, a new part of town with multi-storey offices (admittedly only two or three storeys) and a dominating radio satellite dish. Like other European explorers before me, I had been deluded into basing all my expectations about Timbuktu on its past.

When European travellers like the Scot, Gordon Laing, the Frenchman, René Caillié and the German, Heinrich Barth, first arrived in Timbuktu in the early to mid nineteenth century, they too were disappointed – their expectations and those of their countrymen were based on the accounts of Arabian travellers like Ibn Battuta and rumours, but all were centuries out of date.

Timbuktu had been established as a seasonal camp for Tuareg nomads in the eleventh century, and its importance grew during the Malian empire when trade shifted from the westward routes used during the height of the Ghanaian empire. The city gained a reputation as a centre of Islamic scholarship, particularly between 1492 and 1529 under the Songhay ruler, Askia Mohammed, when scholars wrote significant books and treatises, Islamic texts were imported across the Sahara and the city was home to important libraries. The religious scholars of Timbuktu, known collectively as the *ulama*, participated in the ruling of the city and were members of powerful trading families. When the Moroccans invaded in 1591, they saw the *ulama* as a potential threat, and when there was a revolt against the Moroccans in 1593, the invaders retaliated by killing, imprisoning or exiling many of the *ulama* and confiscating and burning their books. Timbuktu's role in Islamic scholarship was destroyed. Soon, its role as a trading centre also began to be eroded: the cross-Saharan trade that had made the city wealthy shifted to coastal nations, who bartered slaves and gold with the Europeans. By 1826, when

Gordon Laing arrived, the first European recorded to do so, the city's glory was in its past. (By the way, he didn't deliver a verifiable account of Timbuktu because he was murdered in the desert on the way back!)

Despite knowing this history, I had created an image in my mind of a mysterious city surrounded by the shifting sand dunes of the Sahara. Wrong. It proved to be a squalid, depressed and dirty place with Too many flies, Too much open sewage and Too many obnoxious children who followed me demanding '*Cadeau, cadeau!*', and swarmed in a frenzy when I gave them sweets.

In those first few days, after becoming immune to the children, and after their discovering I was a mean-hearted witch who only now told them to '*Allez!*', I was able to wander the streets of the old town and recapture the sense of its past.

The old town consisted largely of grey, low, mud-brick buildings which looked ancient enough but which had probably been remade in the last few years. Mud brick has a tendency to wash away in the fierce rains that come to desert towns. Frequently, the only decorations on the external walls of the square buildings were elaborately carved, ancient-looking Islamic doors. I wandered down the narrow and shadowed, sandy alleyways doubting it had changed much since the nineteenth century and indeed came across plaques marking each of the houses where Laing, Caillé and Barth had stayed. Goats and dogs and donkey carts also roamed these narrow alleyways, and occasionally I came across women baking delicious-smelling bread in large, pudding-shaped clay ovens. Sometimes, I looked into the courtyards of the largest mud-brick public buildings – cool spaces surrounded by internal archways. Had they been centres of learning in the past?

Best of all, I walked out to some nearby sand dunes and watched the town at sunset. From there, I saw the low, grey town emerging from, yet merging with, the surrounding sands. Nearby were the dunes, the humped, thatch-covered dwellings of the Tuaregs, the aristocratic-looking nomads of the Sahara – I had seen their gaunt, serious faces in coffee-table books and knew they were the tribe that roamed the desert and had controlled cross-Saharan traffic for centuries. Their homes and presence added a touch of mystery.

But the mystery was short-lived.

When I actually came into contact with the Tuaregs, my first impression of them was that they looked

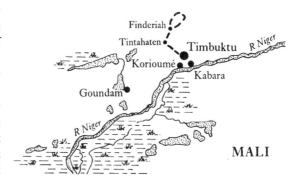

untrustworthy, certainly not noble. I only caught glimpses of their faces from behind their indigo turbans, glimpses which showed leathery, blue-tinged skin and gaunt, hawk-like features. Their eyes gave me most discomfort: they seemed piercing, glinting, avarice-filled, much more so than, say, those of the youths in the Mopti market. With those boys, the hunt for the tourist dollar was a game. Here with the Tuaregs in Timbuktu, there was something else, and I did not trust them. They pestered me unceasingly to buy 'genuine' silver jewellery and knives, and desert camel rides. They seemed to flock like vultures around tourists, on the scent of a kill.

However, I was intrigued by the Tuaregs. I had read about their rich history and seen photos of them looking regal in the indigo robes that stained their dark skin to give it a bluish tinge. As I sat on the wide, shady verandah of the dilapidated Hotel Bouctou, day after day, looking out towards the scrub-covered sand dunes, I started wondering about the possibility of taking a long ride to see some proper *Lawrence of Arabia* sand dunes and to observe their romantic, nomadic life close-up. Baba, the friendly Malian barman at the Hotel Bouctou where I was staying, told me that an older-looking man, Ibrahim, was a Tuareg I could trust.

The problem was *la situation* – the situation – that Omar Hadji had referred to in Tonka, or the rebellion, as it had been called in Mopti. For two years, the Tuaregs had rebelled against the Malian government, and fighting had given rise to unpredictable bandit attacks which closed the Saharan route. However, a few weeks previously, an agreement between the Tuaregs and the government had been reached.

'It should be all right to go outside,' I was told by one local. 'Outside,' was how everyone in Timbuktu referred to the surrounding desert.

'Yes, the security problems have diminished,' Baba assured me.

Someone else said, 'Others have done it,' and even a *gendarme* said it was okay.

So, when I met Ibrahim by chance in a narrow, sandy alley of Timbuktu, I put it to him.

'It is necessary to get authorisation,' he said, 'and you don't want to go too far, but it is possible.'

I guess I should have been warned by the clandestine way in which Ibrahim wanted to discuss the arrangements – away from the hotel, near the dunes. He would go to the *gendarmes* for authorisation, not me. All seemed fine – until the morning of departure.

I asked Baba if I could leave some bags behind. 'Yes, but I will have to tell the *directeur*, Traoré.'

In turn, Traoré had said, 'I must see your authorisation, *madame*.' Traoré was a scrawny, short, unpleasant man, who made a habit of issuing orders. He was the manager, but I guessed he was ex-military. Why should he see it, I retorted. It was nothing to do with him. 'It is to do with me, *madame*!' Traoré screamed shrilly.

When Ibrahim arrived, he took over, but the 'discussion' escalated into a full-scale, high-decibel argument. I intervened and told the manager that he was just being difficult and thinking in terms of lost hotel nights (which I still think was true).

'You don't understand the situation, *madame*,' he said when I told him this.

That made me stop and think. Hmm. What was I letting myself in for? I started feeling nervous for the first time. What were the real dangers of attack? I took Baba to one side, as I had confidence in his opinion. He did not deny what I thought about the manager and said I could trust Ibrahim. That was enough for me. I was still nervous, but there was just one way to find out – to go.

I let Traoré know what I thought of him: 'a little dictator ... a part of the old Republic ... just like Moussa Traoré ...' and so on. Given that Moussa Traoré was still on public trial for treason at that time, this was a pretty nasty comment. On my return, our argument and my comments were well known in Timbuktu. In fact, it earned me some kudos.

'Traoré is afraid of you Australian women,' I was told. 'A few months ago, another Australian woman had an argument with Traoré, and hit him.' Australian women were gaining a Rambo-like reputation in Timbuktu. However, people were also tickled – Traoré was not well liked.

I walked with Ibrahim out to his *campement*, Tintahaten, just 4 kilometres away. Ibrahim was tall and gaunt, his skin pulled tight across his cheekbones. How old was he? Hard to say. His eyes were weary, his movements slow and careful. Perhaps in his forties, but possibly, given his young family, his thirties. He wore a dark indigo *boubou*, faded a steel-grey with age, and an even darker turban. He walked erect and always carried his camel stick, often horizontally across his shoulders. He had an aura of calm and sincerity, yet as I got to know him well over the next few days, I discovered he was a deeply worried and haunted man.

After the arguing, it was late and we decided to rest during the heat of the day. Tintahaten was in the dunes just outside Timbuktu. Low huts were scattered, hundreds of metres apart, in the folds of the dunes. Ibrahim's hut was typical, formed from branches bent into arches and covered with straw matting. It was small – two people-lengths long, one wide and just a metre high. The matting swept close to the ground at the entrance, so we had to crawl. Inside, it provided an escape from the midday sun, already suffocatingly hot in early February.

I met Fatimata, Ibrahim's wife. She was tiny and thin, with the bulge of a fourth baby showing through her worn, dark-blue *boubou*. Her poverty, lack of nourishment and pregnancy made her face look tired and preoccupied, yet the beauty of her thin, carved face, tightly drawn back hair and sad brown eyes, still showed. Despite the heat, she started preparing lunch, lamb and rice with greasy goat's butter. She had to mill the rice and toss it to sift away the husks. She pounded the spice and cut the meat, freshly bought with my money, paid in advance. Ibrahim had left and I did not think she spoke French, so I watched in silence and smiled when our eyes met. I offered to help, signalling chopping or watching the fire, but she smiled and shook her head. I felt a little uncomfortable, like I was being treated as a paying guest. Or perhaps I was being treated as an honorary man. In that role, something I was used to now, I just watched and played with Mana. Mana, the eighteen-month-old baby, was fascinated with the fire and chewed on lumps of charcoal, while Leila, the eldest daughter of about four years, assisted her mother. Mohammed, her son of about six years, just ran around the camp and squealed, the loud noise piercing in the quiet heat.

As she prepared the food she smiled briefly, and commented in fluent French, 'I had to unpack everything off the camels.' It sounded like she was unpacking a boot of a car. She had loaded the camels for our journey, thinking we would be away earlier.

I commented how surprised I was to find she spoke French. 'My parents sent me to school,' she said quietly. 'Before the drought.' She seemed very tired. I asked her where Ibrahim had gone, and she replied enigmatically, 'He will be back soon.' Here was a rare opportunity to speak with a village woman, but she did not seem to have the energy for conversation and, really, neither did I. The heat was debilitating.

Soon, Ibrahim returned and Fatimata and the children lay down to sleep in the shade of a brush wall. Ibrahim and I crawled inside the hut – I was definitely being treated as an honorary man – and talked about the rebellion. Mats were drawn across the entrance to keep out the flies, so the air was still and the light filtered orange. I brought the conversation around to the scene I had witnessed between Mohammed Traoré and himself. I was disturbed. Traoré had been wild, like a madman, and had hurled terrible abuse at Ibrahim. Should I believe Traoré, or Ibrahim? Was I safe? Or had Ibrahim brought me into the desert to make money, regardless of the risks? I needed to understand.

'Was that typical of how Tuaregs are treated?' I asked.

Ibrahim sighed and talked in a slow, low voice. He told me how after the drought in 1970 to 1974, the Tuaregs had asked for cattle to be replaced by the government.

'That was all the help we needed, to deliver our independence again. However, we were told to find work.' He was sad and his voice carried authority. 'Some Tuaregs, the poor ones, moved nearer the towns by necessity, and their children went to school, but they could never get senior positions. There was no assistance and they were treated badly, and it was then that the seeds for the rebellion, which has now endured two years, were planted ...'

I asked if he knew the results of the agreement.

'We are not well informed,' he replied. 'And when we were asked to visit the town [how all the Tuaregs I met referred to Timbuktu] to hear the governor recently, the army gathered and we hid.'

I thought this rather melodramatic and self-defeating. Then.

'Have you got a radio?'

'Yes, I used it when the times were very dangerous, when we were in hiding, but now I have put it away. I don't like the noise.' It was soothingly silent inside the hut.

We talked about the problems as though they were past. The scene with Traoré and the worries he raised started to disappear, subdued by the heat and the quiet of the desert.

In the late afternoon we loaded the two camels and set off for Finderiah, a second *campement*. I was given the big, white camel, Abzul. Ibrahim and his son were on the smaller, brown camel, Ashwar. Mohammed had insisted on joining us as we were leaving, and behaving like an indulgent father, Ibrahim had relented.

Getting onto the camel was interesting. Abzul was resting on his knees when I clambered into the saddle. The beautifully embossed leather saddle sat on each side of the camel's neck and had high front and rear butterfly wings to hold me in place. There were no stirrups and Ibrahim told me to dig my toes into the camel's sinewy neck. There were 'reins' to hold on to, stretching from a bit in the camel's mouth. However, when he signalled Abzul to rise and the camel went onto his knees, lurching me forwards, I let go of the reins and grabbed the front wings. Then, as Abzul rose onto his feet, lurching me backwards, I hastily grabbed the rear wings. I had a lot to learn.

As we set off, it was clear Abzul was going to do his own thing. At first, he seemed to know the way and chose the route, through the dipping and rising dunes. He was moving fast, ahead of Ibrahim, and I concentrated on not rolling out of the saddle sideways and keeping my bare toes firmly gripped on his neck. Then, Abzul decided he was hungry and continually put his head down to munch on the prickly grass that peppered the dunes! Annoying. The third time, I tugged hard on the rope and stopped him – he needed to learn who was in charge.

We arrived in the *campement*, set in a low, scrubby landscape, at sunset. Again, the low huts were scattered over some distance, and I had to look hard to realise that we were not merely arriving at a single lonely hut.

'Tuareg *campements* are like that,' said Ibrahim. 'We do not live like the blacks, all crowded together in towns.' I wondered at the use of the term '*les noirs*' for the Malians. Did the Tuaregs think of themselves as non-blacks? I quizzed Ibrahim, but he explained it only by looking at our skin and saying, 'We are whites.' His skin was a lot darker than mine! (Later, I discovered most Tuaregs thought of themselves as 'whites', the Malians as 'blacks'.)

I was greeted by a group of excited women in dark blue *boubou*s. They had leapt up from resting in the white sand outside their hut.

'*Matula!*' they cried. '*Matula!*'

Of course, they were calling out 'White! White!' There was still some distinction between Tuaregs and myself! Soon, I learnt some Tamachek, the name they give their language and themselves. I reached down to shake their hands. Come down, signalled an old lady, but I had to shrug to show I did not know how. They all laughed, but it was a friendly interaction.

We were invited to stay at the hut of the chief of the village, another Mohammed. I later learnt he was Ibrahim's younger brother, but he looked older and had an older wife, Telemata, and nearly grown family. Darkness rapidly arrived, and I was given a mat to stretch out on by the fire outside the chief's hut. All the family gathered. Ibrahim and Mohammed, the chief, were also stretched out on cushions near me. Telemata sat quietly and prepared the meal with her teenage daughter, Heidera. Unlike Fatimata, they did not speak French, so even during the cooler evening as conversation started, I could not talk to them. Another man, a neighbour, was stretched out on a mat. He wore a bright blue *boubou* and a dark, concealing turban. Ibrahim also kept his turban on, but the chief, in his own home I supposed, removed his. He had a strong, deeply lined face and large, brown eyes. It was a wise, calm face. The chief's two sons, Ibrahim and Ali, both in their teens, left quietly, and then returned. I later found out they were responsible for rounding up the goats and milking them.

We sat talking quietly by the flickering light of the fire. Bright stars appeared in the huge, enveloping sky. We ate chunks of goat's cheese that tasted like Parmesan, then rice and meat with goat's butter. I ate with the men – we ate with our fingers out of a large enamel bowl. I took my cues from them and pulled at balls of rice that I massaged in my right hand and then ate in a single, open-mouthed bite taken from my palm towards my fingers. Mohammed pushed chunks of meat into my depression in the rice when he thought I was not taking enough. When we had eaten as much as we wanted, it was passed to Telemata and the children. The final course was a bowl of warm, freshly drawn goat's milk.

The chief did most of the talking, speaking in deep, quiet tones in the soothing rhythm of Tamachek. He had a restful dignity. Ibrahim translated. I was told that if I had been here before the drought I would have seen this land differently.

'The women were fat and the men were strong. Now they are all thin ...' The chief continued and I found his words magnetising. 'The houses were covered in skins, and not mats ... There were no enamel basins, as everything was made of ebony ... Everywhere you went you would see animals – goats and cattle and camels.'

I watched his calm eyes, not Ibrahim's, as I listened to the translation.

Ibrahim nodded, and intoned, 'You had to be high on a camel to see where you were going, as the pasture was so high ...'

I was told about the problems, *la situation*. I was told of how the people listen for strange noises, and are always prepared to hide. They talked of attacks and the relatives who had been killed. Suddenly, through their matter-of-fact descriptions, the situation seemed real and current again.

I was asked about news from the town, from Timbuktu. 'How do you think the situation is?' I got a sense of their isolation. 'Why do the people in the town hate us?' Timbuktu was the only world they focused on. 'What can we do?'

These were difficult questions that I did not feel well equipped to answer. Was the situation getting worse because the whole Malian economy was suffering from the death of tourist traffic and of cross-Saharan trade? Did the mismanaged southward expansion of the Sahara mean there would never be grazing here for their animals again? Were the people in Timbuktu fearful because of the possible danger to themselves? Was it that they are poor too, and competing with Tuaregs for scarce revenues and jobs? I could offer questions, but not answers.

The chief then asked about my travels.

'It is a difficult voyage you have taken – we always travel in twos, never alone.' The Tuaregs have been one of the great nomadic tribes of this planet, who have survived for centuries following a nomadic lifestyle across one of the world's harshest environments – the Sahara. That they, people I considered great travellers, should recognise my journey as difficult, and somehow elevate my strange obsession with travel alongside theirs, made me feel honoured. I liked the idea of being a nomad. The chief seemed genuinely interested in my descriptions and views of other countries, and I commented on this to Ibrahim.

'We have a song,' said Ibrahim, 'which asks a question, then answers it: what can you keep getting more of, give it away, and still get more? The answer is knowledge, knowledge from travel.'

I was also told about a Japanese man – in 1985 or 1986 – who came and stayed with them. The chief told the story in a gentle way; he could have been reciting a verbal history from a hundred years ago.

'He learnt our language and our ways, and then he voyaged all over West Africa with his own camels. When he came back he even brought news of Tuaregs who we did not know. He returned to his own country and wrote a book, and now he has taken a Tuareg wife, and, I believe, is ambassador for his country to Senegal.'

It seemed an amazing story, and I asked if they had seen him since.

'He started *L'Association Sahel*, which raised money in Japan, and planted trees in the desert,' I was told. 'Once he came. However, we have not seen him again, and the work has stopped now ... due to the situation.' Without this grassroots kind of aid, there could be no hope of these Tuaregs returning to their former way of life.

Then, there was a signal from the chief that it was time to rest. The children left to sleep in another hut. The neighbour left, and Telemata and Mohammed retired inside their hut. Ibrahim and his son stretched out on one side of the dying fire, me on the other. I lay, thinking, watching the stars.

I awoke at the first glow of light in the high sky. As I still lay by the cold fire, I observed the others rising and walking a little way to pray. There were no muezzin calling the faithful in this silent scene. For their ablutions, to cleanse themselves for prayer, I saw Ibrahim and the chief 'wash' their hands in the sand. I walked into the desert for my ablutions ... and also used sand for washing. I felt clean.

Ibrahim said, 'This sand here at Finderiah purifies ... it is not like the sand near the town ... the wind brings all the rubbish to our *campement* at Tintahaten and it is not clean.'

The first task of the morning was to round up the camels, me trailing behind Ibrahim; Mohammed, his son, behind me. We followed their trace in the sand, a trace I could not see. Through scrub we walked, in silence, listening to the wind. The sky was cloudless, a pale blue at this early hour, the low sand dunes were white with stubbles of straw-yellow and grey-green. Ibrahim finally saw the camels when we stopped on a small rise – I did not until we were several hundred metres closer. Their cries at seeing us sounded very much like 'Oh, no!', but they placidly allowed the rope to be put through their nose ring. Their front feet had been tied together with a short length of rope, yet they had still managed to wander two or three kilometres in search of juicier morsels of grass.

Back at the camp, the chief said he would spend the day in the town, gathering information on any movements in the desert, hearing if there was any 'noise'. I trusted these people now, but I knew they were treating the situation with gravity. Another man arrived who had been in the town the previous day. He said there was talk, rumours of military movements, plans. We decided it was wise to do a day trip from the *campement*, returning in the evening to discover the news.

During our morning ride, made mostly in silence, I could see Ibrahim constantly scanning for unfamiliar tracks and for movement on the horizon. I wondered: was he using his centuries-old desert skills to scan for signs of other Tuaregs, to take directions? We came across one- or two-day-old vehicle tracks.

'It must be the rebels or the army,' said Ibrahim. 'No other transport is in the desert now.' I soon found myself watching and listening for the military.

I had asked the night before at the campfire about the possibility of getting credit to buy more animals. I had been still wondering why they were not being more proactive in helping themselves.

'But we have fear,' said the chief.

'Fear of credit?' I had asked, naively, still following my own business world train of thought.

'No, fear. While there are security problems, we can only think of that.'

I could now start to understand that comment, and the impact of fear on their lives. They have been living for two years, looking forward and back; checking information between themselves, in the town; being prepared to hide at any warning sign; having friends and relatives killed in attacks. I was nervous after only one day of imbibing their emotions. This was not a 'noble nomad' experience.

I remembered the discussion with M. Keita in faraway Koundara in Guinea. He had spoken about the lack of justice in Africa. Then, the ideas seemed theoretical and the consequences were hard to imagine. Now, here was something more tangible – a lack of security. I was living with people who ran their lives on fear. It was terrible for the spirit. It took away any ability to plan for a better future. I realised why the Tuaregs in the town looked furtive. At the time I had believed I was seeing avarice and greed, and was suspicious. Now, I pondered that in their intense eyes I had been seeing fear.

Without security, we have nothing.

We talked only intermittently as we rode. I commented on how bad the situation was for them, trying to reach out and let him know that I was sorry. Ibrahim then said, in his thoughtful French, 'We Tuaregs believe that you have to suffer to truly appreciate the taste of life.'

We were travelling through some beautiful dune country, still lightly covered in scrub, when we decided to stop for a picnic lunch. A picnic amongst the sand dunes, or that is what it felt like. Instead of a picnic table and coolbox, we had camel saddles and blackened teapots. After setting the camels free (again with front legs hobbled), we collected brush for the fire. Despite the strong wind, Ibrahim eventually got the fire started under his *boubou*. The steak was dried further on the branches of a thorn tree while we waited for the fire to burn down. It was cooked in the sand, covered by burning charcoal.

'When the meat is completely dry, no sand sticks to the meat,' said Ibrahim. It was very tasty and we ate it with the stale, round breads we had brought from Timbuktu.

Ibrahim tried to make sure I had the most – the meat was bought with my money – but I knew to eat meat was a rarity for them. I looked at Ibrahim's taut body and told him to eat my extra share. Although it seemed obscene, with their generosity, with their insistence on feeding me goat's milk, butter, cheese, meat, and rice, I knew I was putting on weight. It seemed such a ridiculous concern when my friends were struggling to survive.

Green gunpowder tea, with heaps of sugar, is drunk constantly in Mali, and is especially important to the Tuaregs. The ubiquitous, tiny, blue enamel teapot and three small glasses are essential equipment for any family. It is made three times, with each successive pot made stronger, and with increasing amounts of sugar.

'We can survive without food, but we need our tea,' said Ibrahim.

We stretched out in the shade and talked as we drank.

Ibrahim spoke again, 'Many of the old skills and stories of the Tuaregs have been lost. Many old people died in the drought and their learning was lost.' He told of the old abilities to trace many animals and to understand the talk of the birds. 'We knew many things. My father could foresee the future.' Ibrahim had learnt a little from his father and he too could sometimes foretell what was to come. 'I use it for telling me whether any day will be good or bad.' He paused, and added, 'I have better abilities on Fridays.' I supposed that was because it was the Moslem holy day. Today was Friday.

He gathered together fourteen small 'nuts' – goat dung – and tossed them in the sand. He did it several times and I asked him what he saw for my journey. Fortunately, he was reassuring – it would finish well.

We rode back to the *campement* in the late afternoon sun. My camel, Abzul, still did not want to obey me, but I was getting tougher with him. We galloped a little.

News was exchanged as we again settled around the campfire in the evening. Ibrahim translated.

'The chief has said he heard that six blacks were killed in Goundam by bandits. The army then sent out a patrol and rounded up six Tuareg men from nearby *campements*, and killed them. The chief does not know if it was true or not, but this is what he had heard in Timbuktu.'

It was delivered in the monotone of Tamachek and conveyed flatly to me in French. It was horrific – especially their lack of surprise. The discussion continued for hours, but I did not ask for a translation. I was trying to make sense of what I had already heard.

The next morning, I got up early to have some time to myself and to watch the sunrise, while the rest of the *campement* started their morning chores – praying, washing, making the fire, milking the goats. When I returned, the fire embers were burning low and tea was being prepared. Everyone seemed subdued. And the topic of conversation was still the attack at Goundam.

Ibrahim said, 'The chief advises that we do not go out on the camels today. It is better to be in the *campement*, so that should any vehicles approach, there is more warning and time to hide.'

Were they being melodramatic, I wondered, or just cautious? It was clearly real fear they felt, yet I still found it hard to relate to such raw emotions. Ibrahim seemed preoccupied and I sensed that he was worried about his family. I suggested that if we were staying the day in camp, we might as well spend it at his home *campement*, Tintahaten. He was very pleased by this suggestion, although the Chief counselled that I must be happy. They did not want me to be too scared of the situation.

'It is always like this.'

I did not want to be responsible for increasing Ibrahim's anxiety. If I could bring him some peace of mind, even for a day, I was happy. So, it was decided to return. Ibrahim now seemed to me to be a man pushed to the edge of a nervous breakdown.

As we walked back to the chief's camp, he said, 'We suspect the bandit attacks are a ruse, perhaps even executed by the soldiers, as an excuse to kill Tuaregs.' He shook his head and said, 'How can they do that to us?'

He was worried about Traoré too, particularly that he might be in contact with the military. Ibrahim said that Traoré had warned him: 'She [meaning me] will be all right while she is with you, but afterwards you will not be.' I worried for Ibrahim.

As we started loading up the camels, the chief invited me back. By the time we were underway, the day was already hot. The scrubby bush and stunted trees were silhouetted darkly against the burning sand and the wide blue sky. I thought I was getting more control over Abzul – he got up and sat down for me. 'Ooot' for up, and 'Szoo' for down. However, when he got huffy with having an amateur on his back, his pace reduced to a slow creep and he could not be induced, by me, to go faster. I appealed to Ibrahim, who with a few clicks in his throat, would have him moving again. Once out of reach of Ibrahim's stick, however, he slowed his pace again. Very frustrating! Ibrahim claimed he was being so stubborn because he knew he was going away from good pasture. I think I needed more than a week to learn about camels, and thought wistfully of my bicycle. When I wanted to turn, it turned.

Back in Ibrahim's hut, again darkened by the mats pulled across the low opening to keep out the flies, young Ali, the chief's youngest son, who had come with us from Finderiah, made tea. Ibrahim's three young children, domineering Mohammed, quiet Leila and inquisitive Mana, periodically came inside to play and argue. Inevitably, it finished with Mohammed racing off and Mana left crying over something he had done. The contrast between their normality and fun and their father's tired and worried face and bleak words was enormous.

Ibrahim tried his radio, to see if he could find some news in Tamachek.

'Sometimes around noon it is on,' he said, glancing at the sun in the sky, 'but I keep forgetting to bring it out and turn it on.' He looked for a safe place to hang the radio. 'This was left for us by a friend, but it was only afterwards that I realised it was not for us. We have too much sand!'

He told me of the best present given by a German.

'He gave each family a goat. If we can get more goats and camels we can leave the edge of town.' From someone else I would have seen a sly hint for a gift. Before I left Timbuktu, my perspective, my blindness, meant I would have judged this a request for a 'cadeau' from any Tuareg. Now, from Ibrahim, I knew it was a statement of fact. His longing to be free was tangible.

I remembered Sekou Touré's speech: 'We prefer freedom in poverty, to riches in slavery ...' Ibrahim had poverty and slavery.

Ibrahim departed for the town to find out more information that could tell him whether he should flee with his family yet. I spent more time with Fatimata, spreadeagled on the sand, and got to know her better. She had no energy, as much from despair as from being pregnant and the heat. She seemed too fragile to cope with this life.

She told me, 'I was a child, the same age as Mohammed, when the drought struck in 1973 to 1975.' That made her perhaps between twenty-four and twenty-six years old.

She continued, without a trace of emotion, 'My family was rich before then, but the animals died and we were fed by relief agencies. After the drought we had to come near to the town ...' She has been just outside Timbuktu with Ibrahim for ten years now.

'C'est fatigant,' she sighed – it is tiring.

Leila wandered over to play with some sticks near her mother.

'Leila, do you want to go away with Pamela and work in a strange country? Come back to us with money to make us rich?' Leila smiled, without understanding. I wished I could help them. WOMANKIND was not a suitable agency to help – Ibrahim and Fatimata's issues were survival and human rights. How could I help? Money? I gave them some. Publicity? This was one of the first times that the impulse to write about my journey became strong.

Despair was a hard emotion to feel, and I had only sensed it for a few days. I still really did not understand what it was like to live with such fear, without hope.

'Do you make the indigo material for your clothes?' I asked, trying to lighten our conversation.

'No, I buy it in the market. All the Tuareg women wear these,' she said. Then, she started rearranging the folds of her material sadly. 'This is not pretty anymore,' she murmured as she put her finger through a hole.

Fatimata was so lovely. She deserved pretty clothes.

I was sitting haunted by these memories in the gaudy Cherry Bar, an old Portakabin, its doorway alluringly festooned with dangling, faded coloured strips of plastic. I had handed over 600 CFA (US$2.40) for my beer – expensive, but I could afford it. It was cold and straight from the fridge. I sat alone at a table, and took in the decorations – flashing fairy lights and Chinese lanterns. It was gaudy, a kind of weird Aladdin's Cave and it represented money, cheap money, and 'toubab-ness' and having a good time.

My heart cried out for Fatimata and her children. She sits frightened and poor outside the town, I thought, and I am able to leave, to move freely, to spend money. I pictured Telemata and Mohammed at their hut at Finderiah. With the setting sun, a fire would be made. Rice or millet would be cooking, perhaps with the meat of a freshly killed goat. They would be talking of the day, perhaps about me.

Timbuktu's present had delivered an emotional impact far more powerful than any of my previous imaginings about its past. Had I once thought I didn't romanticise Africa? Huh!

But what could I do? How could I have thought of the Tuaregs as avaricious?

Of course, every story is more complex than it might first seem. My consultant mind-set wanted me to know more, to analyse, to come to a considered opinion. I knew little about the 'other side' of the story – the Malian government viewpoint and facts about their actions.

No.

Nobody should have to live like Ibrahim and Fatimata.

(Since being with these Tuaregs, I have become more passionate about human rights abuse. Before I met them, before I left London and my safe life, it was hard to emotionally connect with scenes of horror on television. Now, to sense despair, I just remember my Tuareg friends. These injustices, which take away individual freedom and security, which stop people planning, living and having hope, seem to me the most basic and terrible injustice of all. I have had no contact with Ibrahim and Fatimata since our separation – they had no address. Since my visit, there was calm for a while, then more violence and killing and retaliatory killing, until the negotiation of a new reconciliation agreement in 1996. A fragile peace seems to be in place.)

I took a last gulp of beer, sighed and stepped out into the night in search of food, a meal that would probably contain more calories than Fatimata had eaten in five days.

My journey moved me relentlessly on: tomorrow, I would leave again on a *pinasse* for Mopti, to resume cycling, ever onwards, alone.

Seven

What Do the Men Do Here?

Mopti, Mali – Bawku, Ghana

I returned to Mopti from Timbuktu with another *pinasse*, picked up my bicycle and cycled to Sevaré. At the hotel where I had stayed with Al and Suze, much to my relief, I found a note from them saying that Al had recovered sufficiently for them to cycle onwards to Ougadougou, the capital of Burkina Faso. I hoped to see them there. Leaving Sevaré, I travelled along a tough gravel road up into the interesting and rugged region known as Dogon country. The Dogon were a tribe whose rich cultural and religious tradition had been preserved through the centuries, mainly due to the inaccessibility of their villages built high on the Bandiagara escarpment.

They remained inaccessible to me.

Visiting the Dogon required walking, donkey carts or mountain bikes and several days of time, but I did not stray off the lower main road. Main road? It turned sandy and slow. Still unable to totally rid myself of my management-consultant deadlines, I was anxious to reach Ougadougou. I was aiming for the opening of FESPACO (*Festival Pan Africain du Cinéma à Ougadougou*), a major biennial African film festival that informants in Mopti had advised me not to miss. I might find Al and Suze there, and – just maybe – I might find William, too. In a phone call from Bamako, I had asked him to meet me in Ougadougou. He had been doubtful, but ...

Burkina Faso was another very poor West African country. It was land-locked, about the size of Great Britain, and its dry, flat landscape reminded me of Australia. The savannah conditions and frequent droughts prevailing in most of the country limited agricultural output. There were few mineral prospects and no access to ports, major perennial rivers or cross-Saharan routes to deliver trading wealth. The Burkinabe (as the people of Burkina Faso are called) travel widely to other countries, especially southwards into Ivory Coast and Ghana, in search of jobs and wealth.

Having entered Burkina at the large and bustling regional centre of Ouahigouya, I travelled south-eastwards along fabulous tarmac roads (happily, M. Kounkaye, the retired and talkative taxi driver in Guinea, had been right!); tomorrow, I would reach Ougadougou, or Ouga as it is commonly known.

In just three days, I had found that Burkinabe struck up friendships easily. The people were very open, more informal than the Malians, introducing themselves with their first names, rather than surnames, as was the custom in Mali, and, oddly, given the relative destitution of the country, had more energy in their voices and footsteps.

Even the children said '*Ça va?*' like they really wanted to know, not merely to scream and annoy a stranger. Of course, sometimes there was the accompanying '*Donnez-moi cent francs*' – Give me 100 francs – but not a lot.

In the cool mornings, I was in a bright and energetic mood, enjoying the feeling of rhythmic pedalling, the strength in my muscles and a sense of oneness with the bike. These were the glorious times. Children and women at the pumps, walking along the road or working in the dry fields, greeted me and I waved and smiled back. As I travelled through wide, hazy vistas of burnt ochre soil, dusty grey scrubland and occasional twisted baobab trees, I thought I was the luckiest woman alive!

By mid-morning, though, the constant rhythm and rising temperatures would make me soporific and I would douse myself with cool water. (This was an innovation: I wrapped my water bottles in torn strips of cotton, soaked the cotton when I filled the bottles at village pumps and let evaporation do the rest.)

By midday, my head would be sunk low into my shoulders with the weight of the heat. My arms, exposed below the sleeves of my T-shirt, would sting as they fried in the sun. Sunscreen Factor 5 was not enough and, as I had pruned my clothing, I was no longer carrying a long-sleeved shirt to protect my poor skin. Perhaps I would buy one in Ouga. Perhaps not – it would be too hot.

My head thumped with a headache, and now little children had to be content with a nod, a brief smile and maybe a gruff '*Ça va?*' It was sensible to stop between about noon and 3 p.m. to escape the worst heat, but often villages did not come at the right intervals and, like a mad Englishman, I would cycle on under the midday sun. My energy usually returned with the final stretch in the afternoon – the end-of-day wash and cup of tea was in sight!

Late this afternoon, I arrived in Lay, a

small village 35 kilometres outside Ouga. Its small and closed market was merely a collection of trestle tables by the roadside. A group of men was gathered, chatting there. Asking the group generally about a place to stay, I was answered by the eldest, a man in a grey *boubou*.

'*Attendez!*' As ever, I was told to wait. A child was sent to get someone.

Soon, a serious-looking man in his early thirties and wearing a dark suit, approached.

'*Bonne arrivée!*' he had said, with a happy smile that transformed his features and made him look very youthful and pleased to see me. He was Alain, the *secrétaire* of the prefecture of Lay.

'*Merci,*' I replied. He asked to see my passport. Burkina Faso seemed quite keen on police checks, so I had it handy. Finding everything in order, he indicated I should follow him. Was he taking me to a hotel, a *campement* or his home?

It was nearly dusk, and we walked down dim alleys in the small village, dodging chickens and goats and piles of decaying rubbish, and feeling the heat steam off the burnt clay ground, until we had reached a compound fenced by a low, mud-brick wall, with a hut in the corner. Alain introduced me to his beautiful, even younger, ebony-skinned wife, Judith, who, like me, seemed worn out from the hot day.

'You may stay with us,' said Alain.

It was often like this. Traditional village hospitality demanded that strangers be taken in. For the night, the security and comfort of the stranger becomes their responsibility, and it seemed to transfer to the official world of prefectures. I always insisted on leaving a gift in the morning – not stickers and pins now, but things I hoped were more useful, like T-shirts and food. (I didn't give money because I felt that might attract attention and threaten my security.) However, the freely given hospitality continued to amaze me.

Alain left me with Judith, who was making dinner in a blackened cauldron over a hot charcoal fire. I made my dinner in my aluminum pot over my still temperamental petrol stove. Meat and rice stew for Judith and Alain. Pasta and bland onion and tomato sauce for me. Again. Pasta was easy to carry, onions did not squash and I bought tomatoes nearly every day (I liked to buy things from markets to make contact with locals), so it was my usual meal on nights when I was in small villages and there was no sign of market women cooking. That, or a boiled egg and bread. I probably could have shared Judith and Alain's meal – traditional village hospitality demanded they feed me – but I had stopped allowing this. I didn't like to think that someone else might go hungry for me. As we both cooked, Judith seemed withdrawn and shy, and she did not speak French. I sighed. Although I found my conversations with Fatimata disturbing, they were better than no conversations at all.

I woke up in the middle of the night inside my tent, pitched in Alain and Judith's compound, with something cold and wet trickling down my chin. I

licked at the wetness with my tongue and tasted blood. My cracked bottom lip
had split open. My Akubra shaded my nose, and my nose shaded my top lip,
but my protruding bottom lip – halfway to a sexy pout, I hoped – was cooking
crisply in the sun and wind. I stretched on my mat inside my dark tent and
reached for my torch. It was 3 a.m. The cock in the yard must have seen the
light from my torch because he started to crow, and I sent unfriendly vibes in
his direction. At this hour, I wasn't a happy bunny – in fact, I felt like a
bloated whale. My stomach still seemed to be getting bigger and bigger – it
had been going on for days now. There had been no amorous liaisons, so it
wasn't that, and I was not eating *that* much. I wondered if my period was due.
Due? Well, it had stopped altogether for the first three months (in shock, I
supposed, like its owner), and now it was coming irregularly and with a pretty
pathetic flow. It meant that one packet of precious tampons would last two
cycles – enough to get me to another city with a western pharmacy – but I
wondered if this bloated feeling was because it was all remaining gummed up
inside me. A delightful thought.

I struggled out of my tent to go to the latrine, and nearly poked my eye out
on the low branch of a tree in the compound. Ouch! The latrine was smelly, a
hole surrounded by wobbly planks behind a low mud wall in the far corner of
the compound; at least, in the far corner from the mud-brick and tin-roofed
hut of my hosts. My tent was within whiffing distance. I balanced the torch
for illumination on the low wall, and crouched down carefully. The torch
rolled off the wall and went out. Typical, I thought dispiritedly, you are
bloody hopeless. I groped around the wet boards to find it. It wouldn't work.
I was really irritated with myself now. You're as hopeless as a man!

Men in Africa might have nice bodies, but increasingly they were annoying
me – mainly because they never seemed to be *doing* anything! Each day, I saw
women gathered around the water pump at the edge of a village, working in
the fields, walking along the road home under a heavy load, selling food in the
markets. Because I rarely spoke to them, except in basic greetings, they
seemed like ephemeral ghosts who floated through the background of my
village life. Well, hardly floated – not with a load of firewood on their heads.

At the remote Malian border post, I had been made to wait for about ten
minutes for the guard. Perhaps not long, but I had a 90-kilometre day under a
hot sun ahead of me. What made matters worse was that I could see the man
sitting in the shade, as usual, drinking a cup of sweetened Chinese gunpowder
tea. By the time he came over, my blood was boiling, so that my first
comment was a sarcastic, 'Is that all the men do here? Drink tea?' It hadn't
helped.

During the day at rest stops, a common comment about my journey was,
'*C'est formidable pour une femme!*' – It is amazing for a woman. I was heartily
sick of it, as I felt it implied that it would not be amazing for a man to do it.
The male speaker would be usually drinking tea or drunk. Then, predictably,

the next comment would be, 'Our women could not do a thing like that.' *Aye!* Did they find it amazing for a woman to do her own thing by herself?

Should I be cool? The situation was not so different at home. But there, I wasn't cool about laziness either! Who always did the vacuuming? Who never saw the bin needed emptying?

Then, I remembered a time I had heard some cynicism about men expressed by an African woman. During our few days in Djenné, Suze and I met a schoolteacher, Djenaba, at the local women's cooperative. We both relished the rare opportunity to talk in French with an African woman, and when Djenaba offered to show us the fields on the mud flats outside the walled city where the local women grew vegetables, we leapt at it.

'We come morning and night to do the watering,' said Djenaba, a tall, stately woman, wearing a magnificent pink *boubou* and matching *fula*. Suze and I had joined her near dusk, and many women were working their small plots: some were gathered around the only water pump, others were going towards their plots, walking with magnificent posture and a light step under a heavy bucket, some were bent over their plants watering and weeding. The healthy-looking vegetables shone brightly at this hour of the day, and the women's outfits – ensembles of brightly patterned and spectacularly colourful *pagnes* of material – shone against the emerald green of their amassed crops of tomatoes and lettuces, even radishes, courgettes and peppers.

'You come, too?' I asked, somewhat surprised. Her dress seemed to indicate wealth and I thought that, as a professional, she would have house help to do this. Wrong.

'Oh yes, before my husband wakes, then I return to make his and the children's meal before I leave for my work.' It remained a pattern that educated and professional women in provincial towns and cities were not immune from doing field labour to supplement their family's food or income.

Djenaba showed us her plot, a small parcel of land about 3 metres by 2 metres, crammed with healthy plants. Automatically, Djenaba bent over to start lifting leaves, her long fingers searching out intrusive weeds. 'We would like more land, so that each woman could grow more.' She straightened again. 'But the men will not let us have more.' She pointed toward another barren field of dried, dark-orange mud nearby. 'The *chef du terre* [land chief] allocated this piece of land to the men, a better piece with more water. The men would not stand for us having more land unless they had some too. Yet they have done nothing with their land – it remains barren.'

I went to ask why, but Susanna put a more straightforward question.

'Djenaba,' she said. 'What *do* the men do here?'

At that moment, the muezzin started his mournful call to the faithful over the loudspeaker of the nearby Djenné mosque. Djenaba cast her head toward the sound and shrugged. Her dark-brown eyes filled with a scornful look.

'They pray,' she said.

Now, back in my tent, alone in a Burkina night, I chuckled again and felt my mood lighten. It was a good memory to have at this lonely hour of the morning, a memory of a time when the confusing cultures I was travelling through had again, momentarily, seemed less far apart from my own, when I felt closer to understanding how women thought, especially about their men.

What do the men do here?

I had started asking this question of men, too.

In one particularly quiet Malian village, the sandy streets were deserted in the heat of the midday sun, yet out in the yellow fields, women were working, and as I approached the closed market I glimpsed an elderly woman sagging under a load of firewood. The men were sprawled drunkenly around the benches of the bar. I bought a soft drink, and wandered out to a stall, thinking I would drink under the shade of its verandah. Here, too, all the space was taken by untidy-looking men, stretched out talking or playing checkers. They looked particularly dissipated, and the lack of women made me feel rather uncomfortable.

'Where are the women?' I gingerly asked the group.

'Oh, they are in the fields, working,' said one man in a dirty, pale-blue robe. He sounded like he was stating the obvious.

'And what do the men do here?' I asked, not so innocently.

Now the man was defensive.

'We help with the harvesting, and we do the construction when it is necessary.'

'That does not sound much.' How often was a building needed? And how many harvests were there a year? How about the ploughing, the weeding, the watering and the marketing of crops, and all the home chores, like collecting firewood, looking after children, grinding flour, collecting water, making meals, washing dishes and children and clothes?

The man pulled himself upright and puffed out his chest. In a tone suggesting that the discussion was finished, that men were clearly superior, he said, 'We make the decisions.'

Arriving in Ougadougou required a gear shift upwards in my state of alertness. The passive cycling and daydreaming of my days on the outback roads was impossible. Horns, dust, and the high-pitched buzzing of masses of mobylette engines assaulted my senses, and I had to concentrate on choosing routes, not to mention avoiding death by squashing – overloaded trucks and over-filled bush taxis drove recklessly and stopped unexpectedly. The change of pace was shocking but, now that I had experienced (and survived) Bamako, it was also expected and familiar.

Ougadougou was a city of about half a million people located in the middle of a flat plain (like most of Burkina) and the small city seemed to have spread to fit its available space – the suburbs (or *secteurs* as they were called and numbered, like the *arrondissements* in Paris) continued for kilometres around. A distinctive feature of Ouga was the large number of cyclists on the road. Perhaps bicycles were fun in a flat city, or necessary in such a sprawling city. Either way, the streets looked more reminiscent of China than Africa, with folk weaving in and out of the traffic on black, single-geared, heavy steel horses. If I had flown in from Europe, I may have seen Ouga differently, but after the empty country I had been travelling through, the city seemed busy, full of life and a den of delights (red wine, mail and flush toilets).

Having phoned from a telephone centre in Ouahigouya and been given directions, I found Shell's offices easily. I met Marius Tapsoba, the genial *directeur général* of *Burkina et Shell*, the marketing company, and Somdha, the fresh-faced, enthusiastic manager who had been put in charge of my programme.

'Here is your parcel and mail,' said Somdha. I knew what was in the parcel – it was a goodie parcel that I had assembled in London and sent ahead – spares, new shoes, a T-shirt. But mail! From whom? My parents? Yes! William? Yes! Somdha told me about the hotel they had arranged (very difficult to find in FESPACO week), and then asked about my programme – he took his assigned task seriously. What kind of women would I like to meet? Businesswomen and women working in fields associated with women's issues. When did I need to change money? This afternoon. Why did I need to use a computer? To write the WOMANKIND newsletter. When would I be available for media interviews? Any time. Was there anything else? I needed to obtain a visa for Ghana, and please, could I call Catherine Shovlin in London? I added that I did want to see some FESPACO movies as I was here this week – a hint to give me a bit of time to myself.

Actually, as nice and helpful as he was at that moment, continuing our conversation was excruciating. After eight weeks without news from home, I was hungry to be alone with my mail, but I had to stave off my hunger until mid-afternoon.

Then, settling into a modest but air-conditioned hotel room – yes! – I opened the letter from my folks and the one from William.

My parents were worried, but well – I was pleased to hear they were okay, as I worried about them, too.

William's letter, written in early January (it was now late February) was beautiful. Well, it was totally non-committal (men!), but it gave me one crumb: 'I wish I didn't, but I miss you.' Immediately, at vast expense, I got on the phone. Hearing his voice was wonderful, but it brought bad news. Instead of coming to Burkina Faso, he had gone on holiday to Canada. And he said that he could not handle an independent woman.

That was it then, I thought desolately. Finished. What could I expect really, when I had left him to come to Africa? I was irritated by my reasonableness. I wanted to shake him, shout at him. But you can't do that on the telephone. Why couldn't he cope with independence? I remembered the village men amazed at a woman doing her own thing. 'Our women couldn't do a thing like that.' Clearly, William felt the same. Really, men everywhere were so alike! Why wouldn't he come?! I wanted to hate him. But I didn't.

Getting drunk was one option, going to sleep in clean sheets was another (and very tempting too), but instead I went to the opening ceremony for FESPACO at the sports stadium. Somdha had arranged for his nephew to take me, and besides, I could get drunk and maudlin over photos later. (Homesickness was often worst in the cities.)

The stadium was huge, and bursting with a relaxed, carnival atmosphere. Vendors, all young children, moved up and down the rows selling iced water in hand-tied plastic bags. I was a good customer, buying one for now, one for later. I bit off the corner of the first and sucked happily. Early on, I had discovered that knowledge about water-carried germs was high in West Africa, so I drank what others did. Music played very loudly over the speakers, keeping our bums bouncing to the rhythm, and I amused myself by taking in the scene.

A hot air balloon was being inflated in the middle of the arena – it had a long way to go – and around the edges of the arena were massive signs. '*Sportifs Burkinabe respectent l'adversaire.*' Burkinabe sportspeople respect their adversaries. '*Sport collectif = Joie collectif.*' Collective sport = Collective joy. They seemed like the kind of slogans I would have found in the Communist bloc, and I wondered if these signs at the stadium dated from the years of leadership by Thomas Sankara.

Thomas Sankara was a martyr and hero to many Burkinabe, and a famous name throughout Africa. He was just thirty-four when in 1983 he was appointed prime minister of Burkina Faso, then called Upper Volta, by a military council. Later that year, with fierce divisions in the government between the moderates and the radicals – headed by Sankara – he was arrested for threatening national unity. A rebellion against his detention began in Sankara's own commando unit and spread throughout the country. On 4 August 1983, Sankara seized power and declared himself president.

Sankara became a folk hero. He played the guitar, sang revolutionary songs and loved slogans which fired people up and denounced western imperialism. Initially considered a Marxist with close links to Colonel Gaddafi of Libya, ultimately his policies seemed more driven by idealism to put right injustices and to bond together the many disparate tribes living in Burkina. His methods were criticised as too harsh (reminiscent of Sekou Touré), but his idealism also resulted in popular moves like announcing free housing for all Burkinabe, changing the name of the country to Burkina Faso meaning 'Land of the Honourable', and being chauffeured in a small Renault rather than a Mercedes – a symbol of his simple living and determination to drive out corruption and waste. He even focused on improving the rights of women.

However, Sankara was a poor manager of international relations. He was isolated from France, went to war with Mali and fell out with Ivory Coast. President Eyedema of Togo accused Sankara of conspiring with Gerry Rawlings, the president of Ghana, in a coup attempt to oust Eyedema. Then, fatally, he lost the support of people in Burkina's governing body, the *Conseil National de la Révolution* (CNR).

Sankara was murdered in a coup d'état in 1987 by military officers supporting Blaise Compaoré. That was ironic as, in 1983, Blaise Compaoré had led the commando rebellion that resulted in Sankara gaining power.

I was brought back to the present by movement in the arena. A tall, distinguished and rather handsome man in a dark suit had mounted the dais. Hush descended on the crowd as he started his speech. This was the man himself, the current president of Burkina Faso, Blaise Compaoré.

Compaoré had adopted policies and programmes required by the IMF and World Bank to ensure their continued funding support for the impoverished country and introduced a new constitution with multi-party elections. Although he had no direct involvement in Sankara's death, I had read that the memory of his association with the murder of Burkina's hero had resulted in a lingering lack of popularity for his leadership. However, after banning opposition political rallies, Compaoré ended up being the only candidate in the first elections, and unsurprisingly, he had won.

Suddenly, the balloon shuddered and from being a sorry piece of fabric lying across the ground it grew into a majestic beast. Compaoré continued his speech but no one seemed to be listening. Instead, clapping, cheers, oohs and aahs erupted as the crowd stood to see the magnificent creature come to life.

During the following week, the whole city continued to be abuzz with excitement. Films showed from 4 p.m. till very late, which meant the mornings were devoted to my programme, while from 4 p.m. I was free to go to the festival. If I had imagined I would rest in Ouga, I had been mistaken!

For the first few days of the festival, before pay day, getting into films was easy, then, as the crowds of Burkinabe and travellers arrived, the queues got longer and the disappointments at being turned away more frequent. The consolation prize was chats with friendly people who also missed out on tickets, and often we moved on to find a bar or a *brochette* stall to talk.

'It's great to see Africa through African eyes,' a redheaded French woman, Claudine, said, one evening toward the end of the week. We had both been turned away from seeing an 8 p.m. film and had ended up having a Sobhra (the local beer) together. Claudine was having a *brochette*, but I had been drinking more than eating – my bloated stomach was tender and sore. Was it too much beer? I resolved to go to a doctor before I left.

Claudine, in stylish strappy sandals, designer slacks and pressed shirt, had come directly from Paris for the festival. Next to her, I felt shabby, but she was company and we were both enjoying the festival.

'It is so much better than seeing Africa only as we Europeans like to portray it,' she continued.

I agreed. To me, the best films had been those that portrayed a slice of life in the villages. '*Tillai* was great! Did you see it?' It had been about the problems that ensue when a father marries his son's promised bride.

'Yes, and what about *Denko?* That was extraordinary!' It was a Guinean film set in a remote village. The mother made a deal with a spirit: she would have sex with her son to restore his eyesight, then carry her son's baby. It had reminded me of my encounters with the spirits of the Fouta Djalon.

'But my favourite was *Yelena, The Mutation*,' I said. It seemed to capture Malian manners and mannerisms so wonderfully well – half the movie was taken up by greetings. '*Bonjour.*' '*Bonjour.*' '*Ça va?*' '*Ça va, et la famille?*' '*Ça va.*' '*Et ta santé?*' '*Ça va.*' And on. There were the soft, disinterested handshakes, eyes averted, with anyone encountered. It could be a long-lost relative or a friend of a friend of a friend, and still the same lack of interest. There was the slow walk, the rolling from side to side, arms flapping without any muscle control. 'It was terrific – so true to life,' I explained to Claudine, though I had to admit the story was far-fetched. A well-educated daughter was put in charge of her father's business, and, despite people trying to administer a marabout's magic potions to change her (that part was realistic), she ran the business and chose the man she wanted! In the eyes of men she was a mutation – an independent woman.

We decided to try for an 11 p.m. showing, then around 1 a.m. found another stall for more drinking and talking. A typical long, sociable Ouga night.

Daylight hours were also spent sociably, meeting strong, educated and powerful city women like energetic, elfin Patricia Bouguendza, who ran an office-cleaning bureau. She got the idea while watching a television programme about cleaning women in China, but it had been hard to set up – while women cleaned their homes, they did not think cleaning was work they could get paid for. Her solution was impressive. She organised a day cleaning the streets of Ouga, and when thousands of women turned up – perhaps in response to the offer of a free drink – she stood on a dais and told them to be at her office the next day if they wanted work as cleaners. She had hundreds of applicants! Patricia laughed as she told me stories about husbands who slept outside hotels where their wives cleaned at night so they could make sure their women were not being unfaithful, and about the time a man rushed into her office threatening her with a machete! His first wife was jealous of another of his wives, who through Patricia had an income, and now the first wife would not sleep with him.

Franceline Oubda was a television journalist who talked so much that I wondered when she got things done. Evidently she did – she invited me to a private viewing of her latest documentary (as it turned out, the winner of the

Best Documentary prize at FESPACO), a film about the right of village women to have access to land.

Confirming what I had learnt in Djenné about traditional African societies, Franceline told me passionately one afternoon, 'Women have no right to land. Each woman must be allocated a plot for her use by the *chef du terre*, yet she cannot even approach him directly. She must go through her husband. If her husband does not consent, she does not even get the opportunity to demand more land.' Then she continued, without any need for prompting, 'A woman must work on her husband's land and generally only gets a few hours per week to cultivate her own small plot. She uses her crops for food for her family and to get a small income for children's medicine and education. Worse! If a woman is divorced by her husband, she loses the right to her land. Only if her husband dies does she keep her right of access to her land, but never to his.'

Mme Tami, the local coordinator of the United Nations Development Programme (UNDP) and director of Unifem, the United Nation's fairly new programme for women, was a large woman who gazed at me intently from behind her thick, black-rimmed glasses.

'We have developed a five year plan to address the needs of women,' she said, and gave me an overview. Providing education and work training, access to land, and access to credit funds to help women build more sustainable income-generating activities were priorities. That made a lot of sense, given what I had seen so far about women's lives. She also confirmed attention was now being given by governments, funding agencies and NGOs to helping women to help themselves. I thought it was a pity it had taken thirty years of development aid before the second sex was discovered.

She told me of a programme to sensitise the rural population to the need to educate young girls.

'Religious constraint is not the only problem,' she said. 'Girls may be sent to school for a time, but are taken out to help their mothers, or even if they continue, they're given so many chores that they're too tired to do home-work!'

'As for adult literacy, we have a programme that aims to train fifty thousand women,' Mme Tani continued. 'However, women also don't have time – or if they go to classes, their minds are elsewhere on all their chores. Worse, as the men make the decisions on who goes to the classes, they send the older women of the village.'

'Why do they do that?' I queried.

'Because they fear the younger women will get too independent!' That sounded familiar.

It was comforting to mix in a business and professional environment again, and these meetings were interesting – the women were impressive and friendly, they showed me another side of Africa and I was becoming informed about women's development issues. But I felt a little like I was doing a crash course in gender studies. What had happened to being an Adventurer?

Towards the end of the week I received a note from Al and Suze, and tracked them down at a small hotel. We were glad to see each other, but they had bad news. Al's malaria fevers had come back in full force, and a quinine treatment prescribed was almost as bad as the malaria. Al looked like a pale skeleton, with enormous sunken eyes. What a frightening disease.

I felt fortunate – mosquitoes loved me, and I was always covered in bites, but happily my protagonists had not as yet injected any malaria parasites.

(Only many months later, I received news about what happened to them. Eventually, long after I had left Ouga, Al had felt sufficiently recovered for them to take the bus to Accra, the capital of Ghana. However, in Accra, the fevers returned and once again Al was evacuated by air back to Scotland, where he spent a month in hospital getting treatment.)

Al's misfortune in Ouga was a strong motivator to keep an eye on my health. After returning from a side trip by train to Bobo-Dioulasso, a pleasant town in western Burkina, on the last day before going on the road again, I went to visit Dr André, a short, competent-looking Belgian.

'You have worms,' he said.

'Worms?!' I exclaimed, alarmed. Yuk! The bulge in my tummy took on a different light. I imagined 2-metre-long creatures slithering around in my intestines.

Dr André, however, was all business.

'Take these and you will be fine,' he said as he handed me a prescription for some tablets. He continued blithely – I guess in Africa he had seen it all, but I was still imagining giant aliens, 'Given how you are travelling, you might want to de-worm yourself every two or three months.' Ugh.

I bought the pills and took them before cycling out of Ouga the next morning. They brought little comfort. As I squatted behind bushes, I wondered whether I would pass these creatures. What a terrifying thought!

'Hallo, Whiteman,' called the small children.

'I'm not a white man!' I called back cheerily. I was happy to be in a new country, speaking English. 'I'm a white woman!' The children looked puzzled.

It had only taken two days to cycle the 172 kilometres south out of Ougadougou to the border with Ghana. I entered Ghana at the small town of Navrongo and continued another 30 kilometres to the bustling town of Bolgatanga, the largest regional centre in northern Ghana. The heat was merciless with temperatures well above 40 degrees Celsius. It was mid March. I was desperate to travel southwards, like an arrow, straight for the coast where there would be cooler temperatures and swimming. Even directly, travelling on the main road through Tamale and Kumasi, it was nearly 700 kilometres away. But I had a detour to make.

Bawku was a town in the north-east of Ghana, about 80 kilometres east of Bolgatanga. WOMANKIND funded the activities of the Bawku East Women's Development Association (BEWDA) and I had an invitation to visit. The destination had been fixed in London and, as the journey progressed, it had become a stopover to look forward to. Finally, here would be a chance to see WOMANKIND's activities first hand. This was an invitation I could not miss. Could I? Sigh. Thoughts of a coconut palm and fresh sea breeze were tempting. A swim would be sooo good.

In Bolgatanga, I had stayed with a whiteman, well, actually an English woman. Jane, a brusque young woman who rode a motorbike, was in charge of the local operations of TRAX, an NGO that helped villagers in the surrounding districts with water management. It was a charity that William was involved with, and he had suggested I visit. Arriving in Bolgatanga, I had tracked down their office. 'I think there is one main thing to be aware of with women's projects,' Jane had said. 'Often, we are adding to women's work, rather than alleviating it. As well as getting the water, fetching the firewood, feeding the family ... now they are expected to do literacy training, business training and income-generating activities. They have to work more land and find time to market the produce. The women's days are long enough. They are enthusiastic for new opportunities to improve the lives of themselves and their children, but I sometimes wonder, are we making their lives easier or tougher?'

It was a good, provocative question. The fifties revolution for housewives was about labour-saving appliances, not more work (that came in the eighties). I kept the question in mind as I cycled toward Bawku.

Bawku was a sprawling and ramshackle town, smaller than Bolgatanga, with only a few badly maintained administrative buildings that seemed to date from British colonial times. Gone were the tree-lined boulevards of the former French colonies; in fact, Bawku had few big trees at all. The brick shops that lined the streets were covered by badly stained stucco and had rusty, corrugated-iron roofs. There was electricity (so there were street lamps, power lines and television aerials emerging from the jumble of houses that littered the side alleys) but the power often failed, possibly due to the collapse of the heavily angled poles and their loosely strung load. Of course, signs were in English, a kind of English. Instead of 'Chemist' there was 'Chemical Store'. Instead of breakfast sellers offering coffee and baguettes, here there was rice water and fried egg sandwiches made with a sweet, soft white bread – on tasting it, I decided it must be one of the worst legacies of English colonialism! Instead of the colourful outfits of the women of Mali and Burkina Faso, the look was spartan, practical and poor. But the smiles, fun-loving natures and informality of the people were very welcoming. My trader friend Gaby, I realised, had been an example of a typical Ghanaian!

'At last!' cried Laurencia Azure, the director of BEWDA, when I arrived at the simple mud-brick and tin-roofed office. Bawku was so small that it was easy for her to already know I was in town. A short, stocky woman, with smooth and very dark skin, who looked to be in her late thirties, she wore her hair short and natural; no frivolous tresses for her. Mma Salamatu Sheriff (pronounced Ooma), her deputy, was round and grandmotherly and her eyes sparkled with energy and friendship. She often broke into a broad smile, showing off her lovely white teeth. She had small horizontal scars on each cheek. 'They were done when I was very young,' she told me.

That first day, Laurencia and Mma gave me an overview of the BEWDA credit fund. The fund provided small loans to groups of women in the Bawku district.

'We have made loans to ten different groups. Four are groups of women here in Bawku, the others are groups in villages in the surrounding area,' said Laurencia. 'On Sunday, you will visit the women of Zongo who produce groundnut oil.'

'I will also take you to visit the women in Akara and Lalsa,' said Mma. 'They are villages some distance away where they grow rice and groundnuts and soya beans during the wet season, but now, with the dry season, they have loans to buy seed for growing onions and vegetables.'

Kate Young, the director of WOMANKIND, had asked me to write a report on BEWDA's activities, so I found myself torn between wanting to empathetically understand more about the lives of women in the villages and needing to make assessments. I could feel my consultant's analytical mindset come on.

'How are you organised?' I asked, in consultant mode. 'How are the loans managed?' 'Which groups are in arrears? Why?' 'How do you ensure the viability of the women's loan-funded activities?' Suddenly, I even found myself volunteering to do some financial analyses of the loan book, the women's businesses and the budget. Idiot! I thought inwardly. I did not want to do this. 'African cyclist does financial analyses in remote town.' Ludicrous.

On the other hand, I was unlikely to ever come back as an aid worker, and this analysis might help the credit fund work better for the local women. It was a way I could repay BEWDA's hospitality.

My planned one-week stay turned into two, and I put my dreams of the ocean on hold.

The Sunday morning after my arrival, I went to visit the group of twenty-five Hausa women who lived in the Zongo quarter of Bawku. They cooperated together to get loans for groundnut oil extraction, but were in default on last year's loan repayments. Mma explained that when the groups had problems, she spent time with them to understand the source of their difficulties and to explore possible solutions. 'Is it that there are no sales?'

'Are the sales on credit?' 'Can you sell your product elsewhere?'

We approached a rather weather-worn and discoloured mud-brick house. Two young girls were sitting in the entry room, patiently rolling balls of paste from a huge batch in a wooden bowl. Other women, who had been sitting talking, got to their feet.

'*Lafobay.*' This was the Hausa greeting.

Leaye Tanko, the deputy leader of the group, led us into the courtyard, eager to show us their work.

The courtyard certainly looked like a workshop. A lot of the walls were fire blackened, as was the ground. A cauldron was bubbling to one side, and oil was being heated in a large, blackened pan over another fire nearby. Over yet another fire, a young girl was frying nuts in their brown skins, swiftly turning them all the time. She looked very hot.

We sat down briefly before Mariama Sumani, the group leader, arrived. She was a middle-aged woman with a tired, mature face, quite different from Leaye, who seemed far more energetic and keen to have us there. All the women were short – my size! Soon, we left to see the grinding.

There were actually two stages of grinding. The first stage, where unshelled groundnuts are crushed, shell and all, then shaken to separate the husk, was done in a grinder at the mill. After frying, the nuts were shaken again to remove their skins, then put in a basin, and carried on the heads of the women to the mill for the second grinding – where we were headed now.

'Do the women work collectively?' I asked Mma.

'No, they take the loan collectively and give an equal portion to each woman. The 10,000 cedis each allows them to buy a sack of unshelled nuts.' Then, US$1 was worth 600 cedis, so each woman had borrowed about US$17.

We arrived at the mill, another run-down building, with several women waiting in a queue for their grinding to be completed. There were several machines lying around, but apparently only one was working – the loud engine chugged and paste oozed from the spout of the ancient machine.

'But how do you separate the oil?' I asked Mma.

'We go there now.'

Some young girls walked purposefully with loads of water, paste and merchandise on their heads, passing a group of boys playing football in the street. A group of older men sat quietly chatting in a shady spot. One man held a radio he was trying to tune in.

'Let me introduce you to the landlord,' said Mma

Landlord? I thought. Why do I want to meet the landlord? I shook hands with the man with the radio, an elderly, distinguished man in a handsome *boubou,* and I smiled. We chatted about my journey, then as we walked away I asked, 'Is he the landlord of the house they use for processing?'

'Yes, it is Leaye's husband's house.'

'Why do you call Leaye's husband the landlord?' I asked, puzzled.

'When you marry, you move into your husband's house. It is his property. He is your landlord,' said Mma straightfowardly.

We walked to the end of another street and found women gathered around a large wooden pestle and mortar made of neem tree trunk. They were both black from oil.

'How old are they?' I asked.

'More than twenty years.' Evidently it was a valuable possession – just one was shared by the entire group.

Paste was already in the mortar, and they had been waiting for me to come before starting the oil extraction. Hot water containing a little salt was added to the paste, and then mixing commenced. The pestle was moved around the edges of the bowl – first in one direction and then the other. More water was added, and the colour and consistency of the paste started to change. After about five minutes, another woman took over the pestle.

'Can I have a go?' I asked Mma.

There were giggles as I moved forward and imitated their grip on the pestle. Then I started pushing it. The women had made it look rhythmic, easy. I made half a circuit of the mortar and had to pause. I thought my arms were strong. Huh! I quickly relinquished the work. More giggles and chatter, then Mma translated: 'They say they have done this from the time they were little girls. Their mothers and grandmothers made groundnut oil, too. Like that they are used to the work.'

The stirring continued, then magically, the oil started to separate from the paste. Apparently, the bag of groundnuts that had made this paste could produce 20 litres of oil. I'd never eat a juicy nut again without imagining all that oil concealed within! The women bottled the oil and used the remaining paste to form balls that are fried and sold in small bags as a dry ingredient for vegetable soup. So much work for such a miniscule reward.

We returned to Leaye's house again to sit and talk about their business. Although the subject matter was dry, it was a buzz to have a chance to hear what poor women had to say, even if it was through a translator.

Why had they defaulted? They seemed competent and energetic women, and their explanation reinforced this impression. Apparently, the groundnut crop failed the previous year and they travelled to the coast to buy cheaper, shelled groundnuts. Of course, this both increased costs and the time between sales. Keeping cashflow going with some production and sales helped buy food, but it had made it difficult to repay the loan. They were, however, planning to repay it soon with their new profits.

What changes would they like to the help given them by BEWDA? Again, their enterprising natures came to the fore. Leaye responded through Mma.

'She says they would like a larger loan,' said Mma, 'so they can buy more nuts and be processing one bag, while selling the other.'

As she spoke, I remembered the words of Mme Diallo, the director of
FAARF (*Fonds d'Appui Aux Activités Rémunératrices des Femmes* – Funds
Supporting Women's Income Earning Activities), whom I had met in Ouga.
'Over time,' Mme Diallo had said to me, 'we have found it is better to lend
small sums and only increase slowly. It builds confidence in the women with
credit and gives them more experience at managing the repayments.' I
thought this was probably a good lesson for these women of Zongo – they had
to prove themselves and gain experience by repaying the initial loan first.
However, they knew their production costs and were now making a profit, so
their idea seemed sound.

Another woman added that they would eventually like to have a loan to buy
drums. 'Then they could take their oil to Kumasi and sell it for higher prices,'
translated Mma. 'It is not worth it with only 200 litres.' Very business-wise
and enterprising for illiterate women, I thought.

I asked about their husbands' work. Mme Diallo had said: 'Men have assets
– their land – but they have grandiose plans. They want to borrow large sums
for opening a bar, or buying a plough or a grinder. The risks are high even if
the money does go into the business. And of course, often the money goes on
a television, a motorbike, a second wife or something.' Would these men be
any different?

Mma insisted each woman must talk. 'Otherwise, when I come again, they
will tell me I didn't let them speak to the white woman.' So I listened to
Mma's translation of each woman's response.

Mariama said her husband had been working for a transport company, but
had been sacked, and had used a little money to buy a grinding machine. 'But
most of the time, it is broken and he just uses money he makes when it works
for spare parts.'

Lahdi's husband transported sacks on his back from trucks arriving in
Bawku and so made a small living.

Fati said her husband was not well and did not work, although she looked
old and unwell herself.

Leaye's husband used to have drums – he bought Leaye's oil, and then
went to Kumasi to sell it. However, during the last coup d'état (in 1979), the
government forced them to sell at low prices and the drums had been confis-
cated. As he and Leaye were from the Hausa tribe, originally from Nigeria,
they could not get land to farm, and now, he did nothing.

Maimuna's husband had died and left her with seven children. 'She had
eleven deliveries,' said Mma.

And finally, Habiba. Her husband had deserted her several years ago and
she had never heard from him again. She was left with eight children to raise.

The next day, Mma arrived late. I was waiting for her outside the BEWDA
office – we were going to visit a group of fifty-six women in Lalsa who had

taken a loan for dry-season onion farming. Our plan had been to leave early before it got too hot. Mma had arranged to ride pillion on a motorbike, I was going to cycle.

In the end, we left at 11.30 a.m. – the hottest part of the day. The road ran near to the Burkina Faso border and I caught up with Mma at a customs checkpoint.

'Phew, it's hot!' I exclaimed. 'Let's buy some mangoes.' I had spotted some women selling them in the shade of a tree. It was early in the season for mangoes, and not having pigged out yet, I was keen.

'And break my fast?' asked Mma.

Shit. Here I was worrying about the heat and Mma was fasting – no food or drink, not even water, between dawn and dusk. Mma, uncommonly for these parts, was a Moslem, and it was Ramadan. As I cycled, I thought of my Tuareg friend, fragile Fatimata, who would be observing the fast in the desert outside Timbuktu. How would she be coping?

Lalsa was reached down a track over a yellow, dusty plain. The brown mud earth was cracked, trees were sparse and a heat haze rose in the distance.

'Not far,' said Mma as I arrived at a shady tree where she and her driver were waiting.

A few more kilometres and, again, I saw Mma and her driver waiting under the shade of another tree. There were two huts nearby, one ruined, and the land looked especially parched. It took me a moment to realise *this* was Lalsa.

Women started arriving and settling on the ground under the shade. Mma and I sat on a bench – I felt uncomfortable at the distinction, but I was not in charge of this situation.

'*Kenken*,' said each woman as she arrived, then grasped my extended arm with two hands and made a small curtsey.

'*Naa*,' I said, meaning thank you, wishing they would not curtsey.

It took a while for the meeting to gather. 'When you come to a village, you cannot be in a hurry. I know when I come that everything at home must lay,' said Mma in her original, highly expressive English. I had come to be very fond of Mma. Her motherliness and her common sense were enchanting.

While waiting, Mma told me that the BEWDA loans for the onion seed, both capital plus interest, was repayable in bowls of seed, harvested from the subsequent season and stored in a house nearby. Each woman was repaying a loan of 3000 cedis, plus 20 per cent interest – 3600 cedis. So each woman had borrowed about US$5. Could this really make a difference to their lives?

As if reading my mind, Mma said, 'Such loans help the woman to feed and clothe her children. And she can send them to school and buy them medicines.'

'Her children?' I queried. 'What about her husband? What does he pay for?' Polygamy was common in traditional households, so if a man could support several wives and owned all the land, I thought he'd have enough to support his own children.

'For the husband, they are her children – until they are earning,' said Mma, smiling mischievously, then continued, '"After all," he will say, "I have three wives and fifteen children. How can I support so many?"'

Eventually, the meeting got started.

Lydia Atiiga, the group leader, was quite beautiful: in her early twenties, her skin still firm with only the faintest of worry lines across her forehead. Lydia's right cheek was carved with four vertical scars quite close together, the first near her nose, the last down her cheekbone, each about 2 centimetres long. On her silken skin, the sharp knife cuts had bulged, stretching wide in the middle as happens when you cut a piece of steak, and they had healed hollow with that distinctive bowed shape.

Lydia was wearing a light-blue, western-style cotton shift that fell sideways across one shoulder. She wore a patterned scarf tied tightly around her head. Her skin was dark and polished, her arms were carved like a Michelangelo sculpture of a malnourished *David*. She had thin, straight legs, no shapely curves, and she wore no shoes. Her feet were large and broad; practical feet. She looked more like a determined factory worker, probably a union organ-iser, than a poor village woman.

I was looking forward to hearing her story, but after greetings, Lydia invited me to come to see their onion fields. Immediately, the assembled women, Mma and I all set off across the parched flat country. Did I really care about seeing an onion field?

It was the end of harvest time, and most plants had been pulled from the ground, their yellow, straw-like foliage hanging limply over their lifeless, brown bulbs. Lydia steered me toward some gullies, or were they holes?, surrounded untidily by piled dirt, dried mud. I was puzzled. It looked like workmen had been digging up a road. I climbed to the top of a mound and looked down into a steep-sided gully with muddy water at the bottom, while Lydia climbed down stairs carved into the dried clay sides.

'Each dry season, the women must dig down into the river bed to get water,' explained Mma for Lydia. 'They have a lot of water now it is harvest time, and they are not using so much.' The mud-thick water barely covered Lydia's ankles. 'She says that when they are watering the onions, the holes are dry and they must dig down further each day.'

Lydia had two large, hourglass-shaped gourds in each hand; a hole had been carved at the waist to allow water to enter into the lower bulge – inge-nious watering cans. Lydia submerged the gourds to fill them, climbed back up the stairs and signalled for me to follow her to show me how they watered their crops. She stood in the barren, gasping fields, grasping each gourd through its hole, and tipped. Small, round holes had been gouged into the top bulge, so that the water sprayed out evenly over the now non-existent crops to be evaporated by the harsh sun.

After a passionate interchange between herself and Lydia, Mma explained,

'She says that what the women and the village really needs is a dam. With a dam, they would have better crops from the dry-season garden and more security for their wet-season crops in case the rains fail.' Mma added that she had approached the government about getting a dam built, but there was a huge backlog.

Mma's translations were opening a whole new world to me, but – never satisfied – now I wished I could understand Lydia's words directly. Through an interpreter, I felt detached from Lydia: hearing her issues, but not really building a relationship. But maybe that said more about me.

Mma told me that this group of women had asked to be helped with literacy classes, so I asked how it helped them. One woman, the best student, spoke, then Mma translated.

'She says that when she goes to the hospital with her children, they can mix up a child's card, but now she can read his name, she will know if there is a mix up. Also, when she is giving medicine to the child, she can count the number of times she gives it. In the market, they cannot cheat her because she can count.' The woman remained very serious throughout the translation.

'When they are working,' said Mma in translation after Lydia had spoken, 'they just think, will this thing be surviving my children, or what, so they be working hard.'

I produced the kola nuts that Mma suggested I bring as a present. They were a common delicacy that left gums red and gave a quiet buzz through the body. Everybody – except Mma, of course – eagerly accepted one.

'How much do you eat?' I enquired, uncomfortably aware of how lean these women were. I knew from Mma that the 'hunger season' in this part of northern Ghana, on the edge of the Sahel, lasted from March to July, and then there was a second hunger time in September and October – so half the year was hunger season.

'If they eat three times a day, it will not work,' said Mma, translating Lydia's proud reply. 'The children eat three times a day because they do not know there is hunger. They will cry, cry, cry. The women only eat one meal a day, but they do not feel it.' I chewed on a kola nut too – but some water would have gone down well. I was feeling it.

We got up and walked into the field again and I asked about the onions and their loans. Would they make much money?

'She says they make more money from the loans for wet-season farming,' said Mma, translating Lydia's comments. 'From the onions, they do not know if they will make a profit.' Lydia bent over and used a short digging stick with a pointed end to harvest one of the few remaining scrawny plants. As she then showed me the plant's mouldy surface, Mma continued. 'She says these plants are bent – it means their harvest will not be strong.' Apparently, the plants had been attacked by a disease due to lack of water. 'The problem is that there are too many onions,' continued Mma. 'Prices are too low, and not too many trucks are coming from Accra and Kumasi to buy the onions.'

Finding markets was always a problem for village women. It was often not worth their while to pay for travel, and so buyers from the cities could buy at low, exploitative prices.

I worried the loans might be impoverishing these women, rather than enriching them.

'She says if you are owing somebody and you want more assistance tomorrow, you must pay.' There was a pause, Lydia spoke, Mma translated. 'This year what will be left will be too small to pay for their children's medicine and clothes.' I learnt that on the wet-season loan, Lydia and her group had each made a profit of 8000 cedis, about US$13, just enough to pay their children's school fees and to buy some condiments like salt, pepper and baobab leaves.

Lydia was like many of the women I met during my two weeks around Bawku: they were stoic in the face of misfortune, enterprising and hard-working, limited only by their opportunities. Access to capital, land and education, particularly literacy, was so important to them.

Regional donor-supported credit funds, like BEWDA, were springing up around Africa to provide people with loans for micro-enterprise. When established, they proved incredibly successful for women – men, with their grandiose plans, were generally not interested in micro-enterprise – but, as I later heard, many schemes did not go beyond the prototype stage. An American credit fund manager in Accra told me, 'The governments do not wish to issue licences for more funds, because they fear the women will get too much power.' More men who couldn't handle independent women.

Finally, I asked if Lydia would take another dry-season loan next year, and grow onions again, after this barely profitable enterprise.

'She says, if you are after something, you must grab it,' Mma translated. Lydia was watching with a proud glare. 'Otherwise, she says, you cannot say you are too tired.'

I thought they were wise words, applicable to so much in life – certainly, applicable to my journey.

Before we left Lydia and the other women of Lalsa, they insisted on giving me a present – the digging stick Lydia had used to harvest the onion plants. I was proud to accept and kept it strapped to my rear sack for the rest of the journey, its weight a small price for a constant reminder of their efforts.

As I cycled back toward Bawku in the stifling afternoon heat, I reflected on the grit and responsibility of all these women I had met. It was a relief to finally get to know real people – not just posters and literature – though I still found it hard to relate to their difficult lives. The only personal point of reference I could find was in my grandmother's life – a woman who had migrated to outback Australia after World War I and had to then bring up three daughters, through the depression, alone. I had always felt angry and disturbed by my grandmother's story. Now, I felt the same for what I saw as injustice for these women.

Were these feelings legitimate? Should I judge other people's lives by my western, undoubtedly feminist values?

Aye!

Why did I have to analyse my every bloody feeling?!

A cranky old Brit in a pick-up offered me and my bicycle a ride a few kilometres from Bawku. I accepted, rationalising that these excursions were not part of the bike ride. The Brit had leathery skin, a long, shaggy, white beard and was one of the 'been forty years in Africa' breed of aid worker. He had worked all over the continent, even before the independence of many countries.

'Going to Tanzania? Ain't worth it, dear. Not since '61.' He was referring to the year the mainland colony of Tanganyika achieved its independence from Britain. He was no less outspoken about the plight of women, nor was he hesitant to make value judgements.

'Never give a ride to men, the lazy bastards,' he said. 'Don't do a whiff of work.'

I let the talk wash over me and started thinking about a shower and a cold beer.

'Saw a woman walking along the road earlier,' he continued. 'Load o' wood on her 'ead she 'ad, and a baby on 'er back. Even an 'eavy sack in her arms. And who's walkin' along like King Muck hisself in front of her?' he asked rhetorically. ''Er husband. Got a rich, white *boubou* on, 'e 'as, and an umbrella in his 'and. But 'as he got it over 'er 'ead? No, shadin' his bleedin' 'ead, he was, the ol' bastard.'

Eight

A White Man in a Land Rover

Bawku, Ghana – Elmina, Ghana

As I cycled southwards from Bawku, I entered a world of green vegetation and red clay soils. Not a tame world of clipped grass, a fecund world of fresh, emerald-green undergrowth and towering trees. The blue skies and sun disappeared beneath layered grey cloud; it was slightly cooler but with increased humidity. On the road were muddy patches and small streams ran through the gullies – evidence of rain. That was something I looked forward to – I hadn't seen rain since that dreadful day and night climbing into the Fouta Djalon, in Guinea. (On second thoughts, perhaps I wasn't so keen to see it again.)

With the increasing fecundity of the land came an increasing human population. Gone was the solitude of the Sahelian roads. Calls of 'Hallo, whiteman,' 'Sister, where you go?' and 'You are trying,' rose in a geometric progression to the kilometres travelled southwards.

I had decided not to cycle back to Bolgatanga and down the main road to Kumasi – reputed to be very busy and badly corrugated; rather, I was coming down a smaller, eastern road. It was remote, place names turning out to be small communities with a few shops, a market and simple government rest houses for accommodating stray bicycle travellers.

Having already passed through Nakpanduri and Gushiegu, today I was headed from Yendi to Bimbilla; then, I planned to cycle on to Salaga, cross Lake Volta to Yeji, and go on to Atebubu, Ejura, Mampong and Kumasi. Kumasi was Ghana's second biggest city; I would make a short stop there – perhaps try and find Gaby, who had given me his address – before covering another 300 kilometres on the road to Cape Coast and Elmina on the Atlantic. That made nearly 1000 kilometres of travel between Bawku and my next big destination – the ocean! God, I was looking forward to a swim, and being clean! I sweated profusely in the humidity. My damp hair clung to my forehead, my shorts stuck to my thighs, my palms and clothes were red from dust, my fingernails black from grease, and rivulets of sweat rolled through the accumulated dust on my legs.

Nonetheless, cycling had been terrific this morning. I had been up, fresh, at the crack of dawn and on the road by 6.30 a.m. Before leaving Yendi, I had loaded up with carbohydrates – fried dough balls – and was cycling on a much lighter bicycle.

My moods might be volatile (still an essential part of the African experience!), but it seemed the load I carried oscillated almost as much. I gave away T-shirts, then got more in the cities, ate some food, then bought more, tore up my guidebook, carrying only the relevant pages, then was given novels. But when I had first passed through Bolgatanga and stayed with the TRAX folk, I had made, and implemented, an important decision: I had decided to cut my load in half.

DHL, one of my sponsors, had an office in Bolgatanga, so I had sent the more valuable items home rather than just giving them away. I spent a morning going through each pannier deciding what would be sacrificed.

Out went bulky food bag. Not essential. Out went the stove. Its fuel nozzle had infuriatingly blocked for the last time! Surely I could use my hosts' stoves. Goodbye jumper. When would I need you again? Goodbye Africa outfit made in Mali. Only the new one from Ouga could stay. Goodbye sleeping bag. Inadequate use – the silk sleeping sheet was enough. No more facial creams. Well, except sunscreen factor 15, new from Ouga – my cracked bottom lip was still raw. Keep soap, shampoo, plastic washing cup, body moisturiser, razor, deodorant, toothbrush and paste and Tampax – for a slim toiletries bag. Hooray!

And good riddance, Ouga souvenirs. Still shopping too much. I always forgot about weight once I stopped anywhere. Often, having bought a thing in the city, I would give it away within two or three nights of being back on the road.

With all this gone, I could move my spares and health kit from the front panniers to the space liberated at the rear. *Voilà*! No more front panniers – a mega weight saving!

With this new streamlined form, I had thought, cycling will be a breeze!

Now, three weeks later on the afternoon road to Bimbilla, my morning freshness was already wearing off and the back-heavy loading was making handling difficult. The lighter arrangement was less like pushing a tank, more like handling a heavily filled shopping trolley with a dodgy wheel.

Of course, part of my tiredness was probably due to my fitness – or lack of it. Before leaving Bawku, I had looked back over my daily cycling records, and been alarmed to calculate that in the previous twelve weeks since arriving in Sevaré in Mali, I had only cycled for three weeks! Too many stops. This trek to the ocean was what I needed, both to build muscle strength again and to generate a sense of progress. At my current rate, I'd be on African roads for years!

The road went straight down the slope for 2 kilometres, then straight up the slope 2 kilometres. Of course, without contours, the road had become the shortest route for water to run off and was badly rutted and muddy. Nevertheless, the regular, predictable pattern had become quite soothing – I knew it took twenty minutes per cycle: five minutes to negotiate the ruts down the hill, fifteen minutes to wobble between them up the other side. Twelve kilometres per hour – I had only one and a half more cycles to complete.

Calculating all this had passed some time.

'Hallo, whiteman!' called a man – yes, a man! – working in his yam fields. What a rarity! I should have stopped in honour of this occasion, but I didn't. 'Where you go?' he called aggressively.

The track only had one destination – where did he think I was going? Gritting my teeth, I smiled sweetly and said, yet again, 'Hallo, I go to Bimbilla.' He gave me a broad grin and I felt guilty for my irritation and suspicion.

I negotiated another downward slope, by far the easiest part of the cycle and more conducive to reflection, and thought of Mindy, an American woman I had met on the return from my side trip to Bobo-Dioulasso.

Mindy was an interesting, well, stunning creature, a slim blonde, a couple of years older than me, from Minneapolis whose travel outfit consisted of black leggings, slinky, low-necked dress with black exercise bra visible underneath, and lots of beads and bells tinkling about her person. We met because we were at the same cheap hotel in Bobo. Her balcony was next to mine and one afternoon we exchanged potted histories. I learnt that she was travelling the world over two years – flying between continents.

'I have the Air Miles,' she said rather enigmatically when I asked her how she was affording so much flying, but initially she had been evasive about telling me more of her background. Only after a couple of days did Mindy start telling me more about herself. She told me that she had been a vice-president for sales for a pension investment firm. I was surprised, then she went on to say how she had felt her creativity was being sucked dry in the desiccated, structured and conservative world of actuaries and brokers, and had decided to leave. I was starting to get intrigued. 'I had two worlds,' she said. 'I socialised some with the people at work, but my real friends were Rastas with dreadlocks, creative people, and my passion was travelling, not business. My best friend, Moonstar, would ring me at work, and leave messages like: 'Tell Mindy I love her.' Of course, people at work wondered if I was gay, radical, but I started wondering, who the hell is Mindy Paul?' She spoke of the increasing stress of having a façade – of having to 'put on' her business self, when her soul wanted to be free.

I was excited. It was like meeting a twin! I recalled how my work colleagues had been clearly surprised, even uncomfortable, at coming to my London flat, sitting on the floor, its multi-coloured textures and patterns and ethnic, minimalist furnishings, seemingly not conforming to their expectations of an upwardly mobile young professional's tastes. I remembered my traveller friend, Bronwyn, who had come to a work party and impetuously, passionately kissed one of my blue-pinstripe-suited colleagues on the lips. 'That shocked him, eh?' she had laughed wickedly, clearly pleased with the effect, as we had left. I had loved the pure freedom of it, something done for the heck of it, injected into my generally analytical, controlled world, and it was one of those occasions when I felt I was missing out on something.

Mindy said that the decision to leave just grew on her – the game was done, over, it was time to move on – and she knew the tensions and time demands of work would prevent her from getting in touch with her true self. I knew that feeling too. However, she spoke of how during her first year of travel, the 'transition year' as she called it, she sought a purpose to place on the trip, to justify it in the eyes of others, to justify to herself that she wasn't just a hobo, unemployed.

'People needed a box to put me in, so I said I was in finance, or business,' she said. 'But I went back to Minneapolis after that first year, and I did not fit anymore. The biggest thing was that Moonstar had killed herself!' She laughed but there was considerable pain in her voice. 'She had spent an evening drinking champagne and smoking ganja, then lost control of her BMW on a passing lane, careered into a ditch and went through the windscreen.' Mindy was silent for a while.

'Minneapolis was empty without her,' she eventually continued, 'but also, I got together with my business friends and they talked about deals and new business ventures, and I just wasn't interested.' I wondered if this would happen to me. Could I imagine consulting again? No way. She ferreted in her small, beaded sack, pulled out a business card and handed it to me. 'I guess I'll find out more as I keep travelling – I'm thinking of art classes in Paris or turning professional with my photography – but, for now, that's how I think of myself.'

The card read: Mindy Jean Paul, Explorer.

So. I wasn't the only screwed-up business woman in the world.

As I started the ascent again and the pedalling became harder and the strain on my shoulders and back more pronounced, I thought of how Mindy's transition year related to me. Was I using my involvement with WOMANKIND as a cover, to give the journey a 'worthwhile' purpose?

Probably. Hmm. Mulling on that passed some more time.

And what about the interviews with city women in Ouga? Not the stuff of an Adventurer, I'd worried back there, but I'd enjoyed them, found them stimulating. Was that because I could still hide behind a familiar façade – my business self?

I had wanted to be an explorer – *Esprit de Battuta*, and all that. In my gut, I knew that I truly wanted to free myself, to get rid of all the façades, but to do what, to be what?

I was still trying to control life. Why couldn't I let go?

Maybe I was in transition; maybe it was a matter of time.

I started humming to myself. What was that song?

'Girls just want to have fun …'

I was at the summit – that little trip down memory lane into self-doubt had taken twenty minutes.

Stopping on the crest, I reached for my water bottle and took a swig of warm water. (My refrigeration system didn't work in this humidity – no evaporation.) Another cycle of down and up appeared before me. No sign of Bimbilla. Shit.

I watched a middle-aged man cycle up the slope I would soon descend. As he got near the summit, he stopped.

'Where you go, whiteman?'

Grrr. Is that why I'm here, to answer inane questions, and have my sex misinterpreted?

'Bimbilla.'

A mob of twenty or so children rushed from my left. 'Whiteman!' 'Hallo, sister!' 'Where you go?' 'Whiteman!' And stares. Oh, hell. A mud-brick and tin roofed hut nestled amongst the vegetation. Evidently, it was a school. I was closer to Bimbilla than I had thought.

'I hate kids,' I said bluntly to the man. Crabby. Crabby.

'Oh white lady! Ho ho!'

He burst into laughter, not taking offence, perhaps not appreciating that I was half (er, fully) serious. A smile burst through my petulant lips, and then I laughed with him.

Help and time for strangers was available in vast, free quantities everywhere in Africa, and I was indeed grateful for it, even if sometimes the gratitude didn't show. In Bimbilla, I merely stopped near the small market crossroads and was surrounded by young men, one of whom showed me the way to the government rest house.

After a bucket shower and a change of clothes, I set out on my food hunt. A black, all-enveloping cloud swept overhead and a deep gusting wind blew up. Market women scattered for cover, certain that a storm was due. I would have fled too, but I knew this was the end of daylight and I had better get some food fast.

I was on the look out for fires. I wanted yam chips – a staple of Ghana I had discovered south of Bawku. I loved them. Top carbohydrates with hot chilli. Ooh. What does this woman have? I wondered as I pulled to a halt. Rice and beans. Hmm. Ah, here's another fire at the edge of the market.

'Good evening.'

'Good evening.'

I pointed at her sizzling pan and she lifted the lid to reveal frying dough balls. Ooh. That would do for a snack. I bought two for ten cedis (about 2 US cents), then, gobbling them on the spot and finding them delicious, I bought four more. Mangoes at the next stop – they were common now – and tomatoes from a girl who was packing up in the fierce wind. I didn't really want them, but in case I found nothing else, I could have some tomatoes with some stale bread I carried, and fruit.

I cycled on to another fire. What was there? It was dark now, so I shone my torch to see the interior of the woman's pot. Boiled yams. Yum. But what sauce? Only a meat sauce which I didn't fancy. 'Groundnut sauce?' She pointed to a nearby house. Great. I bought some yams, then cast away for the next stop. The groundnut sauce looked good, so I took a ladle for 50 cedis. There, that's fine. Now a beer. 'Yes, I promise to bring the bottle back in the morning,' I said to the barman, and I was set.

Returning to the rest house, with the first heavy drops pelting from the angry, dark sky, I passed one last kiosk, still open, selling Blue Band margarine sachets. Good idea. Now, I could go home.

I pulled a chair outside onto the verandah, the rain passed as quickly as it came, but the sky was still dark, the musky smell rising from the damp dust was as pleasant as baking bread, and the crickets talked raucously to each other. I set down the kerosene lamp I had been given, opened my beer and settled down to consume my finds.

My beer was a Club; their slogan was: 'It's A Good Life.'

Yes, it was.

But despite that, I was lonely. Although I had met city women in Ouga and village women in Bawku, I had felt more like an investigative journalist, or a consultant doing a gender issues project. Tonight there was no one, not even any forest intellectuals with whom to discuss the woes of the world. The storm had sent people scuttling homewards. My meal over, I pulled out my photos of lost folk, pulled out my notebook and started writing poetry. A kind of poetry, doggerel, I know. But it was from the heart.

An Evening Passes

Clapping
Tin voices, singing, floating on the air
Base insects, burring and clicking
In accompaniment.

Early evening, or
Late evening when you rise
At 5.30 a.m.
A motorbike burbles by.

Looking at photos
Touching photos
Remembering their touch
Wishing them alive.

Visiting memories
In faraway corners
Of the world, or
Of my mind.

I was just a little sozzled.

I thought of William and touched his photo. Jane of TRAX in Bolgatanga had told me she had seen William at a trustee meeting in London in January. She had said he sent his love.

I was suspicious – that did not sound like William.

And that was January – old news, older than the telephone call where he told me he could not cope with an independent women.

Why did we persist in sending each other such mixed signals? I was confused. Was this relationship over, or not? My heart twisted at every piece of news I got from him; yet how could this feeling of pain, and, I conceded, possibly love, last to Dar Es Salaam? Should I fly to London from Accra to see him?

Aye!

It would be so hard then to come back. Something in me felt that if I broke my African life with a European interlude now, I would lose all I was gaining, could gain. I could not pinpoint what was happening to me by being here, but my gut just told me I had to stay.

So, I would not fly home.

I finished my beer. The evening passed and I wrote more poems. I felt a thousand kilometres from the ocean.

*

From Bimbilla, I cycled past giant termite mounds and mango trees to Salaga, where I stayed at another government rest house, and two whites unexpectedly turned up. They were English, new to Africa, a little naïve. They had missed their bus northwards and, being stranded the night, had walked the couple of kilometres to the rest house, without having bought food in the market. What were they expecting to find out here? A 7-Eleven? Remembering all the nights of hospitality I had received in the villages, I fed them.

'Do you stay in these kinds of places often?' the guy asked.

'Sure,' I said, thinking how great Ghana was for easy-to-find, comfortable, *private* accommodation. Of course, there was no electricity, no running water and no toilet – we went round the back in the bush – but that was a small price to pay. It was only in the morning that I remembered the incredulity in his voice. Had I ever been so naïve? Maybe I was becoming more at home in Africa than I thought.

I left Salaga, cycled to Lake Volta and crossed on a ferry to Yeji. Lake Volta was created in the early sixties when the Akosombo Dam was built across the Volta River. It was an impressive project, providing hydro-electricity for Ghana (principally for an aluminium smelter in the port of Téma – not that an aluminium smelter was Ghana's first need) and for its neighbours. However, it had flooded vast areas of Ghana's most fertile lands, and in the more conservation-minded nineties, it might never have been built.

It was the brainchild of Kwame Nkrumah, Ghana's first president. Ghana was the first African nation to receive its independence, in 1957. Nkrumah was another idealistic African leader, very keen on Pan-Africanism, and on investing to create Ghana's economic independence from its colonial masters. His fiery nationalism infected other African nations' struggles for independence, and he invested in a valuable infrastructure of universities and hospitals. However, he repressed opposition groups, built up a personality cult and invested beyond Ghana's means in a lot of prestigious, but ultimately non-viable assets like the Volta Dam, or non-income-generating assets like the State House and big monuments. The disastrous economic impact of his extravagance – and lack of investment in agriculture – was accentuated when the price of cocoa, Ghana's main export other than gold, fell and fell again in the mid sixties. High foreign debt, high inflation and high unemployment led not only to his overthrow in a coup d'état in 1966, but also to fifteen years of military rule, brief attempts at democracy and more military rule. Dreadful, impoverishing corruption and repression was the hallmark of each new regime. In 1979, Flight Lieutenant Jerry Rawlings, the current president, took power in a coup d'état and led the country through years of socialism, anti-corruption campaigns and one-party rule. Economically, not a success. In 1991, under external pressure, he reinstated a multi-party constitution and in late 1992 went to the polls. Despite claims of fraud, he won rather convincingly.

Ghana was now a model country for the World Bank. The government had floated (read: devalued) the cedi – hence, things were cheap for me – and was busy trying to privatise its previously nationalised industries. Not a bad thing. But Ghana was still a country whose exports were limited to minerals and commodities – items where prices fluctuate wildly according to world demand and supply. An economic formula which works for a manufacturing-based economy does not necessarily work for a commodity-based one. Ghana just earned less for doing the same thing. People in the villagers felt no bene-fits, only the pain of unaffordable imports.

Oh well, same old story.

The next day saw me mainly on tarmac: potholed, with some stretches missing, but blissful tarmac! I arrived in Ejura two days later, on Easter Sunday. The main street was filled with men in dark trousers and white shirts, little boys looking like miniatures of their fathers, little girls in lace dresses and women in bright *pagnes* or western dresses, all walking to or from church.

I cycled through town intending to go on to Mampong (about 40 kilo-metres further), but at the police checkpoint on the far side, I noticed black storm clouds gathering. Deciding retreat from the imminent storm was prudent, I asked a policeman for directions to the rest house.

A young boy showed me my room.

'Mmm. What's that lovely smell?' I asked, as we entered the room. I sniffed the air enthusiastically. 'It smells like fish and chips …'

The boy merely looked embarrassed and said, 'I think it is your bike.'

It was then I realised he was being polite. The lovely salt and vinegar smell was me.

Oops. Why did I bother carrying deodorant?!

The next morning, Easter morning, I was headed out of Ejura after a minor disaster: there had been no coffee available for breakfast, only rice water. No caffeine! Ghanaians, unlike Africans from the ex-French colonies, did not have a coffee habit. Desperately, I had mixed a spoonful of my own Nescafé in cold water. Ugh! But at least it had given me a caffeine fix.

The main street was quiet, and I soon arrived back at the police checkpoint. 'A whiteman in a Land Rover is looking for you.'

Who? What did he look like? The policeman, snappy in a blue uniform, said it so casually, like I should expect a white man to be looking for me. 'He did not say,' he said, and added a shrug that showed all whites looked alike to him.

That was very strange indeed. And a shame; I would have liked some company. Oh well.

Then, a little further down the road:

'There is a whiteman in a Land Rover looking for you …'

Again?

A second policeman, this time in a parked police car on the outskirts of

Ejura, waved me over. This white man had been persistent, I thought. Then, considering the looseness of this expression, I thought, it was probably a white woman.

That morning, the world was beautiful. The road was quiet, with new, smooth, wide asphalt and well-graded curves, a dream to ride. It took me through the remnants of rainforest country – majestic, white-trunked trees reaching high into the clear blue sky.

But I couldn't leave the puzzle of the white man alone.

It'll probably never be solved, I mused as I cycled. Whoever it was will be far away by now. Was it a Shell man? But how would they know where I am? And why would they be looking for me? They've never looked before. Unless something Dreadful has happened at home. My stomach lurched. Stop it!

I knew from my list of contacts that there was a regional office in Kumasi. I would be there tomorrow, Tuesday. The office would be open after the Easter break and I could check then.

By 11 a.m., I reached the turn-off to Mampong, my destination for today. A short day, but tomorrow, I wanted to arrive in Kumasi – a big city – fresh. I saw a sign for a Shell service station, the first I had seen in Ghana. If someone was looking for me, they might have passed there.

I found the station and pulled in, ready to give a long explanation, but before I could say a word, a mechanic named Francis came out from under a vehicle in his garage. Wiping his greasy hands on a cloth, he said, 'There is a whiteman in a Land Rover looking for you.'

And no, he was not a Shell man. This stranger was certainly trying hard to find me.

'It was a white Land Rover with red writing on the side, and a red roof ...'

My heart lurched. That sounded like the TRAX Land Rover – I had seen it at Bolgatanga. Could it be William? Steady on, I said to myself. It's probably just one of the TRAX people. But William had donated the Land Rover, driven it from London to Bolgatanga a few years back; he would be able to retrieve it and drive it. It could be him ...

No. I refused to believe it.

'The man was wearing a white floppy hat. He looked hot ...'

I had seen photos of William in Africa in a floppy white hat – and I knew he hated the heat! (Part of our incompatibility.) I started pulling at the miscellaneous junk that was in my front handlebar bag. Bananas, camera, boiled egg, fruit knife ... Finally, I found the tatty, well-thumbed photo. A slim, serious-looking man, debonair in a grey suit.

Holding my breath, I showed the photo to Francis.

'Yes, that is him ... but he looked hotter,' he said calmly, not realising the cartwheels my heart was going through at this news. I grinned madly.

'That's William! That's my boyfriend!' I told him, and Francis grinned and shook my hand.

'He said he was going to Kumasi,' he added. What? The news exploded through my happy daze. It seemed I had only missed him by an hour.

And so I started cycling for Kumasi. By the time I got back to the main road it was 1 p.m., with 70 kilometres to do in the hottest hours of the day. And what if there was another afternoon storm? Really, there was no choice. What had Lydia said? If you are after something, you must grab it. Otherwise, you cannot say you are too tired. And if someone had come from London to search Africa – all right, Ghana – for me, well, I was not going to say I was too tired!

Easier said than done.

Twenty kilometres from the Mampong turn-off (50 to Kumasi), I reached another checkpoint. The policeman waved me over.

'Hallo, sister. Where are you going?' Did we *have* to go through this? I was anxious for news.

'Your husband was here,' he said eventually.

When? Which way was he going? But we didn't understand each other very well. 'I'm sorry. I don't understand your slang,' he said at one point. This wasn't uncommon in Ghana, where English had evolved rather differently to Australian English. But he produced a torn slip of paper. It had William's name and address in the UK, but no message. I was confused. 'He said he was leaving for London on Wednesday.' Leaving on Wednesday, the day after tomorrow? How long had he been looking for me? I cycled on with new urgency.

Don't go, William! You must wait! Fortunately, the road was still paved, not as new and smooth as the stretch from Ejura to Mampong, but it was flat. If William had to be in Accra for a flight on Wednesday he had probably driven through Kumasi and on to Accra. Certainly, he would drive there tomorrow, so my only chance, if he was still in Kumasi, was to find him tonight. I was close to tears. If only I hadn't taken the eastern road – he had probably been looking for me on the main road. If only I hadn't stopped at Ejura.

I cycled like mad. And then – puncture! Not now, not now … I changed the tube and remounted.

Perversely, the nearer I drew, the deeper my despair became. The knowledge of how unlikely it was that I would find him came welling up inside me, and I started gulping air. I had to stop for a bag of cold water from a roadside stand and try to stop shaking.

On and on to Kumasi. At the outskirts, at my first big roundabout and traffic of any consequence since Ougadougou, I took a risk and entered the maelstrom of vehicles – and was nearly cleaned up by a white Mercedes. There was a Shell station on the roundabout, so I pulled in to stop shaking. Again.

'Calm down, calm down, calm down …' I chanted to myself in a mantra.

The attendants had no message from a white man in a Land Rover, but they gave me directions to the Shell regional office. Perhaps William had left a message there.

Otherwise, I thought as I set off into the traffic again, conscious I was entering a city of nearly a million people, how on earth would I find him?

Arriving at Shell, I was taken to see Mr Nkrumah, the regional manager, at his house inside the compound. Mr Nkrumah looked very surprised to have a distressed female at his doorstep on Easter Monday. He knew nothing about me, and nothing about William, but said he would arrange for me to stay at a hotel. As he drove there, I followed, trying to hold back tears of despair.

'I shall telephone the Accra office in the morning,' he said. 'St John Abbey might know where William is.' But tomorrow might be too late! As soon as he left, almost defeated, I flagged down a taxi and asked to be taken to every hotel in Kumasi. The driver looked astonished, but quickly became committed to my quest. A thunder and lightning storm had arrived, the crashing sheets of rain making visibility almost impossible, and some streets impassable, yet we drove around Kumasi for two hours. We both got out at each dark hotel; both of us were soaked.

'Is there a white man with a Land Rover staying here?'

Always the answer was no, or a sad shaking of the head.

Back at my comfortable room, safe from the storm, I passed a desolate night.

The next morning I awoke with a plan. I would fly to Accra. He was probably on the British Airways flight to London and, at the very least, I could meet him at the departure gate. Having telephoned Mr Nkrumah with my plan, I heard back from him within the hour.

'He is on the passenger list for the flight,' Mr Nkrumah told me. I felt empty. It was confirmed, he had been here and he was leaving. 'One of the managers is driving to Accra, you can leave with him if you wish.'

I did, and I returned to my room to fret, to regret, to wait.

Having Shell people pulling for us now made it much more certain that we would get together, but for how many hours? He had tried so hard – and I had tried so hard. Yet still we hadn't found each other. Was this a sign?

Around noon, there was a call to my room: I had a visitor in reception.

William? No, calm down. It will be the manager to take you to Accra.

Then, in the corridor, I heard his deep voice.

William!! Looking thin, looking hot, looking great. A person in the flesh, not a photograph. He was here – for me.

Of course, it was all rather emotional.

He had been in Ghana for two weeks! He had gone to Bolgatanga, learnt I was in Bawku, but had arrived a couple of days after I had left. In Salaga, where I had met the naïve English couple, he had wasted a Saturday when two policemen had claimed I was still in town. He had been told I had crossed on the Lake Volta ferry at Yeji, and at Ejura, on Sunday, he had been told I had passed the checkpoint. That damned policeman! What was he thinking?! He was the one who directed me to the rest house! At Kumasi, he had stayed at a Presbytarian rest house – the one place my taxi driver had not taken me to.

It was only when he had phoned St John to tell him that he had failed to find me and would be returning to Accra, that he got a message.

'Quick!' said St John. (Of course, I later met him, a most astonishingly, infectiously cheerful man. I wondered if when Shell had agreed to support me, they had ever envisaged the role of bringing lovers together, but St John was delighted by his role in our reunion.) 'Rush to the Shell Office. She is leaving for Accra!'

In my euphoria at seeing him, I told William that it was the most dramatic, romantic, wonderful thing anyone had ever done for me! I meant it. It really was an act of great romance!

William was happy, but more subdued. 'Oh … well … I had to come to Ghana anyway,' he said. 'I needed to come, for TRAX.'

'Huh!' I retorted. I chose not to believe him. 'I think you came to find me!'

William only stayed until Wednesday. I left my bicycle in Kumasi and went to Accra with him – thirty-six hours together – then returned alone. Afterwards, I stayed in Kumasi for five days, shell-shocked – alternately ecstatic and bereft. Our time together had been passionate, but William was still coy about making any commitments to wait for me – and I wasn't going home. Was I? His visit was double-edged: I felt comforted that there was someone out there caring for me, but I also saw more clearly the cost of my strange obsession.

During my recuperation time, I visited Gaby and his family – he was a connection with my Africa life and the visit helped to pull me out of wallowing in thoughts of William. My arrival caused a lot of fuss in his street. Terraced houses, stucco covered, red from accumulated dust, stained and mildewed from years of rain, seemed overflowing with people – men were gathered on the stairs talking, the children played football in the streets, the women hung washing or pounded millet in large mortars on the verandah. Urban living without the conveniences, except for television – aerials poked from every roof. When I showed up on my bicycle, I received a village-style welcome. Someone knew Gaby, and a child was sent running to get him.

I was very pleased to see him. He was real again, another special person in the flesh, not just one of the spirits living in my memory.

'Oh, you try!' he said when I told him my adventures coming south. Then, bashfully, he introduced me to his serious wife, his three mischievous children, his riotous sister-in-law and his curious neighbours. Gaby bashful? Amazing. We shared a meal of *foufou* – boiled yam flour – and meat stew, and he showed me the room where there were piles of children's clothes – he was leaving soon for Mali on another trading trip.

After five days recovering, I knew I should move on and was still keen to get to the ocean. Maybe on the coast I could lift my emotional daze. I tapped the wells of obstinacy that seemed infinitely deep in me and found the determination to keep going.

Cycling to the coast was fun, yes, fun. The road to Cape Coast was newly made and downhill from the highlands of Kumasi to the coastal plain. I could average over 25 kilometres per hour and felt incredibly powerful. A nice change after the emotional storms. When I stopped, I purchased food, consumed it rapidly and left. It was like putting a nozzle down my throat, refuelling and restarting the engine. My leg muscles complained if I stayed too long, so it was easier to keep going.

Finally, after three days, I was at the spot I had been dreaming about. Yes! I had covered the 1000 kilometres! I was in heaven – at a palm-fringed beach with waves crashing in.

Of course, heaven is never quite what we imagine.

My hotel was a collection of brick and thatched-roof bungalows, slightly mildewy, very decrepit, by the Atlantic Ocean near Elmina. The bungalows were in a garden filled with coconut palms, but wild storms of recent days – it was the beginning of the wet season – had brought a lot of the tree litter down. In fact, that morning, I was awoken by a terrific storm, and from my balcony watched the storm abate and the forbidding waves crash in.

Despite the grey scene, I was excited. It was the end of April, and I could celebrate 5000 kilometres and seven months down, pedalled, endured, accomplished, completed! It felt wonderful!

Hmm. Amazing what a good road could do.

I started to make out small fishing craft and the hazy silhouette of Elmina Castle, a legacy of an awful slaving past. Many castles used as European slaving bases dotted the Ghanaian coast, but Elmina, built in 1482, was the first and the biggest. I looked forward to visiting it, but now it was 6.30 in the morning and the rain had stopped. It was time to walk along the beach and, maybe, have a swim.

As I walked, I let the waves come and grab at my legs, to splash up and wet my shorts. The water was warm, but it definitely was not a friendly sea and I could pick out rocks beneath the crashing surf.

I nodded 'Good morning' to a couple of men I passed, hoping my initiative would stop them starting further conversation. This was a special moment for me – my first walk by the ocean I had been heading for for so long. But my mood swiftly shifted – I felt more subdued. On a beach I should be with someone – and I thought, again, about William. The emotional daze – and confusion – continued.

What had it meant? It was romantic of him to come, his visit made me feel so loving and loved, yet he had gone so quickly. Some words replayed in my memory. I had asked him to stay longer, and he had said, 'You have your plans and I have mine.'

Was I being punished?

For my obstinacy? My independence?

I felt I could be giving up something very good, but it seemed there was no choice. I simply could not stop. This *was* my life. I was not going back to Europe until this was over.

Yet I damned well missed him Too much! It hurt.

Relationships were not easy! And how could I cope with ongoing separation now? It was Too bloody hard.

Feeling confused and lonely, I headed for the rocky headland cutting me off from the curve of the next beach. I went to climb on the black basalt outcrop, to survey the scene, when I became aware of a couple more men crouched among the rocks.

Oh, oh, I thought. I've stumbled on the men's bathing area. I was used to these from my days on the banks of the Niger River in Mali. I took another glance. These guys had their pants off.

They were crapping!

Delightful.

I did an about turn – not too quick, I was cool. Now, there were three or four other guys crouched on the sand just at the high-tide point. Why there? Discreet enough near the first vegetation, but sure to be washed out to sea at some point? The man I had nodded to on the way out was crouched down. Was he crapping, too? I stole a quick look, and sure enough, he had his pants off as well.

Perhaps coming to the ocean in Africa was not going to be quite the idyllic experience I had been dreaming of. The wind picked up, I knew it was going to rain and I couldn't face swimming in a grey sea probably filled with shit. I would take a shower instead.

The death of romanticism.

Nine

Programmes and Paradise

Elmina, Ghana – Cotonou, Benin

I was in a kind of paradise. I had just completed forty laps of the nearby swimming pool and it was almost frightening to find how fit and strong I was after completing those 1000 kilometres to the ocean. Now, I was lying on a recliner by the side of the large pool, soaking up sun and enjoying my luscious surroundings. The stunning private garden was filled with yellow and purple bougainvillea, palms of all sizes, rubber trees and fragrant frangipani. A waiter, a smiling young man named Kujo, brought a pot of tea from the massive, two-storey house behind me. He was one of at least six staff at this haven of luxury. I was at the Shell guesthouse in Accra.

Recently, my outlook had grown more rosy. Despite the residual ups and downs about William, his visit, overall, had been an emotional boost. Likewise, the good roads since Ejura had made my life easier. The continuing tarmac, tailwind and cooler conditions on the 175-kilometre run along the coast from Elmina to Accra had consolidated my sense of contentment. Now, in the idyll of the Shell guesthouse, I thought exuberantly that cycling was like a metaphor for life! Daily, I struggled and was exhausted, tempted to sit down and swear, but I kept pedalling. And so each day passed. A little was achieved. Sometimes there were frustrations, like not getting as far as I intended. But daily, there were small rewards: the pleasure of having completed another day's journey, the pleasure of the quiet evenings. And gradually, each day's effort built into a substantial achievement - first, 1000 kilometres; now, over 5000 kilometres. Obstacles had been overcome. I had memories of happy encounters, of emotional highs and lows. This was truly living! I like my life, I like Africa, I like Ghana, I like Ghanaians, I like Accra!

Hmm. Amazing what good roads *and* a dose of luxury could do.

I had easily found Shell's offices, having already been there with William. Leaving my bicycle outside with a security guard, I walked into reception to ask for St John Abbey. He was expecting me and came rushing to greet me.

'Welcome!' he cried, his eyes dancing, his round face dazzling with his broad grin. He gave me a big hug. Then, he took me on a whirlwind tour of the two-storey office, introducing me to astonished staff. He even broke into meetings saying, 'May I introduce this woman – she is cycling across Africa!' His colleagues

looked stunned but all shook my hand. The attention was overwhelming. Soon, I found myself at the office of the *Daily People's Graphic* for an interview and photo session! Finally, we reached the Shell guesthouse.

From Winneba, my last stop, where I'd stayed at a cheap hotel for two days and where each night I had tossed cups of water over myself and paced the floor unable to sleep in the still humidity, I suddenly found myself in this exotic Shangri-La.

It was a shock, but not a hard one to accept.

Not like my guilt-ridden reaction to the Calloways' house in Conakry! I guess after so many hard days and hot nights on the road, I needed some good sleep and pampering – and was happy to treat this luxury as a wonderful, rejuvenating gift.

After a delicious dinner, I spent an indulgent first evening, by myself, in the large lounge, furnished with plush sofas, oak side tables and lamps, watching a video, before retiring to my air-conditioned bedroom with its private flush toilet (bliss), and crisp white sheets (heaven).

My senses drank in this extraordinary change in conditions. I felt very kindly toward Shell.

Eight days later, another action-packed stay in a capital city was drawing to a close. Tomorrow, I would be remounting the bike, probably with a softer set of muscles than those I had arrived with (and a bigger waistline), and heading along the eastern road for the border with Togo, a distance of about 200 kilometres.

I was eating my last dinner (of the condemned woman?) with two Shell managers from London, Ian and Ron, who had joined me as guests in the house. Ian was a finance man who spoke enthusiastically about his plans to look at steam engines in Didcot on his return to the UK. Mad as a hatter, I thought. Ron was here to assess the quality of the local company's lubricants.

Having just cleared away the soup course, Kujo was serving us chicken, mashed potatoes and brussels sprouts – aah! He looked very smart in a white uniform, and the table was beautifully laid with white linen, silver cutlery and a gorgeous tropical floral centrepiece. After eight days, I was still in stunned appreciation of this luxury.

I was telling them about my visit that day to see Dr Esther Ocloo, managing director of Nkulenu Industries Limited.

'Marmalade magnate!' exclaimed Ron. 'I think she's making it up.' I found Ron a little mocking, not unusual in a man talking about a woman's achievements.

Clearly, they thought I was mad as a hatter, too.

St John had arranged for me to meet Dr Ocloo – she was apparently well known in Accra, as she had won an African Leadership Award – and she agreed, even though she was coming back from a funeral. She was a fragile, daintily boned lady, probably about sixty to seventy years old, with very shrewd eyes. She was dressed in traditional funeral attire: black *fula* with brown-and-red-fabric, puff-sleeved top and tied skirt.

Dr Ocloo was happy to tell me how she got started. 'I started from a poor family, but at a young age I got a scholarship to go to Achimota School,' she said. Achimota was Ghana's premier school for its future judges, doctors and politicians. 'I had learnt English with a German accent, not a plummy English one, so when I went to the school it caused lots of laughs!' When she finished school, she stayed with an uncle at Osu, a poor ocean suburb of Accra. Times were hard, but one day an aunt gave her ten shillings. 'I knew I must make magic with it – and I went to buy ingredients for making marmalade that cost me six shillings. It usually takes two days to make the marmalade, but I wanted to move fast. The next day I sold it for twelve shillings in the market, so by 10 a.m., I had made six shillings!' Dr Ocloo laughed with pleasure. She told me that she had always been interested in food processing and preservation, as one third of food produced in Ghana is wasted. 'I got a baccalaureate to go to nursing school but I would not go and my parents thought I was crazy. Instead, in six years, I saved enough to go to Britain and study food processing. My money only lasted one year and three months, so I had to come back and save more money. I went back to college after two years and came home in 1962 to build my first small factory.'

It was an impressive story.

Over the years, she bought more equipment and developed more products, like beans in palm oil and cream of palm fruits – a tinned soup base for export to the United States. She also started a foundation for helping women to grow and process food or other products, to create employment for youth and to establish a women's training centre. 'It is the women who suffer – 63 per cent of farmers are women. But there is too much focus on technical training, not enough on business management.'

Ron and Ian did not want to know about all that; they were already talking about Surinam. Surinam?

'I got stuck in Surinam for two days and had to cancel two other countries on that visit and take a flight to Europe to get out!' said Ian.

'Yes,' agreed Ron. 'There's Shell men in the States who fly to Amsterdam to get the direct flight from there – it's the only reliable way.'

I could not add much to a conversation taking a turn towards Air Miles. I wondered briefly if there were many Shell women – certainly, in Africa, I had only met Shell wives – then went back to reflecting on the programme of the past eight days. St John had arranged my Togo visa and for me to have some medical tests done. They had been suggested as a precautionary measure, but nothing too untoward was found – just a sign I may have experienced a bout of typhoid at some stage.

Typhoid?!

It must have been a weak bout! Anyway, the doctor was blasé in his observation, and I had learnt to be blasé, too.

As well as Dr Ocloo, I had met Aba Quainoo, a dynamic young manager at Women's World Banking who talked passionately of expanding her loan scheme for women nationwide. To overcome the issue of women having no assets to offer as collateral and no formal savings track record, she was harnessing the *susu* – women's traditional savings schemes, whereby groups of women saved monthly, pooled the resources and made loans to each other from the pool.

Mrs Tackie, a senior administrative officer with the National Council for Women on Development, had told me about Ghanaian government policy and initiatives for women, and the priority being given to credit schemes, technical training and literacy. 'Initially, our target was to make as many women literate as possible, but women told us they need more money in their pockets!' She also spoke of the priority to change laws to give women more rights, giving me the example of laws to stop traditional widowhood rites and to make widows beneficiaries if the husband died intestate. 'Traditionally, a widow is subjected to various kinds of treatment – from wearing black, to having to stay in her room on her own for a year, to having pepper rubbed in her eyes. The law prevents this now, but some will volunteer anyway. They are made to feel their husband will haunt them if they do not go through the rites. Traditions die hard, but we have made a start.'

The meetings left the impression that Ghana was a country that was tackling the issues of its past and was, slowly but surely, going somewhere.

I also felt good about the people I had met. Somehow, the relationships were changing – from being interviews with strangers, as I had felt in previous encounters, to developing a rapport with professional women. Perhaps I was more comfortable with the issues, with my role, or with the women. Perhaps the cultural gap was not as wide as I had felt. Perhaps I just had more experience of Africa. I guessed I would see how future relationships developed.

'When will you be in Lomé?' Ron asked as the tempting dessert was served, interrupting my reflections.

'Oh, in three or four days,' I replied.

He burst out laughing. 'I'm so used to having appointments to the hour ... it sounds so funny. What's a day here or there?!' We were in two worlds that had briefly collided.

While I was familiar with Ron's world, it was another place. I had finally left my timetables behind and begun accepting the pace of life in Africa – at least, the pace in villages. I guess that was why I was ready – anxious, really – to get back on the road.

The next morning, the transition back to bicycle traveller was harder than the transition to city guest, but, as always, it happened extraordinarily quickly. Within one hour of cheery goodbyes to St John and the staff at the guesthouse, I had battled through Accra's vehicle tangles, and was cycling eastwards through boring, flat, coastal scrubland along the Téma expressway. I was sweaty, dirty, and air conditioning and cleanliness were a thing of the past. Oh well. Here, I had freedom, no one else's timetable, and I *felt* so much when I was on the road – physically, sure, but emotionally, too. There was more time to think and to recognise and explore emotions. The transitions both ways made me appreciate what I was doing, and, I think, helped to keep me motivated.

I was certainly now appreciating how much my physical state affected my emotions and reactions to people and situations. When I was too tired, I was irritable and (seemingly) things went wrong; when I was filled with energy, I was happy and (seemingly) nothing could go wrong. I was learning to respond more effectively to my body now – to take a day off when I showed symptoms of exhaustion. I hoped I could take these lessons back to a London life – I realised that for too long in the past I had suppressed emotions until they (inevitably) bubbled forth, and then I would blame people or circumstances rather than look to myself for a solution.

Despite my new-found awareness, external factors – in this case, geography – were creating constraints. Lomé was only 200 kilometres away on the Atlantic Coast; Cotonou, the major commercial port and capital of Benin, only 155 kilometres east of that; and Lagos, the nightmarish and daunting coastal city of Nigeria, only 120 kilometres further east again. I needed and wanted to stop in each city – Shell was expecting me, there were sure to be interesting programmes arranged, and I needed to visit Lagos to get a new passport at the Australian embassy.

But I felt impatient. How would I get any momentum going with so many city stops in quick succession? Worse yet, I had been told, continuous rains were due from May through July in southern Nigeria and it was already early May! I wanted to make the break out of West Africa into Cameroon and Central Africa – I had been here seven months now, with an eighth in prospect, and felt it was time to move on and explore somewhere else.

From Accra, I travelled for two days to Sogakope on the banks of the Volta

River, then turned off the main road for Keta on the coast. At Keta, the Volta estuary broke through to the ocean, and I had been told to take a short ferry ride across the estuary, then cycle along the coastal road to Aflao on the Ghanaian border with Togo. This would give me the opportunity to see the beaches of eastern Ghana.

However, after a long day's ride to Keta, I had a rude shock. The estuary was too low for the ferry to run – I would have to cycle back to Sogakope and take the main road to Aflao. Damn! Oh well, never mind. That's just Africa.

Ron flashed up in my mind. I bet he wouldn't have been too pleased!

The next morning, resigned to the return, I stopped off at the estuary that had proved my nemesis, when two elderly men approached.

'Good morning,' one said. 'Where are you going?' I explained, and he turned to his friend for a quick discussion in the local language. Then, turning back to me, he said, 'With the bike, you can cross.' I was doubtful – sand and salt – but he continued, 'With the recent rains, the sand should be hard and you will not have to push through much.' Oh, hell, I thought, I'll give it a go.

Having had the way pointed out by the men, I set off. The bitumen soon finished and turned into a muddy track. Concrete breezeblock houses and the ruins of colonial buildings destroyed by the surf gave way to open spaces and fishermen's huts. Then the road became planks – two parallel lines snaking across the damp estuary bed. The sky was a solid blue and the weather windy but hot.

As I paused, a cyclist surprised me by arriving from behind.

'Are you going to Kedji?' asked the young lad. Kedji was the village on the other side of the estuary, and it was exactly where I was going. Garu was a student who lived in Kedji, and we cycled together until the planks stopped and we had to push the bicycles along the shore.

Africa did seem to have a way of making things work out, I thought, if I let it.

It was a long way, the sun was hot, the humidity high. Suddenly, out of the haze, I saw a mirage. No! It was real! It was a boy with a Fanmilk cooler on his head! Fanmilk was a company that made frozen yoghurt and ice cream. It was always surprising to find a Fanmilk seller, but here, amongst shacks with no electricity, it was amazing! I eagerly bought frozen yoghurts for Garu and myself. During the transaction, the inevitable band of little ragamuffins gathered to watch. It was their lucky day – I bought them frozen yoghurts, too.

I was turning into a real softie with the kiddies now. Well, sometimes, anyway.

Finally, we arrived in Kedji, to broken bitumen that emerged like stepping stones out of the sand. Taxis and trucks lined the road, awaiting loading of passengers or goods. Having said goodbye to Garu, I cycled the stretch to

Aflao: a quiet ride down a palm tree-lined road. Neat huts squatted behind woven palm fences. People were walking, cycling and working in their compounds. I was very content, and Africa could do no wrong today.

At the crossroads with the narrow main road from Accra, I was again surprised. I had been expecting a small village in the far-eastern corner of Ghana, but instead, shops were edge to edge along the road, and people were walking, talking and sitting in huddles. It wasn't far to the border but the mêlée increased with people, cars and buses everywhere. I fought my way through Ghana departure formalities and Togolese entry formalities, then began to cycle on to Lomé.

On to Lomé? I suddenly realised I was *in* Lomé. Away from the border post stretched a wide boulevard. To my right was a wide, sandy beach with the Bay of Benin stretching blue to the horizon, to my left, chic restaurants and small businesses, and further ahead I could see high-rises. It was like arriving in Nice on the Mediterranean. However, there were no cars, no people and none of the businesses were open. It was as if everyone had packed up from this gorgeous city and moved next door to live in the bush in Ghana. That, or a neutron bomb had exploded, killing the people and leaving the buildings standing. Bizarre.

Finally, I arrived at a main intersection. A glitzy glass palace, the Palm Beach Hotel, dominated one corner. I stopped to ask a rare pedestrian the way to Shell's offices and why everything was so quiet.

'Is it lunchtime?' I asked, thinking that a long siesta might be the custom.

'It is the strike,' he replied grimly. Hearing reports of 'trouble in Togo', I had imagined wild chaos spilling over into intermittent street riots, not this morgue. I was slow to realise a crisis can resemble a morgue.

I eventually made it to Shell's offices where the security guard instructed me to wait. A short time later, my contact for *Togo et Shell*, arrived. Déti Amegee. A Shell woman! She was the public affairs and commercial manager, very pretty, with her hair in tight tresses, a broad smile and the same height and build as me. My overriding impression was of a whirlwind of energy.

'*Bienvenue au Togo!*' she cried and gave me four cheek kisses. Like St John in Accra, she immediately wanted to introduce me to people. Unlike Accra, we found locked and empty offices. There was a barely a soul in the office. 'Most people have either fled the country or work a few hours a day, or every other day. There is not much to do anyway. We are only providing an emergency service, and everyone is on strike.'

She eventually sat me down in her office and handed me a note from the *directeur général*, Patrice Chanton. Reading it, I found he welcomed me to Lomé, apologised for being away on a business trip, then continued: 'You may have heard we have been living some very bad days for the last two years: state coups, riots, murders ... and the whole country has been on strike for six months now. A lot of people have left the country (there are 400,000 of them

in Benin or Ghana) and in Shell less than 30 per cent of staff are at work …
you must be very careful and also it may be difficult to meet some interesting
people at the time being.' However, action-oriented Déti was not to be
deterred. 'Let's discuss your programme …'

Phew, my head hurt. For a city on strike, people seemed to display an awful
lot of energy. As I prepared my bicycle to leave and worried about the condition of its rear tyre, I reflected on the past four days.

Gruelling activity at a frantic pace. Instead of the two or three meetings I
might have expected, I had about twelve, plus three lunches, two dinners, a
press conference and a television interview – my first in French. It had been
great, and tiring.

There was Dr Moïse Fiadjoe, a gynaecologist, who was quite extraordinary, with Déti's same high energy level and passion for a better future for
the Togolese. He was gynaecologist of choice to the wives of both government
and opposition figures, which in Togo's highly charged political environment, meant he must be good. However, he also did a lot of volunteer work
with poorer women, and he introduced me to one of the initiatives he, Déti
and some others had helped establish – FAMME – *Forces en Action pour le
Mieux être de la Mere et de l'Enfant* (Action Force for the Well-Being of
Mothers and Children). I went to the home (just a spare, sandy lot with no
water or sanitation in an otherwise built-up area) of some of the young,
marginalised women FAMME helped with loans and healthcare (they suffered
from malnutrition and were at high risk from AIDS). The *portefaix* – porters
– were village women who came to Lomé in search of work, ending up in
Lomé's market working as porters carrying heavy loads on their heads. Men
don't carry things, I was told – they were the heads of households. A familiar
story by now.

There was also lunch with an economic consultant, Andrée Kokoé
Kuevidjan. As she arrived at one of the few restaurants remaining open, she
was clutching her Air France ticket in her hand and said, as she sat down, 'I'm
sorry, I cannot stay long. I am flying to Paris tonight for three months. After
the elections I will see what happens.' We talked about the impact of people
going away. 'People are making new lives for themselves and may not come
back. It will take many, many years for the economy of Togo to recover.'

The peculiar thing was that, each evening, after a day spent discussing the
troubles, the government-controlled television news made no mention of a
crisis, or of the strike, or of the flight of refugees. There were, however,
always images of President Eyadéma being fêted by women chanting and
clapping at some ceremony or another. Even the Minister for Social Welfare
and National Solidarity in Charge of Human Rights, Mme Gazaro, made no
reference to the situation. It was as though, for the government, lack of
acknowledgement meant it did not exist.

'Oh my God, what have I done?' Getting a warm send-off, Dakar, Senegal.

Being helped across a small river on those 'roads' into the Fouta Djalon, Guinea.

Dressed for protection against tsetse flies on the road to Labé, Guinea.

A typical struggle to get a better view of the 'alien', Fouta Djalon, Guinea.

Three's company – with Al and Suze during the hazy days of the harmattan, Mali.

Dried fish for sale in busy Djenné market.

My Tuareg friends: Ibrahim (in dark boubou), *Fatimata and their children in the desert outside Timbuktu.*

Brewing millet beer in a village outside Bawku, northern Ghana.

Lydia drawing water from a deep well, Lalsa, northern Ghana.

With Stella, Hamidou and one of Stella's daughters, Benin City, Nigeria.

Having fun with Femi and Fred at 'the most beautiful beach in Africa', southern Nigeria.

'You are not a woman, you are a man,' said the bicycle mechanic (left), *Ibadan, Nigeria.*

The 'short cut' in the mountains of Cameroon outside Bamenda.

Marie Carmen (far right) *with children and friends inside her kitchen hut, Beayop, Equatorial Guinea.*

Caroline carries wood, Loubetsi, Republic of Congo.

Deka and Mputela in the ambulance amongst the pondu, Kinshasa, Zaire.

No money for fuel or fares, Kinshasa.

Pirogue *traders docking at our travelling 'village' on the Zaire River.*

People find space amongst the cargo on the barges.

Philippe and his pet monkey.

'McMonkey'!

Chantal comes to my salon for tea.

Bob and me.

Male silverback gorilla observes us curious humans, Kahuzi-Biega National Park, Zaire.

Watching out for trains near Malagarasi, Dar Es Salaam, Tanzania.

Damned cement mud!

With my parents at journey's end – I'm unable to stop grinning!

As she did not mention the crisis during our meeting, I asked. 'Given the terrible economic and political crisis that Togo now faces, how do you feel that improvements can be made in women's conditions?'

'I will be an optimist,' she said, after a pause (probably thinking, bloody woman, why did I agree to see her?) 'if, after all these problems, we are able to continue with our Head of State. I am close to him, I know that his policies are for improving the condition of women.'

Ugh. Neat side step into political speak, avoidance of my question, and avoidance of responsibility for the current crisis. Was I being too harsh?

Togo had been a German protectorate until World War I. After the war, its territory was divided, with one third being placed under British administration (now a part of Ghana) and two thirds under French administration (matching Togo's current borders). Back then, of course, the impact this would have on tribal groups was not a part of the decision-making process, and several tribes, including the Ewe people of the coast, found themselves separated from family members by a border. When Togo became independent in 1960, Sylvanus Olympio was elected the country's first president. However, Olympio, an Ewe, was reportedly distracted by his main priority, to reunify his people, and neglected to satisfy the economic and political aspirations of people of the poorer north.

Olympio was killed in 1963 by rampaging northern troops who burst into his home. A new president was installed, but in 1967, after four years of economic decline, Etienne Eyadéma (one of the soldiers who burst into Olympio's home) replaced him after another coup. Eyadéma had been in power ever since. One of Africa's old-style military dictators, he was now, in the nineties, in the new world of African democratisation, refusing to let go of power. This was what the crisis and the strike were about.

There had been various coup attempts and crackdowns on opposition during Eyadéma's rocky years of power, but the current crisis started in 1990. Following the arrest and trial of members of an opposition group, massive demonstrations erupted in Lomé. These were brutally put down, leaving many dead. Continuing protests and external pressure forced Eyadéma to legalise political parties, but when protestors called for Eyadéma's resignation, the military cracked down again. A seesaw of opposition strikes, demonstrations and army crackdowns continued. In 1992, in the north – Eyadéma's supposed stronghold, there was an assassination attempt against Gilchrist Olympio, son of Sylvanus and the main opposition leader. Eyadéma's son was strongly implicated in the shooting, causing more demonstrations and another general strike.

Worse had come in January 1993.

'The strike was continuing and Germany and France sent representatives to prod for further moves on democracy,' said my informant. 'The opposition arranged a demonstration to show their desire for democracy and to welcome their assistance. Protesters walked through the streets of Lomé with white handkerchiefs on their heads and carrying candles as a sign of hope and peace. Soldiers opened fire, then closed off the area, brought in trucks and carried bodies away. No one was sure how many were killed. About a week later on January 30, soldiers retaliated for the death of two security officers. They went on a shooting spree near Lomé market, leaving many dead.' The exodus of refugees commenced, the general strike was maintained, Lomé's once vibrant streets became a morgue and its economy died.

'He has robbed the country,' said someone else. 'Now, he is prepared to terrorise his own people and to let the economy sink into poverty and malnutrition rather than lose his ability to snap his fingers and have things happen for him.'

(Togo's history and the events that occurred when I was there were very sad, but what is sadder is that the cycle of protest and repression continues. In late 1993, there was a presidential election. Eyadéma rejected Gilchrist Olympio's candidature and refused to revise the electoral register – even though it had been compiled at a time when the opposition boycotted putting their names on the register as a protest. Eyadéma won. International observers declared the election undemocratic, but Eyadéma maintained repressive power. In mid-1998, there was another presidential election, this time with Olympio standing as a candidate and a revised electoral register. Eyadéma was still declared the winner – even though the announcement came before the ballot boxes of the most important areas of Lomé had been opened, even though, again, the independent observers declared the election undemocratic. People have returned to Lomé, but investors are staying out, the economy remains fragile, and for the future, there is only hope that Togo will not become another Rwanda, another Liberia, and that one day soon, Eyadéma will let go.)

But now it was time to press on.

'Ah, so Shell is lubricating your journey?' asked Déti cheerfully, coming out of the house to see me greasing my bike's chain. A good way of putting it, I thought. Not only was Shell providing lubricants, they were 'lubricating' my journey by providing me with rejuvenating stops and contacts that provided revealing insights into the social and political issues of Africa today. 'I have decided you cannot leave today,' she continued. 'I have arranged for you to meet two of the Nana Benz.' I stayed. Nana Benz was the nickname for the famously powerful women who controlled the fabric trade in West Africa – they were wholesalers who bought from the big manufacturers and sold to traders around Africa. I was very excited by the prospect of meeting them.

'I will introduce you to the Nana Benz because you are a Nana *Vélo*,' joked vivacious Déti. The women got their nickname from the Mercedes they were said to habitually drive, so I guess it was fair I should get a nickname for my bike.

I first met Mlle Marie-Ange Anthony, only twenty-six years old, a young Nana Benz. 'My grandmother commenced the business, forty-three years ago, and I took over when she died recently.' She had studied Business Administration in France and returned when her mother was ill. Marie-Ange seemed a very gentle person to wield such power, but I knew I should not be deceived by appearances. She clearly knew her business well. 'We buy fabric from manufacturers in Holland, Manchester, Japan, Senegal and Ivory Coast. And our clients are international – in Mali, Burkina Faso, Nigeria, Ivory Coast, Benin and Gabon. It is important to know the markets. For example, Togolese women do not like bright colours, Burkinabe women like patterns with the sun, moons and stars, and brighter colours.' She told me she had employed designers so that some of her designs were proprietary. 'It is very different from before. We have computers, stock control, salespeople, tight accounting ... but, of course, here in Togo, the market is closed. All our clients have left the country and all our orders are from Cotonou and Abidjan.' I found her easy to talk to – perhaps because we were talking business.

Marie-Ange was the new style of Nana Benz; Mme Patience Sanvee, the other Nana Benz I met, was one of the original breed. Patience Sanvee met me in the living room of her home. She was elderly – in her sixties – and she exuded power, confidence and importance. 'I started with nothing,' she told me. She had only primary school education and started out as an eight year old in Lomé's central market selling cigarettes and perfume. From her days as a street trader she had become one the most powerful of the Nana Benz. She showed me a book of discoloured clippings – articles about her. A 1987 article from the *New York Times* described her as the 'doyenne of the about fifteen formidable women who control Togo's cloth trade'. The article went on to say how often these women found themselves in conflict with their leaders and how, in 1987, when they protested at the imposition of price controls, President Eyadéma backed down. He was quoted as saying: 'The Nana Benz are the seat on which the government stands. We must all respect them.' It was a nice story.

Nonetheless, Mme Sanvee's Lomé operations had been destroyed in the January 30 crackdown when the military had rampaged throughout the market. Mme Sanvee lost 800 million CFA of stock – about US$3 million at the exchange rates of the time. 'I commenced with nothing,' she said, 'and curiously, the situation has now turned again.' She showed me a letter to a government minister demanding compensation. Then, looking like a warrior for justice, she cried fiercely, '*Le moment viendra! La vérité triomphe toujours!*' The moment will come! Truth always triumphs!

I wished I had her confidence.

(Mme Sanvee has not received compensation and is no longer the powerful Nana Benz she once was. Her health is broken and she has become an old lady.)

Finally, it was the next morning and I could leave Lomé. I was amazed by how much time and effort people here and elsewhere were putting into providing me with informative and controversial contacts. However, I was tired. As with the Tuareg, I found other people's despair and stories of pain and horror debilitating, and the pace of this programme, so soon after that in Accra and demanding such a sophisticated use of my French, had been exhausting. I wanted some time to take it all in – I was feeling information overload – and needed some time to rest.

As I left on Sunday morning, many of the staff and people I had come to know in Lomé turned up to wave me off. I was very flattered.

The 155 kilometres to Cotonou in Benin should not take long to cover – about two days – but Déti had wanted to nail me down, so I said three. There were no Shell operations in Benin, but she had contacts there and had volunteered to come, meet me and give me introductions. We had a date: Tuesday at 6 p.m. at the Croix du Sud Hotel in Cotonou. It would be great to see a familiar face, someone I now counted as a friend, in a new city.

I discovered Grand Popo during my ride to Cotonou to meet Déti. It had been the site of a slaving fort, though the Atlantic had long since taken away any evidence. Nonetheless, seeing a signpost, I left the main road just to take a quick look. I cycled down a potholed, muddy track, past a few scattered houses. A 200-metre stretch of flat, sandy land scattered with tall, skinny palm trees lay between me and the ocean. Old, red, stucco-covered colonial buildings lay derelict, except for one being used as the school. It had twin buildings with peaked roofs, wide gables and an opening arch. One was marked *Filles*, the other *Garçons*. The buildings lay parallel to each other at the far side of the playground and the Beninese flag flew from a centrally located pole. Then, I found the *auberge*.

It was a simple, whitewashed, tin-roofed, purpose-built structure, with a verandah facing the sea. Nearby were palm-roofed rondavels – like gazebos, and across a grassy area were the ruins of another derelict building. In the white sand in the foreground were a sprinkling of blue and white umbrellas and a few tarpaulins for shade. I stopped for lunch to enjoy the sounds of the surf, and it was one of the waiters who mentioned there were rooms in another smaller building back from the ocean.

I could not resist – this place was my kind of paradise. Finally, I had found my ocean. Guesthouses with pools were great, but I adored this simplicity and quietness. I stayed the night, and left reluctantly the next morning.

Already, the day was pressured. There were still about 90 kilometres to Cotonou – and my rendezvous! – and there was an interesting town I had read about, Ouidah, I wanted to visit along the way. Ouidah, like Grand Popo and Porto Novo, the capital of Benin, had been a major trading and slaving centre of the Slave Coast in the eighteenth and nineteenth centuries for the Dan-Homey kingdom (under the French, called Dahomey). This kingdom, remarkable for its skilled and trained female warriors, feared because of its high rate of human sacrifice, had its capital at Abomey, a city 100 kilometres inland from the coast. In the early nineteenth century, a young prince, Ghezo, entered into a pact with a Brazilian mulatto, Francisco Felix de Souza. With de Souza's help, Ghezo was able to take the throne; in exchange he gave de Souza a monopoly over the slave trade. De Souza became the 'Viceroy of Ouidah', the subject of Bruce Chatwin's evocative book of the same name.

As the nineteenth century progressed, the Dan-Homey kingdom had no obvious export alternatives and slaving was only slowly replaced by palm oil exports. The last slaves were exported on Portuguese ships from Ouidah as late as 1885. (Until the development of the petroleum industry during the late nineteenth century, palm oil was the major source of lubrication for machinery; hence, its production became a major industry all along the Slave Coast, as far as Calabar in eastern Nigeria.)

Ouidah's other claim to fame is that it is a centre for voodoo, the traditional religion still practised along this coast today, which was exported to Haiti, Cuba and Brazil with the slaves. Voodoo seemed to be an interchangeable term, used both for the spirits and people who could communicate to the gods. Frank, a barman at Grand Popo (such a reliable source), had told me that the gods could only be talked to through a voodoo priest. People could ask for favours from the gods by making offerings to the voodoo. But Frank gave me an example of how this could go wrong. 'A man could make an offering to win a woman,' he said. 'But in a small village, it was possible his rival might see him make the offering. So the rival might make an offering of wine to get the voodoo drunk, and also surprise the voodoo by rubbing pepper in his eyes to stop him seeing clearly. Then, the voodoo would be confused and could tell the god to make the woman prefer the rival.' Sounded complicated to me – and love was quite complicated enough! He also told me to watch out for pyramid-shaped bales of straw in fields near villages. These were voodoo fetishes which came to life at night and spun through the fields on their missions. I saw the bales; I didn't see them spin.

Ouidah was as interesting as its history, but after a brief stop at its museum – the old Portuguese fort built in 1721 – I left, and the afternoon ride was a nightmare. The road became narrow and very busy, indeed so dangerous that I retreated to the left-hand side of the road to face the onslaught rather than be mown down unexpectedly from behind. Then, I got a flat tyre, found my pump was broken, and faced the prospect of pushing.

Of course, just when I was ready to give up, Africa came to my rescue again.

I had only pushed about 100 metres when I passed a small hut where a man was sitting with an upside-down bike and a bicycle pump. That wouldn't happen in Europe.

The road remained slow and I entered dirty, dusty Cotonou at rush hour – scary stuff as motos, taxis and trucks buzzed by. I stuck doggedly to the hard shoulder, facing the oncoming traffic, despite the glares of pedestrians and despite the shoulder turning to soft sand. I became lost and was late for my rendezvous at the Croix de Sud Hotel. I stopped to ask a man for directions. I must have looked flustered, for he immediately hopped on his bicycle to guide me there. That wouldn't happen in Europe either, I thought, grateful for the help.

Finally, I caught up with Déti in the reception. She looked smart but I looked pretty rough: fixing the flat tyre had left me even more grease-covered and sweaty than usual.

'Ah, there you are,' said Déti, without any sign of surprise. I loved Déti for her enthusiasm and single-mindedness, but I, on the other hand, was astonished I had made it alive. I was tired. 'Come,' said Déti without any pause. 'I have a woman for you to meet.'

This was the hard part of my relationship with Shell folk. I felt like a taut elastic band – the physical demands of the journey were like the band being stretched to its limit one way, then when I got to the city and had to mix with businesspeople, government members and the media and had to use my brain, it felt like the band being stretched to its limit the other way. Good exercise, good fun, good motivation, but to be stretched both ways on the same day made me feel like screaming!

In the end, though, thanks to Déti, my short stay in Cotonou was interesting, filled with meeting more stimulating, kind people.

Most interesting of all was the person I stayed with on my first night: Rébecca Dossou-Gbété, a passionate, well-educated woman with an original lifestyle. She only had one daughter and lived separately from her Beninese husband, who worked with the French government and lived abroad. She had chosen this arrangement so that she could pursue her own career.

'I had a beautiful home in France – really beautiful,' Rébecca told me. 'Marble floors, big rooms, garden … One day I just thought, what am I doing? All those years of study at university, for what? To stay at home? So I went to my husband and told him I had to work. But I wanted to work for the benefit of Africa and there was nothing for me in Toulouse. My husband said, "I am staying in France," so I told him I would go to my family, who would support me until I got some work. People were horrified. "You have left your husband! What are you doing?" And my husband was mad …' She paused, and we could hear the loud calls of crickets from her garden and the muffled sounds of motos from the street. 'That was ten years ago, and he is proud of me now!'

Rébecca had been in charge of a project for the United Nations Fund for Population, and was now embarking on setting up her own business, a consulting firm in career training and community development.

I told Rébecca about the lifestyle and man I had given up to be here. 'You and I could be twins!' she exclaimed. I thought so, too – we had both pursued our dreams, no matter what the risk or cost.

I was lying on the white sand, under the shade of the blue tarpaulin stretched between bamboo posts. Beyond was a cloudless blue sky. If I turned my head, if I had the energy, I could see the ragged, swaying tufts of some coconut palms. The pounding of surf would have drowned out any other sounds, if there were any. But this was a quiet spot. It truly was my kind of paradise.

I was back in Grand Popo and had been there for ten days!

At Rébecca's, I had become ill with a sore throat, constant headache, aching bones and a fever. It may have been malaria – or it may just have been the heat, humidity and dust. I blamed Cotonou – I disliked the city – but then remembered how much my moods and attitudes were due to my physical state. Taking a bush taxi back to Grand Popo to restore my equilibrium had seemed a good idea.

Also, I was waiting for a new tyre. The flats had been coming too frequently, a sure sign I needed a new tyre, and I had sent a message from Lomé to a friend. However, it was mid May and I had forgotten that people in Europe were beginning to go on summer holidays. Nothing had arrived in the few days I was in Cotonou, but, hopefully, I'd have a tyre and new pump waiting for me when I went back.

At Grand Popo, I was enjoying a lazy, wonderful vacation. No gender issues, no politics, no cycling. Hooray! I mixed with about six other visitors – holidaying Peace Corps Volunteers and, unusually, backpackers. Out in the villages, I rarely encountered backpackers – they stayed in bigger places and travelled by truck or public transport. In the capitals, they stayed at cheap hotels while I shared an expatriate or middle-class African lifestyle. It was nice to chill out and have different kinds of conversations. With the PCVs, I compared village experiences; with the backpackers, I exchanged travellers' tales – I enjoyed their stories of wild rides in *taxi brousse* and they seemed to be envious of the freedom of my mode of transport. We drank tea or beer, swam, played *huit américain* – the card game of choice with Africans I'd met, and let time pass.

Soon, my equilibrium, health and contentment with Africa returned, putting me in a better frame of mind to tackle Nigeria, my next country.

Ten

Road Fever

Cotonou, Benin – Calabar, Nigeria

Although I needed to go there for my visa, and for another programme, I wanted to avoid tackling Lagos on the bicycle – it sounded much too big and dangerous. Therefore, after returning from Grand Popo, I cycled from Cotonou to Porto Novo, Benin's capital, then north-east, to cross the border to Nigeria at Idiroko, and continued toward Ilaro, Abeokuta and Ibadan. Ibadan was a big, regional city, Nigeria's second largest, home to more than five million people, 125 kilometres north of Lagos. The brother of Ninon Asuni, my London bicycle supplier, lived in Ibadan, and Ninon had suggested I look him up. I did, and was kindly looked after by Tomi and his wife Martine. Discovering Tomi was marketing director for Fanmilk Nigeria, I begged for a factory tour – with lots of sampling and a ride on a very low-geared Fanmilk bicycle! Then, I left my bicycle with them for a quick and, given its reputation for violence and thievery, dreaded Lagos visit. I would be happier when it was over and I was free to travel onwards through Nigeria and into Cameroon.

The city was built over several small, once mangrove-covered islands. Kilometres of housing and factories stretched over the mainland. As I neared the city, I hit chaotic traffic jams and crept past huge billboards advertising everything from skin lightener to cigarettes to margarine. Then, the city's Manhattan-like skyline rose over the water. This was one seriously big city. With a population of more than ten million, it was in a completely different league to Accra or Cotonou. Nigeria itself was a country about four times the size of the United Kingdom, with an estimated population of over 100 million people, the African nation with the highest population.

National Oil, the retail marketing company in which Shell has a major stake, was to look after me in Nigeria, contrary to their initial decision. The status when I had left London was that National Oil had refused to support me because my journey was too dangerous. Not having support in a tricky country was a pity, but, well, that was that. So, when I heard in Accra that National Oil had changed their mind and would support my journey, I was very pleased.

The managers I had contact with in Lagos ultimately proved as enthusias-

tic as all the other I met. With their help, getting my new passport proved
easy, as did getting my visa for Cameroon.

However, there was an ongoing problem about tyres. I had received my
spare in Cotonou, so I wasn't having any more flats. Nonetheless, I realised I
would need tyres with more traction for the roads in Cameroon. Contrary to
the advice of M. Kounkaye (that talkative taxi driver in Guinea), it was now
pretty clear that I was going to be in Cameroon during the wet. As his other
advice had proved accurate, I sent a follow-up message to my friend, asking
that knobblies be sent to Lagos. Sadly, DHL had nothing for me; so I sent
one last SOS, asking that the tyres be sent to Calabar, my last town in Nigeria
with a DHL office before I entered mountainous Cameroon.

My stay in Lagos was as brief as I could make it – six days – and even that
was longer than I intended, but Orlando Ojo, executive director of oils
marketing, had advised me to stay for June 12, election day.

'We do not know what might happen. It is better you are in Lagos and not
on your bicycle for the election.' Although normally an effervescent man, he
made this point seriously and I listened.

The election was the backdrop to the entire month of my stay in Nigeria; it
was meant to hail a new era of civilian, democratic rule. There were only two
candidates – Moshood Abiola and Bashir Tofa, as there were only two parties
permitted by Major-General Ibrahim Babangida.

The Federation of Nigeria gained independence in 1960, and the Federal
Republic of Nigeria was formed in 1963. Nigeria has a huge diversity of
cultures – perhaps 250 different peoples – and a range of languages nearly as
broad; a federal system offering some autonomy was necessary to bind them
together. The three most powerful, but mutually suspicious, ethnic groups –

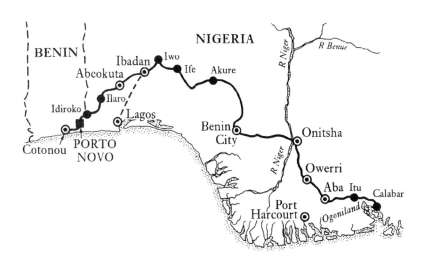

the Hausa of the north, the Yoruba of the south-west and the Igbo of the south-east – had agreed their regions would be run separately, but with a single head of a central government. However, distrust between the groups rapidly escalated, erupted into violence and ethnic conflict, and, in 1966, resulted in a first military coup d'état. Since then, Nigeria has been run primarily by military regimes. Babangida had gained power in a coup in 1985 and had been promising a transition to democracy since soon after his takeover. Since 1990, the elections had been postponed three times and, understandably, people didn't seem to believe it was actually going to happen. What I remember of election day in Lagos was that, finally, the incessant noise of traffic was stilled and I could hear the birds singing. Remarkable!

The infrastructure of Lagos was clearly not coping with its continuing growth. Although no longer the capital – the seat of government had been moved in 1991 to Abuja, a purpose-built city in the central plains – Lagos remained the commercial heart of Nigeria.

'We spend three hours coming to work for 6 a.m. or 7 a.m., and then three hours going home, for a 10 p.m. arrival. When we get there, there is no water or light. It is killing, that is what it is,' said a manager I shared a taxi with one day. I was only trying to get a few kilometres to my guesthouse – comfortable, although nowhere near as plush as the guesthouse in Accra – but we got stuck in a traffic jam for two hours. It *was* killing.

Another day, I walked in Lagos and almost immediately got caught in a major downpour. The rainy days were coming more frequently now. The downpour had caused the street drains to back up. Well-dressed Nigerian men and women, in suits and embroidered robes, had trouser legs rolled up, robes lifted and were wading through calf-deep water; to me, it looked incongruous, amusing. I pulled out my camera, prepared to take a photo and received a lesson that I did not soon forget! Nigerians were very touchy to what they perceived as implied criticism by a foreigner about their country.

I had a mob turn on me.

'What are you doing?' yelled one woman aggressively from her car.

'You must not do that!' yelled another woman, grabbing firmly at my arm.

'This is Nigeria. You do not do things like that!' screamed someone else.

A lot of passers-by stopped, moved towards me, started yelling the same kinds of things.

'Why are you taking a photo?'

'Don't you have things like this in your country?'

I retorted aggressively, 'No, we have drains,' took a photo, then fled. Not very admirable, but I don't react well to mobs.

Someone later told me that Nigerians were so sensitive because they were fed up with foreign media always emphasising the bad things about their country. Certainly, many Nigerians I met felt frustrated by their country's deterioration when it should be a rich nation, by its oppression during the long years of corrupt rule by military 'big men', but they felt the foreign media damned all. I could sympathise with their feelings, though I did not like the impact it had on me.

Soon, though not soon enough, I made my way out of Lagos, collected my bike from Ibadan, and rode out of town. Another place with nerve-racking traffic. I was heading to Ife, about 90 kilometres away, then would travel to Akure, then Benin City, Onitsha, Owerri, Aba and Calabar before reaching Ikom near the border with Cameroon, and on, on, on until Douala, where I would have my next programme. For nearly 2000 kilometres, I had the freedom and rhythm of being on the open road! Hooray!

Oh, shit!

I suddenly lost propulsion and slammed my foot down on the road to keep myself upright. My chain had broken and my gear-cable casing had sheared. What sort of spirit made *that* happen? *And* my chain-link extractor had broken the last time I used it. Damn, why had I forgotten to replace it?

As I wheeled my bike to the pavement, I spied a bicycle mechanic across the road. Again. Like the last time, this was no glossy shop. This was an old man fiddling with a bicycle on the pavement, other bicycles propped up behind him. Africa is great, I thought, my impatience dissipating.

'Good morning,' I said.

'Good morning,' said the mechanic. He was a skinny man in a white short-sleeved shirt that hung over light-blue pants. His English was not good, but he could see my problem and immediately set aside his existing job.

He started trying to fix the chain with a chain link, but – hey! – I had a continuous chain! We had a few fraught minutes as I tried to show him what to do and he wanted to get on, incorrectly. Finally, I convinced him to give me the chisel and nail and I fixed it myself. The gathering crowd watched in awe.

As I righted the bicycle and commenced reloading, the old man said, 'You are not a woman, you are a man!' Perhaps he thought it was a joke.

Five nights later, I cycled into Benin City. It was, as usual, rather alarming.

All the roads in Nigeria were paved, but this only seemed to encourage drivers to go at maniacal speed. And there seemed to be no back roads. I had supposedly come along quieter routes from Ibadan, and even there the traffic was intrusive. Each day, there had been at least one near-miss incident with traffic, one run-in with an aggressive crowd (still sensitive about my photo-taking!) and one act of extreme kindness (an unsolicited gift of food, for example). Each night, I had retreated to a small hotel. In a country with big and frequent urban agglomerations, putting up my tent in quiet village compounds was not possible. Inevitably, I had a room painted bright blue or red, with maybe one bare bulb to see by, and I would sit for a while, trying to recover from the road assault of the day. Each night, I ventured out for a beer, but with thunderstorms regularly arriving in the evenings, there were seldom many people in the bars to talk to.

Now, I rejoined the freeway from Lagos, the only route into Benin City from the west. I rapidly decided to circumnavigate the city rather than going through the centre. The next day, I planned to leave on the eastward road for Onitsha, so if I could find a hotel on that side, departure would be easier. Once I found a hotel, I wanted to backtrack and see the city centre: like Ouidah, it had a famous history.

The kingdom of Benin, contemporaneous with the Oyo empire and the Dan-Homey state, had its capital at Benin City. It had nothing to do with the country now called Benin. By 1500, the kingdom was over 400 kilometres wide, stretching from the Lagos lagoon in the west to the Niger delta region in the east. From the fifteenth century to its decline in the eighteenth century, the *obas* (rulers) of Benin engaged in trade with Europeans, their main exports being pepper, ivory gum and cotton cloth.

In 1897, after a British team trying to negotiate a peaceful takeover of power were murdered (probably not in their negotiating plan), Benin City was sacked and destroyed by the British. Benin had a highly developed court art – bronze busts of the *obas* and copper plaques depicting their famous deeds; during the invasion, these beautiful artifacts were looted. I had seen the booty on view at the Museum of Mankind in London. It seemed a remarkable history.

Hey! What happened to Benin City?

I had only travelled about 10 kilometres, very slowly through dense traffic. I had kept my eyes open for hotels, seen and inspected two – one was full, one was a dive – and had been advised by the receptionist at the dive to continue along the Onitsha road where I would find some more. Now, suddenly, I had fallen off the edge of Benin City and it was 4 p.m. I turned the bicycle around and cycled back 100 metres to a petrol station opposite some large oil tanks. I thought I would buy a drink and ask for directions. As I stopped, my muscles became heavy and I knew I couldn't go any further that day.

'You could ask the woman who runs the store across the road if you could stay with her,' said a soldier in green fatigues who was sprawled by the petrol pumps. His rifle languished in his lap and I thought he looked a bit sleazy. 'I'll take you over to meet Stella – I know her well.' Across the road was a small general store, selling beer and soft drinks, cigarettes, a bit of bread and Blue Band margarine, and I could see a woman serving behind the counter. I made a call – I did not really trust this soldier but it *was* a chance to stay with a woman. Give it a go, I thought. It was better than cycling into traffic again!

Stella turned out to be a willing and kind host, a pretty woman with fine features and a youthful appearance. After she welcomed me, she said I could stay in her daughter Henrietta's room. I thought her spontaneous hospitality was marvellous.

'The bathroom is not fine,' she said. 'It is better to shower outside.' She took me amongst the foundations of a house she was gradually having built next door to have a bucket shower.

I emerged refreshed around 6 p.m., and started joking around with seventeen-year-old Henrietta at the front of the shop. Like her mother, Henrietta was very good looking, with sparkling eyes and a laughing nature. She brought out her best outfit for me to try on over my clothes. The outfit consisted of a top, tie skirt and *fula* made from a silver-and-white heavy cloth, embroidered in purple. I pulled on the top and tied the skirt around my waist.

'Oh, it is very fine!' exclaimed Henrietta. Then, she spent some time teaching me how to tie the *fula* in different styles. I am sure that on tall, slender, hipless Henrietta the outfit looked very fine. I thought I looked like a wedding cake.

I was looking forward to a quiet evening with Stella and Henrietta, but it was not to be. Several soldiers, including one named Hamidou, arrived at Stella's shop for beers. Apparently they were now off duty from guarding the oil tanks. I smiled grimly.

We were sitting on the cement-slab verandah in the dark outside the shop – many cars and trucks were passing, so it was not very peaceful – when Hamidou, by now quite drunk, suddenly said, 'It is just as well you are travelling on Sunday.'

Actually, he was making an assumption that I would leave the next day. Privately, I was contemplating staying an extra day to tour Benin City – after all, seeing artifacts of the Benin kingdom had been one of the motivations for coming this way in the first place.

'The traffic will be lighter,' he continued. 'The Benin City to Onitsha road is the most dangerous in Nigeria! It is straight and too narrow and there are very many accidents and deaths on that road.'

Instantly, I made the decision not only to continue tomorrow, but also to do the 139-kilometre distance in one day. I resigned myself to missing the museum. Coping with Nigeria's traffic on a bicycle and being a tourist were simply not mixing.

The next morning, I left very early, knowing it would be a long, tough day. At least I could look forward to a ride on smooth, flat tarmac. However, it soon became obvious it was too dangerous to be on the road.

To the impatient drivers, a bicycle was only an obstacle to toot at, and run down if necessity dictated it. Necessity could be something as normal as wanting to pass a truck. If I happened to be in the way, too bad – there was *no way* that they would slow down! The road had a narrow shoulder which was badly potholed, and not respected when drivers tried to overtake, but I bumped along there – nervously.

Thick, tangled bush encroached onto the shoulder on either side, sometimes forcing me out onto the road. There were no villages, houses or open scenes, and no other cyclists – no one else would be so silly. Buses and over-loaded trucks dominated, but there were also an amazing number of Mercedes Benz – perhaps only commercial vehicles and the wealthy got petrol. Amazingly, I had been assured the traffic was actually lighter than normal! (Since before the election there had been a petrol shortage in Nigeria, rumoured to be orchestrated by the military government to limit the potential for demonstrations.) I felt battered by the constant flow of vehicles.

And this was Sunday traffic. I did not want to be cycling this road on Monday – that thought kept me going as the kilometres and hours of cycling mounted.

In the late afternoon, after about 90 kilometres of this gruelling day, I saw cars swerving to avoid a log on the road. It was several hundred metres ahead and I watched it take form as I approached. Having little else to think about, I wondered about this log and why it was there. One car even hit it, and it flew sideways.

Suddenly, I realised, this was no log. This was a body!

Or, at least, it was the gruesome trunk of a person. It was bloated into a grotesque balloon and the limbs had been severed, presumably by passing vehicles. I looked away, but couldn't get the image out of my mind. I had to stop – I was shaking and scared. How could I go on?

Hamidou had told me that bodies could be left lying on the side of the road for days. Especially the bodies of bandits.

Whoosh! went the vehicles as they approached. Toot! as they passed. Roar! as they disappeared into the distance. Whoosh! To-oo-ot! Roar! Whoosh! Tooot! Toooot! Roar! I wondered if I'd end up a limbless corpse.

Near dusk, I arrived at a bridge across the Niger River on the outskirts of Onitsha. It was the first time I had seen the Niger since leaving Mali, and it would be my last sighting. After Onitsha the Niger splits into myriad streams that make their way to the Atlantic, and I was not intending to explore the delta region. It should have been a romantic moment, an achievement, some-thing to savour. But a huge thunderstorm was looming, it was getting dark rapidly and I wanted cover from the night – and from Nigeria. I cycled on.

Despite taking Monday off, I still awoke Tuesday with heavy limbs and a dread of leaving. One day off was not enough to restore my optimism and calm, but I wouldn't stay longer – I had caught road fever. I just wanted to get to the border – alive – and to escape into Cameroon, where the roads promised to be more peaceful.

Leaving that day did not turn out to be the wisest decision.

'*Onacha! Onacha!*' called children and adults alike as I tried to leave Onitsha. I was in Igbo country now, and this was their term for a white. I felt they were trying to make me realise my whiteness. Or maybe they were trying to be heard above the traffic noise and the tooting.

It was raining, and people were walking along the road edges, some under umbrellas, some running to get to cover quickly. The roads were slippery. Cars, trucks, buses and vans jammed together, tooting and jostling for position. It was chaos. In this tangle of people and vehicles, I could not bring myself to mount the bike. I was on some kind of dogged automatic pilot as, despite a panicky internal voice crying to go back to the hotel, I just kept pushing, placing one leg in front of the other. I really can't say why I kept going, except to get out of Nigeria.

'*Onacha!*' screamed a middle-aged man, just inches from my face, flinging spittle at me. He was not even a kid. '*Onacha!*'

'*Onacha!*' I yelled back loudly, only afterwards realising I had called him a white. He looked astonished. 'How do you like that?!' I shouted as I pushed passed him. I was always so sensitive when I was tired, but his scream and my anger seemed to jolt me alive and overcome my fear – for a while.

One time, I paused at a roadside shack to buy bananas and caused a flurry of running as people shoved to get a view of the *onacha*. They spilled out onto the highway, causing a traffic jam.

'You must not stop there,' called a man from a taxi, probably meaning well.

'It is not me, tell them!' I shouted, waving my arms like the madwoman I was and pushing through the crowd to escape.

Back on the road, it started raining again. The shoulder became more muddy, but I dared not move further out. Suddenly, the bike slid from under me and I found myself dumped, sprawled across the tarmac. I was terrified, not knowing what would bear down on me. I grabbed my bike and scrambled back to the verge.

A vehicle whooshed passed.

I was lucky. My fall had occurred during a rare break in traffic.

'Well done!' yelled someone from a passing car.

An elderly woman walking along put down the large tin bowl she was carrying on her head and came to help me pull the bicycle upright. 'Sorry,' she said, then offered me a mango from her bowl.

I tried to smile, but nothing would come. 'Thank you,' I said, finally. She was being very kind.

I stumbled a few hundred metres, then paused to recover. Children, adults and a policeman emerged from unseen houses behind the lush roadside vegetation.

'How are you?' asked the policeman politely.

'Terrible.'

'You are trying,' he said. He did not seem to have registered that I had *not* said, Fine, thank you.

'This traffic is trying to kill me!' I mumbled, trying to make him see. I was *not* thinking about the freedom and rhythm of the open road.

'Sorry,' he said, and I realised he *could* tell I was unhappy.

I breathed deeply in and slowly let my breath out, and I tried to become calmer. This was Nigeria, I thought. Despite the chaos, many of its people were friendly, polite, gregarious and full of energy.

'Well done,' they often called from cars with a wave. I even had one man stop and give me money. In Nigeria, good dancers were rewarded by notes being placed on their foreheads. It seemed this stranger was recognising my effort and I was likewise being rewarded. And there was always so much laughter.

Through my exhaustion and fear I registered that I was behaving at extremes – yelling, laughing, screaming – because life was being lived at extremes. It was definitely time for a longer pause, to have a few days off, meet some folk – but first of all, survive today, I told myself.

A few kilometres further and I arrived at a small market town, looking forward to a chance to rest. It was just a nondescript town, but I noticed a crowd gathered at the market despite the rain. An accident? I wondered. As I cycled past, I looked to my right. A *pagne* covered a body – a woman had been knocked down by a vehicle, perhaps moments before, and killed.

Horror burbled up from my stomach and I retched.

'I can't take this country!' I cried to myself, and my eye twitched convulsively.

So much for being positive and calm. I didn't stop.

Ahead a few kilometres, a car lay on its side across the road and again people were gathered around. I held my breath as I passed. The vehicle was empty; no dead body this time.

Further on again, on an uphill curve, I saw a van on its side, straddling a roadside ditch. A tow truck was trying to pull it out. I did not look as I passed, but beyond the wreck I saw a young man, standing, looking stunned. He was probably the driver.

'Was anyone hurt?' I asked, expecting the worst.

'No, it is fine,' he replied.

It was not fine, but I numbed my senses and kept going.

The busy and dangerous conditions continued to Owerri, and through the next day to Aba, where I found a hotel on the outskirts. It had been a long day's cycle (over 100 kilometres). The following day, I was heading directly east for Rivers State to the tiny town of Itu. Almost immediately after leaving Aba, the traffic died away and I was on a quiet bitumen road through lush, green vegetation all day. Even the rain had stopped. The spirits were smiling on me again.

That nightmare ride already seemed years away.

I'd survived, hadn't I? What had all the fuss been about?

In late afternoon, I arrived at the Itu turn-off and discovered Itu was actually on the Cross River, a descent of several kilometres from the main road, and, of course, the same number of kilometres back up to the main road. As I warily contemplated this, some people waved me over from a nearby bus stop. Itu, I was informed, had no accommodation. Oops. Then someone suggested I try the nearby Nigerian Newsprint Manufacturing Company site.

I cycled a couple of kilometres down the road towards Calabar, expecting some old dilapidated African works, but, after following an arrow to the right, I was surprised to find the road had led me to an impressive complex, neatly surrounded by a high fence and security guards. I presented myself at the mill gate, and it was only after I had asked to stay the night that I realised how bold this request was. Cheeky bugger. Back in the UK, would I cycle up to the gate of the Mars factory and ask for a bed?

However, my request was taken seriously, and soon I met with the human resources controller, Femi Fadeyi.

Femi and I hit it off immediately. He was a clown who had me in stitches about nothing. He had a rubber-like face, able to contort into extremes of happiness and despair to illustrate his words. And after there was always the big grin and laughter.

'We have no guest quarters available,' he said, and illustrated disappointment. 'But you can stay at my house!' Now, he grinned and showed happiness.

Oh yeah? Was this the catch? He was about forty years old and actually quite attractive, but had a gold ring on his left finger. Not that this stopped Nigerian (any?) men. I had seen a chat show on Nigerian television. 'Why is a wedding ceremony important?' was a question put to people accosted in the street. 'Well, it changes the status of a woman,' said one male, 'but it does not change the status of a man.'

'No, no – nothing like that!' Femi cried, probably having understood my hesitation. 'I am going to Calabar tonight and won't be back until very late – you will have your own room and the place to yourself!' He laughed again and held out his hands imploring me to stay. I had to laugh, too.

He got in his car, guided me toward the personnel compound – this was a big site – let me into his home, showed me my room, how the microwave and video worked, then left me. It was fantastic!

The next morning, we had breakfast together and he started trying to get me to stay the day.

'We will go to the beach – the most beautiful beach in Africa!' he exclaimed. 'And you will meet my friend Fred.' I was easily persuaded.

Fred was another funny man. He was a DJ on the local radio who hosted the late-night jazz programme, had read all of P.G. Wodehouse and was a master of Bertie Wooster impressions.

'I say, Jeeves, I'm sitting on top of the world with a rainbow round my shoulder. What do you think of that, eh what?'

As we drove down to the beach in Femi's car, Fred wanted to know all about my journey.

'Good Lord!' Fred exclaimed at various adventures, and 'Impossible!' and 'My goodness!' – all in an impeccable Bertie accent.

'What I want to know,' Femi interjected at one point, 'is how you can do without sex for so long?'

It was a good question. The worse conditions had got, the more isolated I became from people, the more I missed William's company. The evenings in the horrid hotels, after a beer, were the worst. I missed him terribly. But loyalty to William, truthfully, was only one constraint to finding someone else. I had little opportunity – I moved on too quickly, and neutered sexuality was my strategy for staying safe, distant from the abundant daily unwanted propositions. Like a gas flame, I had turned my sexuality down low. At least, I tried to.

But I wasn't going to tell Femi this. I knew a proposition, even a joking one, when I heard one, and just laughed. In fact, several Nigerian men had asked this same question. Males of other nationalities might comment on my courage, ask if I was married, but in Nigeria, the men were far more to the point.

'All that pressure building up?' Femi said as he drove through the lush, green scenery of palms, bamboo and mangoes to the coast. Driving was so fast – not like cycling – that I could not take in the scenery I was passing. Of course, I also could not hear the whooshing traffic or the kids crying, '*Onacha!*' Still, on balance, I liked cycling better – *if* it was on quiet roads and *if* I was not in a hurry. Femi laughed his very infectious laugh. 'I could not do that!'

His beach – I have no idea where it was, other than on the Bay of Biafra – was not quite the most beautiful beach in Africa. It was surrounded by swamps and was next to an oil-tank installation, complete with a large flare creating a thick pall of black smoke. After parking the car it was necessary to walk over planks to reach the white sand. The water was at low tide and very brown, churned with sand and minerals or who knows what.

(At the time, none of the issues surrounding Shell's operations and the Nigerian oil industry which were later debated and to which I became sensitised – flaring as a source of greenhouse-effect pollution, the environmental impact of the oil industry on the delta region, the rights to self-determination of the Ogoni and Ijaw peoples – was in the mainstream news. Then.)

Femi and Fred did not comment on the flares. In fact, no Nigerians I met spoke about environmental or human rights issues in relation to the oil companies. At this time, all their talk was about politics, all their venom for the corrupt military government. The presidential election was turning into farce – no results had been announced and it looked increasingly like Babangida was backing off handing over power to a civilian government. But this steamy afternoon, Fred, Femi and I were only interested in playing in the surf. Sitting in the shallows, buffeted by the waves, we drank cold Star beer straight from the bottle. Now, as I rolled back into a wave, I began to like Femi's beach and the world looked bloody good. My life might have its ups and downs, but I had never felt more intensely the good and the bad times in my life.

'Tally ho, Jeeves!' called Fred, lifting his bottle of Star in a toast. 'Let's have a whisky and soda!'

It was another quiet Sunday and I was in Calabar.

Calabar was a lovely spot, the nicest place in Nigeria – like Femi's beach, it was a question of personal taste. Unlike most Nigerian cities, it was on the ocean, well, on the estuary of the Cross River, near its mouth at the ocean. I had been in too many dusty inland towns, and it was good to see a bit of open space and water. Like so many places in the south, the Efik people of Calabar had a long history of trading with Europeans – with slaves, then palm oil.

Now, I was at Calabar Museum, housed in the former residence of the colonial governor – he had chosen a good spot, high on a hill overlooking the port and a bend in the river – and I was delighted to find, from a government notice, that bicycles had played a role in the area's history.

> In the Eastern provinces where, during the heavy rains, lorries are often bogged axle-deep in the main road, the only serious rival to the 'shank's mare' as a means of progression is the ubiquitous and multi-purpose bicycle … In the palm oil season, it is no uncommon sight in the Calabar Province to see troops of forty to fifty of these cyclists, each carrying a load of some 120–200 lbs strung out on a long line, pedalling furiously to the accompaniment of much chatter and laughter as they made for some buying centre by the river or sea … some of the bicycles in these areas were also used to carrying passengers, one first class or possibly two second class (the former paid more and did not dismount with the rider at hills), but the carriage of produce was the primary use.

I had not been so delighted by the idea of axle-deep bogs during the rain, particularly as I had been to the tiny DHL office and there was no parcel, no knobbly tyres. There was nothing to be done, however, so it was no use worrying. I would just have to cope. It was starting to rain now, heavy drops, like a huge hose had been turned on.

It was pretty quiet at the museum and I sat down at the outdoor bar and ordered a tonic. At the bar were the bartender, a security guard, and a young woman. They were all subdued, already talking quietly together.

'No one will vote in another election,' said the barman to the others. 'There is no point.'

'He has disgraced Nigeria in the eyes of the world,' said the security guard.

'He just wanted someone from the north to rule Nigeria. No one from the south is allowed to rule Nigeria,' said the woman.

The previous night, President Babangida had announced the annulment of the presidential election. He said he was still committed to the August 29 transition to democratic rule and was ordering fresh elections – with new rules and new candidates. He banned the candidates in the June elections, Tofa and Abiola (who was rumoured to have won), and announced the unbanning of other presidential aspirants he had previously banned.

'The man is mad!' continued the woman. 'He bans some and he unbans others.'

'I will not vote again,' said the security guard.

'We cannot have another Biafra,' declared the barman. His eyes looked tense. He was in his fifties, old enough to remember.

I did not join their conversation. It was their private pain.

The Biafran Civil War started in July 1967 when Lieutenant Colonel Odumegwu Ojukwa, an Igbo, fearing ongoing repression of the Igbo people after Lieutenant Colonel Yakubu Gowan, a northerner, took power in a coup, declared independence of the Republic of Biafra, in the south-east. Oil had recently been discovered in the delta region; the huge potential revenues raised the stakes. Gowan declared war on the rebels. It was dreadful. The Nigerian Army encircled and besieged Igbo lands, causing near genocide. At least 100,000 soldiers died in the fighting, but the main casualties were Igbo civilians – between half a million and two million were estimated to have died of starvation. I could remember, as a kid, seeing pictures of starving children with huge pot bellies and listless eyes, and filling small cardboard boxes with coins as a donation to help them. The rebels surrendered in January 1970.

In the early seventies, as Nigeria became one of the world's ten largest oil producers, the revenues initially were used to reinvest in the south-east and to reconstruct its infrastructure. In the long run, however, corruption by a military leadership with mainly northern ties had ensured money was diverted elsewhere. Naturally enough, this was a source of many of the grievances of the people of the delta region.

Babangida did resign in August to hand over to an interim government under Ernest Shonekan, a civilian who had been chairman of the United African company, Nigeria's largest conglomerate. In November, General Sani Abacha seized power. He was quoted as saying he would 'save the nation from chaos'. Abacha turned out to be one of the most repressive leaders of Nigeria – banning political parties, arbitrarily detaining opposition members, closing down newspapers, and imposing tight controls on the media. It was he who ordered the execution of Ken Saro-Wiwa. Abacha is now dead, as is Abiola. At the time of writing, General Abdulsalam Abubakar was in charge and promising 'free and fair' elections in 1999.

Poor Nigeria. Individuals I met often expressed the same sentiments. They were fed up with military rule, with corruption, with shortages and nepotism. Yes, they were sensitive to criticism from foreigners, but they had enough to put up with from their own leaders, so I could understand where they were coming from. It was such a tragedy. This country, with its oil wealth and the dynamism of its people, should be a powerhouse for the renaissance of Africa. For now, I was looking forward to being out of Nigeria, away from the madness.

PART TWO

LETTING GO AND SEEING THINGS

'When I let go of what I am, I become what I might be.
When I let go of what I have, I receive what I need.'

– LAO TZU'S *Tao Te Ching*

'We don't see things as they are, we see things as we are.'

– ANAIS NIN

Eleven

Why Do Whites Like to Suffer So?

Ekok, Nigeria – Beayop, Equatorial Guinea

The previous evening, I had left Nigeria at the bustling border town of Ekok, had crossed into Cameroon at the much quieter settlement of Eyumojuk, and was invited to put my tent up on the verandah of the Cameroonian police post. Rain poured heavily overnight, creating a noisy racket on the tin roof. Like so many other days in Nigeria, I had spent my last day there covering a long distance – over 130 kilometres – and did it while climbing steadily through cultivated hillscapes. Thus, despite the rain, I slept solidly. It was only this morning, setting off in a fine mist, that I realised the extraordinary change in my environment.

Forest-covered mountains lazily lay half hidden behind swirling, fluffy, white and grey clouds. Vines shrouded the tall trees, turning them into friendly ghouls and goblins and lush roadside ground cover into an impenetrable tangle. There were no signs of people or villages, and only one car had passed during the couple of hours I had been on the road. It was a fresh, restful environment that smelt musky and damp, with a musical accompaniment of birdsong and buzzing insects rather than whooshing and tooting cars.

That first day, I felt very content to be out of bustling, nerve-destroying Nigeria and into quiet, calming Cameroon – my tenth country. It seemed, then, that I had left the hard days behind.

The road now swept down a jungle-clad valley to a bridge running across a fast-flowing mountain stream, and as I cycled I enjoyed the sound of my tyres squelching through the top layer of viscous mud against the harder layer of clay below. It was raining again. I had my red Gortex jacket on over my T-shirt and shorts. Spatters of mud flicked onto my legs, but I did not care. I thought it was lovely to be cool. I had been watching my bicycle computer, waiting for the milestone to appear. As I approached the bridge, I slowed to savour 6999.9 switch to 7000.0. That was 7000 kilometres completed in exactly nine months – it was July 2. Hooray! Stopping at the bridge, I paused to look down into the tumbling white water and think back over my nine months in West Africa. I wondered what new adventures would come in the forests of Central Africa, in which I had clearly now arrived. Usually, I only thought about three days ahead – to the next biggish town and programme,

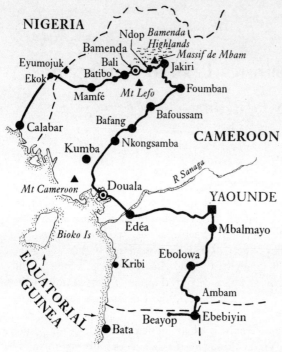

but rarely beyond. Sure enough, even thinking of all that cycling between me and Tanzania made me gulp.

Was I even half-way? I wondered.

In retrospect, this was not only halfway in time and distance, but a watershed period in how I felt about Africa and Africans. My experiences in Cameroon were about to have a significant impact on my way of relating to village people and their lives. For now, to celebrate my achievement, I drew out a pineapple I had bought in Ekok, cut myself a slice, bit into its sweet meat and let the juice dribble down my chin. Excellent.

With the passing months, the pain of being away from the special people in my life – my family and William – seemed to be growing rather than waning. On the other hand, I was feeling pretty self-satisfied that I had finally settled in to my African life. I was confident in my body and its strength to endure the journey, and my programmes had given me good insights into the lives of village women.

Reality, as in all things, was about to catch up with my complacency.

I cycled on, up the valley, down and up another. The road was still climbing and, with the ongoing rain, was becoming sloshy – a challenge to cycle along, but quite fun. Within a few kilometres, I came to a wide clearing where a small collection of wooden huts was strung out along the road. Oddly, the road was barred. A police check?

As I paused at the barrier, a male voice called out, 'Pamela! *Salut!*'

I looked towards the hut where the voice came from – it was a bar up a few concrete steps, Guinness bunting strung brightly across the front beam and a verandah to the side. Standing up waving at me was a man in a green Cameroonian police uniform and red beret. It was Anastase, from the police post where I had camped out last night.

'*Salut!*' I called, as I took off my sodden hat and bicycle mitts, and stripped off my rain jacket. Before mounting the stairs, I ferreted in my handlebar bag for a hairbrush and tissue to wipe my face, fearing I looked a big mess. I liked Anastase – my, what a body! Were all Cameroonian men going to be so cute?

His eyes looked bloodshot and weary, but I knew he had been on all-night guard duty. Now, he was drinking Guinness at 11 a.m. Still, his lithe, muscular body was beautiful: his skin was a shiny coffee brown, his palms a lovely contrasting mocha, his fingernails neatly trimmed, and his lips thick and sensual. He wore his uniform loose and his red beret askew – most dashing.

'Haven't you been in bed yet?' I asked in French.

Where was all this coming from? It seemed my attitude to African men was softening, just a teeny bit … Tut, tut. Ah well, men everywhere could be lazy, infuriating and dangerous little sods, but everywhere, some men, like this one, could be so very attractive. And so much for my sexuality being on low burner. Maybe it *was* hard to go without sex for so long.

Anastase merely shrugged and smiled.

'Sit down, Pamela,' he said a little slurrily, but with the wonderful intonation, breathy on the 'P' and long on the last syllable, that only French speakers put on my name. 'The road is closed. What do you want to drink?'

I accepted an orange soda, then asked why the road was closed.

'It is because of the rain – the road is too muddy, but it will be opened again soon, maybe in one hour.' The rain had eased and there were even a few rays of sun penetrating the heavy cloud, so I hoped the wait would not be too long. Although, with this company, who cared?

We started talking about Nigeria.

'*Ils ne sont pas sérieux,*' said Anastase. They are not serious. This was tough talking – it was what African women had said to me about African men! Tough talking about Nigeria – that is, generally knocking the country and its people – was common amongst many non-Nigerian Africans, but I found it was a favourite pastime here in Cameroon, perhaps because of the long-standing border dispute over the Bakasi peninsula (a strip of coastal land between the two countries, said to be oil rich).

We had not got far in exploring Anastase's views when the loud roar of an engine came from the direction of the border, and an overlander truck lumbered into view. It was a private truck, not one of the main companies that operate truck trips across Africa, and this one looked like a home-made conversion with an open-sided cabin built onto the flatbed. Standing for a better look, I could see some whites on the roof and in the rear section. I was amazed – I hadn't seen any European travellers since Grand Popo, nearly two months before.

'They'll come over,' said Anastase. Moments later, there was the sound of a second engine – a vehicle that had been parked further up the road beyond the raingate came back and a man rushed to lift the barrier.

'Ah, that is my car,' said Anastase. It was his colleagues who had been at an office, or another bar, further along the road. Evidently, they were returning to the border. He rushed to finish his Guinness, wish me good luck and leave. *C'est la vie*, I thought. My gorgeous friend was gone, opportunity lost.

'Hi, I'm Dave,' said a new voice, in English. 'Are you on the bicycle?' It was a guy from the truck, a cute, smiling chap with curly black hair.

'Hi,' I said. 'Yeah, that's me, I'm Pamela.' Another brief friendship commenced, and again, I thought that life on the road was pretty good.

I made Mamfé that night. It was a pleasant, small town, with a fresh, mountain air feel, and, as part of Anglaphone Cameroon, was English speaking.

A German colony before World War I, Cameroon was captured by the allies, then separated into an English section, roughly one fifth of the country in the south-west (where I was now travelling, but confusingly called the North-West Province), and the rest, which was French. At independence, a huge political issue for Cameroonians was whether to reunite as one country or whether the English section should join as a state of the Federation of Nigeria. In a United Nations-sponsored plebiscite, the majority decided to reunite and the country received independence in 1960.

I was eager to be pushing forward in this new country. From Mamfé, I would head into the mountains to Bamenda, then go higher across the Grassfields and Ndop plains of the Bamenda highlands to Jakiri and Foumban. From there, I would lose altitude to Bafoussam, Bafang, Nkongsamba and Douala, the main trading city on the Atlantic coast and next Shell stop. It was a distance of 750 kilometres, so I should be in Douala in about two weeks. There was a more direct route to Douala via Kumba, but all the roads in this English-speaking North-West Province were marked as 'partially improved earth roads liable to be impracticable in bad weather', advice not be taken lightly. A complaint of the Anglophone Cameroonians is that, under the two leaders since independence (Ahmadou Ahidjo from the north, and Paul Biya, the current president, from the south) they have felt their part of the country has consistently received less than its fair share of political representation and of investment – for example, in roads. Still, I figured if I was going to have bad roads I might as well have good scenery – and the roads of the Bamenda high plains were all marked on the Michelin as being exceptionally beautiful.

Mamfé to Bamenda was marked as 205 kilometres. Only one other town was marked on the Michelin between Mamfé and Bamenda and that was Batibo, 123 kilometres away. As I quit early from Mamfé the next day, I planned to make Batibo that night, and Bamenda the second night.

'The road is not fine,' Anastase had said, as had a grease-covered truck driver I met near the Mamfé market. As had the young lad who served me a beer at the small hotel in Mamfé where I stayed.

I had known bad roads before. I was a veteran of the rubble of the Fouta

Djalon and the sands of Mali. Their comments could not faze me.

For the first 20 kilometres, the clay road was okay, if a trifle slippery in places. Then, I reached the Bamenda junction and took a left turn, heading for the high plains. The vegetation was a little like the border road to Mamfé – lots of foliage fighting for light. The road was very narrow, just one car width with passing places, and this emphasised the sense of remoteness. There were mileage markers by the side of the road – yes, miles. Did this suggest the road hadn't had significant repairs since the time of the imperial British? Villages, people and vehicles were few and far between, but it meant I could clearly hear the sounds of birds and insects. There seemed to be an awful lot of insects.

After about an hour's cycling on relatively flat terrain, my quiet world was suddenly turned upside-down. Cycling around a bend, I found myself in a section of road enclosed by walls of mud and was alarmed to see a sedan skidding and zigzagging wildly towards me at full rev. With uncommon speed, I lurched the bike toward a mud bank! Happily, the driver regained control, zagged the car away and missed me by inches. Almost immediately, though, the sedan's roar turned to a whine – it had got stuck in another deep trench of mud. By this time, several muscular, shirtless, clay-coated men had come running down the road, passed me without a second glance, and surrounded the vehicle to push it out. Following that, a sorry line of people, probably passengers from the sedan, came picking their way more carefully through the mushy substance. Women held up their *pagnes* and men had their trouser legs rolled above the knee, but they were all in sludge up to their calves. I gawked at them, wondering what I was going to do to get through this section.

I started trying to push my bicycle ... but only slithered sideways and landed on my bum. Suddenly, like the vehicle, I was surrounded by four eager, mud-caked hunks who grabbed at the bicycle. In an instant, the bicycle with its heavy load was lifted into the air and carried forward about 300 metres through the worst of the mud trenches. I could only scramble and slide behind.

'Dash me something,' said one of the men as I arrived to retrieve my beloved friend. I had been a bit worried to be separated from him.

'Dash me,' called another, with lovely, long-lashed eyes.

These local villagers had a business helping push vehicles through the mud – 'dash me' meant give me some money, a tip, and, for once, I was happy to oblige.

I asked if the road continued like this.

'The road is not fine,' said one of my strapping assistants. Oh.

'It is bad like this at mile twenty-two,' said another. Apparently, villages and places on this road were referred to by the mileage markers. I was near mile seventeen.

Nearly as muddy as the men, I mounted the bicycle and cycled forward.

The road started rising, winding its muddy course into the mountains. The sticky mud kept forming clumps under the mudguards – mud catchers was a better name – and I frequently ground to a halt, needing to dismount and carve the mud out with a stick, or, in desperation, with my fingers. I looked like I had been in a brawl with a tub of chocolate ice cream!

Sure enough, at mile twenty-two there was another long stretch of deep mud trenches. Before, I had felt a twinge of guilt at letting others push the bike and wondered whether it was a Rule of the Journey that I had to do my own pushing. Blow that, I now thought, as I paused, waiting for handsome village assistants to appear.

No one came. Blast. No entrepreneurial spirit here.

I heaved and tugged and slid the bike through.

The day became an ongoing endurance test. I stopped taking in the lush vegetation which enclosed me and instead concentrated on the defects of the road. Frequently, it turned to edge-to-edge viscous mud and water holes. Initially, I dismounted and pushed my way through, letting the wet mud seep into my shoes. The mud squelched between my toes, and, of course, had a way of transferring itself from my legs to my hands to my face. Perhaps it performed cosmetic miracles – free clay pack treatments! Soon, however, I got bored with dismounting – there were too many of these wet patches – and I discovered that, with strong arms, I could stay upright as the bicycle and I slithered our way through the clay.

Rapidly, in these difficult conditions, I started identifying with the bicycle as a team – together, against the odds, we would make it! I guess I was already feeling a little lonely.

In late morning, I arrived at a small collection of huts and stopped. After carrying the weight of mudguards for over 7000 kilometres, I hit mud and discovered they were superfluous. My bicycle was about to become very streamlined. A small crowd of children, men and women gathered to watch me unpack the bike, turn it upside down and remove the mudguards.

'White!' called one small child, setting off a chorus.

'White!'

'White!'

I wondered how they could tell. My skin had taken on an ochre hue.

Finally, I was finished and dashed the front mudguard to a startled villager. I kept the rear one as I wondered if I was being a little precipitous in giving them away just yet, and strapped it to the back sack. It lasted ten more days before it too was given away.

Despite the ongoing difficulties of the day, I was more cheerful than I had been on Nigerian roads – at least with mud, I knew I would arrive alive.

However, I would arrive slowly. During the day I kept revising my destination back from my original target, Batibo, at mile seventy-four. In early afternoon, I met a rare passing villager and asked about another, nearer village. Widikum, he told me, at mile fifty-four. By mid-afternoon, I knew that was too far and asked another villager I encountered for an even nearer destination. Kendem, he told me, at mile thirty-seven. That would do. By now I was getting worn down by these road conditions and things weren't quite as much fun.

The sight of neat huts edging the road and people working in their compounds cheered me up considerably. It was Kendem, a mere sixty-two kilometres from Mamfé, yet it was near dusk and I had been on the road for ten long hours and, for the first time in Africa, was feeling remarkably cold. Now, knowing a stop, shower, dry clothes and food were imminent, my energy and good spirits bounced back.

My dirty appearance in their midst near dusk must have surprised the Kendem villagers, but they took it in their stride.

'White!'

'White!'

'Dash me something!'

Well, almost in their stride.

I paused in the light drizzle and soon three young men gathered around me. After exchanging greetings, I asked for a village chief so I could find somewhere to stay, but the youths looked at me blankly. I asked about the police or administrative centre. One boy in a muddy yellow T-shirt suggested I stay with him, but I wasn't keen, and soon discovered that further along there was a health centre with a verandah – important for pitching my tent on what promised to be another very wet night.

Arriving at a cement building, I halted and young children gathered around me. I asked for the doctor; two boys ran to the building across the road and soon, a short young man in white shirt and black pants picked his way across the road under an umbrella. He showed more surprise at my arrival than the villagers, but rapidly agreed to letting me put up my tent on the centre's verandah. However, he seemed agitated to get back inside his dry home. I could see his wife preparing his dinner in the compound, and I didn't blame him. (Of course, his wife was getting wet!)

A little rain and cold weren't going to keep the children from their enter- tainment, so, feeling playful, I mimed a magic performance and, after unloading the panniers, erected the tent with a flourish. First, I flung open the tent roll, flapping it in the air as if to show there was nothing inside. Then, letting it lie, I waved a cluster of short, folded poles in the air. Unknown to the children, the poles were connected by an internal elastic. I held the end of one pole and made an underarm throw, letting the others sweep free. *Voilà!* Click, click, click! The internal elastic flipped the aluminium sections together to create a single long, flexible pole. What magic! My audience took a step backwards and bewildered stares turned into shy giggles and happy laughter.

Having set up my home for the night, I asked about bathing. My energy was flagging, and the sooner I could get past washing to the eating stage the better.

'You can go in the river,' said one teenage girl who was watching. She told me her name was Celia and said she would show me the way with her friend, Rose.

'Go away,' I told the other children and waved goodbye. I wanted to have a private bath, and adopted African directness to put my request across. As expected, it had little effect, and Celia, Rose and I were followed by an enthusiastic and growing crowd to the river. It was like being the Pied Piper.

I lathered up in my bra and undies, feeling incredibly self-conscious in front of my vast, squealing audience. Another man was washing further upstream and we studiously avoided each other's gaze, but, apparently, children did not have the same rules of etiquette. From a variety of lookout points, at least fifty children stared.

I sighed, gritted my teeth, and tried to still that screeching internal voice. My Africanisation had not gone as far as I'd hoped.

As quickly as possible, I finished lathering and leapt into the cold, clean, fast-running water for a rinse. Rose took my mud-encrusted socks to wash and after a lot of scrubbing and beating they emerged remarkably white again. Of course, she used half my cake of soap.

'Dash me something,' called Rose. I gave her the remaining soap, which she liked because mine had scent.

'Dash me something,' asked Celia. I gave her my moisturiser. My toiletries bag was becoming very slim indeed! Of course, I could replace everything in Bamenda.

'Dash me something!' cried children from their lookout points.

'Dash me ... dash me something!'

I had started a riot and, now, I was getting fed up. I was clean, and having finished dressing, had on dry clothes. However, I was tired, aching and still very hungry.

'No,' I said, and huffed off to my tent in the gloomy light, my mob scrambling after me.

Night fell quickly, so I could not take my muddy bicycle to the river for a bath. A fierce thunder and lightning storm also started, and with it came a very heavy downpour – too heavy to venture out to find food and anyway, with the coming of the storm, probably most cooks would have fled home.

I clambered inside my tent and foraged in my food bag for supplies. There wasn't much. Somehow, I had ended up with a cabbage and Bournvita drink crystals. The cabbage was bought in Mamfé. Normally, I hate cabbage but I was getting so few green vegetables that when I saw it in Mamfé market I pounced on it with the glee I normally reserved for pizza. Tonight, I hated cabbage again and wondered at my sanity in carrying the thing. Without a stove, I could only eat it raw anyway, so I ate the Bournvita instead.

By 8 p.m., I had pulled on all my dry clothes – only a couple of T-shirts in addition to my one cotton Africa outfit (my jumper had been jettisoned in hot Ghana) – and was inside my silk sleeping sheet shivering, hungry and wishing the doctor had invited me to join him for dinner.

I dreamed of being in a warm bed with William, but that didn't help at all.

In the morning, I was ravenous and stiff.

The first chore was to wash my bicycle. He was taken to the river for a bath, and the wee mob gathered to watch this eccentric behaviour too. I think I spent more time on getting him clean than I had on me yesterday afternoon. Then, when I returned, I found the encrusted mud had stretched the brake cables and I needed to do some adjusting and lubricating.

Finally, I went in search of food. I was hungry enough to pass a death sentence on any chicken available for roasting. All I could find was a cheerful woman selling some boiled potatoes and fried plantain. They tasted very good and provided fuel for the road. As well as paying her, I dashed her the cabbage. But there was no coffee for sale, so no caffeine boost.

The road from Kendem to Widikum was steeper than that of the previous day and there were further deep mud holes to contend with. Being wet and covered in mud was even less fun than the day before. I was still hungry and there were no villages, only a few collections of huts, and no women cooking. Late morning, I found one woman selling puff-puffs – dough balls fried in oil. I bought a few and devoured them hungrily.

The buoyancy of the past few days was behind me and I was beginning to feel very lonely on this quiet road, more so than in Nigeria, where, during the day, the traffic kept me preoccupied with survival. I kept revisiting William and my parents and friends in my mind, a kind of metaphysical transportation away from my present circumstances. I could see the images clearly. Fragments of conversations or words from letters replayed in my head, but these visits seemed to be making me feel lonelier. How could I overcome this? It was becoming another burden, a kind of hollow emptiness, sometimes a physical ache in my gut, and it accompanied the physical tiredness and aching of the long trudge.

A woman walking downhill came around a corner and our eyes met. She looked bloody tired too and walked at a slow, heavy pace. She carried a large cluster of plantains, freshly cut from a tree, on her head.

'*Aysha!*' she called. She sounded fatigued.

'*Aysha!*' I said back, having no idea what this meant, but hoping I had said hallo, and had not called her a white.

I kept going and saw an elderly man. He was sitting on a bank, seemingly in the middle of nowhere, holding a large, boat-shaped plantain leaf over his head as an umbrella. Perhaps he was having a rest, I thought.

'*Aysha!*' he said as I passed him.

'*Aysha!*' I said, giving him a tired smile which he returned. He looked very old and wrinkled.

The road kept going up through a dark cave of vegetation that smelled of decay. I kept pushing and every now and then reaching down to scratch my legs. They were very itchy – damned insects had bitten me.

A young man in a wet cotton shirt and trousers that clung to his skinny frame came freewheeling down the hill towards me on his large, clattering Chinese bicycle. He paused by me.

'Why do whites like to suffer so?' he asked.

Did I look like I was suffering?

I didn't know what to say and anyway I didn't have much spare energy for talking. I shrugged and smiled and then he was gone. However, his comment struck a chord – I was suffering; I was here by my own choice – and as I trudged along, I started wondering why I was putting myself through this pain and loneliness, what I was gaining that made it worthwhile.

Was I finding myself? Huh! What a fool thing to search for that was. Did I think my true self was going to appear around one of these corners? Or magically, my inhibitions and crotchetiness would slide away and I would be a different person? If anything, I had confirmed I was the same person here or in the city – stubborn and moody, interested in business and women's issues, and needy of clean clothes and flush toilets. All I was getting was bigger muscles and scars. All I was finding out about was pain and suffering, and only sometimes having rollicking fun. Did I need to come to Africa for this?

And what about Adventure? Was I finding that? Well, yes, but it wasn't an adrenalin rush-giving event. This was no bungee jump. For me, the rush was the freedom I had and the unpredictability of where I might end up any day and who I might meet. Living on my wits and physical resources felt good. Actually, I realised with a start, a lot of the adventure was that I was feeling life, I wasn't watching it.

In my luxury retreat in Accra, I had enthusiastically likened my journey to a metaphor for life – I was persevering despite setbacks, achieving little by little. I liked the emotional ups and downs – the essential part of the African experience – because they made me feel alive. Was adventure best in retrospect?

I supposed I was finding out more about Africa, although parts didn't seem that different from anywhere. Men seemed incorrigible and sexy simultaneously, as the world over, and women seemed to have too much responsibility for too little reward, as the world over. That was a big insight, I thought. Worth all this loneliness?

My village nights and city programmes had taught me about African big man politics, and western collusion, but I'd known something of that before. The new knowledge gained was about the second tier of life in Africa – daily life in the villages, the part that clearly kept the continent going despite everything else. I knew about the injustices, caring, responsibility, hard work and suffering that made up village life. But so what? What good was it going to do me? Or the people I was meeting?

Why didn't I just go home, escape this daily struggle, this suffering, this awful, gnawing loneliness and just go back to my nice little life and man? That day, I was too tired and depressed to think of answers to these very good questions.

Eventually, late in the afternoon I made Widikum (at mile fifty-four). It had a real cowboy town feel to it. Houses were made of wood with broad verandahs, and people bustled with energy I had not seen since Nigeria. The miniscule town, just a large village really, was located in a broad clearing and it was good to see daylight after the claustrophobic dark forest tunnel of the road. I searched out some food – more plantain and puff-puffs. I was too late for breakfast and too early for dinner so, unfortunately, there were no stews available. However, I bought some rice, onions and tomatoes. During the day I had been looking out for dry twigs and branches – not very successfully in this damp climate, but had accumulated a little pile I was now carrying in my food pannier. The rice, vegetables and wood were my insurance that tonight I would have a hot meal.

As I ate my last puff-puffs by the road, I guess I looked a wet and bedraggled creature. A bush taxi arrived from the direction of Bamenda. Traffic was rare – this was the first car I had seen today. A man extricated himself from the taxi, needing to climb over someone else to get out. He was in his thirties, dressed in a suit that looked incongruous here. He dusted himself off, then saw me. We exchanged greetings; he asked about my journey, I asked about his work. He was a clerk who worked in a government office in tiny Widikum and had been in Bamenda for shopping. Abruptly, he asked the same question as the young boy on the bicycle.

'Why do whites like to suffer so?' And he followed up, 'We work to get money and comfort, to stop ourselves and our families suffering. We see the videos of whites living in beautiful houses with beautiful women. We see whites pass in big, air-conditioned cars, looking clean and rich. Then we see whites like you, dirty and struggling. You don't need to be here. Why do you take on our suffering and struggle like us?'

Even with my earlier reflection, I found it a hard question to answer.

'I feel more alive and free here,' I said, although was the suffering today making me feel alive? I guessed it was. 'Maybe I'm just a bit crazy,' I laughed, my first laugh today.

The man related to that, nodded and laughed too.

'How is the road between here and Bamenda?' I asked, trying to change the subject.

'It is not fine,' he said, and added with a wry smile, 'You will suffer.' Shit.

Later that afternoon, I decided to stop at a small hamlet perched on the side of a mountain, just short of Batibo. I could not go farther today – my legs were like cement and would not budge. During this long, difficult day of pushing and trudging, I had only made 30 kilometres. It had been debilitating to push not ride, and by day's end I was like the Duracell bunny running out of battery power. Kinetic and mental energy were very, very slow. I felt more dead than alive.

One youth in a blue tracksuit and spiked running shoes came forward from the small group of two or three families who gathered at my arrival – I think it was because he spoke the best English. His name was Peter and he was a quiet, serious lad of about eighteen who I immediately liked. He showed me where to pitch my tent – a little way from the mud-walled and straw-roofed huts on some flat, high ground. At last, I had emerged from the darkness of the forest into the more sparsely vegetated high plains. The air was fresh and I had a magnificent view down towards jungle and crop-clad valleys, and up towards sun-covered grass-lands. The rain had stopped and the skies were clearer than I had seen for several days. Only a few people remained watching me erect my tent, and it seemed more personal than the mobbing by children in Kendem.

Peter guided me to a nearby stream to bathe, and left me in a little fairy grotto with a burbling stream. I stripped and used my plastic cup to scoop the icy water over myself. It was invigorating, helped my energy come back and I stood shivering on the mossy stones, looking down into the crystal-clear water. My ankles started aching from the cold, but I did not care. This was why I suffered, I thought, to experience magical places like this. Tough adventures were not only best in retrospect, they helped me appreciate small joys at the end of the day. I went back to my tent with a lighter heart and the ability to smile.

An old lady, probably a grandmother, from one of the families was walking down the road as I returned.

'Good evening,' I said.

'Good evening,' she replied. She was quite short and bent over, wearing *pagnes* that had been washed threadbare. I told her I had been bathing, and she shook her head sadly.

'Ah, the water is too cold!' she exclaimed, surprising me with her comment as well as her English. 'It gives rheumatism.'

It was near dusk and I walked to the edge of the steep hillside to watch the sun setting behind the mountains I had climbed through. Peter approached me, quietly, and we sat together for a while. Mist was forming in the valleys and the sun was an orange ball, descending fast. I sat watching the fabulous sunset light up the sky behind the silhouetted mountains and saw glorious, heart-lifting beauty.

Suddenly, Peter spoke. 'This land is so bad – so many hills and valleys, such steep sides – it makes working in the fields very hard.' I started seeing it with his eyes, and nodded in agreement.

Near dark, I went back to my tent, and in the rapidly spreading dark, tried lighting a fire on the flat ground nearby, using the twigs I had collected during the day. I was very hungry and badly wanted some hot food. However, after many matches and much blowing, I was still only getting smoke, well, steam really. Of course, I had a small audience and was embarrassed by my manifest lack of fire-lighting skills.

'Can you help me get it started?' I asked Peter, who seemed a competent young man.

'Oh, no,' Peter said in amazement. 'We always use kerosene stoves!'

I resigned myself to a cold meal of tomato, onions and puff-puffs. It was pretty awful, and afterwards, I sat shivering outside watching the stars. It was dark, there was no moon, and the families had returned to their huts. I scratched at the itchy bites from the insects of the dank forest world below me, and thought about my series of misperceptions tonight. I saw a magical bathing place; the grandmother saw cold water that gives rheumatism. I saw a glorious sunset; Peter saw hard work. I tried cooking over a fire; villagers preferred kerosene stoves. So much for my knowledge of village life, I thought wryly. It was so hard not to ascribe my own values and feelings to the lives of others.

Only a few days before on the road to Mamfé, I had been self-congratulatory that I didn't sentimentalise villager's lives. 'What a shame that television is coming to the villages!' exclaimed one of the Europeans I had met from the truck. 'They will lose their culture. They don't know how lucky they are.' A load of sentimental claptrap. These villagers knew their lives were hard, I had thought, and that there should be a more comfortable way. Television would not make them *want* change.

But tonight, and probably at other times, I had fallen into the same traps and been guilty of treating them like specimens, their lives like a *National Geographic* documentary. These people knew what their priorities were. I had a lot to learn.

After two more days of slow travel and little food, I was only a few kilometres outside Bamenda. The road had not been fine, but now I was in a heavy rainstorm and rivers of muddy water rushed down or across the road. At some points I had to wade through deep, fast-flowing streams. Too bad! Nothing was going to stop me getting to Bamenda now.

Just as I crossed onto bitumen, letting out a cry of joy, the rain ceased. Houses appeared and suddenly I saw Bamenda Modern Bakery and smelt fresh bread. I screeched to a halt, and with hat and rain jacket dripping water, I marched into the shop for a *pain au chocolat*.

'You have come from Mamfé?' asked the shopkeeper in a shocked tone. Yes, after four days, I had arrived.

Bamenda, capital of the North-West Province, was a large town with a friendly feel, crisp, clean mountain air and plenty of pine trees. Commercial Avenue was the main shopping and commercial strip, and one of my first chores was to buy a new stove. No more wood fires nor bucolic sentimentalism for me – I was going to use Camping Gaz.

Bamenda was also politically important: it was the home of John Fru Ndi, the popular leader of the main opposition party, who was a bookseller here. Since 1982, Paul Biya had been the unelected president of Cameroon, but presidential elections had been held the previous October, as agreed under the newly agreed multi-party democratic constitution. John Fru Ndi had supposedly lost – polling 37 per cent of the vote to Biya's 40 per cent – but observers described the elections as a sham. Poor Cameroon was suffering from another dictator who would not accept that his time was up, that people did not want him. Although opposition to Biya's rule started in the Anglophone provinces, it was now widespread. In 1991, a general strike had been called; it was still being practised. People were on strike from Monday to Friday, resulting in a '*ville morte*'. Commerce, usually the purchase of essentials, took place after hours – if at all. The economy of what had once been one of the wealthiest African countries was in tatters. The opposition had won a new constitution, but Biya was still in power. In fact, demonstrations since the elections had resulted in the house arrests of Fru Ndi and other opposition leaders, and reports by Amnesty International of mass arrests and deaths in the western provinces.

I looked for Fru Ndi's bookshop but couldn't find it.

While walking around Bamenda, I met an Australian coffee-processing expert, Tony Marsh, who was working there. Bamenda is wealthy from the coffee grown in the surrounding highlands. Tony invited me to stay with himself and his wife Jacqui at their home at Upper Station, the residential area for wealthy Cameroonians and expats that was located at the top of a high scarp above Bamenda. It was a tough ride up the steep scarp road (I insisted on cycling – still choosing to suffer!) but superb to be looked after for two days, to have coffee and croissant breakfasts, and to wear clean, dry clothes borrowed from Jacqui while she washed mine in the washing machine. In fact, I think the best thing was wearing something different from the modest wardrobe I carried and which rotated on a short monotonous cycle.

But soon, it was time to face the elements again. I was setting off on the ring road, a scenic road around the Grassfields, said to be an area of high, hilly meadows and a highlight of the Bamenda highlands. My plan was to leave Bamenda, take 109 kilometres of this road eastwards to the tiny towns of Ndop and Jakiri, then leave it and turn south for another 100 kilometres to Foumban (not a provincial capital, but capital of the Bamoun people who lived in this province, and therefore an important centre). Given my experience on the road from Mamfé, I expected this to take four days.

At morning coffee before my departure, Tony and Jacqui suggested I take a short cut to Sagbo, a tiny village, not on my Michelin, but which they said was a few kilometres past the junction of the short cut with the Bamenda to Ndop section of the ring road.

'It's very scenic that way, as well as shorter,' Jacqui said brightly.

The ring road for Ndop left from lower down in the town and then required me to climb out of the Bamenda basin, again. I was already high, I thought, so surely this scenic short cut would be a better proposition.

Famous last words.

The first 5 kilometres were vehicle-churned, damp mud that was difficult to cycle, but not impossible. Then, the road became steeper, and it became clear I was crossing a desolate mountain pass that even a goat would find difficult. Rain soon arrived and the road surface turned into a shiny slick of slippery mud. I stopped cycling and pushed, but slithered further back down the hill than I progressed up it! In one uncontrolled slide backwards towards a ravine, I aborted with a neat belly flop, became as slick with mud as the road surface, and gave up. I unloaded the bike, and walked up the mountain 100 metres carrying the panniers in two loads, and then went back on a third trip for the bicycle. I repeated the process until, two hours later, I finally arrived at the col just as a wild thunder and lightning storm broke around me. I saw a lonesome, small tree, and sought imaginary protection from the icy pellets of rain.

Breakfast with brewed coffee seemed an age away.

I was freezing and ate a Cameroonian chocolate bar (I had stocked up with them in Bamenda) for an energy boost.

The road down was as slippery as on the ascent and I knew any attempt to ride would be like hopping on a plastic mat and taking a water slide down the mountain. I dug my heels into the mud before bearing the weight of the bike, and leant backwards into the mountain using my weight against the fierce pull of gravity – and still had several frightening slides downhill.

Finally, after starting at 9 a.m., at 4 p.m. I arrived at a small village and had covered just 11 kilometres! The village was just a few wooden houses with tiny, well-kept gardens of flowering bushes and tiny hedges, but it felt like a return to civilisation. The rain had stopped; I tried riding – the road was continuing downhill, but at a lesser gradient – and landed on my backside. So, still more pushing – I wished I had my knobbly tyres.

However, as I continued walking out of the village, the sun began to shine, the sky turned bluer and the world seemed a friendlier place than it had been on the exposed col. In fact, now that I could see for more than 10 metres, I realised the scenery was dramatically beautiful. The narrow, shining, ochre road swept between high, emerald-green grass dotted with dainty flowering plants. Grassy tombola hills and exposed, high granite cliffs glistened from the rain. I could hear people's voices, a bubbling brook and chirping birds. All was fresh and bright and open.

Then, I saw an old man standing in the road, watching my approach.

'Where is your man?' he asked abruptly, when I paused by him.

'I don't have one!' I said proudly – but I wondered where mine was. I conjured up William in my mind as I pushed forward and he stayed there a while, until there was a stabbing physical pain and I did not want to remember him any more.

'*Aysha!*' called an old woman who was walking towards me, hunched over with a load of what looked like lavender on her back. As she raised her neck, her eyes, glazed with what looked like extreme tiredness, caught mine.

'*Aysha,*' I replied, thinking my eyes probably looked pretty glazed too. I kept pushing, resolving to find out what that word meant – tomorrow.

The mud seemed stickier now, less slippery. After a couple of hours without rain it was drying, so I mounted the bike and started cycling, slowly, through the rolling green scenery. At 5 p.m. and 15 kilometres completed, I did reach the main Bamenda to Ndop road. It had been an eight-hour scenic short cut!

At this late evening hour, in a rain-cleansed light, the scenery became even more spectacular, reminiscent of the Scottish highlands. At each bend, a little waterfall appeared and mist hung on the high mountains. In the dimming light, the rock faces shone brightly.

After a couple of kilometres, I reached Sagbo, a small town where I might have stayed the night. However, Tony and Jacqui had recommended I push on to Bamessing, where there was a Presbyterian mission and some Swiss people they knew.

'It is only 10 kilometres beyond Sagbo,' Tony had said. I should have known what to do with their advice by now – but I kept going, lured by the thought of a shower and a dry night. What I had not realised was that Bamessing was at the base of a 10-kilometre zigzag descent to the Ndop plains. The road started going down almost directly after leaving Sagbo. Fortunately, the 10-kilometre descent was tarred, a unique treat in the North-West Province. Unfortunately, it started to rain again. Icy, hurting rain. Then, I realised this was not rain – it was hail! Big bullets of ice were pelting me at 6 degrees north of the equator in Africa.

Down, down, down went the road. I had never imagined that down could be bad. The road was steep and slippery, running with water, and, despite gripping the brake levers tightly, the wet brake pads slipped against the tyre rubber, only slowing my speed marginally – barely enough to maintain steering control and avoid going over the edge! By the end, the pain in my hands had me screaming out loud!

Finally, reaching the flat, I could stop the bicycle – in the middle of a river flooding across the road.

Soon, I found the Presbyterian mission and, kindly, with little fuss, they gave me a bed. After a massive 27 kilometres today, I was too tired for conversation, took the bed gratefully, felt happy to be inside from the wild night, and slept deeply.

As usual, by the next morning my energy and optimism had recovered, and I left early to pass through the lowlands of the Ndop basin. These were the Grassfields – there was high, green grass and ripening maize and the scene looked pretty against a backdrop of craggy, grass-covered mountains and a blue sky. It was a Sunday, so as I approached Ndop, I passed a lot of men, women and children in their Sunday best, going to or coming from church. I paused for a drink and a few passing families also stopped.

'*Aysha!*' said one man. He was thin, wore spectacles, and a small girl in a lace dress held his hand.

'*Aysha!*' I said, then took a chance and asked him what *Aysha* meant.

'*Aysha,*' he repeated, then continued seriously: 'It means, I recognise your struggle.'

I thought it was a Very Fine greeting.

I continued across the plains, but by early afternoon, the sun disappeared, clouds rolled in and the rain started. Blast. The road became muddier and I slowed. My energy reserves were depleting, and despite bites of chocolate, within an hour I felt weak. The bicycle and I suddenly took a slide in a slippery patch. The bicycle and panniers on one side, were covered in gooey, brown mud. My shorts were sticky with mud and my shoes had become mud-heavy galoshes. I kept going for a short while but when I saw an open-sided shelter amongst fields by the roadside, I took a composure stop. I used my stove to boil some water and make myself coffee while the rain pelted down outside. I was really fed up with mud.

Suddenly, an old woman emerged from amongst the high corn. She looked like she was heading homewards after a hard day in the fields. Her clothes were ragged and as wet as mine.

'*Aysha!*' she called, and as our eyes met I could see the exhaustion and pain in her eyes. It was a common look in this part of the world. We were all feeling the same way.

'Thank you,' I said. '*Aysha!*' I said it kindly, and I meant it.

Later that afternoon, I struggled up another lonely, mud and rock mountain road, this time to Jakiri, up from the Ndop Basin. It was perhaps better than the previous day's mountain pass – at least I did not have to unload the bike. However, it was still very hard – sweaty pushing in intermittent rain through greasy mud. The effort required to keep going today, and yesterday, had been relentless, and my batteries were running down again.

Suddenly, a couple of vans appeared, surprising me. Vehicles were still very few and far between.

As they approached I saw the messages painted on their nose. 'Nothing Good Without Effort!' said the first as it flashed by. 'Patience!' was written on the second. Good advice.

Eventually, arriving into a small village, I stopped at a bar to ask about the route to Jakiri. The incurious men suggested a short cut. Another short cut? Given my experiences, I was wary, but as it was already dusk, I could certainly use one.

'Is it up?' I asked. This was my primary route-selection criteria.

'No. It is fairly flat,' said one man. After more probing, they agreed it was about 2 kilometres, that I would save 4 kilometres. With some misgivings, I decided to take their advice – the light was failing.

The 'short cut' turned out to be a slippery walking track – better described as a stream – fairly flat, but clinging to the side of a steep hill. There was one point where I spent some five minutes slipping and sliding, certain I was going to break a leg, as I tried to get the bicycle and I up a small slope.

By the time I rejoined the main road, my batteries were completely dead and not even a chocolate boost could revive me. I had to switch to emergency reserves – pep talks, out loud, alternately scolding myself for putting me here, and soothing myself that it would be all okay soon. Either way, the bottom line was keep going; my legs obeyed and I trudged on in the dim light. I could not trust myself to cycle, even on the gentle downhills appearing now, as I just did not have the energy.

Where the hell is Jakiri?! In a burst of anger, I suddenly yelled this to the wind, but even the energy to be angry was fleeting.

I fell into a numb silence and pushed on through the now enveloping dark night.

Suddenly, there were headlights, a lone car came toward me, then stopped.

'You are staying here?' the driver asked with a grin. I managed a faint nod. 'The only hotel is back there,' he said, and I realised I had passed it.

There was no sign for the 'Trans-African Hotel', as he called it, but the man showed me the turning, and some young boys, appearing magically from the night, helped me push the bicycle up the mud slope to the simple, quiet hotel. I had arrived.

A man showed me to a concrete-floored cell, left me and I wheeled the bike inside. I unloaded the sacks, then lay on the hard bed, feeling very strange – my eyes were open, but my mind and body had shut down. Finally, sleep came.

The numbness in my brain was still there the next morning. My mind took in images and processed ideas slowly, my heavy body felt like it belonged to someone else. The ride from Mamfé and the last two days had sapped me of my energy and for once, I could not bounce back. I lay in bed, processed that I was still in my wet clothes, and saw my bicycle in the corner, unloaded of his sacks, filthy with mud and looking forlorn.

'Good morning, Ibn,' I said in an exhausted slur. From somewhere in my tired brain, I had decided my closest companion should have a name and that he should be called Ibn, after Ibn Battuta. It means 'son of' so his name would be Ibn Watson, son of Watson. Appropriate, really.

Eating and packing were done in slow motion. I went to shower, again saw my bicycle in the corner looking muddy and registered that Ibn could be wheeled into the shower.

So, I took a shower with him.

Oh, hell. What was I thinking? Ibn had such a thick mud coating that the run-off completely clogged the drainage system. Muddy water backed up and created a lake in the bathroom. I knew I should be horrified, but felt numb. Emotions, as well as thoughts, were just not registering very well. I got into slow-motion action, trying to mop up the lake with toilet paper, but with very little impact – even after a half hour. There was just too much mud. I wondered what could I say to the man from the hotel?

'I took a shower with my bike and clogged up your drain.'

I might have stayed another day, but now, feeling cowardly and guilty, I just packed up, left some extra money in the room and stumbled out.

As I left the small town of Jakiri for Foumban, which I expected to be two muddy cycle days away, I barely registered what it looked like. Cognition, emotions, reflections remained subdued. What I noticed was the minutiae of my existence, and I was very sorry for myself. The mud was sticky and clumping on the tyres, so within minutes of starting cycling, I had to stop and peel back mud with my hands. Again, I had mud thick beneath my nails, over my clothes and splotching my legs. It was raining, so rapidly the skin on my fingers wrinkled and would remain that way all day. The insect bites I'd scratched were now infected and, while wet all the time, had no hope of healing. Each time I mounted Ibn I felt scared I was about to drop him and take another slide. I had had too many falls over the past few days and did not want to be totally coated in mud again. But nor did I want to push. I did register that the vistas of cloud-capped mountains were beautiful, but it was hard to raise a smile. I was too close to tears.

What kept me going? I was too tired to think about alternatives. I focused on getting to Foumban, getting out of the Bamenda highlands and getting to tarmac, and let some dogged automatic pilot take over the physical output.

That night, staying in a small village rest house, I awoke shivering in bed, and by the morning, I felt like a steamroller had run over me. I had to lever myself from the bed, only because I needed to get to the toilet. It was a very difficult process – I was extremely stiff and sore.

I stumbled to the loo – it was a stomach-heavingly smelly hole in the ground.

My distaste for smelly village toilets finally had one benefit – I decided there was no way I could allow myself be sick here. I drew on final reserves of willpower to keep going for one more muddy day's cycle ride to Foumban, hopefully a large town with a water supply and sanitation system.

You can be sick there, I told myself sternly.

I did make it to Foumban that night, found an old colonial hotel, Le Prunier Rouge, and moved into a dilapidated but airy room with a real bathroom and toilet. Despite getting afternoon sweats again, and needing help to carry my panniers and Ibn up the stairs to my room, the first thing I did on moving in was to clean the bathroom and toilet – in Africa, even after all these months, they were seldom clean enough for my taste! I planned to stay a while, cleaning made it my home and now, any extra dirt would be mine. Perhaps I was feverish.

The sweats returned again the next morning, making malaria very likely to be the cause. What caused what? Was it that all the effort of the past two weeks in the rain and mountains had worn me down and made me susceptible to malaria? Or had the misery of the last few days been intensified because I was weakening and coming down with malaria?

Through Al's experience, I'd learnt that mosquitoes carry the malaria parasite to the blood of their host. Diagnosis can be difficult, as symptoms vary widely between malaria strains, and under the microscope, the malaria parasite is not always easily detected in a European's blood. However, delay in treatment can mean the parasite multiplies in the bloodstream, then, during its dormant phase, goes to hide in the liver. Once there, as happened with Al, it's much harder to zap it! So, instead of going to the doctor for tests, I immediately took Halfen, a malaria cure I carried. The sweats stopped coming and, remembering Al's pale, skeletal form, I counted myself lucky that the strain I had was so responsive. But I was still very weak. I decided to give my body four days of total rest before putting it back under physical stress.

I knew I needed a rest from the mental stress, too.

I could not bear the idea of being wet, and as it was still persistently raining, I spent most of my time inside my room. Foumban, built over several lush, green hills covered in rusty roofed, red–clay–walled houses, mango and papaya trees, banana and date palms and budding corn, was an interesting place, I was sure. There was the German architecturally-influenced Royal Palace of the sultan of the Bamoun people built by the sixteenth sultan, King Njoya, in 1917; there was a rich crafts and antiques village; and there was a bustling market. Eventually, I got to all three, and even bought some fabric in the market and commissioned a tailor to make a fresh Africa outfit, so I could toss out my old, worn clothes. However, my visits were made without much interest – except in the imminence of rain. Happiness, instead, was blinking at the flashes of lightning and crashes of thunder, hearing rain pelting on the tin roof, gazing out from my window on folk fleeing under banana leaves and upturned basins, and seeing flash streams flooding the clay streets, all from a dry place.

During this time alone, my loneliness became excruciatingly painful. Without the distraction of being on energy-sapping roads, even more of my attention was focused on the constant gnawing pain in my gut. I was not interested in venturing out to meet people, even to the bar. I wanted William, and my parents and brother, as well as my friends, and I set out their photos on the desk in my room like a shrine – and talked to them! Knowing I could blame no one but myself for being here in Africa, for several days I berated myself for my selfishness in persisting with this journey, the fear and unhappiness it was bringing for others and the pain for myself. If there had been an international airport in Foumban, I would have been on a plane out of Africa.

Instead, on one of my few sorties to the market in Foumban, I purchased some paper and coloured markers, and back in my room, wrote long letters to people expressing my feelings, and drew them pictures supposedly depicting how I felt. I became convinced that colours represented emotions, and after that it was an easy step to use colour combinations to represent how I felt about certain people. It seemed obvious to me. (Later, unsurprisingly, I heard the recipients were very perplexed!)

I spent five days recovering my energy, until I felt strong enough to continue. Going back out into the rain was daunting – the thought of being wet made me cringe and my infected sores weren't healed – but I had renewed my sense of wonder at what the next day or week or country might bring. I was ready for adventure again.

As I packed to take to the road for Douala, I gazed at my tiny collection of photos for one last time.

'Goodbye,' I said to each person, in turn.

Quite bizarre. I could no longer cope with the painful split between wanting to be there with them and, simultaneously, wanting to be here in Africa. For now, I had to accept that they were not part of my life.

As I looked out the window, I imagined pushing, sliding in mud and having soft, melting skin again.

'*Aysha!*' I said to myself. I recognised I was struggling, but it was okay. I needed to accept the good and bad of being here. For now, this was my life.

Incredibly sentimental nonsense, eh? Surely, totally meaningless too! After all, in the months to come, I still spent evenings gazing at my photos, trying to wish people alive and to send my spirit to them. At the worst times, I still beat myself up for putting myself through this suffering and loneliness.

But, I wondered. Something was changing in me, in the way I felt about my village life and the people I met. Had my bicycle journey indeed become a metaphor – for the life of villagers? Could I better sense their struggle through my own? Had I simply become so lonely that I had to reach out ... or was I finally letting go?

About three weeks later, at nightfall, I arrived in a tiny village, Beayop. It was a cluster of wooden buildings in a clearing on either side of the road. As I paused, a group of four or five grim men, including one very serious-looking policeman wearing dark glasses, came forward and surrounded me in a tight circle.

'*Buenas tardes,*' I said, intimidated, wondering what would happen next.

I was in Equatorial Guinea, my eleventh country, an ex-Spanish colony, and therefore one with a new national language, Spanish – which I could barely comprehend.

From Foumban, it had taken five more days in the mountains to arrive in Douala, the port city and commercial capital. Fortunately, they were days without mud – from Foumban there was tarmac – though there was plenty of rain; and by the time I limped into Douala, I was, yet again, fairly miserable and sorry for myself. I had suffered nearly three weeks of battering on Nigeria's roads, I had struggled three weeks in the lonely mountains of Cameroon, and one of my insect bites had continued festering until, by Douala, it was a huge tropical ulcer. I was in desperate need of a rest and recuperation stop. Shell again provided that, starting with a 'Welcome Pamela Watson' banner strung across the road into Douala, and including a comfortable stay at the fabulous house of the *directeur général*, medical help – it took two courses of penicillin to contain the infection – and, of course, another stimulating programme. I also finally got my knobbly tyres. They were waiting in Douala with apologies from my friend who had been away – in Australia!

From Douala, I travelled on tarmac to Yaounde, the large, modern capital of Cameroon, then south to the small but pleasant provincial town of Mbalmayo – where I fell off the edge of my well-used Michelin 953 of North and West Africa and switched to my new Michelin 955 of Central and South Africa. A real landmark! I swiftly travelled southwards to tiny Ambam, before crossing the border to Equatorial Guinea and arriving at the small town of Ebebiyin. From Ebebiyin, I cycled through dense rainforest on unsealed, dry roads – it was not the wet season here – to Beayop, and this unfriendly reception.

'*Buenas tardes*,' replied the policeman, eventually. He seemed to be eyeing me suspiciously. He threw a few questions to me in Spanish, but I shrugged in incomprehension. I had heard the word *dinero* – money – but ignored that. No one was very forthcoming about a place to stay.

Then, a small, strong woman, probably in her thirties, and dressed in brown rags with a heavy load of wood on her back, stepped forward. She had clearly just emerged from a day working in the forest.

'I am Marie Carmen,' she said coolly. She asked me a few questions in French; I replied. The others did not seem to understand our exchange.

'Come,' she said in her calm, authoritative manner. 'You can stay with me.'

Marie Carmen turned to the men, spoke fiercely to them and, finally, the men stepped aside to let us pass. Marie Carmen strode purposefully forward, still carrying her load and I followed.

'They wanted money from you,' she said over her shoulder, almost spitting the words. I had guessed and felt grateful for her rescue.

We arrived at a small wooden hut.

'This is my kitchen,' said Marie Carmen. I left my bicycle outside and followed her into the dim interior. Inside were several low cane beds and a larger cane shelf unit filled with tin pots.

'They are all for your family?!' I gasped. She had at least five times as many pots as I did in my London kitchen.

'We are a large family,' said Marie Carmen seriously. Oops. I felt like I'd put my foot in it. Our rapport was not yet strong. 'We are two wives,' she continued blandly. I sensed tension and wondered whether she was happy about that. Or maybe she just thought I'd disapprove.

Marie Carmen left me to go and change. 'I have just come back from the wood,' she explained as she disappeared in her brown ragged shirt and top. Maybe, like me, she just had end-of-day tiredness and blues and needed a pick-me-up shower and a few minutes of rest to restore her calm.

When she returned she had on a colourful skirt and a frilly blouse, a scarf tied tightly around her head, cheap white plastic beads around her neck and plastic sandals on her feet. Her youngest baby was clasped to her hip and her strong arm and leg muscles showed. She was not conventionally pretty but she was striking for the fire in her eyes.

While waiting, I had been entertaining a gathered group of rascals, but now I was given a bucket of water to have a shower.

'The shower is being constructed,' said Marie Carmen as she led me to another hut for my shower.

I returned clean and refreshed.

'I can invite you to stay here,' she said proudly, indicating her kitchen. 'I built it with my own money.' I gathered the house was her husband's, to stay there would need his permission. However, I was keen to stay in my sealed tent – there were too many insects in the forest. Also, I knew it was much more convenient for all if I stayed in my own place: my hosts would not have to move to make room for me, and I would get a restful, mosquito-free night of privacy.

Of course, I was now better at explaining all this in a way which would not cause offence. 'Thank you, but the tent is my home. When I travel to a different place each night, I can sleep better in my own familiar bed.' Marie Carmen understood. Erecting my tent caused the usual commotion and, as I had perfected my flourishes with the poles, was great entertainment for the children. It was also a useful way for breaking down lingering suspicion and for making me feel more in control of the situation – and my audience. Slowly, I was reaching an easier relationship with Africa.

Soon, the light was dimming, and we returned inside the kitchen to talk. We were joined by several children plus her husband's sister. I prepared some tea, but Marie Carmen refused a cup.

'It is not worth it,' she said. She had never tried tea and was not interested.

When some meat was prepared, the men appeared and I was introduced to her husband. He was a handsome man of about thirty-five, but seemed a little drunk. After the men had finished eating, the children consumed the left-overs.

I asked Marie Carmen how she came to learn French in a Spanish-speaking country. It was still a rarity to find a woman I could speak with directly. However, as I'd become more comfortable with myself and my life on the road, I had also become more adept at spotting better-educated women.

'When Macius came to power, my parents fled to Cameroon,' she explained. Macius Nguema was the first, monstrous president of Equatorial Guinea following independence in 1968. In eleven years of terror before he was overthrown in 1979, he is reputed to have murdered thousands and caused two thirds of the country's population of 300,000 to flee as refugees.

We were talking by tilly lamp now, and I asked her about her children.

At first, she just talked about three, the three in the kitchen with her. There was an older girl of ten, and two babies, perhaps just a year apart. Eventually, with emotion cracking her voice, she told me she had six children, but three had died – two at childbirth, one when he was four years old. She looked to be in her mid-thirties; my age.

There was a pause, a comfortable silence. I admired Marie Carmen's strength. Before, I might have seen only the differences between our lives, but tonight I felt a growing bond, felt less like an intruder. I remembered Ibrahim's words, said in the desert outside Timbuktu all those months before: 'We believe you have to suffer to truly appreciate the taste of life.' I thought my daily suffering helped me appreciate my end-of-day showers, but perhaps it was more than that. Through my suffering, had I come to appreciate the taste of her life?

After a while, I asked about what the work was here in the village.

'The women grow food – manioc, sugar cane, peanuts. It is for our families, but if we have enough, we sell some.' Manioc (another name for cassava, especially for cassava flour) is grown, harvested, pounded and fermented, then individually wrapped in banana leaves, called batons. This is a major source of carbohydrate in Central Africa. (I thought it tasted off.) She told me the women would make three hundred batons; this would provide about US$25. There was another pause.

'It is the women who suffer here,' she said quite suddenly. Struggle and suffer were common words in village vocabulary, and were always said without any whingeing, only with realism.

Marie Carmen went on to tell me that she also cooked food which she sold at the market in the village for travellers passing in bush taxis. And she was the health worker for the village. She had done three months training with her husband to get this position, although it was not paid. Her husband had done the course too, because he would not support her going otherwise.

'So, I work in the field, I work at the health centre and I work in the house.' She did not seem to count her work selling food. Marie Carmen's determination and hard work reminded me of Dr Ocloo in Ghana, the marmalade magnate who had made magic from ten shillings. In a less oppressive 'big man' political environment, if Marie Carmen was given a little money, I was certain she would make magic with it.

'The men do nothing,' she said scathingly. 'They help with the ploughing and sometimes they do construction.'

Marie Carmen never stopped while we were talking. It was like visiting married friends with children in London. The children were fed and washed. Her middle son, a toddler, had an infected toe, so she cleaned that and he screamed.

'We try,' she said despairingly, over his screams, 'we try, but the children are always ill.'

As I helped her peel peanuts, she said, 'I sell these for money.'

She swept the floor, then she disappeared outside to bring in firewood, and I followed. There was an enormous pile outside the door.

'We are having a fête this weekend,' she told me, 'so I needed all this wood.' There was a party Saturday night, followed by a baptism and communion on Sunday. She showed me the basket she put the wood in – I had seen her with one load when I arrived, but now she told me that was her second load that day. 'Normally, this would last a week.' She told me it was hard to find dry wood and that she had to wander for perhaps an hour in the forest to find this load. Then, she had cut it with her machete for perhaps another hour.

'When I go to sleep at night, my body just aches everywhere,' she said.

This comment was like an empathetic missile to my gut. These African women I admired carrying their loads were not superwomen. Their work and their childbearing made them old before their time. My body ached at night, to the extent I was always taking aspirin and Piriton – an antihistamine which helped with the itching from my insect bites, but which also helped me sleep. I understood how Marie Carmen felt and as I looked at her lean, muscle-bound body, I thought, '*Aysha!*'

I helped her pile the firewood inside.

'So, do you have a different chore each day?' I asked.

'Yes, tomorrow I must gather the manioc and pound it and roll the batons in preparation for the fête.'

Later, we sat near the charcoal fire that burnt in the rear of the kitchen, near the door opening to the blackness outside. There was a loud background noise of insects. Marie Carmen was roasting peanuts, using her hand to occasionally turn the peanuts in the blackened pan. The fire seemed to create little smoke, yet all night my eyes smarted and my nose ran.

Marie Carmen's mother-in-law sat quietly by the fire, warming herself with her spindly legs outstretched toward the burning coals. We were quiet for a few minutes, just listening to the insects and watching the burning embers. I felt very comfortable.

'You will have many things to tell,' said Marie Carmen suddenly. 'You are certainly in Africa now.'

Her reference to my other life made me feel hollow and heartsick. I felt kinship with this woman and so could empathise deeply with her, yet one day my journey would end. I would step out into a different world of opportunity and hope.

She compounded the gulf between us when I asked her what would be her next project, after her kitchen, if she had more money.

'I would build a room for my children,' she replied. 'I only have one room in my husband's house and it will be crowded as my children get older. I would like them to have a room.' Then, after another pause in the dappled firelight, she added, 'I would like money for my children's education. I would like her,' and she pointed at the sleeping form of her eldest daughter, 'to have more education than me.' Marie Carmen had done three years of high school, but had stopped her education to be married. 'I have more education than most of the women here, but I would like her to have more.'

Her hope was for her children. My hope was to get to Dar Es Salaam and find myself.

We talked a long time into the night before I retired to my tent. I heard the sounds of women talking and taking bucket showers long afterwards. There were no sounds from the men.

I pounded the pile of clothes that were my pillow. Marie Carmen and I were both humans with the same emotions, yet we were a chasm of hope and opportunity apart. I did not want to sentimentalise her life, but I couldn't get away from knowing her pain: appreciating the taste of her life was not comfortable. I felt angry at her lack of hope for herself, then despair with the knowledge that the real differences between us were just a matter of where we were born, and sheer bloody luck.

Twelve

Nothing Happening in Equatorial Guinea?

Beayop, Equatorial Guinea – Luba, Equatorial Guinea

After leaving Beayop and Marie Carmen, I still had about 150 kilometres to cycle westwards to the Atlantic coast and Bata, the main port for Equatorial Guinea on the mainland. This road through Rio Muni, as the mainland is called, should have been an easy one – rolling and unsealed, but thankfully without mountains or mud – except I had developed a bad cold with running nose, headache, fevers and sneezes, which made cycling difficult. Also, I was agitated by the environment of my route – dense forest.

Perhaps part of my nervousness came from the stories I had heard from Shell folk in Cameroon during a farewell dinner. Discussion revolved around forests, wild animals and spirits.

'You think you have been in the forest,' Yonn, the sophisticated marketing manager, said challengingly. 'No, wait until you see the forests of Equatorial Guinea and Gabon.' He spoke of how dense and dark they would be, then switched to giving me strategies for coping with wild animals.

'If you get caught between villages at nightfall,' – of course, according to Yonn, villages would be 40 kilometres apart in the 'real' forest – 'do not climb a tree. You may meet a snake there. Yet on the ground, you may meet a hyena.' So reassuring. 'You should stay in your tent, but don't sleep! That's always when the wild animals come. Make a lot of noise, but don't shine your torch – animals are attracted by light!' I could imagine myself in my tent in a damp, close forest nervously awaiting the growl of an approaching hyena or spirit and singing and clanging on my pot with my spoon!

I thought Yonn's stories were pretty tall, but others had said much the same thing; and the forest on the Nigeria–Cameroon border road, which had seemed so tranquil and beautiful the first day, certainly soon became lonely, claustrophobic, dank and full of biting insects! The memory left me with some trepidation about travelling southwards in Equatorial Guinea and Gabon through thousands of kilometres of dark forest with few villages. What would it be like?

'Do not worry,' continued Yonn, having seemingly read my thoughts. 'I shall be there with you – my spirit will come to protect you!'

Another employee gave me a leather bracelet *juju*. 'There are many evil

spirits, but this will protect you,' she said, somewhat alarmingly. 'Beware of crocodiles,' she added, then, 'Also, be careful of bandits – there are many, many bandits in Gabon.' Great.

Now, I was travelling in the forest. Lush grass, ferns and palms fighting tall trees for light had commenced in southern Cameroon after I left Mbalmayo. As I travelled, the vegetation became denser, and here in Equatorial Guinea, on quiet roads with hardly any traffic, the forest seemed far more intimidating.

The road from Ebebiyin, the Cameroon–Equatorial Guinea border town, to the coast was like a dim, stiflingly humid canyon through towering, quiet trees, that smothered sounds of life within. Kilometres of red, dusty road carved a narrow thread through the tangle of green. The road was repetitive – it curved down towards the right, then, inevitably, it curved back on a gentle upward slope to the left, then another turn and a gentle downward curve to the right, and on. Tall trees cast gloomy shadows, cool shade. There was just one discernible shade of dark green, but a variety in size and shape of leaves, and in height of trees and plants. Sometimes, some trees stood higher, and I registered them silhouetted against the sky, but most of the time it was an unending biological wall.

Birds squawked and cried as they emerged into the road canyon; the sounds echoed loudly and startled me. Hawks glided silently into view. Strange large black birds flapped their wings with such force that they created reverberating, helicopter-type sounds.

Tiny villages nestled in sunny clearings every 3 to 5 kilometres, but often they seemed deserted. Doors and windows of the tiny, closely huddled wooden huts were closed. Frames and doors were painted a bright blue or yellow and the compounds around the wooden huts were swept clear. Somebody was active and caring, but where were they? Sometimes there was a dead monkey or bush rat tied by its legs from a pole, clearly for sale, but with no seller.

Larger villages, every 20 kilometres or so, were only a little livelier. I would know I was approaching one when I encountered one or two boys careening down a hill on a scooter fashioned from wood – even with solid wooden wheels. '*Hola! Hola!*' the boys might call excitedly but, in the sticky heat, they never had the energy to chase me very far. Here, I would also see a collection of huts in a slightly larger sunny clearing, but the main difference was a bar, always identifiable by the L & B and Dallas cigarette bunting. Experience had shown me the few shelves would be sparsely stocked with tiny bottles of Beaufort beer in a distinctive green bottle with a green label, some familiar, Cameroonian 33 beer in brown bottles with a red-and-white label, and red Tetra packs of Vino Tinto, imported Spanish red wine. The latter was a rare treat in Africa. Cigarettes were sold singly. The only food available would be a few faded packs of Marie biscuits. I didn't like to stop because there would always be a small cluster of men, often, drunk, with usually at least one in uniform, wanting to see my papers and make my life difficult.

On my way to Mikomessing, a small town about 30 kilometres beyond Beayop, I was passing through one of these larger, anonymous villages when I saw an aluminium casserole by the bar, a sign that food might be for sale. Feeling hungry, and being an opportunist (food was not always available when I wanted it), I decided to cycle over and take a look. On opening the lid, I saw greasy pieces of meat, looking like tubes of brown and grey rubber lying there. A group of men were sprawled under the shade of a communal shelter near the bar. They were drinking home-made palm wine and 33, and playing checkers. I remembered similar scenes in Mali. These men must be doing a lot of decision making.

'*Buenos días!*' the men leered drunkenly.

'*Buenos días,*' I replied. 'What is it?' I asked, pointing at the casserole, thinking one of these chaps must be the barman. I used French and hoped someone would understand.

'*Singe,*' – monkey – replied a particularly drunken old man dressed in pants and a shirt, both a dirty white, and I decided to buy a packet of Marie biscuits instead.

Then, one man, dressed neatly and cleanly, but not in uniform, got to his feet and officiously asked for my papers. He was wearing dark sunglasses even in the shade.

'*Non,*' I said tetchily, not caring if he understood me or not. It was clear that Equatorial Guinea's style of government had not changed much since the days of Macius Nguema. In fact, Macius had been ousted by his nephew Teodoro, who was still in power. While I was in Equatorial Guinea, Teodoro was going through the motions for a democratic presidential election. (Later, I heard a report on the BBC World Service that no electoral observers had been sent by the US, UK, France or other European countries, the election had been boycotted by the opposition and the US government was quoted as saying that 'the election is a travesty of democracy in keeping with the brutal and repressive regime in power'.) Today, this man's officious arrogance made me angry, and I continued, 'I don't just show my passport to anybody.'

The drunken old man moved uneasily.

'Show him, this man is important.'

I remained stubborn and eventually Sunglasses pulled out a plasticised identification card. All I took in were the words *Securidad Presidencia*. Display of defiant bravery (or stupidity?) over, I showed him my passport, bought the Marie biscuits and got out of there as quickly as I could.

A little further along the quiet road, I stopped for a drink and damp Marie biscuit. The world seemed muffled, but as my ears began to tune in to the silence, I picked up the background noises. Bird cries floated from the tree-tops, and the sounds of insects emerged from down below. (I was well aware of *their* presence – my scalp was lumpy from the bites of tiny insects that had infiltrated my tent's netting a few nights before.) I could even hear human voices faintly, from deep in the forest and the sounds of a machete being hit against a trunk.

Suddenly, a woman stepped out onto the road from a forest track I could barely discern. We both jumped, startled. She was in brown rags, with a machete in her hand. A rope made from vines passed around her forehead and was tied to a wicker basket filled with cut wood, that hung down her back. This was typical of the few women I saw on this road.

'*Hola!*' I said.

'*Hola!*' she replied, still looking a little worried by my presence. As I sneezed and blew my nose (no tissues, too horrible to describe), she smiled – spirits would not have colds – and set off at a slow pace down the road.

I resumed cycling, had passed her, and was picking up pace down the slope, when I screeched to a halt.

A short, green snake had slithered across the road in front of me and I had barely missed hitting it. Or had I? I dismounted and checked under the panniers and even under my seat to make sure the damned thing hadn't jumped aboard! Marie Carmen had told me that the biggest danger for women working in the forest was snakebite, and I vaguely remembered someone telling me that deadly mambas were short and green. I checked again. Nothing.

Soon, I arrived in Mikomessing, just a crossroads, a couple more red, dusty streets, a few whitewashed wooden buildings with rusting tin roofs, a couple of bars with their familiar bunting and a church. It was a metropolis compared to the villages in tiny clearings. My idea of a metropolis had changed since West Africa! Miserable little Koundara in faraway Guinea had been a huge town, and Labé a thriving city, compared to the small, quiet communities in the sparsely populated Central African forest. For now, however, it was good to break free from the dim forest and in fact, perhaps because we were just two degrees north of the equator, the light had a clarity reminiscent of the mountains. Mikomessing looked good to me and, as I really felt under the weather, I decided that if there was somewhere to stay, I was going to bail out. There was a man in uniform at the crossroads, and I called to attract his attention.

'*Buenos días*,' I said cheerfully, trying to build rapport, and directly followed with, 'Is there a hotel here?' That way he'd know I was a harmless *turista*.

'There's a white here,' he replied without a greeting or a smile, 'at the mission.' Then, suspiciously, he demanded to see my papers. So much for building rapport. The atmosphere in this country continued to feel sinister.

Having been led to the Salesian mission by the policeman, I met Antonio, an elderly Spanish priest, who spoke French and welcomed me warmly. He led me to a room in the cool wooden house lived in by the few priests who stayed in Mikomessing, and after a shower, a light lunch with the priests and some visitors from Bata, I slept the afternoon and the worst of my cold away.

Near dusk, Antonio walked with me through Mikomessing's four streets. I liked Antonio – he had a quiet peace about him, and I asked him whether he loved Africa.

'What do you think?' he smiled. I knew. It was a silly question – he had been in Africa for thirty years. So, I asked him what he found here.

'It is this,' he shrugged. We were walking very slowly, stopping every now and then for Antonio to greet people. The sun was going down, and with the slightly cooler evening air, a few people were coming out, strolling, arm in arm, even the men. On promenade. Perhaps, this was a legacy from Spanish colonisation. 'It is time passing, time to care, valuing time spent with others.' I felt that, too, and I was starting to wish I could stay a longer time with the people I met. Antonio went on, 'When I go back to Spain, I don't belong. I see the cities, the rush, all that noise. Here there are no newspapers. In Spain, there is news being bombarded at you from television, radio, newspapers, but it is all the same, it is all too much.' I wondered if I would feel the same way when I went back.

I asked Antonio why the villages seemed so empty.

'Well, they are empty,' he replied. 'Most people leave for Cameroon and Gabon to find work. There is nothing in Guinea.' He used the Spanish term, *nada*, for nothing. I had heard the same from a visitor to the mission over lunch.

'What is manufactured here in Guinea?'

'*Nada*,' he said. 'They only export the trees cut from the forests.'

'What is the ideology of the president?'

'*Nada*, his only ideology is to continue in power.' I learnt that Teodoro, like Macius before him, was from the small village of Mongomo on the Gabonese border in the east of the country. Apparently, the country was being run as a private fiefdom, with all positions, work and wealth going to relatives of those who were from Mongomo, and to those from their tribe, the Fang.

I asked about why people just shrugged and even laughed when I asked about the economy and politics of Equatorial Guinea. 'They don't seem to have the fire to want to change things that I felt in other countries with political crises.'

'The people here have suffered much,' Antonio said. 'The fire is gone, they are too afraid and they have learnt to endure. For them it is *nada, nada, nada.*'

I was feisty with the policeman at the post outside Bata. Not his fault, I supposed. He was just another official in this blood-curdling country doing his job for, as I had been told, '10,000 CFA a moon'. Before the radical devaluation of the CFA later that year, this was about US$40 a moon; afterwards, it was about US$20. I had become accustomed to showing my papers, my issue now was the continuing red, dusty track. Why hadn't the bitumen started? What kind of a piss-pot country was this when there was no bitumen at 5 kilometres outside the estimated *el centro*? My cold was not making me a happy bunny.

I lifted my Akubra from my head – it now had a lot of character, and holes. Not only were my clothes covered in red dust as per normal, but a few kilometres before, I had ripped the crotch of my trousers as I had dismounted. I now manoeuvred myself somewhat awkwardly to preserve decency.

'*Buenos días,*' I said, my tone showing my vexation.

'*Buenos días,*' he said, his tone showing his masculinity and authority.

Oh, shit. I knew what he wanted and retrieved my passport from my handlebar bag – it resided there when there were so many calls for its presence – and handed it over.

He flipped through the pages, I pouted my lower lip. He landed on the front page, with all the details and my photo. I did not think he could read English. He turned it this way, he turned it that way. Come on, I thought, let me get going into Bata. Then, he started examining the photo. He looked at the photo, he looked at me. He stared at the photo and again, dubiously, compared it to me. I frowned and glanced down at the photo. A bubbly woman with curly brown hair and blue eyes wearing a suit jacket and a bow-fronted shirt smiled at me. I looked at the policeman; he definitely seemed sceptical. As our eyes met, I burst out laughing and so did he. He was quite right. We were two different people.

As I cycled into Bata, finally on the bitumen, I received cheers from the children.

'*Turista!*'

'*Turista!*'

Yes, yes, but where was *el centro*?

Eventually, I arrived at the waterfront. The air was still with heavy humidity.

The waves rolled placidly in to shore, a disused pier reached out into the lazy, grey sea. This was still the Atlantic, on the north–south coast of Africa. I had turned the corner of the armpit, but remained in its choking embrace. There was some evidence of Spanish architecture, a few crenellated walls and Spanish tiles on roofs. There was an interesting clocktower and building at what I took to be the central market. Clever of me, that – in the stalls there were clothes and fruit and dead monkeys – still strung up by their tails – for sale.

'*Turista!*' continued small children, and a few adults looked up in surprise. Bata was a quiet town. Here, there were maybe more people, but there seemed little more energy than in the villages. Knock, knock, anyone home? Was there *nada* happening in Equatorial Guinea?

Yonn, of Shell in Cameroon, had suggested I look up one of his clients in Bata. The client, Olga, managed the office of a shipping company, CONARE, and was helpful because I wanted to make a return voyage to the island of Bioko, part of Equatorial Guinea and home of the capital, Malabo. Both places had different names under their colonial past – the island was the exotic Fernando Po, the capital was Santa Isabel. They were one of the first sites occupied by the Europeans as they started their nervous crawl around Africa, and were important trading posts for slaves and gold in the eighteenth century. CONARE had a ship that ran the route between Bata, Malabo and Douala.

'*Dona Elvira*' – the name of their ship – 'is in port now and will leave for Malabo once loading its completed,' Olga told me at our first meeting. I found Olga difficult to fathom. She was in her thirties, of Equatorial Guinean and Spanish origin, her face was badly scarred, she was not easy to get to know, but she had an inner strength and a story to tell. Of that, I was sure. She invited me to stay aboard the *Dona Elvira* until it left. Fabulous.

Paco, a chunky and ebullient Spaniard, was the captain of the *Dona Elvira*, a small tub for cargo and passengers. I'm sure Paco would hate me describing her as a tub. I'm not much of a ship/boat/yacht person, so what would I know? She was berthed at a wharf a few kilometres out of Bata, and I cycled down there and moved Ibn and myself aboard. We waited four days for her to sail – and during that time, I totally lost contact with Africa, Equatorial Guinea and Bata, and instead had the wildest fun!

The mornings began late. I rolled out of the bunk in my cabin and trotted along to the dining room for lunch.

'*Hola Paco! Hola Marie Luce! Hola Ramon!*' I exclaimed. Marie Luce was Paco's honey-coloured, smooth-skinned, very young girlfriend from the Ukraine; Ramon was a rugged, grey-bearded Spaniard who I thought was the engineer. I only thought so. When I asked him directly, 'Are you the engi-neer?', he replied, 'I am an expert on women.' Right. That was about the level of the conversation, in fact an advanced level, as my Spanish was so limited that my contributions were in accusative nouns and laughter at what I could gather about jokes. There were a lot of jokes, undoubtedly sexist, but frankly, through an alcoholic haze in the company of gregarious, generous people, I didn't care.

Sometime during lunch, Genaro arrived. Genaro arrived to see me. Genaro was a very hunky Spaniard, with huge, dopey brown eyes, dopier when they looked at me, who spoke zero French or English. Well, nearly zero. He managed '*Je t'aime*'!

In another time and place, I undoubtedly would have been offended by his presumption. Once I would have said that I was attracted by men with brains and good conversation, not by muscular bodies. But that wouldn't be true, would it? Genaro was a sexy animal and, after the loneliness and hardships of Cameroon, I accepted the attention and finally let myself have fun.

We all squeezed in around a laminated table on the lower deck. A bench seat, padded and covered in vinyl, ran either side. A small fridge was at table height and usually Marie Luce was seated next to it. She briskly emptied its contents of butter, ketchup, rolls of salami, and other spiced meat and cheeses. Then, she would start on the drinks.

'*Biere, coca, vin?*' she would ask me, having produced something of everything for the others. Apart from Olga, who occasionally turned up for these lunches, she was the only one who spoke French. I learnt that asking for a *coca* was no way of avoiding alcohol, as inevitably someone, usually Genaro, would slosh whisky into my glass. As a result, I usually started with red wine, then moved on. It was not at all like my white-wine spritzers in Covent Garden restaurants.

Lunch would appear in the hatchway leading into the kitchen. 'Starters' always consisted of an enormous platter of freshly cooked, unpeeled prawns. These prawns were nothing like the tiny, squelchy, pale-orange ones I had refused elsewhere (too likely to deliver an upset stomach!) These were fine, 8-centimetre, fat, fresh, red prawns with a delicious flavour. Everyone tucked in, pulling up handfuls connected by their feelers and tails and dumping them on their plates. Baguettes were reached for, a piece torn off, and the eating and drinking began. The conversation and laughter never stopped. I could not understand most of what was being said, but usually I knew the cause of the laughter – some playful tormenting between the captain and Marie Luce, or some joke of Ramon's at the expense of Genaro or myself. I found myself eating and drinking far too much.

There was a sign on the wall. '*Ne pas fumer.*' Why was it in French? I remember wondering. Why was it there at all? Ramon and Paco puffed away.

A main course of some meat stew would follow, or we would tuck into salami and cheeses. Ramon always had the job of making coffee in the filter machine tucked in the corner. He made a strong brew which demanded sugar, and to which somebody always added whisky.

I would feel my mind stepping out, watching the lunch proceed, taking in everyone's faces. Ramon had sparkling eyes fringed by thick, curling lashes, Marie Luce had a bubbly laugh and an effervescent face. She was constantly all over her captain, not behaviour I would emulate (no, never!), but it made me wish I had someone to love and be loved by. The captain, although in his forties, had the same silky, flawless skin as Marie Luce, a slightly darker colouring and tightly curled, short dark hair. Genaro was Genaro, very chunky, very muscular, very olive skinned.

Why did everyone on the *Dona Elvira* have wonderfully happy, alive eyes? They should have been dull from drinking.

Suddenly, it would be over. People stood up and started inching their way out, gathering plates and putting them in the hatchway as they left. No good-byes, it was just back to work for them. I would make my way up to the upper deck clasping the handrail tightly, lurching ever so slightly (and we were in port!) and find a sunny seat to catch an afternoon snooze, before dinner.

Several days passed this way. In a rare sober moment, I wondered whether this non-stop partying was because there was nothing else to do in quiet Equatorial Guinea. I also wondered how Genaro imagined I might get involved with him. We did not share a common language and he clearly needed a distraction. Maybe I needed a distraction. I let Genaro pour me another drink.

Dona Elvira finally left port to make the short overnight voyage to Malabo on Bioko Island and my decadent days were over, or so I thought. Just after dawn, I rushed to the deck to watch our arrival and saw a conical mountain rising from the grey sea, covered in forest and shrouded in cloud. Actually, the island was made up of two volcanic cones; the one I was seeing was Mt Malabo. Suddenly, the clouds parted and on the horizon another enormous cone appeared – it was Mt Cameroon, away on the horizon. Clearly, Bioko's two peaks and Mt Cameroon were sisters.

After docking in Malabo (distinguishable from far out at sea by a huge gas flare), and saying temporary farewells to my friends (I would return to Bata with them when they made their return run from Douala in about a week), I set off to find accommodation and explore the area.

Malabo was an extraordinary time capsule of Portuguese and Spanish history. It became one of the first sites of European settlement with the arrival of the Portuguese in the late fifteenth century. In the eighteenth century, the Portuguese relinquished control of the island to the Spanish, and during the nineteenth century, several European powers used the island for slave trading. Britain established a naval base in 1827, and Spain's interest in the island only became strong after cocoa plantations were established late in the nineteenth century. Superficially, today's Malabo, a small city of colonnaded shops and plazas, reeked of that colonial past. Houses were very individual, some stucco covered and painted gaily, others wooden, with second-storey balconies that usually displayed terracotta pots of red geraniums. From the narrow streets where I wandered, I caught glimpses of cloud-topped Mt Malabo, green with rich forest. There was an elaborate cathedral, and in the nearby town square were iron arches covered in flowering vines and straight-backed seats covered in tiles. Although many tiles were missing, those remaining depicted scenes of village women, pounding millet, dancing, weaving each other's hair. It was a welcome change to see women on public monuments – most depicted warriors, hunters and chiefs – but I was a bit dubious about why they were all young, nubile and naked from the waist up.

At sunset, life commenced with children playing on the streets, old folk chatting at street corners and well-dressed couples on promenade. Sir Richard Burton, my explorer hero, was Honorary British Consul to Fernando Po from 1861 to 1864. I imagined him on promenade here in Victorian long-coated jacket and top hat.

However, this was the superficial, historic Malabo. Any romantic vision was spoiled by today's heavy air of authoritarianism and violence. Walls were peppered with bullet holes. Police cars cruised the streets, uniformed soldiers with automatics slung over their shoulders stood at street corners, walked on patrol. Intimidating men in plain clothes were saluted, police asked to see my passport often, and I felt watched. I saw no other tourists. One evening, two men introduced themselves to me, chatted about my journey, then revealed they were members of the presidential guard. Of course, they were Moroccans – none of Africa's dictators could trust their own people as their personal guards and, from the accumulated stories I heard in other countries, it seemed it was generally Moroccans and Israelis who provided these distasteful leaders with their crack troops. I wondered if the men talked to me deliberately.

In Malabo, the closest I got to political discussions were people shaking their heads and saying, 'the politics are bad'. Another passenger on the *Dona Elvira*, a woman who had been trading in Bata, on a visit from Nigeria where she now lived, had told me her memories as a young girl in Malabo during the Macius years.

'Many girls were raped – he killed many people. The schools were closed and the churches too. Many people, we ran to the bush, or left in small boats. My aunt was put in prison, but she had it too bad. They put her in with many ants. We used to take her food, that's all she had to eat, but the guards would tell us to taste it ... and taste it ... until all the food was gone. Only people from Mongomo got the benefits.' She spoke Nigerian English. She had even-tually been put on a boat to escape the madness. Nigeria, so chaotic to me, had become her safe haven.

I wondered how different things in Equatorial Guinea were today.

Disliking the menacing atmosphere in Malabo, I decided it was time for Ibn and me to move on, to take the 57-kilometre muddy road to Luba, the only other town of any consequence on the island. It was a jump from the proverbial frying pan into the fire.

Luba had a placid feel, an end-of-the-world feel. It was two grim and dilapidated streets of Spanish buildings clinging to the edge of a circular bay, cringing below the heights of the other perfect volcano, Mt Isabel. After checking in to the only hotel in town, a pleasant colonial building where I got a big, airy room and a balcony overlooking the bay and dilapidated wharf, I went on promenade to meet the locals.

Mangaram's was the only general store in town; I went in, and as usual, groceries were on shelves behind the counter, the range only slightly wider than in villages on Rio Muni. As usual, too, the general store was also the bar, and standing drinking a beer was a middle-aged, black-haired Spaniard. I bought a beer, joined him, and soon discovered his name was Choochi, he worked for *Cooperación Española*, and had been in the four-wheel-drive, the only vehicle that had passed me on my way from Malabo.

Choochi told me he was waiting for some officials.

'They are the big men here in South Bioko,' said Choochi. I didn't detect any contempt.

We were soon joined by Bernado and Thomas, the big men. Bernado, a middle-aged, overweight, overbearing man, was the party controller for South Bioko; Thomas, a thinner but equally self-important man, was the party controller for a nearby village called Batete.

Bernado seemed to rapidly take a shine to me, even though I thought he was sleazy. Before long, through Choochi's translations, I was hearing about all the property Bernado owned, undoubtedly taken by force from their owners. He insisted I walk outside so he could point out his house, a Spanish colonial mansion, encrusted with bullet holes, lying nearby. I wondered at its history.

'Whose is that one?' I asked Choochi who had joined us, bringing out our beers. I was pointing to an attractive, two-storey, Art Deco-style building at the end of the road, before it swept up the hill and back to Malabo.

'That is the house of the commandant,' Choochi said, after putting the question to Bernado. 'He says that from there he can see everyone who comes and goes from the village – so there are no problems in Luba.' Big brother is watching you, I thought.

Very late, after a lavish meal and several beers at my hotel, Choochi, Bernado, Thomas and I drove in Choochi's vehicle up a muddy and winding mountain road to Thomas's tiny village of Batete. The road was potholed, the mountain forest shrouded, and I wondered where we would arrive.

After about an hour, we came to cleared land, and by the light of the nearly full moon that peered from under a gauze covering of clouds high in the sky, I could make out Batete. There were wooden houses, many two-storeyed, sprinkled across the cleared mountain side and it seemed larger than Luba.

However, there were only two buildings which were served by generators and which showed lights. One was Thomas's house, where we immediately drove.

We stood on the wooden open verandah drinking more beer, looking out over the ghostly town, to the faraway orange glows from Nigeria's offshore oil platforms and to the perfect, dark cone silhouette of Mt Isabel. It was turning into a wild Guinean night and I felt comfortably detached from what was happening, from myself. Drunk again. Bernado started flirting with me, or he thought he was. He kept brushing himself against me and gazing longingly at me every time I looked at him. Horrible from a sleazy man, and I was pleased when we left for the other building with a generator, the disco. It was Saturday night.

We walked to Batete's disco through the deserted dirt streets, attracted by the loud music and electric-light glow. The dance floor was dark – light was only outside – so that eliminated the possibility of any further meaningful eye contact from flirtatious men. The loud, fast-beat Cameroonian music drowned out the need for conversation. I was very drunk already, but accepted more beer as I was pulled onto the dance floor amongst the shuffling, gyrating crowd. I switched partners as men draped their arms around me, while women took my hand and tried to teach me to move my hips to the gyrating rhythm. Everybody, including myself, seemed to be moving in slow motion. It was a very strange, almost out-of-body experience.

Teach me to get so drunk, I guess.

We drove back to Luba in the middle of the night, back to the Luba disco for more dancing, more beer, and more dancing.

About five in the morning, having lost the others, Choochi and I walked out on the disintegrating wooden wharf of Luba, drank more beer and watched, through a bleary haze, the moonlit sunrise over the ocean. The dark shadow of Mt Isabel loomed above us, and, momentarily, I thought this was a paradise. Then, Choochi's words shot through my reverie.

'People are disappearing,' he said. 'Friends, people, you know, are disappearing, being shot.' His despair was tangible, his dark eyes potholes of pain.

All that alcohol and it was still not enough to escape. He seemed to be living in a dual world of friendship and respect for these high-ranking Guineans, and anger and despair at what was happening.

'There is so much fear. I love this country, I was born here, but I think I must leave.'

It was so sad. Through my own pierced numbness, I wondered whether a lot of the drunkenness and determination to have wild fun was people's way of coping with hopelessness in a desperate situation. I thought how wrong I had been in thinking that there was *nada* happening in this country.

Thirteen

Respect For Life

Cogo, Equatorial Guinea – Brazzaville, Congo

Crossing the frontier from sinister Equatorial Guinea into Gabon seemed like breathing in fresh air. Huh! I was soon to be disillusioned about that! After returning from Bioko Island to Bata, I had travelled 130 kilometres south to Acalayong for exit formalities and to Cogo, still in Equatorial Guinea, for the night; in the morning, I crossed the estuary to Cocobeach by motorised *pirogue*, and left directly on the 135-kilometre cycle ride to Libreville, capital of Gabon.

Libreville was beautiful. Gabon's oil wealth showed in modern glass towers, the huge presidential palace and a stunning, broad boulevard along the palm-fringed estuary, but like all cities, it had two contrasting sides: the sophisticated world of the wealthy and the gutter-edged world of the poor. Even the boulevard displayed that – vehicles were either new, tinted-windowed four-wheel-drives or decrepit, rust-bucket taxis and trucks stuffed with people and sacks. During my time there, I experienced both sides.

As usual, Shell's local marketing company looked after me well. Anatole Bourobou, the *directeur général* of *Pizo Shell*, took me out to dinner at a chic downtown restaurant. He was a kind and urbane man, about fifty, with deep-set, jet-black eyes, who, over drinks, started talking about the forest.

'I grew up in a small village in the forest,' he said. 'I love being in the forest,' he added in a nostalgic tone, and his eyes took on a faraway look.

I was still not that keen. My last stop before Libreville was in a wooden shack of a hotel in a small town surrounded by trees and darkness. I awoke in bed to the feel of a rat's dancing claws on my leg. I started, it fled, then I heard it scrabbling in my food bag for the rest of the night. Not ideal, but these small trials of my life with Ibn did not distress me now – or, if they did, the emotion flashed like a bushfire and was gone. I was in a buoyant mood, I was in Africa for the long haul. Of course, I had not done much long-haul travel recently! In the past six weeks since my arrival in Douala, I had only spent one day in three on the bicycle. When not cycling, I was having drunken fun; when cycling, compared to the trials of Cameroon, life had been far easier. So far. After Libreville, I would be headed out on mainly unsealed roads for over 1000 kilometres until my next big city, Brazzaville, the capital of Congo. There would be a lot of forest and village life to experience. I wished I could get to like it better.

'I hate it,' I said to Anatole. We Australians are known for plain speaking. 'Can you help me understand what you like about it? Then, maybe I can see what you do.'

'It is quiet in the forest,' he began. 'It is peaceful. I can think more clearly there. I like to walk there, beside the streams. It is cool in the forest. I like to hunt there.'

'But it's the unseen, lurking animals that worry me! How do you hunt?'

'I hunt the animals with traps,' he said. 'If it is for an animal that walks like this, like gazelles,' he marched his well-manicured fingers across the crisp, white linen tablecloth, indicating animals that walk sure-footedly, 'I make a trap with a hole in the ground. For other animals, I set a trap with a spring-loaded stick and food. When the food is approached, the animal puts its neck through a hidden noose, and when the stick flips up ...' he used graphic hand gestures to illustrate, '... the noose tightens and the animal is garrotted!'

I liked the sound of this and briefly considered whether I should get him to

teach me his technique; it might come in handy, at the very least for rats!

'Attention,' Anatole continued. 'If the stick is down, nothing has come by. If the stick is right up, the animal has eaten the food and gone away. However, if the stick is halfway up, beware! The animal is caught. He may be dead, or he may be very angry.' He was clearly enjoying worrying me. 'You may have caught a panther or a gorilla, and then you must be prepared to fight it!'

Scrap hunting, I thought.

But Anatole was away remembering images of the forest near his beloved village. 'The streams are very beautiful in the forest,' he murmured. I could hardly hear him. 'And the hills and valleys. The forest changes, you know. It is beautiful everywhere.'

I could recognise his love – it was how I lyricised about subtle changes in desert country or the moods of the ocean. Hearing his passion did help me to better appreciate the forest as I moved on. And it was better than yet another bandit or evil spirit story!

Dinner was served. Anatole's meal was bushmeat. The *maître d'*, who knew him well, had ensured he was served the part he would like – the braised head!

'It is the best part!' exclaimed Anatole, as he foraged in the skull for tasty morsels. Anatole wore a beautifully tailored suit, had a goblet of red wine at his place, and was foraging with a silver knife and fork. I could not see him living in a village again, no matter how nostalgic he was for the forest. Meanwhile, I had a different kind of nostalgia to indulge – I foraged in my pepperoni and pineapple pizza.

At the other end of Libreville's social spectrum were two young women I met, Valerie and Grace. They were prostitutes.

I met them quite deliberately. Earlier in my stay, I had met Suzi, an American Peace Corps Volunteer whose job involved helping administer the Gabonese government's AIDS programme. Suzi wanted to talk to prostitutes who worked the upmarket hotels stretched along Libreville's foreshore, to find out their awareness of AIDS and to give them condoms. I wanted to meet them because, elsewhere in Africa, I had often found bar girls to be sassy, independently minded women with dreams and lots of stories to tell.

We saw two young women standing together opposite the Novotel Rampochombo, the premier hotel of Libreville. Under the pooled light of a solitary street lamp, there did not seem much business around, so we strolled over and introduced ourselves. Valerie was happy to chat, while Grace initially hung back in the shadows, nervously watching us.

Valerie was like a young antelope, tiny in stature, with a fine bone structure. Her face was framed by gorgeous brown curls – she was wearing a lavish European-style wig that gave her long shiny tresses – and she wore thick red lipstick. She was ornately dressed in a red mini-skirt and yellow frilled blouse, with a sparkling chain belt around her waist, and expensive costume jewellery – lots of coloured glass and gold hung from her neck. She looked very fragile, very pretty. Grace was like a frightened fawn in comparison. She was dressed in a mini-skirt of cheap, black, stretch cotton and a black stretch-tube top, both of which emphasised her thinness. Like Valerie, she wore high stilettoes, but she wore no jewellery and no wig – her hair was not even tressed, just left in its close fitting cap of tight black curls. Grace kept her eyes averted and she looked very young, very shy.

Valerie seemed to adopt a protective, big sister role toward Grace, but there must have been barely any age difference between them.

Rapidly, we discovered they had come five months ago from Mamfé, the English-speaking part of Cameroon, so we switched languages. I was not surprised they were foreigners – in Gabon most menial and trading work is done by Africans who have come to make their fortune in oil-rich Gabon, to the extent that, even in the villages, shopkeepers I met in Gabon were more likely to be from Mali, Cameroon or Equatorial Guinea! Initially, we stayed on neutral subjects. Valerie said they were sisters, but this could have been in the broader African sense of comrades from the same extended family, tribe or region. Then, Suzi asked how they liked Gabon.

'Life is too expensive, too hard here,' said Valerie.

'Why did you leave Cameroon, then?' I asked.

'In Cameroon, life is hard too,' answered Valerie. 'Our president is playing games with our country, making it very hard to make money.' I had certainly witnessed the truth of that.

We talked a little while about what a nice country Cameroon was, and laughingly agreed that the roads were very bad. But when I asked if they missed Cameroon, Valerie didn't quite get my question.

'What do you mean? A Miss Cameroon contest?!'

After a little explanation, she exclaimed, 'Oh, too much! We are very homesick. We talk of Cameroon all the time.' She went on to add that they had no friends here in Libreville. 'It causes too many problems.'

I was not sure if Valerie meant jealousies, or that they were worried that news of their 'nice little job', as she said they described it in letters to their father, might get back. Suzi told me later that, as in other trades, all the prostitutes were foreigners, and moreover, many were from Cameroon.

'We did not plan to be prostitutes,' continued Valerie, 'but it was necessary.' They had found Gabon too expensive and could not afford the money for a *Carte de Séjour* – a work permit. It was only through prostitution that they could live and get enough to send some money home.

Suzi was pleased to discover they always used condoms, although she did not believe it – condoms were expensive, there was little budget for the Gabonese AIDS education programme, and HIV positive cases were on the rise. She gave Valerie and Grace some samples, and both giggled and were shy about taking them.

'The men here are not serious – the Frenchmen or the Gabonese,' said

Valerie. 'They won't even buy us a drink, they just want sex and to be finished.'

At this Grace, who had been coming closer, added her own view.

'Some of these men try to leave us at the edge of the forest,' she said in a quiet, timid voice. 'They are very bad and we must get a taxi back.' I shuddered at the thought of being in the forest at night.

Valerie started telling us about other problems with men. 'There are groups of young boys, with knives, who rob us, and the police are always wanting money!' She continued, 'One time, they took me to the station and they were going to shave me and whip me, but luckily, there was a policeman there, a friend of mine, and he told them to let me go.' Then she laughed and pointed to her wig of curly brown, European hair. 'That was before I had this,' and I wondered if another time she had not been so lucky.

They had dreams. 'Oh no, we will not be prostitutes when we leave Gabon.' Grace wanted to study medicine, to be a health worker, but Valerie had different ideas. 'I would like to study literature, or I would study computers,' she said. 'I think that will be useful in Cameroon. But I would like to go to the Europe or the US.' They saw no romance in working in the fields or cutting wood in the forests. They were only nostalgic for people, not the discomforts of the way of life they had left behind.

I told them I thought they were very courageous to have left their own country and come here alone, but Valerie would not hear of it.

'It is just like you, no? You voyage from country to country by yourself.'

I shrugged and smiled, but wondered how true it was. Maybe we were both pursuing fantasies that required us to take risks, but my discomforts seemed small compared to the dangers of their path, and I was educated enough to know better.

After an eight-day stay in Libreville – with another busy programme – it was mid-September and my mind was focused on the road ahead. It would be a long haul to Brazzaville, but quiet – I hoped. On my route inside Gabon, I would pass through Lamberéné on the Ogooué River, then Fougamou, Mouila and Ndendé, but once inside the Republic of Congo, I would pass through nothing but villages for nearly 300 kilometres southwards until the railway town of Dolisie, with still another 350 kilometres of remote travel eastwards to Brazzaville. I would be treated to only 120 kilometres of bitumen before nearly 1000 kilomtres of unsealed, only partially improved roads to Brazza. Phew. It was time to get started.

As I cycled more deeply into Gabon, I did start to see the forest as something richer and not so intimidating. I appreciated the different kinds of trees, bushes and vines, and listened for the cries of different birds and insects. The mood of the forest did indeed change over the kilometres. Generally, the red, dusty road was broader than in Equatorial Guinea, so the cavern I cycled through was not as claustrophobic. However, in some straights, the dense vegetation closed in, and I cycled through dark shadows. On other sweeps, the vegetation became coloured with flowers, dappled with sunlight, alive with white cranes nestling in high branches. Then, it was like cycling through a bright tropical garden.

Mary Kingsley, the Victorian explorer who had travelled on rivers and tracks (not on roads, like me) deep into the forests of Gabon in 1895, wrote about learning to see and read the forest.

> On first entering the great grim twilight regions of the forest you can hardly see anything but the vast column-like grey tree stems in their countless thousands around you, and the sparsely vegetated ground beneath. But day by day, as you get trained to your surroundings, you see more and more, and a whole world grows up gradually out of the gloom before your eyes. Snakes, beetles, bats and beasts people the region that at first seemed lifeless ... It is like being shut up in a library whose books you cannot read, all the while tormented, terrified and bored. And if you fall under its spell, it takes all the colour out of other kinds of living.

One day during her travels, Mary, leading the way along a forest track, fell into a 5-metre-deep elephant pit and landed on the fire-hardened points of nine 4-metre poles.

'You kill?' asked her closest follower.

'Not much,' was her reply. 'Get a bush-rope and haul me out.' Her stubborn insistence on wearing a Victorian hooped skirt during her journeys, instead of the recommended lightweight trousers, had saved her.

I hoped there were no elephant pits on this road.

There were, however, villages, and these were not 40 kilometres apart (or further) as had been ominously predicted in Cameroon – more like 8 to 10 kilometres apart. There would be a small, swept clearing and a cluster of wooden houses. As in Equatorial Guinea, these villages were often quiet places, much smaller and more modest than in West Africa, and deserted during the day. I only met people on the roads, emerging from the forest, usually accompanied by dogs.

I disliked their dogs. Especially when I was on a bicycle displaying vulnerable legs that looked like tasty morsels to a rabid, hungry hound.

'You must keep cycling and shout at them, or pretend to throw stones at them,' said a laughing villager on my first day out of Libreville, after his golden-brown, short-haired, muscular creature, with long, pointed snout, yellow teeth and mad eyes, had chased me. I had fallen off the bike and landed in stinging nettles, and did not really want his advice, only his restraint of his bloody dog. 'You must not be scared of dogs – they will always know you are afraid.' How could I not be scared when memories of the dog attack in Guinea rushed to the fore as frequently as their dogs rushed at me? Ultimately, I became an expert at skidding in the gravel, leaping off Ibn, and holding the bicycle between me and the animal. Ultimately.

On my final day of bitumen before Bifoun, I was rushed at by a growling dog, and this time my frightened application of brakes and inevitable skid on the loose tar and sandy verge took me and the bike down. My ring and middle fingers on my left hand were pinned by the handlebars as the weight dragged across the bitumen. The nail was ripped off my ring finger and a large hole was drilled in the nail of my middle finger.

A woman rushed from a nearby house – I had been passing a village clearing. She threw some stones at the dog, raced at it and thrust at it with a rake she was carrying. Finally, it slunk away.

'You must not be afraid,' she said. 'He is not vicious.' Huh. I sat in a heap on the road, thick blood pooling on my fingertips, feeling faint and nauseous from the pain. Then, I eyed her rake and plotted revenge. Come back doggy, I thought. I was ready to kill the mutt.

'Respect for life was the cornerstone of Albert Schweitzer's philosophy,' said curly haired, sparkling-eyed Pierre.

Having arrived the previous day, I was staying at the Albert Schweitzer hospital at Lamberéné. Pierre, a pharmacist, was president of the Swiss Trust, one of three trusts which provides funding for the hospital.

The hospital was a collection of old and new buildings nestling in a large, flat clearing near a broad bend in the grey Ogooué River. Modern clinics were built alongside squalid, rusty-roofed housing for staff and families of patients. The hospital demanded that patients were accompanied by family members to nurse and feed them. In Schweitzer's time, this had been perceived as revolutionary sensitivity to Africans' needs.

'Essentially, his philosophy was about respect for others,' continued Pierre, 'for other people, other animals, insects, vegetation ...'

'Even dogs?' I asked.

Albert Fry, godson to Albert Schweitzer, and almost a living replica of the man – he was stooped, stocky, with tough, suntanned skin, white hair and white, pointed beard – was with us. He was a Protestant preacher who loved talking, mainly about Schweitzer. He and Pierre were showing me a replica of Schweitzer's old home. There were photos of Schweitzer as a young man – large and black haired – and as the more familiar, stooped, white-haired old man in pith helmet and white clothes. Always he was surrounded by women. We had seen the desk at which he wrote, apparently at all hours of the night. There was a wooden stool at the desk. Albert said Schweitzer used this for his consultations and his writing, and only at seventy years of age did he finally accept a cushion on the stool. Apparently, he believed in pushing his body to the edges of endurance. Albert continued with a story.

'If someone swatted a tsetse fly that was sitting on Schweitzer's shoulder, he would rebuke them. "That was my fly," Schweitzer would say. "I had the right to decide if it lived or died."'

Interesting illustration of respect for life, a little like fascism, I thought, though I was more alarmed to think there might be tsetse flies lurking in the forest for me!

'René, Schweitzer's daughter, tells the story of the time he went back to Europe when she was a little girl,' continued Albert. 'She met him excitedly with a bunch of freshly picked flowers and he said, "Why have you done this? These flowers will live no more!"'

'Really, the philosophy is not that special,' said Pierre later, probably controversially. 'At its base, it is the same as for all the world's religions.'

Undoubtedly, it was too easy for me to find contradictions, as from Gabonese I met, it was clear that respect for Schweitzer's work, dedication and brilliance runs deep in the nearby communities. But to me, it seemed an ironic philosophy to be espoused in Africa.

Three nights after leaving Lamberéné, in a small village between Fougamou and Mouila, I stayed with the local chief – an elderly man, with loads of dignity, a mournful way of speaking and gentle eyes. Despite my status as only a woman, as dusk fell, he invited me to eat with him – possibly because he seemed to be the only person who spoke French. We had dinner together inside his hut, eating alone; the women were outside pressing sugar cane – part of the process of making palm wine. 'It is the best thing for making money,' the chief had told me. The women and their children would eat the leftovers, outside, afterwards.

'Please, I will eat my own food,' I said, pre-empting the offer of mashed plantain and fish stew. I had to do some creative explaining so as not to offend. 'I have eaten a lot during the day – to have the energy to cycle, so now I am not very hungry.'

In fact, before leaving Lambaréné, I found apples in the market – New Zealand apples! A slice of temperate heaven in the tropics! Other than bananas, fruit was not something I frequently found in the forest, and since Libreville there had been a drought even of these. I usually had to beg a papaya. (These grew like weeds but were considered too lowly a food to actually sell.) Knowing it might be my last chance before Dolisie, I bought twelve apples! Some things were worth their weight. Tonight, I sat with the chief eating apple and papaya fruit salad and two-day-old, slightly off yoghurt.

Most peculiar, I could see the chief thinking, but I had given up trying not to be peculiar.

On the road to Lamberéné, having passed the equator marker and crossed into the southern hemisphere, I had stopped at a stall for a celebratory drink. The stallkeeper, a Cameroonian, of course, not a Gabonese, had addressed me. '*Vous êtes terrible!*' he had exclaimed, and I had been a little taken aback. After all, that means, you are dreadful! Talking with him, however, I discovered that he meant I created dread in him, and, he said, in all Africans. 'We think you must be in league with the spirits to travel – a woman, a white, alone like that.' All bad things rolled into one. It helped me see there were some cultural bridges I could never cross. I figured I might as well keep some pleasures, rather than adopt all ways that were foreign and uncomfortable for me. If eating fruit for dinner was strange to villagers, too bad. So was cleaning my teeth. So was my mere presence. Was this cultural insensitivity on my part, or a necessary adaptation to give me some sense of control in my still tough life? I hoped the latter.

The chief and I talked by the light of the kerosene lamp on the wooden table. He talked of how the people suffer here in the villages.

'The work is so hard. You must be strong. Then, you can get everything you want from the forest. It is hard work, but you can live well.' He told me that money was needed regularly only for soap and kerosene, for the lamps.

As we walked from his hut to the rear of the compound, listening to the music of the crickets, enjoying fresh air after a rainstorm, the thoughtful chief started lamenting how the young men were not satisfied with life in the village.

'They get education, but cannot get work – they don't want to work hard in the forest like us. They want things that cost money and some go to the city.'

To date, I had tended to think of my experiences in African cities and villages as so divergent as to belong to different, parallel worlds. I had not given much thought to the influence of one world on the other.

'In the city you need money,' continued the chief. 'And there is a problem, too. The young go to the city and cannot find work and there is no one to support them. Here in the village, problems can be solved because everyone is here to help. If someone is sick, money is found to send them to hospital. But in the city, you must wait until the end of the month! You go to die.' There was clear evidence of what the chief was saying.

Often for young men, with more education and freedom than young women, the lure of the city would be strong. But, with administration jobs disappearing as the public sector is reduced, with economies stalling due to poor leadership and lack of access to capital or export markets, and without a strong trading tradition like women, young men were only finding unemployment. In Libreville, as in other African cities, there was high male unemployment, which in turn created social problems like increasing drunkenness, thieving and violence. Not so different from parts of the UK and Australia.

It was not only through direct human rights abuse that Africa's old-style leaders, the big men still in power in so many countries I had passed through, were affecting people's lives. By not spending their countries' money responsibly, they failed to create the investment, employment opportunities and stable social fabric necessary for Africa's renaissance.

The chief moved away to smoke, and I recalled again my time in the desert outside Timbuktu. This time, I remembered the still night under a starry sky spent with the Tuareg chief who had told me about the Tuaregs' woes and fears for security. Both chiefs had spoken mournfully with deep concern for their people. Why weren't there responsible people like these chiefs reaching political leadership positions at the national level?

I stayed in the compound, drawn by the full moon, the silhouetted trees, and the scent of fresh, earthy air. The women had finished their work and were gathered with their children around a charcoal stove at the far end of the compound, eating. I smiled at them, they smiled back, then resumed eating. At night, the villages were peaceful and quiet, a treasure for the city-jaded soul, but as I rolled my shoulders and felt the usual ache, I could understand why people tried to escape the physical pain of this life. The drift from country to city was a familiar one the world over, and, despite the chief's concerns, would surely continue.

The chief came back suddenly and handed me a glass of foggy liquid.

'Drink that and you will fall down,' he said good-humouredly, and moved away. It was a glass of palm wine.

As the bright moon moved high in the clearing sky, I sipped at the strong, pungent liquor, and thought darkly about irresponsible big men.

Several times during my ride southwards through Gabon, I had been buzzed over by aeroplanes and helicopters. President El Hadj Omar Bongo and his entourage, I guessed. The presidential election in Gabon was two months away, but Bongo had started campaigning via a countrywide set of flying visits. Why didn't he use the roads, I wondered, to see how he could have used his country's oil revenues? If he used the badly potholed road, which rapidly turned to mud as the rainy season arrived, he might spend more money on them.

The chief had said that he was worried by the elections. 'Our current president has been in power for twenty-six years and we have had peace and contentment.' The chief's legitimate concern was for stability. However, he did not seem to hear any contradiction between this comment and his lament about the hard work endured in the villages, and the lack of work in the cities. He did not seem to wonder why Gabon's oil wealth had not reached his village.

Gabon should be a wealthy country. In 1992, it had a GDP of US$4.6 billion. Much of its income comes from oil, but it is also rich in minerals like manganese (an estimated quarter of the world's known deposits), iron ore, chrome and diamonds. Gabon's population is only about one and a quarter million, so its per capita GDP was nearly US$4000 – a lot for Africa. (For comparison, Nigeria's 1992 per capita GDP was only US$256.) Yet this village was not accessible by a sealed road, and it had no electricity, sanitation or water to show for twenty-six years of this extraordinary per capita income. For all its faults, Nigeria's roads were sealed, and places I stayed were electrified and at least had water pumps – this in a country nearly four times as big as Gabon. Few aid organisations operated in Gabon, reasoning that it should have the income to provide for itself. Where had the money gone?

'*Il a bouffé l'argent,*' was a favourite expression in Gabon – he has eaten the money.

The huge presidential palace I had seen in Libreville cost US$800 million to build – in the seventies!

Two days later, I arrived in Ndendé, the last small town in Gabon before the Congolese border, and found it in a state of excitement. President Bongo was arriving the next day. I decided to stay. In fact, I had to stay – the border would be closed during his visit.

The crowd was gathering near the regional prefecture about 9.30 a.m. The president was due at 10 a.m., but of course he was late. People waited, dressed in their best clothes – old gents' suits were decorated with medals, and the women wore embroidered outfits or *pagnes* and T-shirts emblazoned with Bongo's image.

'Those women have been trucked in from Congo,' said a Gabonese woman standing next to me. 'There are not enough here in Gabon.' I was puzzled, then saw these women being ushered to the front. When the helicopter bearing Bongo, his wife and followers touched down, they performed the welcoming dances. So, was it that there were not enough dancers in Gabon? Or not enough women who supported Bongo? The answer remained unclear.

The district president offered a cordial welcome to the president and thanked him for 1 kilometre of bitumen here and 500 metres there. But this was not the beginning of the usual political pleasantries, for he then read out a long list of problems, which he said was not limited to, but included: lack of water pumps, no reliable telephone service from such a strategically important border town, no bank, and lack of books at the school. He concluded by saying that Ndendé had really received nothing and they were keen to hear what the president could offer. He received hearty applause as he sat down.

President Bongo went to the microphone. He was a short man, debonair, dressed in a very smart, dark-blue suit. His wife remained seated and anonymous behind dark, clearly expensive sunglasses. When Bongo spoke it was as though there had not been any criticism. He spoke at length about the warm welcome he had received, then made an unspecific offer to talk with officials afterwards about future unspecified promises.

That evening, listening to the radio, I understood why it did not matter. The Gabonese national radio station only played Bongo's reply.

Democracy was better than military rule and dictatorship. At its best, as in Ghana, it gave the opportunity for freedom of speech and raised hopes that the majority could influence change and empower leaders who strived to deliver an improved quality of life for all. African democracy was imperfect – like everywhere, really – but sadly, in many African nations, the unleashed hopes of many that change was possible were being dashed. Disillusionment had led to a spiral of violence and human rights abuses.

Later that day, I was about 15 kilometres out of Ndendé, headed towards the border when I overtook an elderly man in a wheelchair. In Central Africa, I'd previously seen this design: it was something like a tricycle with propulsion via hand pedals connected by a long chain to the rear wheels. Neat, except this man's chain was broken, so he was having to propel himself along a zigzag course by pushing the wheels.

'I saw your president in Ndendé today,' I said, after stopping to help.

'And what did he have to say?' asked the wise old fellow.

'Not much,' and I explained about the list of problems and the evasive response.

'Well, he won't be there for much longer,' he said. 'The fifth of December and he will be gone. Twenty-six years is too long for one man.'

(In 1993, despite allegations of corruption, Bongo was elected president for a seven-year term – leading to rioting in Libreville.)

It had taken me two weeks to cover the 500-kilometres from Libreville to the Gabon–Congo border, including a three-day stop in Lamberéné. For the last 200 kilometres before the border – really, since my night with the chief – the land had started getting drier and the scenery had changed. Gradually, lush, high forest had changed to scrubby trees and low grass and shrubs. Now, as I entered Congo, the scenery became even drier. I was in a land of low horizons, big skies and luminous light – green grasslands with just a few trees poking their heads above the lower growth. Bizarrely, to me, a lot of the trees were coconut palms. They looked out of place in this inland landscape.

The road continued to be a slither of red dust – I had been off the seal for over 400 kilometres now – and it was corrugated down the main route, deep dust pockets near the edges. If I tried to venture into the bush for a toilet stop, I ended up in flour-like dust to my ankles, so I tended to choose a long straight where no people were yet in view, squat quickly by Ibn and get it over with. Fortunately, the dust was highly absorbent and I left no trace – important, as no matter how quick I was, someone would always turn the corner before I got away.

On my first night in northern Congo, I stayed in Nyanga in a nightmarish hotel room that was suffocating when I lit the kerosene lamp and turned into a whirling cave of bats when I doused it. Now, I was stopped by the roadside, somewhere between Nyanga and Loubetsi. I was never quite sure where I was in Congo as my Michelin had few towns marked, and confusingly, contrary Congolese governments had changed village and town names after independence in 1960, then had recently changed names back to pre-independence names. For instance, my next major town, about 250 kilometres south-east of the border, was called Dolisie by the French, then was called Loubomo, and was now Dolisie again. Even more confusingly, different people referred to the same place by their different names, probably according to their political allegiance.

After my rapid ablutions, I pulled out a piece of tough, stale baguette for a carbohydrate fix. I ate that quickly, too – I was listening for logging trucks. Evidently, there were still forests in northern Congo, and massive logging trucks passed frequently, leaving me in a fog of fine, red dust – I choked on it, my clothes and skin were coated by it, Ibn's chain and gears were clogged by it, and if I was eating food that would be covered in red dust too.

Fortunately, at this stop, the truck passed as I gobbled my last gritty mouthful of bread. The dust settled and I held out my arm to examine it. Quite artistic, really. My forearm rippled with muscle, the skin was a pleasant rouge streaked by sweat, and my strong, now broad hand was capped by grease-packed fingernails (on my right hand – on my left hand, two fingers were without nails.) I wore 'dead whitemen's clothes' now: second-hand cast-offs from wealthy Europeans: Africans, who could not understand any living person giving away clothes of such quality, called them as they were perceived – dead whitemen's clothes. My once white shoes were a mix of black from ground-in mud and grease, and red from the dust – one was even badly chewed by mice. Funny to think how back in Guinea I'd been concerned about getting my shoes wet! I did not even bother cleaning them now as cleanliness was too ephemeral in these conditions. I pulled out my mirror to look at my face. I saw myself in full-face or full-length mirrors so infrequently that I found it strangely reassuring to check that I was still there, still okay.

I quite liked how I looked these days. My hair stuck to my skull – it never dried in the clinging humidity; my cheeks were gaunt; and my shoulders, while broad, were muscular and defined. And there was a wildness and bold-ness in my eyes that had not been there when I left London.

As I sat grimacing in the dust, a solitary man approached on foot.

'Have you fallen off?' he enquired solicitously.

That evening, I arrived in Loubetsi, a large village – a commune, in the administrative parlance of formerly Marxist Congo – and the home of a Protestant mission. I later heard the mission was once staffed by the Pentacostal church of Norway or Sweden, but there had been a falling out and now it was an independent Protestant mission, with no white missionaries. I received a very warm welcome from the head of the mission, the charming and elfin Pastor Germain.

'Welcome, welcome!' he cried excitedly. He was a short man, very wiry, with intelligent eyes filled with mischief and fun. 'You must stay with us, the house is full, but you are very welcome!'

I knew I would be better rested in my tent. Behind his house, I spied a flat piece of ground with shady trees, far from other compounds, and asked if I could erect my tent there.

'Over there?' He seemed surprised, even confused, at my request. 'You want to stay out in the open!' I explained with my usual story, and finally he let me, the perplexing white guest, do as I wished.

Towering mango trees, surely at least fifty years old, stood magnificently, only metres apart, like sentinels around my preferred camping spot. They cast a shade over the flat, swept-clay ground that was welcome even at that late hour of the day. There was a small structure at one side of the grove, like a picnic shelter. It was flat roofed, about the size of a small room, framed with wood. The three walls and the roof were covered in dried palm fronds. There was a fence of bamboo stakes along the open side, and when I had washed myself and my clothes I found the fence useful as a clothesline. Most attractively, the nearest compound was at least 50 metres away. Perhaps I would get some privacy, and the grove looked so peaceful.

It was a tranquil evening. After the usual spectacle of tent erection, the crowd dispersed and I was left with unusual peace at sunset. There was competition between voices soaring from a nearby church and drumming from surrounding compounds. While the singing ceased, the drumming continued, pleasantly echoing from different compounds throughout the evening.

I was up with the light, and walked over to my water bag hanging from Ibn's handlebars. I took a swig, and then washed my face and hands with a dribble. Shards of sunlight were breaking through the overhead canopy of branches and leaves, but the air was still hazy; the sky, where I could see it, a glint of silver. My nearest neighbour's mud-brick house and matching clay ground shone a bright orange as the sun found a hole in the haze and lit their compound. The mother emerged, brush in hand, and immediately bent over and started vigorously sweeping the compound. Hens and their chickens pecked energetically before her, desperate to find tasty morsels before they were swept away. Two little boys, not looking at all sleepy, played together in the far corner – they had a hand-made wooden toy truck that one could pull and the other chase. Around the parcel grew picturesque coconut palms.

It was a Sunday, and I was alone as people gathered at the church for singing and prayer. This morning, the congregation's competition was from birds twittering from the trees above. I was in no hurry to pack up and move on. I had another dust cold, but life seemed very good.

I started boiling some water on my Gaz stove, arranging some stale bread and my Nescafé, when Caroline, Pastor Germain's daughter whom I had met briefly the day before, and who apparently was skipping church this morning, approached. She was in her early twenties and was very like her father – petite and strong, with sparkling, intelligent eyes. She was wearing a bright white T-shirt and a blue, flowered *pagne* around her waist. Her hair was tressed tightly to her skull, leaving her face clear to show her fine cheekbones.

'Whites do drink coffee in the morning!' she immediately exclaimed, startling me as much as she was clearly startled herself. She laughed mischievously – also like her father. I was astonished that even my caffeine habit was now an object of amazement.

'What do you do?'

'I just get up and go to the fields – I might have manioc around 10 a.m.' She said it matter-of-factly, but she still looked perplexed. 'I have seen it in videos, where whites wake up and drink coffee! And you do, too!' She was laughing at the idea. 'I even saw one where the man would not get up until he was given a cup of coffee! So, it is true then.' She was shaking her head with remaining bewilderment, making me also feel bewildered. There was so little I could do that was not strange.

'This is a beautiful, quiet place,' I said to Caroline as I drained my cup of coffee. She had not accepted my offer of a cup, but she had remained watching me, making me feel like an interesting specimen. The sun had strengthened and now sunlight dappled the ground. There was more activity in nearby compounds and people were walking along the road at one edge of the grove.

'Yes,' said Caroline. 'It is where we hold evangelical services.'

'Services?' I gulped with stirring unease. 'You mean this is an open-air church?'

'Yes, and that,' she said, pointing at the 'picnic shelter', 'that is the altar.' I looked across to the altar to where my undies and T-shirt were fluttering, dry now, in a wafting breeze. I was aghast.

This was crass behaviour on my score card, yet it was treated like my drinking coffee. Caroline merely shrugged and laughed at the bizarre white. I immediately leapt up and pulled my clothing off the altar, and went to dismantle the tent.

'Why don't you stay another day?' asked Caroline. I was tempted. The dust cold was making my chest burn and my sinuses throb. All that red dust had got into my lungs – given the embedded coating on my T-shirt, I hated to think what their interior was like – and was now being expelled.

'Should I put the tent somewhere else?' I queried, not wanting to continue my offence.

'Why? Don't you like it here?' So, it was decided, and when Caroline left me, I crawled back into my tent, gave myself permission to be ill, and went back to sleep.

All morning I struggled out from my tent to greet curious new visitors, but fever began to take hold. Each time my visitors left, I crawled back into my secure cave and flopped again. It was not until the afternoon that I felt well enough to socialise properly.

I walked over toward Pastor Germain's house. Pastor Germain was not about, probably working hard on Sunday, but I could see Caroline under the shade of one of the mango trees, deftly tressing a young girl's hair.

'How many children do you have, Pamela?' asked Caroline directly as I sat down. She had a very assertive way about her. I noticed she had not asked if I was married, the usual first question from a man.

'None,' I said. 'How many do you have?'

'I have two, from my husband. We are divorced now.' Divorced in her twenties. This seemed unusual.

As we talked, I watched Caroline work. Caroline took a small strand of 1-inch-long, tightly curled hair, divided it into three, made a tiny tress, then laid it down against the child's skull – no cotton was needed to tie the end off to stop the plait unravelling.

'Here, feel it!' cried Caroline, pulling at my arm. I touched the young girl's hair and found it felt like steel wool, much stronger and wirier than other hair I had felt during my travels. The girl, not Caroline's daughter, giggled and reached out to my hair, as did Caroline. They found it strange, and Caroline left her work for a moment to brush it for me. It could have been soothing but I had too many knots!

Caroline resumed her work and I picked up our conversation.

'Why did you get divorced?'

'He used to take other women, and he would beat me,' she said. She sounded emotionally detached from the experience. 'He was military, and would drink too much. Men ...' She left the word hanging, shaking her head and not looking at me. Perhaps her emotions were not that detached. 'When they drink too much it is very bad.' She paused and then, with more spirit, said, 'He wanted to take a second wife, but I would not support that!' She told me how, one night, her husband had not come home and she had gone searching for him. At the time, they had been living in Brazzaville, the capital of Congo; she knew where to search. 'I found them at a hotel and I beat and screamed at the door until he let me in. I started attacking the woman and she fled downstairs into the hall with nothing on.' She stopped her work and looked directly at me. Her deep-brown eyes glinted.

'And what did you do to your husband?' I asked.

'He ran away!' She laughed, although I could see there was still some pain. 'It has been hard on my family. With the divorce, the money that my husband paid for me has had to be repaid ...'

Emmanuel, Caroline's younger brother, had joined us, walking over from the house, as Caroline was finishing her story. He was a tall, lanky young man, with doe-like, brown eyes. Unlike his sister, he had a calm disposition, but he was also very friendly.

'How much is paid for an Australian woman?' asked Emmanuel.

'Nothing,' I said.

'Nothing!' exclaimed Emmanuel. His doe-like eyes woke up with interest. 'Your parents would be paid nothing for you?' Even Caroline found this idea amusing, and Emmanuel was probing the consequences. 'You mean I could come to Australia and take an Australian woman?!' He was clearly very excited.

'Well, she might put up a fight,' I said. It was hard to explain this bizarre new white habit.

In the cool of the afternoon we walked to the river to have a swim and to wash my clothes, again. Caroline insisted they were not clean; she was right.

We went to a shady pool, the women's place. As it was the dry season, there wasn't a lot of water left, but it looked clean. While I frolicked with the children, Caroline took my leggings and T-shirt in hand – literally. They were soaped, beaten, scrubbed and pummelled with strength (and patience) I still did not have. However, it still took her fifteen minutes of persistent scrubbing to get the T-shirt white again.

As we walked back up the track to the village, Caroline starting talking about her plans.

'I would like to be a doctor, but I am still studying for the bac,' she said. Congo must have adopted the French baccalaureate educational system. 'I have failed it twice, but I will keep studying until I pass. It is always the physics that fails me!' I told her that physics was my worst subject, too.

Back at the village, I walked with her to collect some firewood which she then carried on her head to another compound. It was nearing dusk and I wasn't sure where we were going. By way of explanation, Caroline suddenly said, 'Tomorrow I must go to the fields but *mes règles* [my period] is giving me problems. This is the home of the traditional healer.' The firewood was payment.

We walked around the back and found a number of people waiting outside – old folk and mothers with children, including twins. Eventually, Caroline got her turn, went inside, then returned for another wait. That had been the consultation, now she awaited her medicine. After about a half hour, the healer's wife gave her a glass of red liquid, warm from the fire.

'It works very well,' said Caroline, 'but it makes me very sleepy.'

I was sleepy too, and I returned to the peace of my tent to make myself dinner. I was sitting outside, watching the stars that filled the black sky, when Caroline walked across from the house. We sat companionably together for a while, listening to the drumming again coming from nearby compounds. It had been a lovely, peaceful day.

'Why have you come back to Loubetsi?' I asked Caroline. She had lived in Brazzaville with her husband, and I imagined that she was here because of her divorce, or because she was waiting for her bac results.

'It is because of the civil war,' said Caroline in her usual straight manner, but surprising me.

I knew that from a trade unionist uprising in 1963 until 1990 Congo had been a Marxist state, though during the presidency of Colonel Denis Sassou-Nguesso (1979–91), this had been more in ideology than practice. In 1990, Marxism was renounced; in 1991 Sassou-Nguesso was forced to resign; and in 1992 a new multi-party democratic constitution had been approved. In ensuing elections, Pascal Lissouba – who had been appointed as prime minister in the first 1963 Marxist-Leninist government – won the presidency, but without a parliamentary majority in the senate or the national assembly. Lissouba called fresh elections in 1993. Lissouba's party won their majority, but the results were disputed and fighting had broken out all over the country between the armed forces and supporters of an opposition alliance that included Sassou-Nguesso's party.

'There is too much fighting in Brazza. It is not safe there anymore,' said Caroline. I thought the fighting had quietened down, but I supposed I had better find out more.

On leaving Loubetsi, it took two days of cycling hell to reach Dolisie.

'When I was a young man, I cycled to Loubomo in five hours,' said Pastor Germain as I was leaving. 'The roads were good, but now there are corrugations.' Too bloody right! My poor body was pounded by the ceaseless thud of the ridges and ruts. These ran edge to edge, so there was no escape – my arms felt like they were operating a jackhammer. At one point, just after 10,000 kilometres ticked over on my cycle computer, I stopped to grease the chain. Its links, thirsty for oil, were slipping on the dry, dust-covered cogs of the chainset. As I drew my water bottle to take a sip, the holder broke from metal fatigue. Oh Ibn, I thought, you are as tired as I. I let my bum drop back behind my haunches and I sat in the deep dust, causing small orange cloudlets to rise. The T-shirt Caroline had cleaned was red again. I just stared at the broken holder and at Ibn. I was numbed from exhaustion and from the heat. For several minutes, I rocked myself – back and forth, back and forth – and continued staring. I was only barely aware that I was near my limit.

After I recovered – through sugar and time – I wondered, do African women feel this way every day?

Dolisie was a large town with a French colonial feel, but it was barred and shuttered because of the recent fighting. Discovering a train for Pointe Noire was leaving that night, I decided to make a quick return excursion to the coast on the Congo–Ocean Railway – the train that runs between Brazzaville and the Atlantic port. Forced African labour was used for its construction by the French between 1924 and 1938, and thousands of workers died. This experience, together with the ongoing brutal exploitation of Congo by the French, resulted in the radicalisation of the trade unions and in the country's leaders turning to Marxism after they gained independence. But, to Ibn and me, the railway merely gave a comfortable overnight ride through gorges and bush to Pointe Noire.

At Pointe Noire, some Shell folk, who ran a small renewable forestry operation, took me to their farms (the eucalyptus smelt of home), and to a refuge for young chimpanzees orphaned from hunting and logging of their habitat in the rainforests of northern Congo. The chimps were excited to have a female visitor to their large forest compound, and at one point I had about eight baby chimps clinging to my limbs and torso, anxious for a milk drink!

Then, goodbye to the Atlantic (or so I thought) and back to Dolisie to resume the eastward leg to Brazzaville. Under the hot sun, and back on the badly maintained road, it did not take long to feel tired again. And to feel tired for six days.

Eventually, 90 kilometres outside Brazzaville, the bitumen had begun, and now, finally, I was cycling into the outskirts of the city, pleased to be out of the beautiful but disquieting countryside of Congo.

Certainly, in long stretches, the road from Dolisie had been captivating. Despite the corrugations, gravel, dust and mud, there had been rolling grass-lands with high, wide, cloud-sculptured skies and two Sierra Madre-like dry, scrub-covered mountain passes to cross. Throughout, the light had the clarity of fine crystal and on the mountain passes, away from villages, the road seemed quiet: I had frequently heard nothing but buzzing flies and a few chirping birds, and had wished I could record the quality of the silence.

That is, until the heavy humidity delivered black rainclouds and a powerful storm while I was on the final mountain pass. The wet season had arrived in this part of Africa. Darn it, I had thought while cycling up the mountain road, lightning flashing around me. It could have waited until I was dry in Brazza!

But the storm had added to my existing disquiet about this road. For the past four days, at the outskirts to villages, the silence had disappeared, and with it, any sense of peace and security.

'*Arrêt! Arrêt!*' and '*Cadeau!*' had been the aggressive calls of brooding youths – teenagers, twenty year olds, all male – as they had looked malevo-lently toward me and demanded their gifts. They had even grabbed at me a few times as I cycled past their village, but fortunately I had been able to find the speed to evade their grasp.

Sister Marie had been right. On the second night out of Dolisie, I had stayed at a monastery, where I had met Sister Marie, a French nun, who had been in Congo twenty-eight years, and Father Thomas, a French priest, here for thirty-two years. (There were a lot of missions and religious orders in Central Africa, and I consistently found them welcoming places to stay.) Over dinner in the refectory, they had told me more about the situation in Congo.

'In the nineteen sixties, this was a country with a lot of promise,' Father Thomas had said. He had white hair and a long, pointed beard and seemed ancient – but was probably in his late fifties. 'People had ideas. They wanted to change the country for everybody.'

'Now things are done for the president,' Sister Marie had added. She was a lithe woman with dark hair, probably a similar age. 'The country was terrible in July. People from the president's tribe and from the opposition's tribe started killing each other, chasing each other from their homes.'

'There were barricades put up by the youths everywhere, all over the country.' This had been Father Thomas. 'They demanded money, broke windscreens, were very violent …'

'And now they remain very insolent and menacing,' Sister Marie had continued. 'No one ever stopped them or punished them, so they think they are kings.'

The menacing had started at villages the next day, and the pervasiveness of the problem had been confirmed two nights later when I had stayed in the small village of Kinkembo. The elderly chief had welcomed me, but when I told my story of wanting to sleep in my tent because it was my home, he had shaken his head adamantly.

'I cannot guarantee your safety outside my house. You will put your bicycle inside and you will sleep with us,' he had commanded. Then, more sadly, he had added, 'It is the young men, they have come back from Brazzaville but do not want to work in the fields. There have been thefts and violence.' He had looked subdued. 'Things are very bad.'

It was depressing to realise that in Congo, not even the villages were safe havens from economic unrest and political violence.

Soon, I was cycling into downtown Brazzaville, also not a safe haven. The city had sprawling suburbs and in the centre were neat boulevards, office blocks and monuments. The fighting was not evident – until the next morning when I saw the damaged buildings. (In fact, the fighting continued in Congo, exploded in 1997, and resulted in heavy destruction and loss of life in Brazzaville. In 1998, Sassou-Nguesso was president.)

Now, at dusk, it looked a calm place. I cycled along the Corniche de Brazzaville wondering where I would stay the night – there were no Shell marketing operations in Congo: Elf was king here – so I was on my own. I was spellbound by my first view of the Zaire River, perhaps a kilometre wide, brown and laced with floating reeds that zipped downstream in the fast current. Across the other side was the skyline of Kinshasa, clearly a far bigger city than Brazzaville. I was excited to cross over, to get to Zaire, and to find out if the steamer to Kisangani was running. Along the way, I had heard it was not, but I was optimistic. One way or another, I would soon be travelling by boat rather than bike, heading for the wild interior of Zaire.

Suddenly, there was a scream of sirens and I swung over to the kerb. Policemen on motorbikes sped passed, then armed soldiers inside four-wheel-drives. I wondered what was happening. The president perhaps? But no. Following the soldiers at high speed was a hearse. A hearse?!

I asked a fellow bystander.

'It is the wife of an ancient president,' he said. 'She died in France.' It turned out that she was the wife of a president who had been assassinated. My companion was sardonic. 'We assassinate them one day, and revere them the next.'

Fourteen

Patience

Brazzaville, Congo – Kinshasa, Zaire

I passed quickly through Brazzaville and crossed the river to Kinshasa, a sprawling city with over five million people, and the capital of a vast country of over 42 million – the enticing Zaire. Fortunately, Shell had a presence here: after the long ride from Libreville, I was once again happy to let myself be cocooned inside another palace – a massive, though spartanly furnished, two-storey house with a pool all to myself – and to be invigorated by another programme.

Kalonji was my minder. He was a big man, like a bouncer and very opinionated about women's issues – basically, he believed a woman's place was in the home looking after her man – but he got things done. One of the first tasks for which I enlisted his help was to find out about the steamer (or *courrier* as I discovered it was called, because of its role in delivering mail and news) – was it running?

'ONATRA,' he said, referring to the government transport company that ran the steamer to Kisangani, 'has only managed to schedule one *courrier* this year.' It was late October. 'The best thing to do is to travel by cargo boat – they leave all the time, but conditions are hard. Will you manage?'

I was disappointed the *courrier* was out of the question. This was an infamous journey – an old colonial steamer, three storeys high with dilapidated staterooms and even first-class cabins (with doubtful facilities, but some privacy), made the journey to Kisangani while pushing several barges loaded with people and goods. It was a journey that had been written about and photographed, and seemed the *pièce de résistance* of great river-boat journeys of the world. I had cycled this far south primarily to experience the *courrier*, and now it was not running. What is more, the only road route out of Kinshasa went south-east into Shaba province, well away from Kisangani and the route I planned into Tanzania.

Besides, I wanted to travel this great river, used by Henry Morton Stanley between 1887 and 1889 to cross the continent. Of the 620 men who travelled with Stanley on the dreadful expedition, only 225 returned. The rest were killed along the way by disease, starvation, wild animals and hostile tribes. The expedition's objective was to rescue the German, Emin Pasha, governor

of Equatoria – a remote province in present-day Uganda; yet when they found him, Emin Pasha was not only better fed and better dressed than his rescuers, but able to produce champagne for a toast! He had no desire to be rescued! If Stanley and his men went through all that for so little, then whatever the conditions on this river, I could manage a cargo boat. The only question: when was one leaving?

Of course, then, I had no idea how long I would have to wait, nor what emotional turmoil waiting could bring.

The day after my arrival, Kalonji and I visited the port. Against the grass-covered river bank and ancient wooden wharf lay rusty pushers and barges four and five deep, with other, smaller craft moored prow-first between them. Rusting hulks lay on their sides or were propped up on stilts on the dry mud, but there was not a lot of work in progress. The port seemed like a jumble yard.

Amongst the jumble, we sought the office of Mboliaka, the company which ran the cargo boat Kalonji had heard might be leaving later that week (though it was Thursday already). I followed Kalonji past a number of containers that were laid side by side, then up a steep, metal-runged ladder laid against one of them. Where were we going? At the top was a double-width metal container, with holes cut for windows and a door – the Mboliaka office!

A woman behind a desk greeted us. She wore glasses with thick lenses that enlarged the size of her eyes.

'I am Mme Kabamba, can I help you?'

When we enquired if the boat was leaving tomorrow, she revealed they were waiting for fuel. 'Fuel is coming Monday and will be loaded Tuesday.' Her tone implied efficiency, speed. 'The cargo ... well, it will arrive when the customs are ready.' She smiled wryly. 'Come again on Tuesday, and then try each two days after that.'

'You see that time is flexible here in Zaire,' said Kalongi.

Back at Shell, Pierre Zumbi, the energetic personnel director, said much the same.

'This is the Z factor, Pamela,' he said cheerfully. 'Time passes without consequence. It is what we battle here in Zaïre!' He sounded like he enjoyed the battle.

However, I was cool. Clearly, I would be in Kinshasa at least a week, but there was plenty to experience here.

With Ibn laden only with the handlebar bag and an empty rear pannier, I could cycle through downtown on shopping trips for supplies for the great river journey.

'You must bring your own food, and be responsible for your water,' Mme Kabamba had said.

A week later, I cycled down Boulevard 30 Juin, the main six-lane highway that defined the heart of downtown Kin (as the locals called the city). Office buildings from the Belgian colonial period were massive, made of granite, with a prosperous, Gotham City look. There were modern office buildings and shops, but most were closed, windows protected by metal shutters. Soldiers sat outside every building or strolled the streets. People everywhere were out walking – men and women in suits and traditional *pagnes*. They all stared at me. I expected that in the villages – it was one of my ongoing burdens that I now accepted playfully, or resented gloomily, depending on my level of tiredness – but I usually had more anonymity in the cities. Not here: Europeans do not normally walk, much less cycle, in Kinshasa.

'You should not cycle, Pamela,' Zumbi had warned me. But when I walked, I was followed; I preferred the speed of my bike.

A city train, a long articulated bus, rumbled past, people hanging precariously from the doors. There was a lot of tooting from a procession of cars coming toward me; I pulled over to watch.

'It is a funeral, *madame*,' said a man near me, 'for a soldier.' The line of cars and military vehicles was on its way to a nearby cemetery. People in the cars waved tree branches from the windows, the coffin was in the back of a pick-up truck, guarded by seated soldiers, their rifles visible. The tooting faded as they passed and I remounted, heading for *Supermarché* Select, the main source for tins and western goodies.

When I arrived, it was 1 p.m. and it was closed. Again! For three days, I had arrived to be told they had closed – Monday at 3 p.m., Tuesday at 2 p.m. and today at noon. Always too late! They were closing to adjust their prices upwards to account for the plummeting exchange rate. When I had arrived, it was 9 million Zaires to the US dollar, today, a week later, it was 45 million! I had changed my dollars at a 20 million rate so I needed to find something to spend my money on, quickly.

The money situation was surreal. Not only was there 1000 per cent inflation, but prices were in many millions of Zaires – when I had arrived, a carton of orange juice cost 35 million Zaires – while the highest denomination note was 1 million Zaires. People walked around clutching satchels and briefcases filled with money, transactions were done with wads of cash. I was carrying 200 million Zaires – a pile about six inches thick.

I cycled to the *Marché Central*, a huge place covering the equivalent of several blocks that, despite the hyperinflation, was a chaos of activity. Goods tumbled over each other – fabrics, food, cosmetics, clothing, hardware and household items – as did sellers.

'*Madame! Madame!*' people called, trying to attract me to their wares.

For over a year now, by necessity I had bought seldom and frugally, but now I had an excuse to spend. Much as a visit to Harrods department store in London might stimulate an urge to buy, I now felt a materialistic urge to 'own'. I headed for the plastics section, a corner devoted to buckets, bowls, plates, cups, baskets all in bright shades of blue, orange, red, purple, yellow. After careful considera-tion, I selected a blue bucket with a lid for holding drinking water on the boat (and other uses, I thought, remembering Al and Suze in Mali!), a new lilac plastic cup for scooping water, a green bottle with handle for attaching to a rope and drawing water from the river, and a blue lunch box because I liked it – and handed over a fat wad, 100 million Zaires! I was in a spending frenzy and, excit-edly, I realised I still had 100 million Zaires to spend!

Within weeks, the Zaire currency was to be replaced by New Zaires, at a rate of 3 million old Zaires to 1 New Zaire – but the government had no foreign exchange backing for issuing the new currency, and no guarantees it would be accepted in the marketplace. A previous attempt to introduce a 5 million Zaire note to pay soldiers had been blocked by market women who refused to accept it. Zaireans, who mainly held their money outside the banking system (most of the economy was in the informal sector), were anxious to convert their money to goods while their notes still had value. A vicious circle of panic buying, wild inflation and more panic buying was fuelling itself. Nobody was sure where it would end.

This was Kinshasa under the final years of President Mobutu Sésé Seko Koko Ngbendu wa za Banga, who had come to power in a coup d'état in 1965. Although facing considerable external and internal pressure to democratise, Mobutu, whose self-adopted name meant, in full, 'the all-powerful warrior who, because of his endurance and inflexible will to win, will go from conquest to conquest, leaving fire in his wake', was not going to give up power easily. A National Conference to draft a new multi-party democratic constitution had been called in 1990, and in 1992, a new prime minister, Etienne Tshisekedi, and opposition-dominated government had been elected, and recognised by the opposition and National Conference. Mobutu had retaliated by appointing his own prime minister, Faustin Burundwa. The power struggle was intense.

Early conversations in Kinshasa were peppered with a French word – '*pee-yage*'. I thought it was a tollway (*un péage*), but the sense was wrong. I kept hearing, 'Before the *pee-yage* … During the *pee-yage* … After the *pee-yage* …' Finally, I had to ask.

'Qu'est-ce que c'est "un pee-yage"?'

'It is rioting and looting by the people.' Oh. What I was hearing as *'un pee-yage'* was *'un pillage'* – a pillage. What the Visigoths did in Rome.

It was a strange word to hear in common use, but I discovered there had already been two pillages in Kinshasa.

The first had occurred in September 1991. Some maintained it was orchestrated by Mobutu – to destroy opposition wealth; others said it was an uprising by rebellious unpaid soldiers. Either way, it started with the soldiers in Kinshasa, but spread to the general population, and resulted in businesses, offices and homes being stripped not only of small, valuable items, but also of their wiring, flooring and roofing. The second pillage occurred in January 1993, resulting from Mobutu's unsuccessful attempt to pay soldiers with the new 5 million Zaire note. Finding the note was not accepted by traders, the soldiers again went on a looting rampage, this time not followed by the general population.

'I saw a mama walking with a television set on her head, just like it was a basin of bananas,' said one Frenchman at a dinner party I attended.

'I saw a man swimming to Brazza, using a refrigerator as a float,' said another.

The expatriates who had experienced the pillages were generally those with their own businesses who had spent many years in Zaire. They had stayed or had only briefly evacuated, while the expatriates on two-year contracts left quickly – and often for good! Amongst the long-term expats, there was a curious one-upmanship for the most outrageous or awful tale to tell. Some stories were terrible – about rape victims contracting AIDS, having been held by gun to their forehead, being left with no water for days, being separated from their children and not knowing what had happened to them – but it also stimulated camaraderie. Those who had been through the pillages would stay now, come what may.

And they weren't sure what was coming.

'It is not the politics that may start them this time, but their stomachs,' a Belgian who had lived for many years in Zaire told me. 'With the price rises, people cannot afford the food. They are hungry.'

Zumbi of Shell had confirmed, 'The worst problem in Kinshasa today is hunger.'

I knew what they meant – a few days ago, a small baguette had cost 2 million Zaire, in the afternoon it cost 3 million Zaire, the next day it was 8 million Zaire. A salary for a driver was 30 million Zaire per month, for a company director 130 million Zaire a month. Government workers had not been paid for eight months. People were walking on the streets of Kinshasa, not for a cosmopolitan promenade, but because they could not afford to pay bus fares.

'You must carry your radio and keep it on at all times,' commanded Zumbi when I first arrived, referring to the two-way radio I had been issued that connected all Shell employees on a private frequency. 'In case the situation blows up, we all assemble by the river at the *directeur général*'s house.' During the second pillage, Shell staff had fled to the director's house to leave by boat to Brazza across the river, but they had been fired on. The marketing director, Nkobo Makabi, had been shot in the arm and was still in Belgium, receiving medical treatment. When I cycled around Kinshasa, it was with a radio aerial poking from my front handlebar bag. On the one hand, the situation made every day feel full of adventure. On the other hand, I wondered, where would this madness end?

Of course, while I was in Zaire, all the focus was on getting rid of Mobutu. When I offered Zumbi my observation that African leaders had failed their people, he was fierce.

'We would have got rid of Mobutu long ago, if it had not been for the Troika!' He was referring to Belgium, America and France, the three countries with the greatest vested interests in Zaire's future.

Others I met echoed his feelings. Another professional and well-educated Zairean said, 'Bush George,' – in Zaire, people were referred to by their surnames first – 'received funding from Mobutu, as did Mitterand and Chirac – he bought their support. We are not sure about Clinton Bill, but of the others it is clear. Gistang Valerie comes to Zaire for holidays with Mobutu, and a son of Mobutu is best friends with the youngest son of Mitterand.'

These kinds of accusations about foreign interference in Zaire's self-determination were common at Kinshasa dinner parties and amongst the general population. What was clear was that, for many years, Mobutu's corruption and diversion of funds to his own pocket and to those who supported him, had been well known. However, during the Cold War, having Zaire – a huge country at the heart of Africa – led by a pro-western leader suited the western powers. Moreover, it had extraordinary mineral wealth, and many lucrative mining leases were potentially available.

(As of this writing, Laurent Kabila has a tenuous hold on the country's leadership. One of his first acts on taking power in 1997 after Mobutu's death from prostate cancer was to rename Zaire the Democratic Republic of Congo (DRC) and the Zaire River as the Congo River. It was a popular move: the name Zaire had bad associations with the past. Kabila took power with the support of the Ugandan and Rwanda governments, both Tutsi controlled, and the Banyumalenge, the DRC Tutsis who also live in the Lake Kivu region, an extremely tiny minority in DRC's patchwork of 250 tribes. By mid 1998, Kabila had lost their support, and fierce war erupted between rebels and Kabila's forces. The rebels are a mixture of Rwandan troops, Banyamulenge, soldiers once loyal to Mobutu, and ex-supporters of Kabila. Kabila obtained support and military aid from Zimbabwe, Chad, Angola and

Namibia, as well as loyal Zaireans who feared a foreign Rwandan/Tutsi-led takeover of their country. At stake is the wealth of Zaire and its existence as a single nation. The interference of the Troika – on different sides – is again rumoured. At this writing, rebels hold eastern Zaire, Kabila is threatening a big offensive to push them out, African-led peace negotiations have fallen apart, the likelihood of a break up of the Republic increases, and the cycle of madness continues for ordinary Zaireans.)

While I was at the *Marché Central*, tying down my plastic purchases to the rear carrier, my radio telephone crackled into life.

'Kalonji for Watson, Kalonji for Watson, over.'

I answered my call.

'I have contacted Mme Kabamba at Mboliaka, over,' crackled Kalongi. My heart leapt. The boat would be leaving and I hadn't finished my purchases.

'Yes?' I replied. 'Over.'

'They are still waiting for fuel and cargo,' he said. 'She says they may not depart for one or two weeks yet.'

Ugh. I had been waiting for one week already. Now, maybe, I would have to stay three weeks. I was starting to experience the Z factor – in full.

'She says to call each day to get news,' continued the crackling Kalonji, and then he added, '*Patientez-vous, Paméla.*' He knew I would be dispirited. 'You think a day is twenty-four hours.' I could hear his chuckle. Zaireans loved chuckling at whatever life threw at them. I had learnt that much in one week. It was the source of their resilience. 'In Zaire, a day is seven days. Over.'

When on the corrugated, red-dust road from Libreville, at times I had wanted a home where I could be clean all day and do domestic things. My wish had come true. Teach me to be careful what I wish for, eh? To combat the Z factor by having fun, I developed a basic early morning routine of swimming laps in the pool of my palace, cycling a circuit around the upmarket *quartier*, Gombé, then coming back to make myself breakfast of banana, papaya and coffee – to be taken by the pool, of course. Some days, I went shopping (still trying to unload my Zaires, but shops had been emptied of stock and few were opening at all now), organised my visa, wrote my newsletter, explored by bike, or visited the port for news about boats for Kisangani; and despite the increasing monetary crisis and rumours of pillage, a programme kicked into gear. Two women I met became special friends.

'They are the *grandes dames* [big women] of the Ministry,' said Zumbi, when he was first telling me about them. Both were *chef des services* in the *Ministère des Affaires Sociales, Familles et Solidarité Nationales* – Ministry of Social Affairs, the Family and National Solidarity. Mme Bolie Odette was the director of legal services, while Mme Mputela Antoinette was the director of services to promote the socio-economic development of the family. Both were passionate about their responsibilities and the issues that were their personal priorities.

Bolie, a big woman physically, hair always pulled back tightly from her attractive face, and often dressed in elegant *pagnes*, could be very formidable. 'The law says a woman can only work with the permission of her husband,' she told me forthrightly. 'So if a man has fallen out with his wife and is going to divorce her, he may ring her employer and say he does not want her to work. The employer is obliged to dismiss her! It is not right and will be changed!'

Mputela, a smaller woman who was very unpretentious in dress and appearance, had equal spirit. 'Does anyone talk about sanitary napkins?' asked Mputela energetically. 'No, because it has to do with the menstruation! Yet, there are none available anymore, and those that are imported are too expensive. What can women and young girls do? Something must be done!'

However, both agreed there was a more immediate and compelling issue facing people in Kinshasa – hunger.

'Health is a luxury now. Tuberculosis is coming back because of malnutrition and women do not have money for even the most basic ointment for their children,' said Bolie.

'People are more concerned with getting something to eat. Women must grow food or earn money to buy food – even ourselves. We have not been paid since March, and even if we are paid now, it will be worthless!' exclaimed Mputela energetically. 'Feeding our families is all that matters.'

Together we visited an innovative group who described their *Fonds Rotatif des Lapins*. Rotating Fund of Rabbits? Had I heard correctly? What was this?

'The fund lends rabbits,' said the leader. 'A male and female is lent to the women. For every male lent, they should repay a total of two, for every female lent, they should repay a total of four.'

Why rabbits?

'They are a good source of food, easy to keep in a small allotment, but more importantly they reproduce quickly … in thirty days, a woman could have a litter of ten or twelve rabbits!'

It seemed an innovative, sensible response to a high-inflation environment and the need for food. So sensible that Mputela and Bolie wanted to know the date of the next training session – they wanted to keep rabbits!

My third Saturday in Kinshasa, at 9 a.m., I waited to be picked up by Bolie and Mputela for a planned visit to Manenga, a village some distance outside Kinshasa.

'The Ministry helped the village women to purchase land from the old chief, to build a health centre and a day-care centre for the children,' Mputela had explained earlier. 'But now there is a new chief and we have heard that he is not letting the women work the land, he closed the health centre and destroyed the day-care centre!'

'These chiefs do what they want,' Bolie had said with angry resignation. 'It is like that.'

'We need to meet this chief and resolve it,' Mputela had added fiercely.

It sounded an interesting situation – but what was more interesting was when Bolie and Mputela turned up, two hours late (more Z factor), in an ambulance!

'It was the only vehicle that was working,' explained Mputela nonchalantly. For them what was special was having fuel. Due to the monetary crisis, fuel, like other goods, was not being imported and there was a shortage. (Hence my difficulty in getting a boat.) Deka, a young doctor I had met previously at a health-care centre we had visited, was driving.

We rapidly got caught near the *Marché Central* in a seemingly impenetrable tangle of turning vehicles, walking people, hawkers, their carts and bicycles, but a half hour of skilful and patient manoeuvring by Deka resulted in our escape – into more traffic jams and road blockages in the *Cité*, the popular but poor district of Kin. Open drains next to the roads were littered with rubbish, and often the tarmac disappeared under gushing water, or just disappeared. Houses, some mere rusty tin shanties, were crowded together. Roadside verges, in fact any open spaces, were converted to plots, with neatly planted rows of manioc, tomatoes and other vegetables. People walked along the road edges, jumping over obstacles or out of the way of swerving, alarmingly driven vehicles. Deka had to snake around vehicles queuing for petrol – they radiated in all directions from each open station. Even closed stations had queues as rumours spread quickly across the city about where the next petrol supply would be made. Deka drove the robust ambulance, really a van, over verges and median strips to find a track around a blockage. He made U-turns, then was foiled by more tangled queues in the other direction.

'Life is very hard here in Kinshasa,' he called at one point. Mputela and Bolie agreed, but all three laughed and were enjoying the battle.

I thought that life had a certain surreal quality in Kinshasa – and I loved it, too!

We discussed the rumour that a petrol station had been pillaged, we discussed inflation and the rumours that the new currency would be refused in the opposition-controlled province of Kasai, we discussed whether a Mboliaka or an ONATRA steamer would ever leave. But it was banter with lots of laughter, and as many turns to the conversation as Deka had in his driving! Whether battling the traffic, or politics, or the Z factor – life seemed very vivid, very daring.

It started to rain and the people walking along the road held umbrellas, banana leaves, briefcases or material above their heads to protect themselves from the sudden downpour. Unexpectedly, we stopped to pick up a tall, thin man whose jacket hung loosely on his bony frame. It turned out he was a friend of Deka's, apparently the chief statistician with the government, concerned with measurements of the cost of living in the informal economy. Deka and he chatted for a while, then we were introduced.

'Do you calculate a poverty line?' I asked wondering how it kept up to date with hyperinflation.

'We used to,' he replied, 'but in the last pillage, all our computers and diskettes were stolen. We don't have any records anymore – only very old statistics on paper. We are forced to start again.'

We made a detour down a muddy side street to drop the statistician near his home. It was 12.30 p.m.

'The mamas will be waiting for us,' said Mputela with a grin. 'We were to meet them at noon.' We had still not left Kinshasa and had 30 kilometres of country road to cover, but no one seemed very worried.

Another stop was made, this time at a street tyre repairer to mend the spare.

When we finally arrived near Manenga, after a drive through a lush valley of small farms, it was nearly 2 p.m. Leaving the ambulance, we crossed a white-water river by a precarious-looking bridge made from suspended vines and planks, then traipsed up a steep, manioc-covered, emerald-green hill along a treacherously muddy track to the village. Women emerged from their mud-walled, thatch-roofed huts to greet us.

'*Bonjour!*'

'*Bonjour!*'

But the chief was not there.

'He has stayed away deliberately,' said Mputela.

'Where is his son?' asked Bolie of one elderly woman, and we were led to a whitewashed building where the woman called out. Petit Thomas, the chief's eldest son, looking very much at home with a towel around his waist – he had been washing – emerged from the building: it was the health centre. The chief and his family had moved in!

Petit Thomas got a grilling from the *grandes dames* from the Ministry. Eventually, drinks were served – palm wine, which tasted more palatable with each sip – then, a woman brought out a casserole dish.

'What is that?' I asked as the casserole lid was removed to reveal small, white lumps.

'*Ce sont les chenilles,*' Bolie said. Caterpillars!

'*C'est la protéine,*' said Mputela as she picked up a few in her fingers.

'*Très bon!*' cried someone else, and everyone was grabbing fingerfuls and popping them in their mouths.

I was already aware of the Zairean habit of eating insects – I had seen them for sale in squirming basins at the *Marché Central*. 'They are a good source of protein when meat is so expensive,' said a man nearby – he had seen me grimace. Now, I tried them. I sniffed one – it smelt like mushrooms. I popped one in my mouth and swirled it about – not much flavour. I bit into it – it was crunchy. Everyone laughed at my timidity, I ate another fingerful and we drank more palm wine.

The afternoon seemed very inconclusive and, as we departed, all in a good mood, I asked, 'Why *was* the day-care centre destroyed?'

'Petit Thomas said there was a big snake living in the building,' answered Mputela. 'It was threatening people in the nearby houses so they burnt the building to kill the snake.' Mputela and Bolie both laughed raucously at the bizarre explanation. Life was definitely surreal.

Near the spot where the ambulance was parked was an enormous market for manioc leaves – *pondu*, as they are called.

'It's our basic food,' said Bolie as she haggled with a seller. Manioc root and leaves cooked in different ways were the staple foods of Central Africa and I eventually had learned to like it.

'It is like spinach,' said Mputela, also in serious negotiations. It seemed *pondu* cost 3 million Zaires a bunch out here, versus five times that in Kinshasa. 'It is best prepared with salted fish,' continued Mputela, taking ownership of many tied bunches.

We finally left for the return drive to Kinshasa around 5 p.m., in an ambulance where people were no longer visible – the entire interior was crammed with bunches of *pondu*. The day was not totally inconclusive!

On Wednesday, three weeks after my arrival, the monetary crisis was near boiling point, but I had a decision to make – Kalonji had finally given me the news that a Mboliaka boat was leaving tomorrow.

'You must get out of Kinshasa while you can,' offered one expatriate. 'It is getting very hot here.' 'You should not leave Kinshasa – there are military everywhere, and the pillaging will happen in Kisangani as much as Kin,' said another. 'The captain can keep the boat in the middle of the river if there is trouble,' said a third. 'You should go.'

Kinshasa was alive with calamitous rumours and expatriates who had arrived after the previous pillages were especially fond of giving me unsolicited alarmist advice. Expatriates who had been through the pillages were more sanguine. Kinshasa was always alive with calamitous rumours which never came true, I was told, and the worst occurrences were never predicted.

However, I had other issues than impending pillage to consider.

During my first few nights in my Kinshasa palace, ironically when I was not in the protection of my sealed tent, my legs had been badly bitten by small, black insects. Stupidly, I had scratched them, and in the past couple of days, many of the bites had turned to open, infected sores. I had been cleaning the sores with antiseptic cream, but it was clear they were not responding. Kalonji knew and was doing his best to find antibiotics in closed-down Kin. However, this was the day before joining the boat for a twenty- to thirty-day journey to Kisangani, in steamy, unclean conditions.

I had been through this before many years ago on a boat journey on the Nile. Infections on my legs became so bad that I became delirious. Fortunately, three

Dutch travellers were aboard; they cared for me and took me to a hospital for treatment when we finally arrived in Juba in southern Sudan. I was barely conscious.

To leave Kinshasa now, before I knew the sores were responding to antibiotics, while they were still open and pustulating, would not be the prudent decision. I had a stomach of iron (more or less) but I knew battling infections was not my body's strength. Having come so far, how could I risk, at best, having a miserable boat journey, or at worst, ending up in a hospital or being flown out, ill, from Kisangani?

But I badly wanted to go. While on some days, Kinshasa's surreality and unpredictability made me love Kinshasa and feel alive, right now, I had had enough. I hated being stationary, and in these days of fuel shortage, who knew when another boat would be scheduled?

Kalonji arrived at the palace the next morning. I limped downstairs to greet him, my legs were wrapped in bandages. He had the antibiotics.

'*Tu pars ou tu ne pars pas?*' he asked solemnly. You leave or you don't leave?

'*Je ne pars pas,*' I replied, close to tears, tears of frustration. I wasn't leaving, I could not risk it, but I was close to despair.

'You are just getting Kinshasa inertia!' exclaimed one expatriate friend, Jason. He and his wife, Suzanne, were Canadians who ran their own business and had been in Kinshasa with their two children through both the pillages. After my decision to stay, it became clear I needed to fend for myself – shortly, I would be evicted from the palace by the arrival of two managers from Europe and, anyway, I felt I risked outstaying my welcome. Jason and Suzanne came to my rescue with an offer to stay with them. 'Lots of people keep saying they will just stay a bit longer and it ends up being years!' continued Jason. 'Life is so good here.'

Then, he realised what he had said, and we all burst into laughter.

Initially, it was hard to perk myself up. My sores responded to the antibiotics – and as is the ironic way of these things, this depressed me. Should I have gone? I hated using up my welcomes. Now, when would I get away? I worried about so much time passing when I could be spending it with my parents, my brother, William. Should I fly out? But then I received mail from a friend in Australia with good advice: Never Give Up!

The crisis peaked in late November, the week after my decision to stay. A benefit of being in Kin was that I would get to see the outcome of this taut thriller! (Or so I thought.) The New Zaires were introduced, accepted in most places but prices took another leap forward as, rather than dividing by 3 million Zaires to the one new Zaire, shopkeepers just knocked off the zeroes. Hence, the 18-million-Zaire baguette which should have cost 6 New Zaires, cost 18 New Zaires. The tension over the potential for pillage continued – but I had become more used to it.

As the days wore on, two possibilities for a boat to Kisangani emerged: the ONATRA steamer and a cargo boat. I got excited and my energies went into tracking them down; then, I had to suppress my frustration as the news continued to be inconclusive.

I now haunted the office of M. Wampileka, manager of programming for the ONATRA steamer, just in case. To see him once I had to make several visits, because often he was not in – probably moonlighting on another job, as was the norm for most unpaid government workers. At least going there, trying to see him, made me feel like I was doing something to overcome my stationary fate.

'No, *madame*, it is not yet programmed' he invariably said once I located him. M. Wampileka was a likeable man, but whether the steamer travelled or did not seemed of little consequence. He would grin and add, '*Patientez-vous.*' However, at least there was a steamer, the *Kokolo*, that had returned from Kisangani. Where there was a ship, there was hope. 'We are waiting for fuel, *madame*,' said M. Wampileka. 'However, it will not be long. ONATRA is an important company – they must give us fuel.' Oh, really?

Kalonji kept me informed about the other boat, but the situation was the same.

'No, it is not yet programmed, *madame*,' he would say over the radio, which I still had, despite my decreasing contact with Shell. '*Patientez-vous.* Over.'

The Kinshasa experience was one of intense ups and downs and contradictory emotions, all in the same day, every day. It was that essential part of the African experience that Suze had so aptly described in Mali – magnified one thousand fold!

To battle the Z factor, to steady the emotional turbulence, I kept busy.

With the passing weeks, as I came to know even more people, I was invited to talk to various groups, including schools, and even to the Rotary club. Ibn and I spruced up – as much as we could – for a luncheon at the Intercontinental Hotel with the great and good (males) of Zairean and expatriate business. After I had finished speaking, the director of the Office for Tourism, a debonair-looking man, rose to give a vote of thanks.

'It is probably appropriate that this task fall to me,' he began. 'At last, I have some work with the arrival of our first tourist to Kinshasa this year.' There was a roar of laughter. It was December 10.

'And it is good to meet someone who does not demand security,' he continued. 'When I was in Europe last year, all the travel representatives I met in each country, could only talk about that. I gave them assurances that security was absolute in Kinshasa, then, when I got back we had the second pillage!' The house was brought down.

Yes, I was busy, but was I going anywhere? Jason said it all when he came home one evening.

'Phew,' he said, sitting down at the table for dinner. 'We had a Zaire kind of day. Everybody worked hard but nothing was achieved!' This was the battle against the Z factor. Sometimes it made everyday life a challenge and exhilarating. Sometimes.

By mid December, I had been in Kinshasa for seven weeks, and *still* no boat was programmed. The news from the cargo boat was that it was probably not going to leave until the New Year, and what about ONATRA? I had not been to bother M. Wampileka for a while. Then, while visiting Shell, I met Zumbi on the stairs.

'Have you heard?' he said, smiling. 'The ONATRA boat is scheduled to leave on Sunday.'

What?!

I immediately cycled to see M. Wampileka. He was in. I tried to be cool.

'How is the position with the diesel?' I asked nervously.

'*Ça va,*' he replied.

'*Ça va!*' I exclaimed.

'Yes, we have the fuel,' he was smiling. 'But now we have a repair to do. The *courrier* may be programmed to leave in the New Year.'

I cycled back to Zumbi with my distressing news, but he could only guffaw.

'Oh, Pamela! You think that when Zaireans say A, they mean A. No, they always mean B.' He rocked himself with his own, solo laughter, then added, '*Patientez-vous.*'

To restore my patience, and now knowing no boat was leaving until the New Year, I decided to travel west to see the Atlantic. Again.

I travelled westwards overnight to Matadi – the port of Zaire, the town furthest inland along navigable stretches of the Zaire River – in a logging truck run by a company called COTRAZAL. From there, I travelled via various vehicles to Muanda, back on the coast. In Muanda, I had a second Christmas in Africa with new-found friends: it was spent in the waves, eating crab, drinking too much Primus beer and dancing all night to the noisy, fast-tempo, wonderful *soukous* of Zaire. It was good to forget travelling eastwards for a while, but before New Year, I was back in Matadi, to join another COTRAZAL truck for the return to the capital.

During the long ride back, on a remote stretch of road, the friendly driver, Kwase, and I were forced to halt behind a backed-up queue of trucks and vehicles. After a drenching storm the night before, a culvert over a small river had collapsed, taking part of the road with it. The remaining slither of bitumen was laced with cracks, while the far side was subsiding mud, clearly with no support beneath and in danger of imminent collapse. Nonetheless, with a crowd of others, I watched a truck accelerate down the final approach to the precarious stretch over the culvert, saw its wheels subside in the mud and the load lurch to a sickening 60-degree angle to the ground. Would he tip? The driver corrected the skid, then ground to a halt, the truck's wheels scoured deep into the glue-like mud. Phew.

The next act was the lumbering arrival of a grader marked *Office des Routes*.

'It is the *Office des Trous*,' said a droll young man standing near me – Office of Holes.

A steel-mesh cable from the grader was attached to the truck, then the grader reversed and pulled the truck free from the mud and onto steadier ground.

Soon the entire performance was repeated, this time for a Kinshasa-bound truck.

'It has been weakening for ten weeks,' said the young man. I had discovered he was a teacher who lived in a village nearby.

'Why hasn't a diversion been built?' I asked. This Kinshasa to Matadi road was an important artery connecting the capital with its port, and was used daily by hundreds of heavy vehicles. It enabled produce, logs and minerals brought down the Zaire River from the interior to be exported, and provided access for imports to the main market of Zaire. It was strategically important but, despite stories that the sealing of the road had been funded by donors three times, there were only two short stretches of rapidly deteriorating bitumen, a long gap of disastrous track in between, and now this road collapse.

'We have things like this in our country,' said the teacher. 'It is caused by the leadership.'

There was another breathtaking near disaster with an old, rusting bucket of a truck.

'These trucks are making it worse,' I said. They were gouging trenches that would weaken the culvert further, yet after the drenching of the night, the day was now clear and the equatorial sun was bright and fierce. 'Why don't they at least wait for the mud to dry?'

'Oh, we Zaireans,' said my friend, without apparent humour, 'we don't like to wait!'

My patience, or at least my optimism, had returned over the New Year break. Pillage hadn't broken out and the monetary situation seemed to have stabilised for a while at 125 New Zaires to the US dollar. This was a devaluation of over 400 per cent. At least with stabilisation, fuel and other goods might be imported and available once more. On the first working day after New Year, a Tuesday, I went to check on boats.

Nkobe Makabi, the marketing director, was back from Europe, and I went to meet him.

'Call me Mak,' he said. He looked frail and had lost the use of his right arm from the gunshot wound he sustained in the last pillage, but he was extremely friendly.

'Let me find out about your boats,' he offered. 'The cargo boat from Zaire SEP, and ONATRA?'

I went back to his office later in the morning to get the answers. One would be leaving, I was sure.

'The cargo boat left on Saturday,' he said. What? It had gone without me! And ONATRA? 'It is not yet programmed.'

Anguish! After all the waiting, one boat had gone without me, and the other – well, the other, I had never expected to go. How long would I be stuck here? More battles against the Z factor – no! I had to get out.

I was sunk in a chair, in darkest despair, then Mak continued. 'I have found you a boat for Wednesday.'

Next Wednesday? Only eight days away! Hooray!

'No, it is leaving tomorrow,' said Mak.

I leapt up and hugged him. Finally, I would leave Kinshasa – after ten long weeks of waiting.

Fifteen

Africa Moto!

Kinshasa, Zaire – Kisangani, Zaire

It was late afternoon on day two of my journey on the Zaire River. We had left Kinshasa at dusk the day before.

'*Plus ou moins vingt jours*,' – more or less twenty days – was the greatest precision the *commandant*, Jean, offered about how long the journey would take. He had said we would stop at Mbandaka, Lisala, Bumba and Isangi before arriving in Kisangani. I could see each place dotted along the blue arc of the Zaire River marked on my Michelin, but did not know what to expect of them.

More importantly, I had no idea how powerfully this journey would affect me.

I was on a cargo boat, a pusher plus four barges lashed together. The pusher was a sturdy pitbull of power and practicality. The diesel engines barked and strained below and discharged water behind in white, churning streams. The top level was the wheelhouse (emblazoned with red letters – GAP – the name of the company that owned the boat), the *commandant*'s accommodation, and a covered rear deck largely filled by two enormous freezers, while at water level were the engines and one squat toilet for passengers. Each barge was a rusting, flat-topped hulk, about 30 metres long and 10 metres wide. Three lay one in front of the other, while the fourth lay to the port of the second barge. Their holds carried diesel, while the surface supported various cargo including vehicles, and perhaps five hundred passengers squashed together.

I was the only white aboard and had been offered the same privileges as the four or five military officers aboard – I accepted them quite shamelessly: I knew enough about pain and suffering now to grab at chances of comfort when they were offered to me. Not only was I allowed on the pusher, I was able to use the toilet and shower in the *commandant*'s cabin and to put my food in one of the freezers, and was given access to the roof, a rare place of space on this crowded boat.

I had one rooftop companion – Freddy, a tall, gangly lieutenant who had been wearing army fatigues, but now, out of sight from Kinshasa, was wearing bright green shorts and a T-shirt. He had helped me strap Ibn to the electrical box on the roof and to secure my tent via elastic bungee cords to various hooks and bolts.

Climbing down the ladder, pulling my heavy blue sack of most precious possessions behind me, and entering the mêlée of the barges, was not something I had been ready for, and I had sat on the exposed metal roof throughout the heat of the day.

Overnight we had left the lake-like vista of Stanley Pool – the stretch of river where Kinshasa was located. All day we had been travelling through a narrower stretch of river, perhaps just 500 metres wide, edged by low hills that rose directly from the water and were lightly vegetated by emerald-green forest. The dominant feature was the sky, a sultry, enveloping, grey-blue canopy. The water was dark and rippled from a light breeze and it concealed whatever life hid below. Clumps of water hyacinth, the floating weed of African rivers, slid by.

Around 1 p.m., dark clouds had emerged and swept the Republic of Congo, which was on our left; the river marks the border. As the clouds raced towards us, people rushed to move their possessions under cover – I put mine in my tent. Soon, the rain was upon us, bucketing down; then, just as suddenly, the sun was out, beating down.

The barges provided an ever-changing mosaic of life. In the early morning,

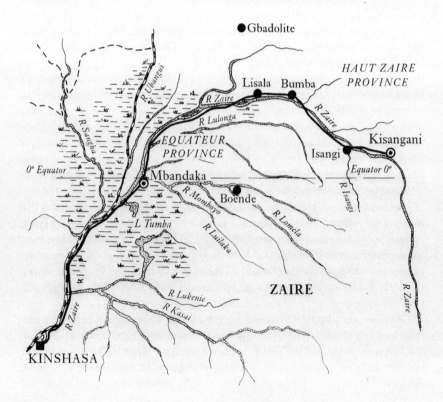

young men fished for water using empty tins. Tied to a string, the cans were tossed into the swirling currents and pulled back, the thrower taking a thirsty draught or using the water to clean his teeth. During the day, women emerged from their hidden camping spots, and crouched or sat on wooden, three-legged stools, tendering charcoal burners, washing dishes or scrubbing clothes in buckets. About a metre around the edges of the barges was left clear for people to pass and do their chores. Flurries of activity occurred in every spare inch of space.

A few *pirogues* emerged from tiny villages on the banks, waited ahead of our path, then, with great skill, were manoeuvred into tying up with us. The village traders might have dried or fresh fish, bundles of *pondu* or other produce to sell. Usually, one of our eager passengers snapped up the goods, then the villager clambered aboard and shuffled around looking for a bargain. It seemed our passengers were carrying goods for trade and markets were set up around the edges of the boat, just out of my sight.

The rest of life on this first barge was concealed by five khaki-green MAN military trucks. Four were parked two abreast; the fifth was in the centre at the farthest end of the barge. They were chunky and ancient, their wind-screens lowered flush with the bonnet, and I thought they looked like something out of *M*A*S*H*. Initially, each had its back covered with a tarpaulin, but soon after leaving Kin, the tarps had been pushed back and the truck cabins had become homes to young men.

One truck had a sleek speedboat as its load. Revealed by the removal of a covering tarp, it provided a paradoxical image. Seven young men, attired in Hawaiian-style, patterned shirts and bright T-shirts (only a little dimmed by time) had moved in, and were seated comfortably in the plush, beige vinyl chairs, idly chatting and smoking cigarettes. They looked like young mafiosi who had mistakenly become beached on an old tug.

Life on the two barges in front of the first was less visible from my roof vantage point. There were a couple of Land Rovers on one and various goods covered by tarpaulins. The barge to one side, which I could see more clearly, looked like Hyde Park on a summer's day. In the morning, some men had erected cane poles, and unrolled two large tarpaulins. A group effort resulted in these tarps being neatly tied from the poles, creating a shady parkland. People seemed at ease. Some sat on cane chairs, comfortably watching the passing scene and talking to their neighbours. I felt these folk must be old hands at boat travel.

I must venture down to make a tour, I thought. Tomorrow.

Despite my months living in uncomfortable village conditions, today I knew I was in a kind of culture shock. In Kin, I had lived with a Canadian family and had mixed with Zaireans and an international crowd in govern-ment, business and the embassies. There had been dinner parties, talks, interviews, visits and chats with varied and stimulating discussions. Now, in terms of quality of conversations and standard of living, I was back in the villages.

People looked at me and cried, '*Mundele!*' – the Lingala word for white.

Freddy was kind but had little conversation.

'I am for change,' was the first thing he said to me, then added, 'you will be safe while I am here.' When I looked at him, he repeated his reassurances and grinned inanely. Was he all there? I wondered unkindly. I was not reassured. In fact, with so many military and civilian males aboard, I had taken my own security measures – I told everyone I was '*madame*'.

William seemed part of another life now – mentally, I had said goodbye to him in Cameroon. Nonetheless, we still talked on the telephone from the cities and exchanged letters and he was never far from my thoughts. However, in a letter I received in Kinshasa, he expressed concern that I did not match his ideal woman. Humph. What did he want? A Home Counties wife who would breed babies and stay at home?! His words made me feel outcast, but for this journey, he became my make-believe husband.

At noon, when the heat had been at its fiercest, I had ventured down onto the rear shaded deck. One of the crew members had come up to me and ponderously said, 'This side is Zaire, *madame*, and that side is Congo.' Thanks for the insight.

Having discovered the *commandant* took the night shift and slept in his cabin during the day, I had gone to use the squat toilet down at water level. There had been a long queue, and people had called, 'Are you married?' '*Ça va?*' '*Mundele!*' 'What's your name?' 'Where are you from?' '*Ça va?*' '*Mundele!*' 'Where is your husband?' I had answered their questions but had once again felt watched and isolated. How was I going to reach out to such a vast boatload of strangers? Then, I chastised myself. What arrogance! Why were city conversations 'better'? How quickly I seemed to have forgotten how rich some of my village conversations and relationships could be.

The Zaireans were putting considerable effort into their grooming in these humid, dirty conditions – the men washed out at the back of the pusher with water drawn by bucket from the river, the women washed themselves and their children inside the dark, hot, metal-box toilet by the same method. My leggings and T-shirt, fresh yesterday, and my sweaty white skin looked grubby. I decided to see if the *commandant* was up yet and, if so, to have my own bucket shower in his bathroom.

After clambering down the ladder, I found that the *commandant,* a stocky, handsome man who seemed intelligent and serious, was in the wheelhouse. Emile – a cheerful man with eyebrows that registered constant astonishment, whose role was cook and general assistant – gave me the key when I asked. I retrieved the bath bucket and went out to the railing. There was a plastic container, something like a 2-litre milk bottle with its mouth cut wider, attached by its handle to a rope. I had seen others toss the container into our side wake to collect water and pull it back on board. I tossed the container out. The container bounced along the top of the waves, staying quite empty.

'Oh, *mundele!*' cried people from the lower level. They had looked up and seen who was the incompetent container thrower!

'Like this,' said Emile, taking the bucket from me and demonstrating a rapid fill. It seemed the trick was to give the rope some slack, capture a little water in the container, then let gravity do the rest.

I tried, and tried. Eventually, I filled it – but it seemed to have happened with the same luck as catching a fish. Then, having tipped the water in the bath bucket, I went back to try again.

The toilet and shower space were in a damp, hot, metal cubicle off the *commandant*'s cabin. There was only one hook for clothes and towel, and of course they dropped on the wet, mildewed and hair-covered floor. The cubicle was directly over the engines and the noise was deafening.

This was a privilege? It was a hot-box hell-hole.

As it neared dusk and got cooler, I started feeling hungry. In the freezer, I had frozen baguettes and yoghurt, and in a box in the *commandant*'s cabin, I had a box of tinned food and a bucket of drinking water. (Mme Kabamba of Mboliaka had been clear about providing my own food and water – so I had!)

While I was leaning over the railing, cooling down after my shower, Lefé, another of the crew members, came up. He was a small, friendly man who seemed to do general chores and had helped load Ibn and my baggage. I had got to know him and a couple of the other crew members, Papy, a gorgeous young hunk in jeans, white T-shirt and red baseball cap, and Willy, who was older, wore shorts and had very sexy legs. Both took turns at the wheel.

'You have very much food, *madame*,' said Lefé. Already, a couple of passengers in the toilet queue had murmured to me, '*J'ai faim, madame*' – I am hungry.

I was gutted. Any remaining sense of being sensitive to village life was now completely smashed. How could I have been so thoughtless about the food I had brought aboard? Buying the tins in Kin had been fun, a challenge against closed shops and the falling value of my money. I knew the suffering the economic crisis was causing to people who did not have dollars, yet clearly I had been out of touch with the emotional impact of being hungry. Village and boat life quickly put me back in touch.

I felt stupid and guilty – so I retreated to the roof, with a baguette, no tin, and dined frugally. It was proving difficult to make the transition to boat life.

By the fourth day, a routine was developing. Well, almost. At first light, I blearily unzipped my tent ready to emerge for a new day, wondering at my sleepless night. On the roof was a massive spotlight which was used intermittently to light our channel at night. It had proved a powerful lure to huge flying insects which swarmed against my tent walls. Their silhouettes reminded me of Alfred Hitchcock's *The Birds*. Lucky my tent was sealed. Now, as I put my head out, I saw the entire roof was covered in the bodies of dead white moths.

'You see?' said Freddy. 'There are no hills.' He was referring to the scenery. Indeed, it had opened out to a wide, flat landscape; the river ahead was littered with low-lying mangrove-covered islands. Fisherman's huts were built on stilts on the banks. There were a few scattered clouds that looked exquisitely bright, like silk, and the brown-green water was glassy smooth – it reflected the clouds. 'We are in Equateur Province now,' said Freddy.

That might have been interesting, but I was too distracted. What about the moths?

He could only tell me they were attracted by the light. Freddy called to Lefé to fetch brooms and we swept them into massive piles, then shovelled them overboard. There were thousands of the poor creatures.

As I drank my coffee and ate a stale piece of baguette, offering both to Freddy, I watched the morning scene.

Life was relatively quiet on the barges, the first charcoal fires of the day were started, and people were drawing water for cleaning their teeth or shaving. One of the young men in the speedboat was peering into a tiny piece of mirror and trimming his moustache. He saw me watching, waved and I waved back.

The real excitement was the arrival of the *pirogues*. It seemed that every fisherman's hut, every concealed village, sent *pirogues* to meet us. Away to the horizon, I could see *pirogues* idling mid-stream, waiting for their chance to link up with us. For remote villagers, the passing boats were their only access to trade. Now that we were further from Kin, the numbers had increased and watching them attempt to intercept our barges provided an exciting spectacle.

Two villagers in a single *pirogue* paddled hard to link up with our pace and direction. At the seemingly last possible, breathtaking moment, the front villager thrust down his paddle and reached over to grab hold of a barge. He missed and the *pirogue* slipped back along our length. A *liane* rope – made from forest vines – was quickly pulled from the bottom of its hidden floor and tossed to a passenger to help haul them in. Three young men laughingly pulled on the rope, and were dragged a few paces before they won the battle against the strong current.

The newcomers brought aboard manioc and fresh and dried fish to sell, and quickly disappeared into the market throngs. Everybody was moving about at this cooler morning hour. It was amazing to me to see the small quantities for trade which made the tough and treacherous paddle worthwhile. Perhaps these two men would buy a bar of soap or a small pack of salt, and then return to the *pirogue*. Trade, I had discovered, was what this boat was all about.

Another two villagers were already leaving, having completed their trading, and were being cast off by helpful passengers. I watched as they paddled furiously to get outside our wake before being able to turn the *pirogue* and continue the more leisurely drift down river, back to their village concealed somewhere in the forest.

Finishing my breakfast, I decided to go on a tour of the barges before it got too hot, to try to find some fruit for sale and simply to see the trading spectacle close up.

As I climbed from the pusher onto the first barge, a fish rack fell on my head.

'*Mundele!*' came the exasperated cry, like it was my fault. I rubbed my head and felt a bit dazed. The man who had dropped the rack called '*Mundele!*' again, and others echoed his cry and laughter. Dried fish were being sold by visiting villagers to our intrepid passengers. They were kept intact inside elegantly formed and tied bamboo racks. The racks were hung from every high point on the boat's structure, so that circulating air would keep the fish dry. Dead, and smoke blackened, the fish were ugly-looking creatures, and very heavy! I disentangled myself from the confusion of charcoal burners, plastic buckets, Chinese bags and feet that blocked my path, and moved forward.

'*Mundele, mundele!*' came the constant cry as people sought my attention. 'Come and sit with us.' 'What is your name, *mundele?*' In fact, there were a sprinkling of more intimate calls. '*Bonjour, Paméla!*' and 'Pamela, come sit with us!'

I was not so intimidated now: I had done my first barge tour yesterday and had already got to know a few people, by sight anyway. I waved, said '*Bonjour,*' and moved on down the starboard side of the barge, past the first MAN truck. The pathway was less than a metre wide now as passengers, who sat under the truck, or squashed into gaps, had set up charcoal stoves on which they prepared food or mats with their trading goods laid out. To my right, the barge fell abruptly away, without a rail, about a metre to the water below. The metal surface of the barge was wet with river water and slippery from fish scales and palm oil – leftovers from food preparation. I picked my way slowly and carefully through the debris. Others pushed and shoved their way forward – it was like rush hour on the Underground, but I worried about slipping over the side.

I eyed the merchandise on the mats, scanning for useful items. Small, yellow tins of Blue Band margarine; tiny plastic bags of salt and sugar; cigarettes, sold individually; a single pair of thongs; two or three *pagnes* of material; second-hand T-shirts and clothes in unruly, unsorted piles; some AA and D cell batteries; freshly roasted peanuts. The sellers, peering hopefully from their cramped positions, were surrounded by sacks of belongings, bags, cooking utensils and family.

'*Mundele!*' 'Pamela!' The greetings continued and I made a royal progress of waves, greetings and smiles.

Then, to the side, I spotted a *pirogue* approaching with a pineapple in its base. As ever, the fruit caught my interest and I continued with sudden purpose. However, by the time I arrived where the *pirogue* had tied up, at the end of the first barge, it was too late – the pineapple had already been sold.

Under the awning of the second barge were the families and the lone women, their areas defined by the size of their straw mat, and the barricade of their belongings and purchases. However large, it was never enough for the number of inhabitants. Bodies lay in foetal position, people sat crouching, huddled into corners, children lay in mothers' arms. There was no ease here, and so little air, yet there was activity everywhere – trading, cooking, hair tressing, barbering, food preparation, card games and laughing.

A young, smiling woman, her short, natural curls tied into three mischievous-looking clumps on her head, smiled shyly and held up a blackened, dry fish she was selling. I could see that the fish had been gutted and opened out into the shape of a yeti footprint. Certainly, it looked prehistoric enough. Behind her were stacked high racks of more dried fish. The sharpened teeth of a piranha-like fish smiled ghoulishly at me. They looked so ugly, but they did not smell. In front of the woman was a low charcoal burner piled high with fish she had bought and was drying.

'They will be very valuable to sell in Kisangani,' she said.

By her side was an enamel bowl with the freshly acquired fish. A black, long, shiny eel slithered on top and a huge cod, its skin a spotted, slippery grey, lay beneath this monster. So many different shapes and sizes, so many varieties. This was what lay hidden beneath the surface of the Zaire River. I asked her what they were called.

'I do not know, but they are all good to eat,' she replied. Quite rightly, that was all that was important. And that she could sell them for a profit.

An older woman sitting next to her took her pot of *pondu* off her burner and held it up for me to see. Evidently, she thought I was on the prowl for food, but I only wondered at how tough her skin must be to hold the scalding pot.

'*Paméla! Viens ici!*' – Come here! The call was from Odette and Chantal, whom I had met the previous day. Their spot was just ahead underneath a tarpaulin canopy, a 5 metre by 3 metre area marked off by mats and posses-sions, which they shared with some five or six other women and numerous small children.

Chantal was an air hostess with Air Zaire. She was tall and wore cheerful Carnaby Street-type clothes – black flares, a cropped T-shirt and white rimmed sunglasses. She looked great, but it seemed strange to find her here. 'I am visiting relatives in Lisala,' she had told me. Today, she was tressing a child's hair and minding the trade mat of one of her group – there was one pair of nylon panties, two *pagnes*, some thread for tressing hair and three pairs of thongs.

'Did you know these people before?' I asked her, as I found a sack to perch on. I was intrigued.

'*Non,*' she replied, 'but now they are my sisters.'

Odette, a serious and stocky young woman, was preparing a meal. Meal preparation seemed to happen at all hours of the day. She was mixing tomato paste and chopped onion with tiny fish. She reached for some tearings of banana leaves which she arranged cross-wise.

'How are you cooking the fish?' I asked.

'Steaming it,' she replied, 'in a bain-marie. I will put the fish in the leaves, tie them tightly and then put them in this pot.' She took the lid off a small pot already sitting on the charcoal stove. A small amount of water was at the bottom. Her boat cooking arrangements looked a lot more organised and sophisticated than my own. I was subsisting on bread and jam, still too horrified to open a tin of tuna or vegetables, or even cook my usual spaghetti and tomato sauce. I decided that tonight, I would cook.

As she cooked, I asked Odette about her plans, wondering if she was visiting relatives – I knew she was leaving at Lisala, too.

'I will buy maize and take it back to sell in Kin,' she said.

'That is what I plan to do, too,' piped up Chantal. I should have known. Everyone on this boat seemed to have schemes for making money. The situation demanded it, and unlike in Gabon, the resilient and optimistic Zaireans rose to the occasion. Perhaps the Zaireans' situation was worse, perhaps by nature they were more energetic and self-reliant, but certainly, I had yet to meet a Zairean who was not an entrepreneur.

'I want to travel to Europe this summer,' continued Odette. 'So I must make plenty of money now.' She told me that a US$2000 purchase of maize in Lisala would fetch US$20,000 in the markets of Kinshasa.

'Money is easy to make in Zaire,' said Chantal. I had heard this so often before. Was it just wishful thinking, or was it true?

'That is what the whites do here,' said Odette. 'If you have capital, you can make plenty of money.' The riskiness of the situation created high upside, and downside, potential. I knew businesspeople in Kin priced goods so as to get a payback on any investment inside six months. It was a place for cowboy entrepreneurs.

I invited them to come some morning for coffee on the roof, then left them, moving on to the front barge where young men and military with families had established themselves. It was peaceful here, almost silent, so far from the throbbing engine of the pusher. I could hear the water rushing beneath our barge, signalling our progress. The river vista lay wide ahead, not interrupted by the sight of busy humans. I lingered a while before heading back along the port side of the barges.

Soon, I was called over by Jimmy, another friend from yesterday's barge tour. Jimmy was from Anglaphone Liberia – he spoke English with me when we weren't with other French speakers – and had an acute sense of humour. He was long and lean and wore his hair in a box cut. He had a moustache that drooped around his red-lipped mouth towards a tightly cropped beard. He looked wicked. Jimmy told me he was a diamond dealer, a 'businessman' who travelled a lot. Certainly, he had big stories to tell. He had been in Guinea and Ivory Coast, other diamond areas, and had travelled through Ghana and the other countries around the coast. Today, as I sat with him in his airless space on the second barge – in fact, nearly opposite Chantal and Odette – he told me about his business ideas.

'There is a lot of money to be made here. It is Very Fine here. Not like other places. Here there are no controls,' Jimmy confided in me. I laughed. I enjoyed hearing colourful West African English again, and his enthusiasm and confidence reminded me of Gaby, my trader friend from Ghana. 'But you must be part of *le système*,' he continued.

Curiously, I asked what that was.

'You know, *le système*.' There was a tone of wonder in his voice. How could I not know what the system was? 'For example, when I arrive in Kisangani I will go and see the *commandant* for the town. "Hi, I am Jimmy," I will say. "Nice to meet you," and shake his hand.' He shook my hand by way of demonstrating the smooth manner in which a bill would be transferred from palm to palm. 'I need some protection, so that if I have problems I can call on the *commandant*.' In fact, after that, I heard '*le système*' a lot in Zairean conversation.

Having returned to the pusher – my 200-metre tour had taken over two hours – I passed some time hanging over the rail near the wheelhouse. The entire boat quietened as people snoozed through the worst heat of the day.

The senior military aboard sat on a bench in front of the wheelhouse. I knew most of them now. Bob, the ranking officer on board – a two-stripe lieutenant, whatever that might mean – was going to a new posting in eastern Zaire. He was a tall, large man with a big tummy. He sported a thin moustache, hedging luscious lips, and his eyes twinkled with shrewdness and vitality. I liked Bob because he was a jovial chap who liked a joke. Guy was Bob's wiry, shy second-in-command, who was travelling with his wife and children. They had a spot on the front barge. Then there was Philippe, a commando – an intimidating man who perpetually wore a black beret, dark mirrored sunglasses and black cotton parachute suit, complete with commando rope, knife and bottle around his waist. 'I am with the presidential guard in Kinshasa,' he had told me. A tough, select cookie. I guess I should have found him repulsive, a symbol of Mobutu's Zaire, but he had lovely, ripply muscles and deep black, satin skin – so, true to type, I found him magnetic and attractive.

This afternoon, loud Zairean *soukous* music boomed from Papy's large cassette player. Whenever Papy was at the wheel there was music. Papy, in his mid-twenties, was not only tall, muscular and terrific looking, but also a great dancer – which he showed even while he had the wheel! He and his mate, Willy, danced rhythmically as they steered the barges between invisible sand-banks. I was happy to let my hips move to the up-tempo beat of the spirit-lifting music, too. I hung on the rail, watching the river flow past, *pirogues* arrive and condors swoop on pieces of fish tossed overboard.

During the afternoon, I wandered into the wheelhouse and took a look at the mapbook. It sat on the only table in the wheelhouse and was open at the page for our location. On the cover, it showed that it was printed in 1973 and that the route from Kinshasa to Kisangani was 1753 kilometres. Phew. Perhaps not much compared to the 11,500 I'd travelled on my bicycle, but a lot further than I had travelled in the ten weeks of waiting. I started flipping through the pages, each of which covered about 20 kilometres of the river. So far, in seventy hours, we had covered about 330 kilometres; not much. Even so, I was amazed to be making any progress without pedalling – though not without sweating!

Yesterday, we had passed the confluence with the Kasai River, a major river in its own right, but a small stream compared to the Zaire. Today we would pass the Ubangui River on the port side and leave the Republic of Congo behind – after that the river flowed entirely inside Zaire. We would not arrive in Mbandaka until the day after tomorrow. Mbandaka was on the equator – the Zaire River swung north-east in a huge arc and I would reach 2 degrees north again at Lisala before the river swung south and east toward Kisangani which was on the equator again. Our route was marked in pencil and weaved its way through deep channels. Sometimes an old route was rubbed out, or hatched, with a '*Non!*' next to the rubbing out, speaking of past accidents and sandbanks.

'The river is high now,' said Willy, who was taking turns with Papy at the wheel and had seen me pause on a page with many rubbings out. 'We're unlikely to have accidents.' Fine.

At sunset, after another amusing battle with the container and river for bath water, I retreated to the roof. I had luxury now, a straw mat to sit on. (Freddy had offered to act as my intermediary with the *pirogue* vendors.) It made life a lot more comfortable, clearly defining my space.

As I sat enjoying the view, waiting for water to boil on my Gaz stove, Bob arrived. He had visited on other evenings and already knew my habits. He arrived with his cup and I made him and Freddy a cup of tea. In the cooling evening, the boat became busier again. People started moving around, preparing for night; they jostled up and down the edges of the barge and the *pirogues* continued to arrive.

'It is like an attack,' I said to Bob as six *pirogues* were paddled furiously by their villagers to come and join us. Bob, unlike Freddy, had joined me on the mat to watch the spectacle. I enjoyed his company. He had told me about being stationed in Muanda on the Atlantic coast during the pillages but claimed to not have been involved. I believed him.

'Yes, and it is very dangerous,' he said cheerfully, referring to the linking-up process, and cheekily he held out his cup for a second cup of tea.

The older men seemed the most cool and competent, timing their approach to miss the higher bow waves, and then with a couple of paddles, and a twist, they were alongside. Young men were the most rash and always looked closest to capsizing.

That said, now a woman and her young son approached on the starboard side looking in danger of doing this. The middle-aged, muscular woman was in the rear, the steering position, and as she brought the *pirogue*'s nose towards the barges, her son reached out to grab a hold, but his small hands slipped on the metal. The woman was not going to allow the chance of a fish sale to pass by: she leapt from her steering position into the already moored *pirogue* and pulled her own to a halt. Her son, who had made an ill-timed grab for another dug-out, stood up, looking pleased with himself, oblivious to the help he had received from his mother.

We watched another *pirogue* handled by two men come in fast near the bow and get a fearful battering. They grabbed at another *pirogue*, slipped, passed further down the length of our boat, grabbed at the prow of another *pirogue*, but again the wet wood slipped out of their grasp. At the final chance, the young man in the rear manoeuvred the canoe in, and the front man leapt into a tied-up *pirogue*. He did a quick turnaround, and grabbed the prow of his own boat. There were a few claps from the onlookers. Everybody was enthralled by this never-ending entertainment.

Of course, when the *pirogue*rs missed, as they frequently did, there was nothing for them to do but look a little sheepish for their audience and let themselves drift homeward.

Suddenly, there was more drama. A different woman fell out of her *pirogue* into the river and a cry went up from nearby onlookers on the port side. I turned towards the sound and first saw the *pirogue* drifting fast beyond the pusher, empty. I stood, so did Bob, and people on the barges, straining to see. My heart beat faster for her. I caught sight of the woman being swept along next to the barges more slowly, as she unsuccessfully tried to grab hold of several tied *pirogues*. At the last boat, her hands reached up and grasped the edge. A quick-acting youth leapt into the *pirogue* and reached down to pull her in. The woman, once dragged from the water, stood and modestly realigned her *pagne*, which had slipped, and retied it. Her naked form was still silhouetted through the soaked, thin material.

There was another splash. A young boy had jumped in, and I wondered if he was the woman's son. He swam a kind of frenzied dog paddle downstream and, with the current, was rapidly swept into the distance toward the runaway *pirogue*. In the dimming light, the son became a black dot in the enormous stream, but he seemed to drift closer to the faint line of the canoe. I could only hope so.

'Yes, it is dangerous,' repeated Bob, with a grin. I could hardly see his face in the dimming light but his eyes twinkled. '*Mais ils sont habitués,*' – but they are used to it. I caught my breath and wondered if this was true – and wondered if Bob would be back for morning coffee.

After another day of travel, we arrived mid-morning in Mbandaka. As we approached, from the river we could see the wharfs, with their rust-roofed offices and warehouses. We passed vast numbers of rusting barges and pushers, some moored, some sinking.

'It was a good town allowed to fall into the ground,' said Jean, the *commandant*. He was a man of few words and I wondered what story lay behind his comment. When we docked, it was prow first, into the bank, and planks were laid from the front barges to the shore. People started streaming off, but I stayed near the wheelhouse. I wanted to take Ibn off but could not see how to get him from the roof, along the barges and across the planks to the shore. Bob had the answer.

'This man will take you to shore,' he said pointing to a young man standing with two others in a *pirogue* that was moored against the pusher. He had negotiated for me to exit via *pirogue*! Rapidly, with several helping hands, Ibn was passed into the *pirogue* and then I clambered in, too. One youth wore my Akubra and held Ibn upright. The base was waterlogged, so I stood, too, while the two other men poled our way to shore.

'Are you leaving us, Pamela?' called several people from the barges, but I reassured them I would be back.

I had two chores. The first was to find photographic film. After ten weeks to prepare for this journey in Kin, I had managed to leave with just one roll. Idiot! My hopes were not high as I cycled down the quiet boulevards of Mbandaka. It had been a substantial town, but the signs of pillage were everywhere. There had been little reinvestment and the devastation seemed more apparent than in a big city like Kin. Windows and doors were barred, most establishments were closed, some buildings were derelict and there was little sign of commercial activity. At a main crossroads, the *Centre d'Achat*, clearly once a large general store, was empty and barred, while the nearby *Pharmacie Centrale* was a derelict shell.

I went into a small shop that was open – behind the counter was a Pakistani shopkeeper and a few cartons on shelves, not even unpacked.

'It is not a time for tourism,' he said, when I enquired after film. He told me how his shop was looted bare during both pillages, then he asked me how to get an Australian visa. 'I want to change countries.'

Amazingly, I did find film, at a specialist camera dealer, so then I went on to my next chore – to find drinking water. I had boarded at Kin with a full bucket, but it had nearly all been used – on lots of coffee and tea! Emile had told me to try the Catholic mission, so I cycled back to the waterfront road, along the coconut palm tree-lined, potholed boulevards, past the derelict service station and the quiet government offices and found it where he said I would. I had my blue, lidded bucket with me, and asked a father if I could use their pump. As I filled my bucket in the mission's courtyard, we talked about the impact of the pillages.

'You must pray for us in this country,' he said.

I strapped the heavy bucket to the carrier and as I cycled back to the boat, again registering the air of dilapidation, I thought I understood the *comman-dant*'s comment.

I returned to the boat via *pirogue* and was welcomed by my fellow passengers with grins, thumbs-up signals, and a few cries of, 'Pamela, you came back!'

We left Mbandaka about 4 p.m., and at sunset I was once more on the roof, watching the *pirogues* and making tea for Bob. Jean was outside the wheelhouse, shouting at his men to cast off *pirogues*. We seemed to have attracted a huge number – forty to fifty on each side – while moored in Mbandaka. Many villagers were hitching rides with us and there were so many that their weight was slowing our progress!

Bob had brought me his photo album and showed me pictures of himself, his wife and children, his parents, brothers, sisters – the lot. In one, he was young and thin, wore bellbottoms and a psychedelic T-shirt, and had Afro-style hair. He looked awful!

'I play the guitar,' he told me, as though this was an explanation. Of course, photos of me in the seventies would be as ghastly – I just never looked at them. 'I can sing too – do you know Bob Marley?'

'Another Bob,' I said, and in the gathering gloom, he started singing. 'One Love', 'No Woman No Cry', 'Buffalo Soldier', and 'Get Up, Stand Up'. He had a very mellow voice and it was a lovely way to spend an evening. He got a third cup of tea, we ate tinned macaroni heated on my stove and shared a pineapple I had bought in Mbandaka. Although he was married, I regretted having said I had the same status. Bob certainly had distracting charms.

By now the Milky Way was bright overhead, the lighter grey sweep of the enormous river lay in front of us, the banks were marked by a darker grey and then, to the sides, there was heavy blackness where the forest lay.

Although the barges were in darkness, there was some Zairean music playing from different parts and the echoes of people's quiet voices. Murmurs came from the attached *pirogues* as people rearranged their positions for the coming night.

'In the first couple of days, everyone was asleep early,' I said. Initially, we had all been sleeping by 8 p.m., tonight it was already 9.30 p.m. 'Now, everyone is awake and chatting.'

'Yes,' said Bob, slowly. 'It has become our way of life now. *Nous sommes habitués.*'

True, I thought. I was relaxed, content and had friends. My loneliness, I reflected, was really a choice. I could overcome it by my state of mind and how I reacted to others – as with so much else in life, the kinds of relationships I had with others were entirely up to me. I also realised that I was not the only one who had initially felt isolated. Perhaps like any tour group or cruise, we had all found it difficult to adjust to being amongst strangers in a new environment. Now, as we got to know each other, it was becoming our home.

I found a use for all my tinned food – I started holding parties. Bob called the roof my salon. He was right – the tent was my bedroom, the area inside the flap, out of the wind, was my kitchen and the straw mat was my living room. People came for morning coffee, brunch, sunset tea and supper. There was Bob, of course, and Guy, Philippe, Jimmy, Chantal and Odette, and even sometimes Emile and Lefé. Not Freddy. He had bought so much palm wine from a passing villager that he was knocked out cold most of the time.

'It is a cold,' he told me. 'This fixed me,' and he showed me a jar of Vicks Vapour Rub.

'No cold made you sleep for twenty-four hours,' I told him. 'It was the palm wine.'

'That?' he laughed innocently, 'Nooo, that is a *sucré*' – a soft drink.

Jimmy and Chantal came for *petit déjeuner* on the roof a couple of days after we had been in Mbandaka, day eight of the journey. I had suggested it was bring your own cup and water, and we sprawled on my straw mat as I boiled water on the stove and spread stale baguette with jam. Tinned fruit with yoghurt was for second course. The sun was getting hotter by the time it was all ready. Chantal was today dressed in a geometrically patterned shirt and black flares, and wore hot-pink lipstick but no sunglasses. 'Someone lay on them during the night,' she lamented. She wanted to pray before we started eating, which led us into a conversation about religion.

'I wasn't always like this,' said Chantal, and I prompted her to tell the story of how she found Jesus. 'About three years ago, my uncle, a pastor, came to my house and asked me to come to his church. I said no, but he kept coming every day. Every day I had an excuse. I was too tired, I had to wash my hair, I had eaten too much. I didn't know it then but he knew it was the Devil at work in me. One day, to, I don't know, to satisfy him, I went ...' She took a bite of baguette and drank some coffee before she continued. 'When the pastor, my uncle, spoke, I was touched, but when we started to pray I don't know what happened. I could feel myself filled with the Lord. I thought of all the bad things I was doing with my life. Then, I was not like now. I used to tell lies and I had friends ... I wasn't married, but we made love, and in the church I started to cry. My uncle came up to me. "What is wrong?" and I told him. "It is the Lord," he said, and I knew it was true. And from that day my character has changed.'

Jimmy had been nodding a lot during this revelation, so I asked him if he believed in this way, too.

'Sure! You too will go back to Europe filled with the Lord after meeting Chantal.' He spoke with fervour equal to Chantal.

I asked which church he belonged to.

'The Charismatic Church.'

'And you, Chantal?'

'Yes, the Charismatic Church also.'

'If so many people are praying to God here in Zaire, why is the country devastated?' I asked them both, but it was Jimmy who mainly did all the talking – for ten minutes or more, his food and coffee forgotten. Apparently, Zaire's parlous state was all because of the belief in, and use of, fetish.

'God is jealous! He says believe only in me!' said Jimmy. 'But here in Zaire, people believe in fetish and go to the medicine man. For example, if I saw Chantal and I thought she was a pretty girl but she was taking no notice of me, I would go to the fetish man and get an ointment. I would rub it on my hand, then go and see Chantal. I would shake hands with her and *voilà*! She would not know why, but she would start to want me. She would come looking for me and I would be hiding to see that it worked.' I was surprised by his religious fervour. Chantal was nodding agreement.

'Yes,' she said, 'and if he did it to you, you would start wanting Jimmy without even knowing why.' Sounded interesting stuff, I thought as I drained my coffee.

'If Chantal wanted to be more beautiful,' Jimmy continued, 'she would ask for a perfume and she would put that on and become more beautiful.' Chantal smiled, but nodded again.

'What's the problem, then?' I asked.

'So, God is jealous,' said Jimmy. 'He let us play, have a good time.'

'Before, there was no place like Zaire,' said Chantal. 'It was so rich and we just danced all the time. Then He made things stop working – when the water stopped coming out of the tap, or the electricity stopped, we just kept dancing. And now it is like this.' She cast her hand toward the barges, packed with passengers.

Well, that was one explanation, I thought. It was sorcery that had done Zaire in – and I guessed the same could be said for the rest of Africa. It was God's lesson to His children, not mismanagement, incompetence, foreign interference and exploitation, and corruption.

'I don't believe that – why should God punish Zaire like this?' I asked. 'Ordinary people here do work hard. And in England and Australia, many people don't even go to church and don't believe in God any more. Why aren't they punished?'

I heard a lot more about why I should find the Lord. It soon became too hot to remain on the roof and this party was over. Phew! We had to agree to disagree. A lucky escape from being saved, I thought. Now, I wonder where I can get some of that love potion and beauty perfume?

Another day. The river scene was just the same – wide, lazy, brown-green river, a few clumps of water hyacinth (less than lower down), low emerald and dark-green forest, with a few mango trees turning a pleasant, autumnal orange. From the mapbook in the wheelhouse, I could see we were travelling down a channel between mangrove-covered islands, seeing only a small section of the wide river. Sometimes, the entire river was 5 kilometres wide! I spent my time watching the slowly passing, slowly changing scene. I found I was mesmerised by the smallest details of life. That was where drama was for me now.

One morning, late, but before the smothering heat arrived, I hung over the rail watching a woman at work in her large *pirogue* which was attached to our boat. She was one of our hitchhikers taking a ride closer to another village further upstream. Her *pirogue* lay alongside the pusher, roped by its nose to the last barge. She looked middle-aged, wore faded *pagnes* and sat on a small wooden chair near the stern of the *pirogue* cleaning rice using two enamel bowls. She dipped one, containing the raw rice, into the brown river water, decanted into a second bowl until there was a small residue, presumably husks, dirt and stones, then washed this away in the river and started again. She was completely involved, just as I was in watching her. I was intrigued by the detail of her world; it seemed important.

I took in her hands, strong and wiry, her feet the same. Next to her was a beaten iron pot sitting on the charcoal burner already heating some water; to her left was a small pile of assorted enamel and plastic bowls, a few spoons and an enamel cup; in the toe of the *pirogue* was a mirror, comb, two tooth-brushes and a plastic bag, probably containing soap and a scrubbing cloth; strapped in the centre of the *pirogue* were her trading goods and meagre possessions – a barrel and a couple of bags and sacks, contents concealed and shaded by a grass mat and a dirty blanket.

The woman finished the cleaning, scooped handfuls of the rice into the pot, then cleaned the bowl. Having put the lid on, she washed the bowl, picked up the scoop and scraped grey water and sludge that had accumulated at the bottom of the *pirogue*. I caught a glimpse of a small gold earring, a valued possession for any African woman. She used the last couple of scoops of river water to clean her feet. Despite the engine noise, as she sat down in the small chair the sigh of her movement was audible. She unwrapped her *fula*, revealing hair plaited in four long tufts. She was about to sit back, then looked at her hand and thrust it in the water to clean it.

At last, she was able to sit back, put her feet up on the edge of the canoe and wait for the rice to cook.

So, I watched people, and people, likewise, watched me. Was it because they were intrigued by the detail of my world; did it seem important? Or was I their resident soap opera?

Jimmy told me that people on the barges were discussing whether I was his woman or Bob's woman. I was a little put out to be thought of as anyone's woman. To be honest, I was attracted to both Jimmy and Bob, well, especially Bob. But this was clearly not a thing to tell Jimmy.

'I am my own woman,' I told Jimmy, but he just laughed.

It was time to do some washing. I borrowed the bucket from the Jean's bathroom, heaved water aboard from the plastic container attached to the rope – I was quite adept at collecting river water now – and found a corner to wash my clothes. I scrubbed them with one bucketful of water, then hauled in another bucketful for the rinse.

After finishing my washing, I sat next to Philippe, the commando, on the bench in front of the wheelhouse. I had learnt he had eight children, his eldest daughter of twenty-two had two children, and that he was forty-five. I was surprised, having initially put him at ten years younger. Of course, I had previously found my guesses at women's age usually put them a decade (or two) older than they actually were.

Philippe had bought a tiny female monkey from a trader and he was playing with her. It made him seem more human and vulnerable, especially when he assured me she would be kept as a pet, and not eaten.

'You carry yourself like a man,' he said suddenly. He continued, 'You are open and direct. People on this boat see this. If anyone tried to harm you, they would protect you. Do you understand?' He paused, then added, 'You seem wise and calm.' I loved these guys who could observe you, talk to you for five minutes, then sum up your character. He did not know what I was like in the morning before my first coffee! 'I think your parents must be wise.' Well, maybe that was nearer the truth.

However, I liked his compliment. I was not sure exactly what he meant, but I did feel like I belonged and that people could sense my comfort with them, and I felt people were comfortable with me. The highs of this journey were changing ... from tough adventure on rotten roads in Guinea to being content to be myself, chilling out and relating to others. I played with his monkey and he gave me a swig of raffia wine from his water bottle and a taste of some fried grubs he was eating. I had come a long way.

One morning – day nine, I think (I was losing track!) – hairdressers set up shop on the roof near my tent. Enterprising, I thought, and watched their male customers have their short, curly hair trimmed into a new style: usually

a straight front or with a slight box effect by close trimming at the sides and a
longer square left on top. Interesting, I thought. Until I started eating a
mango and observed tiny black curls landing on my fruit, on my knife, stick-
ing in the juice on my fingers – the wind was blowing these small but prolific
offcuts straight into my tent and over me. I might even have consumed a few.
Yuk!

I showed them my openness and directness. '*Allez!*'

Another day, as I made my morning constitutional around the barges – the
200 metres could take three hours now as I stopped to chat and because the
course had become more congested with goods and people – I saw a wild boar
arriving from a *pirogue*. He was fat and brown, like something from *Asterix*, I
thought.

As I got back to the pusher, Emile asked if I had seen the pig. 'It is over
there,' he said, pointing over the rear railing. Going to have a closer look, I
found the little animal had been turned into raw slabs of meat! Urk! I am definitely a Tesco pre-packed meat shopper.

As nearly always now, that night, Bob came to dinner – this time with a
present.

'Here is some pork!' he said, pleased with himself. Despite my squeamishness, we ate the boar – fried in my pot – and he was quite delicious.

As we watched another night settling over the boat, a surprisingly cool one,
I asked him about where he would be staying in Kisangani.

'The commando camp is on the *rive gauche*,' he said. Only he and his
second-in-command, Guy, were travelling on the boat, and he would join his
new force in Kisangani for an initial six weeks of training. 'The training is not
like before,' said Bob. 'When I joined, we had weapons and training from the
US. Now we have not had new uniforms since 1987.' Interesting that 1987
was the end of the Cold War and the end of America's need for anti-commu-
nist governments in Africa ...

Bob said that after training he would be sent to a military post in eastern
Zaire, either north or east of Kisangani or near the Rwandan border at Goma
– he pointed them out on my map. 'There is gold mined here. Here, there are
diamonds, and at this post, near Rwanda, there are many very wealthy
commerçants crossing.'

I wondered at the relevance of all this to a military posting.

'We are just sent there,' he said. 'We are paid little or not at all. I will arrive
and search the means to survive.' I asked him to explain how he would earn
money. 'Well, if am posted near the Rwandan border, perhaps the Rwandan
commerçants will give me a truck, so they can import thirty without duty,' he
said quite straightforwardly.

'Isn't that corruption?' I smiled.

'No, it is *le système*.' I shrugged. He was right – it was not corruption, it was
how Zaire worked. It would take more than one man to change a system.

'What about if you are posted to the diamond area? How will you earn there?'

'Well, perhaps there are two men who have found diamonds, and they have an argument about how many each should have. I will be called in to judge and perhaps I will offer to sell the diamonds and give each half. Then, afterwards, one may come to me, and offer me some – if he can have more. It works like that.'

I nodded. Military, as government officials, were only paid, if at all, months in arrears, and hyperinflation eroded the value of their salaries. They must do the best they could to fulfil their duty and make a living by it at the same time. I could see through Bob's eyes. There was no firm distinctions of right and wrong in Zaire. In this wild world, it was all a question of survival.

The next day we arrived late into Lisala, a small town distinguished by having been the birthplace of Mobutu – according to Bob. Certainly, as we docked I could see a large, white mansion high on the hill above Lisala, and on my map I saw a road from Lisala to Gbadolite – Mobutu's family village in the north and main home. The cargo boat that had left without me was also in port and now I was pleased to discover it was delayed by a repair.

'There are whites on the Zaire SEP boat,' said Lefé excitedly. He wanted to take me straight over to meet them, but I was cool.

Actually, I was rather excited and looked forward to a traveller's exchange again. These would be my first European travellers since the truck on the road to Mamfé in Cameroon last July. However, I was not going to rush over the minute we landed like a dog with my tongue hanging out. Rather I stood at the rail and watched our unloading, and later strolled over, tongue hanging out, to meet them.

They were Lisa and John from Australia, backpacking through Africa. We exchanged a few tales, especially about Zairean culinary treats we had tried.

'Have you tried caterpillars?'

'No,' said Lisa, the more talkative of the two. 'But I'm more cautious – John eats anything. The other day he ate a grilled canary!' Gross.

In fact, like me, they seemed comfortable in their own world with their current companions, so after a short dose of traveller talk, we parted.

Chantal and Odette were leaving, so I helped them unload, then walked into the town with them. I was with Ibn and my empty bucket, and after a sad goodbye to the two women, set off to look for water. Lisala had a few administrative buildings but was really a large village, and the only water supply I discovered was a spring, busy with villagers also filling buckets.

The next morning – day eleven – we were underway again and I felt the rumble of the engines beneath me. I felt pretty rough. The boys (half the boat) and I had gone to Lisala's *boîte de nuit* – nightclub. It was a small shack, but, it being Saturday night, the generator was going and the joint was jumping! After a raucous evening of Primus beer and dancing (lots with both Bob and Jimmy – it kept them and the boat guessing, and kept my options open!), we had stumbled back well after midnight. To get to the pusher and my tent, I had had to negotiate the dark barges. Drunkenly, I had stepped over sleeping people, charcoal stoves and produce: one 'log' wriggled as I stepped over it – a baby crocodile! (Fortunately, with its jaws tied by *liane*.) Finally, I had made the tent, but this morning I was definitely in need of a second coffee. No friends were with me today – perhaps they needed longer than me to sleep the beers off. Or maybe they moved onto palm wine before bed. I wouldn't have been surprised.

There was a sizzling noise behind me and a smell of burning. What's that? I wondered. Freddy was definitely deep in a palm-wine sleep – so he wouldn't be cooking. I looked back to find the source. A young man was on my roof holding out a monkey by the tail. It was a half-burnt monkey, dead, looking not unlike Philippe's pet. He was holding it up against the boiler exhausts and singeing off its fur! I took it calmly, I think.

That evening, I had Bob with me for sunset tea, and then dinner. A storm was blowing up – it was cold in Equateur Province! To keep warm, I had on two pairs of leggings and two T-shirts. Bob and I had been talking for a while – it was dark now and people were settling for the night. Bob was kind, attractive and a good friend. As the days and evenings passed, we shared more of out hopes, thoughts and fears. He wanted to seduce me, but I hadn't made up my mind. I liked him, but did I want a relationship? Friendship was less complicated, but my word, it *was* hard to go without sex for so long!

'It must be very uncomfortable on the barges,' I commented. I knew Bob slept more comfortably than the others inside one of the MAN trucks that had a covered back. 'There is so little space.'

'It is better than coming the other way,' he said. 'From Kisangani, there is much more cargo.' I found that hard to believe.

Unexpectedly, the spotlight went on and there was a roar of approval from our boat. I looked up and saw the crew had put the spotlight on a boat approaching from upstream. It was heavily laden, yet I only caught a glimpse of the merchandise piled high and the precariously placed passengers atop. After a second and third sweep, matched always by accompanying cheers from our mob and waves and jumping up and down on the other boat, I saw the boat was a pusher with about four barges. The same as us, but the merchandise rose to several storeys high. Bob was right!

The spotlight of the other boat streaked out to touch us and the crescendo of its passengers' cheers reached across the stretch of river dividing us.

'Ah … Zaire!' mused Bob fondly, '… ah, Zaire.'

'Ah, Zaire,' I thought contentedly. This bizarre world of suffering and vitality was addictive. I felt very much at home.

The next morning, on day twelve, we arrived in Bumba. This was a bigger town than Lisala, and it was a railhead for river distribution of sacked maize and manioc flour that had been brought on the train from further north. That's if the train worked – the rolling stock and warehouses I saw looked pillaged. It was a short stop for us but it provided a shock for me. We were joined by several new passengers, including another military officer, Baudouin, who had been in Bumba purchasing maize for the Kisangani *Garde-Civil*, and four whites.

The whites joined our boat for the trip onwards to Kisangani and made themselves at home on my roof.

At first, I found myself shy with them, then, as I discovered their weirdness, I dubbed them Gung Ho Gary, an American who styled himself as their leader and who thought he knew everything; Follower Lucy, a wet Canadian who let Gary be their leader, Wet Walter, an even wetter Canadian than Lucy, and Supercilious Hillary, a blonde American completely out of her depth in Africa, coping by withdrawing into herself. What a bizarre bunch of whites, I thought. Of course, I gave no thought to how they perceived me!

Gary and his gang had come from London on a truck tour with twenty or so others. They had been on the road for about three months, yet from the isolation of their truck and group, even they realised they were not really experiencing Africa – other than its appalling roads. These four had decided to leave the truck on the Central African Republic border with Zaire, travel independently to Bumba by bush taxi, take the boat to Kisangani, then travel with a cargo lorry to Goma in eastern Zaire where they planned to rejoin their group. They had given themselves about three weeks and were in constant anxiety about missing their rendezvous in Goma. They had been waiting at Bumba for five days for a boat when we arrived. I could not be sympathetic. They had endless discussions about the same subject. I wanted to shout at them to just let the days happen. There was nothing they could do – they were committed now, and could only go as fast as Zaire would let them.

Then Walter began whining that Lucy had taken too much water – they only had one water bottle between them.

'You never think, Lucy. You don't share ...' I ended up giving them some of mine. But the pedantry continued. 'I bought two packs of peanuts for everyone last night.' Walter again. Apparently, they were sharing their food bills. 'I shouldn't have to contribute so much today.' How old was he? How much were peanuts in Africa? Why were they so petty? I wondered. Was this what whites were like?! I found them fascinating and repulsive – then wondered if Africans found me fascinating and repulsive too. The four never washed and their clothes were very grubby. A village woman I knew on the barges asked me why Lucy did not wash her skin when she saw black, greasy marks on Lucy's arms and feet. I could not answer, but I was horrified that she thought I would know. Why *were* they so dirty? I was finding people assumed I knew these whites intimately, we now seemed to be categorised together – we were the whites. I hated my loss of identity.

Of course, perhaps this is what racial minorities feel anywhere. Awful.

And there was an element of jealousy, my jealousy. I was not the centre of attention anymore. My salon breakfasts and sunset dinners were not the same. Jimmy and Bob still came, but the conversations were not as peaceful, nor as intimate. Bob and I didn't have private evenings to share our pasts and dreams anymore. Jimmy joked with the others. And when I made teas and coffee, bought palm wine and opened tins – the whites joined in! Initially, I offered, but then started wondering why I should subsidise them. At this stage of the journey, I had been giving tins away to crew members and people on the barges, and buying local food, then sharing it with children or friends. These whites had the means to buy these things; it was their choice not to.

One evening, they had a pointed discussion about the bland sauce they were making.

'Wouldn't it be nice to have something to liven it up?'

I offered them a tin of mushrooms at a price of 200 New Zaires (about US$1.60) – the price I had paid. They declined.

Another afternoon, Jimmy took me aside.

'Why does Hillary stay so alone?' he asked. 'She does not come down to the barges and mix. One day, she will need help and she will not know anyone.' Aloofness was a puzzle to sociable Africans – and I thought that she hadn't yet learnt how painful loneliness can be. Actually, of the four, Hillary was the only one I found sympathetic. At least, in watching Africa, and not donning the adventurous but loathsome front of the others, I felt she was being true to herself.

I realised there was also a greater truth. In some of their attributes that annoyed me, like Hillary's culture-shocked insularity, Gary's concern about time and Walter's irritability, wasn't I seeing myself? Hadn't I withdrawn to my roof at the beginning of the boat journey? Hadn't I been concerned about time in Kin, and at the beginning of the journey? Hadn't I been known to argue and be irritable in my time?!

Moreover, it *was* nice to have some white company with whom to talk about Africa from an outsider's perspective and to compare experiences. I had known city expatriates, in the main, but now I realised truck travellers had few encounters with Africans. When not travelling, they spent a lot of time taking turns buying food in town markets, preparing it, guarding their trucks and sleeping, often in their trucks or in tents in the bush. In the mirror of these whites' experiences – and their very presence – I realised how much I knew (and still did not know) about village life, and how sympathetic I was to villagers and their struggle.

Soon, I also found ways to escape, to have time to be alone with my African friends. The second night after leaving Bumba, I bought some palm wine (at least, I provided Jimmy with the money and empty bottle and he bought it from a villager on one of the *pirogues*) and escaped to Jimmy's quiet spot on the barge and played cards – *huit américain*, of course – with Jimmy and his mates.

Then, the next night, the night before we arrived in Isangi, I sat with Bob on the bench outside the wheelhouse. The barges were quiet, everyone seemed to have gone to sleep for the night, it was very dark, and I kissed Bob.

Very pleasant ... and, finally, I didn't analyse my emotions. This was not a time for confusion or misgivings. I just let it happen.

After our long kiss, Bob told me I did not smell like a white.

'We think whites smell like dead people,' he said. We discussed why that could be. I speculated that, after fifteen months of eating African food – lots of starch cooked in palm oil and little meat or vegetables, my smell might have changed, but I did not really care. I was very pleased to smell like a black woman. It made me feel like I belonged.

Into Isangi, another sleepy clearing in the forest, our last stop before Kisangani. We arrived in Isangi on day fifteen since leaving Kinshasa, and Gung Ho Gary and gang were hopeful that Kisangani would only be two or three more days ahead. I was unconcerned; a stop here perpetuated good company and put off cycling – it was awful to contemplate that it would start again soon.

But before I could think about it, a new bit of news began spreading quickly around the boat. The pusher and barges were leaving us to make a trip up the Isangi River, a sizeable tributary to the Zaire, to the GAP palm-oil factory. There, they would unload the diesel from the barges, then return to collect us. In the meantime, everyone needed to disembark and all our possessions needed to be offloaded. I was unconcerned for myself but felt sorry for all the folk who had so much to offload. It was a horrendous task.

Some people talked of moving to small local hotels, others (the majority) moved their possessions as far as the riverbank and camped there. It was not clear how long we would be stranded but the easiest thing for me was to fall in with what my military friends were doing. Bob, Guy, Philippe and Baudouin (who I now knew as a humourous and very generous fellow) talked of staying at a small hotel nearby and told me to come with them. Gung Ho Gary and gang were concerned about the price and stayed behind on the riverbank. I was happy to lose them.

Of course, it caused more talk about Bob and me. Despite having kissed Bob late, in the dark, ever so discreetly I thought, Jimmy was jealous, and the whole boat was talking about it. In the eyes of the passengers and crew, I was definitely 'Bob's woman' now, and although I disagreed with the sentiment, in some ways they were right. It was wonderful to have someone saying nice things to me, about me, and it was lovely having someone to hold. I could not complain about the gossip.

Once I started analysing my emotions, I wasn't sure where this relationship was going. I was conscious that the boat had created its own world and that in many ways, this was probably a shipboard romance. He was married and going to be stationed in eastern Zaire, so what future was there in it? And what about William? Yes, what about William? His words had made me feel an outcast, while Bob's words about my smell (and other nice things) made me feel the opposite.

One day, two days. Where was our boat? I went down to the riverbank to see if people had any news and was dismayed at the conditions. Everyone was close together. The slum of the boat was now the slum of the riverbank.

'Why do you all stop here like this?' I asked a young man I knew from the barges. 'On the boat you said you suffered because of lack of space. Now you could spread out, but you choose to stay so close together.'

'Ah, but when people are close like this,' he replied, 'it creates an ambience.' Very true.

No one had any news.

On the third day of waiting, I decided to cycle out to the GAP factory – it was only about 30 kilometres. I thought I could bring news back, but it was also an escape. I was fed up with the whites moaning about time, I was fed up with Jimmy's jealousy and I was fed up with Bob wanting to sleep with me. (I hadn't decided on that, yet.)

I rode out late in the afternoon and arrived at the lonely wharf to find the boat and hard-working crew. Papy, Lefé and Emile gave out cries of greeting as I pushed the bike down the final bank having emerged so unexpectedly out of the forest. Even serious Jean, the *commandant*, gave me a smile. Fortunately, the unloading of the fuel was nearly complete, and so that evening we cast off to make our way downstream to Isangi.

The boat and barges were very different without the load of passengers and *pirogues* – it was incredibly quiet and peaceful. Even the engine did not disturb our peace as we glided down the centre of the black Isangi River under a dark sky speckled with stars. It was beautiful, moving to my spirit.

Papy produced his cassette player. He had been working hard, as had the rest of the crew, and the *commandant* let everyone rest during this short hop. Papy set his music up on one of the now empty barges, and we all started dancing, carefully, on the diesel-spattered deck. Zairean music roared into the dark space around us and we danced for the night, for the forest and for ourselves. It was exhilarating!

One chorus was common to all the songs on Papy's favourite cassette: '*Africa Moto, Poto Mulele!*' It was chanted over and over again, so I drew Papy aside to ask him what it meant.

'It means Africa is hot, burning, on fire – *moto*! Life is hard, but life is hot!' Then he grinned. 'And *Poto* means Europe. *Poto* is cool – that is *mulele*. Europe is cold, but also everything is cool there. Life is good.'

'Africa Moto! Poto Mulele!' Africa Hot! Europe Cool! There was a double meaning behind each phrase, but tonight, I thought African life was hot, excitingly, vibrantly hot! And Europe was too cold for me. We all started singing it, but the surges of energy, the biggest grins, from all of us, were for Africa.

Suddenly, we could see the blackness lightening. We were approaching the confluence with the Zaire River. Isangi and our people were on the banks around the corner. The music was turned up, and we sang even louder.

'Africa Moto, Moto, MOTO!' Africa Hot, Hot, HOT!

We rounded the bend and the barge's spotlight was turned on the five hundred spirited and self-reliant souls camped on the bank. A huge roar went up from them. We were back. I did not want this journey into the mysterious heart of Africa to end.

Two nights later, on day eighteen, we anchored at the Isle de Belgica, just 50 kilometres outside Kisangani. Boats were not allowed to arrive in Kisangani after 5 p.m., so we had pulled over to await daylight before setting off on our final day's travel.

Near dawn, I was awakened by a heavy downpour.

'Oh, shit,' I heard from Hillary as she gathered up her sleeping bag and rushed away. She, Lucy, Gary and Walter had been sleeping under mosquito nets outside. There was a general rumpus from outside on the barges due to the untimely rain, and I went back to sleep.

First light and another rain started, together with a fierce wind, and I put my head out of the tent in time to prevent their sleeping mats blowing over the side of the boat.

'Hillary, Gary!' I called and they joined me to help me keep their belongings on the roof. But they had grim faces.

'There's bad news,' said Hillary sullenly. 'A man has fallen overboard, disappeared, sure to be drowned ... but we may have to wait two days. They say we have to wait for the body to surface.'

I went down to the wheelhouse to find out more. A death was shocking, but not all that surprising – the decks were very slippery now. What was worse was the idea of not moving on to Kisangani. We had mentally prepared that the journey was over, illness was creeping up on us all, and there was little food left aboard. With the rain, shivering, miserable people clasping damp towels and *pagnes* around their shoulders were seeking shelter under the rear canopy. Rain poured down, and every now and then, someone would reach up to poke the canopy and release an immense lake of water over the edge. There was not much talking, and not much more information.

Bob passed by at one stage and he merely confirmed the news. A young Malian travelling with his brother had fallen overboard and disappeared. Now, there was an investigation in the *commandant*'s cabin, and Bob, being the senior military officer aboard, was in charge. However, normal procedure was the boat must stop for at least twenty-four hours, and normally forty-eight hours, or until the body surfaced. In this current? I thought. Surely it would have been swept downriver by now.

I went down to the squat toilet on the lower deck of the pusher, joining the queue in the rain. The gloomy faces in the line told how discouraged people were by the news.

'When will we leave?' asked one woman in the line. I was considered a source of reliable information, being close to the *commandant* and the lieutenant. I told her of the delay. 'We suffer, people are sick,' she said.

I agreed, and when I went up and saw Bob again, I was angry.

'We must leave,' I said. 'There are five hundred people living here. One has died and it is sad, but these people are suffering. We cannot sit here for two days! It is nineteen days now, women and children are sick, the rain will bring malaria. We must go.'

'How do you know they are sick?!' he asked. 'Are you UNICEF or *Medécins sans Frontières?*' he added scathingly.

I was mad, probably too bloody self-righteous, and he was discounting my comments.

'And the men? They are not sick?' he asked reasonably. The day before, we had had an unsatisfactory exchange about women's position in African society. Today, Bob was not budging and I had stopped listening. Men made decisions.

I stayed on the roof throughout the morning. Everyone was subdued by the death and by the uncertainty it had created. The rain had stopped, but still there was no news from the investigation going on in the *commandant's* cabin.

Lefé and Emile climbed up to tell me latest rumours. 'When the rain stopped, the Malian went up to the front, maybe to pray. He got up, passed his brother, and fell, just like that.' said Lefé solemnly. 'People started shouting someone had fallen, but he came up only once, then disappeared – just like that.' He paused, as though the fact he came up only once was very significant. 'He stayed at a hotel in Isangi,' he finally added, 'and the mirror broke, without his even touching it!' He shrugged, and I nodded knowingly. This was the explanation.

Emile added, 'Yes, it is clear a bad spirit was at work.'

More waiting, then the cargo boat I had seen in Lisala passed us. Lisa and John waved madly at me and I waved back! Gary and Walter came onto the roof. 'Why weren't we on that boat?' moaned Gary.

'If only we had caught that boat, we would be getting to Kisangani today,' whined Walter. Finally, thankfully, they went below again.

Unexpectedly, Bob also arrived on the roof. Perhaps the investigation had reached a conclusion, but I ignored him – I was not talking to him. However, fortunately, he was more forgiving and started recounting something of the evidence.

'The woman in the *pirogue* nearby, she said it was not normal, the way the Malian slipped, there was no reason, and then the way he disappeared so fast was also not normal,' he said solemnly. 'His brother said he could swim. Did you hear about the mirror ...?' He left the sentence unfinished. I nodded and he continued. 'These Malians, they have many fetishes.' The spirits had been found guilty.

Bob finished his explanation and left – there was no decision on how long we must stay.

A short while later, I heard the *commandant* start issuing instructions from below in the wheelhouse. The engine of the pusher was started and the barges were unhooked. I wondered what was happening? Gung Ho Gary and gang suddenly scampered up the ladder to the roof.

Gary called exultantly, 'We are going to the Zaire SEP boat. We can join them!' They must have been moaning downstairs and Jean, the *commandant*, was giving the whites the opportunity to leave.

Without the barges, the pusher raced through the water like a speedboat, and rapidly we caught up with the other boat, now around a bend in the river.

'Quick, get your tent packed!' Gary called to me as he and his companions rapidly assembled their gear. He was taking charge of me, too.

It was happening too fast. I was white, I was being given an opportunity to leave, but I was torn. My eyes were stinging, I had a throat infection and a fever, like most others on board the boat. I badly wanted to arrive in Kisangani, but did I want to go with the whites? When travelling, whites often gravitated together due to common backgrounds, to exchange experiences, and because they were outsiders in a strange culture together. We could talk about Africa together, couldn't we? They thought like me, didn't they?

About ten minutes later, the pusher returned towards our awaiting barges and I was alone on the roof. Bob and Jimmy could be dismissive, possessive and annoying, but I knew I felt more comfortable with them. I wanted to be with them. I had let the whites go.

At first, a few people on our barges saw me, then others. They stood and pointed, then cheered me and waved at me, and I knew I had made the right decision. I was happy, I was content, I was grinning like an idiot! I was back with my friends, in the life I sometimes understood, and accepted, sometimes happily, as my own. I felt a deep, centred sense of peace. I had come home.

Sixteen

Like Nowhere Else

Kisangani, Zaire – Bukavu, Zaire

We stayed moored at the Isle de Belgica until mid-afternoon, then, the engines were re-started and we left for Kisangani. What had happened to the requirement that we must remain for one or two days? Bob came to tell me that people were ill and he had decided we should continue. Hmm …

It was sunset when we first saw the signs of housing stretching several kilometres along the *rive droite* – right bank, which was, perversely, on our left – and it was almost dark when we saw the more imposing silhouette of the port and downtown Kisangani. What had happened to the regulation that we could not arrive in Kisangani after 5 p.m.? I suspected *le système* took care of that.

There were a few, scattered high-rise buildings, perhaps four to six storeys high and, at the port, a cluster of light-coloured cranes reached high into a cobalt-blue sky suffused with pink. I knew it was a city of more than 600,000 people, one of Zaire's largest cities, capital of the province of Haute Zaire. However, its presence and size, an apparently modern urban agglomeration, after travelling through thousands of kilometres of forest down a wide river highway, seemed very, very strange.

The roof was quiet now without the other whites, and only Bob and Baudouin sat with me watching our arrival. For Bob and me, this was a new place; for Baudouin, it was home. People in the barges were standing, all straining to see, and as we reached the port, crowds lined the banks to cheer our arrival.

'Is it a big thing for Kisangani, when the boat arrives?' I asked Baudouin.

'Yes, it is very important,' he replied. Wearing a bright pink *Tintin* T-shirt, he looked non-military and very relaxed. I had warmed to him enough to see he was a handsome man with a short cap of black, cropped curls, a thin moustache and a wide smile of brilliantly white teeth. However, he looked tired – his vibrant eyes were tinged with the red of infection – and excited to be arriving. Like all of us, probably. 'We bring food, supplies, things to sell. We bring news and, most importantly, we bring money.'

Baudouin suggested that Bob and I leave our possessions aboard the boat – in the *commandant*'s cabin, return for them in the morning, and spend the night with him.

'Both of you can stay in my brother's house – it is close to the port!' I wondered what his brother would have to say. Never mind – in the company of friends, I was content.

We moored along the riverbank near the port and wobbly planks were laid out for our disembarkation. So this was Henry Morton Stanley's Stanleyville. This was *Heart of Darkness* territory, Kurtz's Upper Station! At last! It was thrilling. But leaving the boat, knowing the journey was over, felt very sad. I should have known I was in for a challenging emotional time.

We walked in silence through dark streets – there were no street lamps, although some houses had power. With the help of bright moonlight I could make out large, Belgian colonial-style houses, with small, shuttered windows, arched porches, high gables and steep roofs – a useful design for letting snow fall off, but just a bit ridiculous on the equator!

'This is the administrative area,' said Baudouin. 'The Belgians lived here during colonial times. Now it is for government officials. Apparently, Baudouin's brother, Tony, worked for the government.

As I looked more closely, I began to see signs of dilapidation. The gardens, in particular were wildly overgrown.

'That is the problem here in Africa,' observed Bob, who was drinking in the surroundings like me. 'People don't look after things.'

'Part of the problem is the lushness,' laughed Baudouin. 'Cut the grass in the morning and you can almost see it growing!'

Soon, we were inside one of the houses, settled in armchairs under a rotating, cooling fan, exchanging news with Tony. He was a short, wiry man who had been pleased to see Baudouin and took the news of our invitation to stay the night equably.

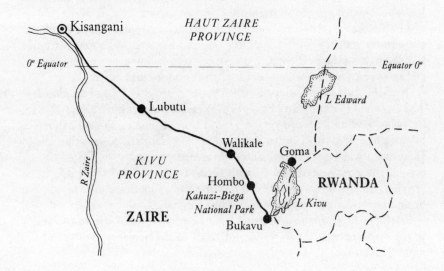

'The dollar is 125 New Zaires,' commented Tony.

'Ah, that is what it was when we left Kinshasa,' said Bob. It was good news that the new currency had stabilised. (In July 1998, the New Zaire was replaced by the Congolese Franc. At the time of writing, the dollar is 3.40 Congolese Francs, the equivalent of 340,000 New Zaires.)

'You will see that prices are higher here than in Kin,' said Baudouin to Bob and me. 'It is because of the diamonds.' He went on to explain that Lebanese and Belgian diamond traders lived in Kisangani and bought diamonds from miners who came in from the fields or from traders like Jimmy, who bought them off miners then returned to Kisangani to sell them at a higher price. The fields were not developed by any commercial companies – at least, not after the pillages – and mining was undertaken with picks and shovels. Primative perhaps, but then there was no De Beers to monopolise the buying. Baudouin finished by declaring, 'There is a lot of money to be made in Kisangani!'

Tony's wife prepared some manioc-flour *foufou* and meat stew and a young lad brought us some Primus beers. As I sat back under the fan, happy to listen to the conversation of others, I felt that the boat journey – such an intense emotional and visual experience – was already slipping away from me, becoming a memory of another world.

The next morning, going back to the still crowded boat for Ibn and my possessions, proved equally disorienting.

'*Paméla, donne-moi un cadeau!*' – give me a present. Over and over and over.

I gave my bucket and most other plastic containers from the Kinshasa *Marché Central* shopping spree to Bob. He had asked for them during the journey and I was happy for him to have them. I gave my remaining tins and various souvenir pins and stickers to the crew and to the passengers I regularly greeted. Yet, I caused uproar and unleashed jealousies.

'Why did you give to him and not to me?'

'*Tu n'es pas gentille, Paméla,*' – you are not kind.

'*Tu es méchante,*' – you are naughty.

This was from those who missed out, but even those I gave presents were jealous of what I had given someone else.

'Do you have another pin with a koala, Pamela?'

'I wanted the Nescafé. Why did you give it to Emile? *Tu n'es pas gentille.*'

It went on and on. I was kind if I gave them a gift, not kind if I didn't, not kind if I didn't magically produce the gift I had given someone else, naughty because I hadn't an endless supply of presents. Was that the value of my friendship – how many tins or pins I could supply? I left the boat wondering what friendships I had really made. Even Bob was upset when I gave Freddy the straw mat. For heaven's sake! For a quiet life, I gave Bob a stool I had also bought along the way and which I had intended to give to Philippe. When we were parting – he was going to the military camp on the *rive gauche* – I said I would come and see him soon. Would I? I wasn't sure.

Were my friendships with Bob and the others genuine? Was this also part of *le système* – that by giving presents, I received transient friendship? How could I trust relationships like this? I left feeling hurt and very confused.

A week later, I sat drinking a beer on the open-air verandah at the dilapidated Hotel Kisangani. I was the only client. Three young girls, peanut sellers, slouched at another table nearby. Their circular metal trays, holding a few tiny plastic bags of shelled and grilled nuts, were laid on the table. They seemed to have nothing to say to each other. They were just letting time pass. Like me.

The barman sauntered out from the interior, stood at the edge of the verandah, cast his eyes up and down the deserted, wide street, hummed a little, then went back inside.

The night sky flashed with lightning – broad, low eruptions of light, rather than jagged knives. The storm had passed overhead earlier, and now we were watching its farewell performance.

I was feeling very dazed and impassive about the passing of days, about moving on. Was it that the boat journey had overwhelmed my senses, exhausted me and now I needed time to recover? Was it that, having not cycled for over three months, the thought of travelling by myself along tough roads through the forests of eastern Zaire was too daunting? Or was I just absorbing the impassivity of Kisangani and following its slow rhythms?

Probably a bit of everything, but certainly Kisangani had a compelling feeling of being the calm vortex at the centre of Zaire's giant whirlpool of energy. It was surrounded by forest, and there was no mail or telephone system to connect it with the outside world. News came from the folk off the boats from Kinshasa, the truck drivers from the north and east, and from the missionaries and diamond traders who flew in and out by small aircraft. Daylight, and a few days of exploration on Ibn, had revealed Kisangani to be a large place devastated by the pillages. Avenues were broad, speaking of earlier, more prosperous and busier times, but most were badly potholed and the undulating gravel had clearly not been graded for some years. Grass grew long on the road edges and median strips. There were few vehicles on the road as petrol was still scarce. The market, a sprawling collection of trestle tables and tin-roofed wooden stalls, was Kisangani's busiest spot. Yet, the market had little in variety of fresh food or goods. Each stall sold tins of Blue Band margarine, Nescafé, Nido powdered milk, mayonnaise, jam, cooking oil, bags of sugar, bars of soap, pens and batteries. There was little else. No wonder my tins were popular, I thought. I should have been more understanding about the demands for *cadeaux*. I reminded myself that survival meant being opportunistic here.

Many offices were closed, many buildings were without power and showed signs of pillage – panes of glass missing, wiring hanging loose, boarded doors and gateways. Only a few hundred metres from the Hotel Kisangani were the ruins of the Coca-Cola factory, abandoned after the last pillage just twelve months earlier and already overgrown by grass and vines.

I frequented the same shop each day. It was a large place that had once been a delicatessen and patisserie. Now, its freezers were empty, the shelves contained a small sampling of the standard range of tins and jars, and five men were always there to serve me, often their only customer, with a rare and unexpected treat – soft-scoop ice cream.

I was still following the lifestyle of the boat, which also seemed to be the lifestyle of people in Kisangani – hanging out, chatting, eating, watching the world go by. It was fun, I was content, yet I felt bewildered by my behaviour. What had happened to my drive? Like the locals, I seemed to have given up.

I met people at the hotel or on the street. The pace here was so slow that there was time for folk to stop their car when they saw a stranger, and wave me down. I accepted invitations to lunch and dinner from Zaireans and expatriates. It was kind and I liked them, but the acquaintances felt shallow and brief. It felt like I was giving them a distraction and entertainment for an afternoon or evening. In return, I got food and company.

Was this wrong? I wasn't sure. It just seemed to be the way friendships worked here.

Baudouin invited me to his apartment to have lunch and meet his wife.

'Zaire is like nowhere else!' laughed Baudouin as we sat sprawled on the cool terrazzo floor of his verandah, eating *foufou*, meat stew, cooked *pondu* and fried plantains. A young boy was summoned to buy beers. I paid for them all, including those for several neighbours who fortuitously, or opportunistically, just happened by. It was a very pleasant way to spend an afternoon.

Cycling around, I had met a twenty-three year old Lebanese on a motorbike. He was an extremely handsome diamond dealer named Ali. I sensed he was lonely and wanted sex. I was alarmed that I had yet another fellow after me in such a short space of time. What signals was I sending out? Were we all sex starved? Despite my misgivings, I accepted a dinner invitation – to have virile companionship for an evening and to watch his promised video collection. Then, I frustrated him by saying I was going home.

Nearly every day, I went back to the port to see people from the boat. The crew were indulging in leisurely lives aboard the now empty barges, but my enterprising fellow passengers had set up an impromptu market on the river-bank nearby.

'Do you have a present for me, Pamela?' Still it went on.

'*Tu es méchant!*' I now replied.

Tonight, after a week in town, Jimmy turned up at the bar of the Hotel Kisangani. I was not staying there, yet people seemed to know where I was, what I was doing and would find me – if they wanted to. He had heard I knew Ali and wanted me to introduce him to this diamond dealer, a good contact for him.

'When can you arrange it, Pamela?' He had been aggressively insistent and I got annoyed. I felt used – he had been another person who had given me a cool farewell from the boat when I hadn't given him a good enough present (or because of Bob), and whom I had not seen since.

As for Bob, earlier in the week I had seen him once for dinner. Now, I was avoiding him, and at the military camp he did not have abundant free time to wander Kisangani looking for me. He had left a note at my hotel, telling me he loved me and missed me, but I doubted it. Did his declarations of love and friendship have a price, too? Present relationships were simply too confusing.

Meanwhile, relationships from the distant past seemed completely severed. Without easy communications to the outside world, my folks, William, friends would not know where I was, that I was safe. But in the lost world of Kisangani, it did not seem important that they should know.

Two young men shuffled their thonged feet across the hotel's verandah, the sound drawing me out of my thoughts. They hung over the railing facing the street, lit one cigarette and shared it between them. A couple, arm in arm, sauntered slowly passed the hotel, seeming to savour every step. People were about at night, but they had no money and nowhere to go.

What is wrong with me? I wondered. Am I sick? Have I got a fever? Why haven't I left, or even made plans for leaving? Am I happy or depressed? I felt truly directionless, perplexed by my own behaviour, mystified by relationships and indifferent about continuing the journey. Day followed day and I just existed. I had seen the other whites briefly – they had remained deadline-driven, and, after a few more days of tortured waiting, found a truck to take them to Goma. Ah well, I sighed. One day I might feel like them, like leaving.

Early during the second week in Kisangani, I walked with Frank and Ed, two travellers I had met in town, to Wagenia Falls, the big tourist attraction of Kisangani. Named Stanley Falls (by that modest explorer) until Mobutu's decrees to localise names during his 'authenticity' campaign in the early seventies, the falls marked the end of the navigable section of the Zaire River upstream from Kinshasa.

Frank and Ed had recently entered eastern Zaire from Uganda, having come up with an adventurous scheme to buy a *pirogue* in Kisangani and travel in it downstream to Kinshasa. I had been trying to convey to them how big this river was, how rough it could get, and how easy it was to capsize a *pirogue*, but they were determined.

Fair enough, I thought. I knew that determined feeling to do something – even though I didn't have it now!

Frank was a young East German from Leipzig who had grown up under an East German Communist regime and who seemed enchanted to be out sampling the world. He sported an Arab man's headgear – a red-and-white-checked scarf kept in place with a black braided silk cord (bought in Egypt) and a dirty safari suit (made in Kampala, capital of Uganda). Like my various Africa outfits, his clothing marked his travel route down the Nile from Egypt, through the Sudan to Uganda. Ed was a likeable, eccentric, middle-aged Dutchman with an unkempt red beard and thinning red hair.

'I sold my house three years ago, and I have been travelling ever since,' he said defiantly. Apparently his family, an ex-wife and children, thought him mad. He had met Frank in southern Sudan, and they had been travelling together for a couple of months.

I had already been to Wagenia Falls during my first week in Kisangani. I had paid a young guide to take me there, as I wanted an easy life and I was in the frame of mind to be generous. The falls were more like wide, granite boulder-strewn rapids. What made them interesting was the wooden structures built across the rapids by the Wagenia fishermen who lived nearby. *Liane* ropes were attached to the structures and used to raise and lower conically shaped bamboo fishing baskets to catch huge and delicious *capitaine* (perch).

Frank and Ed were not interested in the falls – they wanted to see if the Wagenia people would sell them a *pirogue*. We stopped on the outskirts to their village.

'You must pay US$5 to see the falls,' said a man who clearly wanted to be our guide.

Ed explained their purpose, but the man would not let us pass without payment.

'The chief says everyone must pay.' That sounded like *le système* to me – a convenient rule imposed (and possibly composed) on the spot to extract money. It was easy to spot *le système* – I had experienced it several times in Kisangani already.

'You must not bring your bicycle here, *madame*,' a surly policeman had said when I wheeled Ibn through the quiet lanes of the Kisangani market during my third visit. 'You will need a permit.' Right. Instead of paying, I had left. When I went to get a visa extension, the immigration officer said, '*Tu as pleuré beaucoup, madame*,' – You have cried very much, Madam, after I had complained loudly at the extortionate price he had wanted to charge. Then, he had arbitrarily cut the price in half. In the end, I had paid, still sure I had been providing him with an income. Taking photographs had also resulted in a demand. '*Madame*, you need a photograph permit.' Apparently true. 'I can let you take a photo if you pay me.' This part had been *le système*.

It was a game, understandable in the dire economic circumstances, integral with the current government, and you either played or did not. Today, we were not interested in playing the game.

The man at the outskirts of the village of the Wagenia people was becoming very agitated, so we did not attempt to pass. We turned around to walk back into town.

As we walked, I was chattering on about Kinshasa, when Frank piped up.

'What's a "*pee-yage*"?' he asked.

I laughed and laughed, almost hysterically, as I remembered my own question and the emotional journey I had been on in Zaire. I started telling them about Zaire.

'In Kinshasa, there was money just blowing along the streets, in the wind – it was worthless.'

'People here have incredible resilience – they laugh at problems, even tragedies – which occur every day. They don't say "*Ça va*" here when you ask them how is it, they answer "*Ça va aller!*" – It will go!'

I told them about the two pillages, the two prime ministers, the money reform, the Z factor, '*Patientez-vous, Paméla*', *le système*, monkeys being grilled against boiler exhausts – but it was hard to explain. As I talked and saw their astonishment and incomprehension, I knew they would need to experience Zaire and learn its disorienting, enchanting ways for themselves.

Talking to Frank and Ed also allowed me to recall the memories of what I had seen, who I had met, what I had done during fourteen weeks in Zaire. No wonder I was overwhelmed, disoriented and exhausted, I thought. Zaire was like nowhere else.

(Frank and Ed did undertake their *pirogue* journey. Before they reached Mbandaka – a huge, impressive effort – Ed came down with typhoid, Frank also got very ill, and eventually they had to be flown to Kinshasa from Mbandaka to recuperate.)

I met Michel, a Belgian businessman, in the ice cream shop. He had been in Kisangani for many years, and had stayed through the two pillages. Now, I was in his office chatting before we headed out for a drink and dinner.

'Zaireans are the complete entrepreneur,' he said. I had sensed both admiration and bitterness in his voice. 'If I made someone the doorman to control entry to the office, he will sell that power to give and refuse entry. If you pay, you will always be allowed in. In part it is *le système*, but I think a lot of it is in the mentality. Despite their apparent warmth, the welcome they give you, it is always with a price. They want something from you,' he had said. 'And they do it to each other as well.'

He showed me his ledger. He recorded his *cadeaux* under 'General Expenses'.

Michel was a very quiet, gently spoken man, thoughtful and intelligent, but he sounded sad and disillusioned. Perhaps he had been here too long.

'There is no such thing as friendship as we know it,' he continued. 'As long as you keep giving something you will have their friendship. But once you stop or refuse, it is over. When I first came to Zaire, I thought I could have some real friendships with Zaireans, but I lost many in this way.' He looked thoughtful. 'One must be careful in a friendship with a Zairean. I have learnt that. Unfortunately, you must always keep a little bit guarded.'

Was this racism? I wondered, when applied to a whole nationality like that? Surely, this was as gross as saying all Englishmen were emotionally frigid, or that Australian men's idea of romance was a night out with a six-pack (possibly true). Anyway, all friendships have a contract of give and take involved in them, I thought. Hadn't I had friends I drifted away from once we no longer had things in common? Wasn't this just human nature, not a Zairean trait? But he was only saying things I had thought. And it was also how I was now behaving. Were these 'natural' human traits exaggerated and distorted here? Like so much else? Perhaps I had also been here too long.

Finally, after nearly two weeks, I went to see Bob on the *rive gauche*. He was expecting me. The day before we had met down by the port and he had invited me to lunch. After we had met at the beach, he took me to his quarters. We walked down orange clay paths between the long grass before entering the military camp. Inside the camp there were more children than outside, and they squealed to see me. His quarters was a small semi-detached, concrete house, up a few stairs to a verandah, into a main living room and out to a kitchen and back bedroom. The walls throughout were plaster-covered, but holey from previous inhabitants' rough use and dirty with years of growing mildew.

'Do you like it?' asked Bob. He had gone to some trouble: his possessions were in neat piles, he had proper candlesticks (there was no electricity), he had a fresh flower in a bottle vase and he had a second stool on the breezy verandah – with mine.

'It is very good,' I said. 'It catches the fresh air – but you should whitewash the walls.'

'It is not worth it,' he replied.

'Why not?'

'It is not my house – it is the army's. They must maintain the houses but they have not the means. I will only be here a while.' True, but still ...

We soon got to work on the verandah, cooking dinner. At least, Bob did. He had bought meat, onions, tomatoes, spices, palm oil, *foufou* flour and Primus beers. He borrowed a charcoal stove from his neighbour, heated the palm oil in an old, blackened frying pan, and fried the onions before he added the tomatoes, meat and spices, then let it simmer. For the *foufou*, it was a matter of adding boiling water and then pounding it a lot. I got that job. We both drank our beers.

It was a very domestic scene, but I wondered what Bob expected. I liked him a lot, he was kind to me, we talked easily about all manner of things. I was still attracted to him, but our lives were going down separate paths. As we ate the delicious meal, Bob got to the point.

'I want to marry you,' he said.

'But you are already married and have children.'

He just shrugged. 'I will come to Australia with you.'

'And what will you do there?'

'I will be a farmer.'

I had to break it to him that I was leaving, that this dream wasn't going to happen.

'You don't love me,' he said, sounding very hurt.

Men. Exasperating creatures. Just the same everywhere. But some were so very handsome. How much of what he said was true? How much did I care for him? Or didn't I really trust whether his love was for me or my visa? In Michel's words, was I keeping a little bit guarded?

Poor Bob. I got a lot from his friendship; I hope he felt he got more than his few tins, plastic containers and a stool, from mine. That evening I left him, and although I sent him notes trying to explain, I never heard from him or saw him again.

And so, one day, about two weeks after arriving, I decided it was time to get moving. I had waved Frank and Ed off on their big adventure, I had resolved my emotional ties (or copped out of them), I had said goodbye to the folk from the boat – I had given them some final presents and received some big grins and good wishes. I had even found a doctor to take some of my letters with him on his flight to Uganda, to post them on from there. My resolve had returned.

I felt like I had woken up.

I turned over my Michelin. On leaving Kisangani, I would cross the middle fold of the Central and South Africa map. There was the Indian Ocean and Dar Es Salaam. Now I only had to cycle approximately 700 kilometres south-eastwards from Kisangani, via Lubutu, Walikale and Hombo to Bukavu, which was on Lake Kivu and at the border with Rwanda. Then, I would cycle over 400 kilometres southwards through Rwanda and Burundi and cross into western Tanzania. And finally, I would leave Kigoma, a Tanzanian town on Lake Tanganyika, and cycle about 1500 kilometres directly eastwards, following the railway line for two thirds of the way, into Dar Es Salaam. That made roughly 2600 kilometres – about two months if I was lucky and if I pushed it. Now that I had chosen to continue, I wanted to finish quickly.

It was the second week of February, fifteen weeks since I arrived in Kinshasa, and the thought of all that cycling was terrifying! Quickly, I refolded the map to show only my route for the next couple of weeks to Bukavu.

Then, I cycled out of Kisangani.

The road was reasonably flat and paved – just a narrow strip of potholed bitumen, but that seemed excellent to me – and I was passed by a few trucks and bush taxis. However, about 50 kilometres outside Kisangani, a bridge had collapsed and vehicles could not get past. Truck drivers, who sat smoking near their parked vehicles, told me the bridge had been down for a few days and they did not know how long it would take to repair. I pushed Ibn down the steep bank, waded the stream, and continued on my way. The road was quiet after that – I only shared it with other cyclists and pedestrians.

The first evening out, after a 70-kilometre day, I was fresh and impressed that I was still strong, or at least less unfit than I had imagined I would be. I also enjoyed my evening in a small village chatting with a school teacher about the difficulties he faced when parents had no money for school fees, books and pens. Was I simply becoming calmer? More at peace with myself? And more accepting of others?

By the third evening, I was less fresh and less confident about my fitness level. I was also far enough from Kisangani, in a remote part of the forest, for my arrival in a small village near sunset to cause a major commotion.

The wooden huts of the village were in a clearing cut shallowly around the road but which extended along the road for about 2 kilometres. As I cycled along the length of the village, looking for the market, a tiny food stall or somewhere bigger that could be a chief's hut, I gathered a following of excited, laughing children. Soon, they were a screaming horde.

Seeing an old man, who I hoped might also shoo the children, I pulled to a halt.

'*Bonjour,*' I said.

'*Bonjour,*' he replied. He, too, seemed astonished by my appearance.

'Can I see the chief?' I asked. Then I realised he did not speak French. Finally, by pointing at the setting sun, mimicking sleeping and repeating '*chef*', he came to understand my meaning, and I was led by a young boy, surrounded by my almost hysterical audience, to the chief's hut.

The chief, an elderly, small and wizened man, came out, but he spoke no French either. He called for someone, and soon his eldest son arrived, a lad of about twelve. He knew a few words of French, enough to understand I was asking to stay and relay this to his father who nodded agreement. However, trying to convey the idea of a tent and camping was too hard! Eventually, I pointed to an open space near the hut, unloaded the bicycle and started erecting the tent. Everyone, and by now it seemed I had the entire village as an audience – children, men and women – was mesmerised. I did it as entertainingly as I could: I wanted to be a good guest, even though I began, yet again, to feel intimidated by such a large, staring crowd. Then I asked about bathing. I learnt there was a river, and a young woman who spoke no French was appointed my guide. We walked along the road beyond the village for about a kilometre, trailing the larger part of my audience. Only at the river did the young men veer away, but I had to bathe in front of about thirty women, and at least triple that number of children. It was very intimidating, more so because there was no conversation to lessen the intensity of their stares.

It was after dark, though, that I really began to feel the loneliness of the nomadic village existence swell in me again. I was not alone – even in the pitch black before moonrise, I was aware of the enclosing circle of children and adults – yet, we had no means of communication. I was just a spectacle, a bizarre object, and that made me feel very lonely.

I shone my torch at my radio to see the dial, then shone it out toward my audience. I hoped to see friendly faces, a smile or two, and find that maybe someone out there spoke French. Instead, I created a stampede. Children and adults screamed and scuttled off in all directions, one child must have fallen over and his crying started a wave of others. They were hysterical, so scared of me. I felt awful.

My torch dimmed, then the batteries gave out all together.

'*Madame, madame.*' It was the chief's eldest son and he sounded quite nervous, too. He held out a lit kerosene lamp. 'For you, *madame*. My father said to bring it.'

It was the family's only lamp. I had seen them using it around the kitchen fire behind their hut. It took extraordinarily precious currency to buy kerosene. I shook my head but he would not accept no, so feeling dreadful, I took the lamp, and the boy ran back to the safety of his parents.

Why am I doing this? Sixteen months in Africa, away from my people, my life. And now, I thought rather desolately, when I had the chance for a different life, one where I had found rapport, I let it go. For what? To continue alone, in the bush, and to scare people half to death?

It was as if I only valued the comfort of having a social network and a stable town routine once I had lost it. I forgot all the disquiet and confusion now that my existence was nomadic again, now that I was experiencing an especially lonely night.

Feeling a need for some contact with these people, I walked towards the fire, taking the lamp with me. I would leave it there as, afterwards, I would sleep. For now, I hoped we might at least laugh together, at least share something. I walked into the family gathering, the lamp adding illumination to the scene. Everyone froze, wide-eyed, looking at me. They were a snapshot of family life in a remote village.

In mama's lap nestled a sleeping toddler; from a nipple of her exposed breast hung another baby. The seemingly middle-aged woman was pounding manioc and the baby bounced in rhythm to the pounding and sucked contentedly on her nipple. The chief, in the shadows away from the fire, was talking in low murmurs to another man. Another daughter, seven or eight years old, was dozing. The eldest son was not there, so I realised there would be no conversation. However, it did not matter – my gaze was held by the sight of the younger son, about ten years old, who was hovering close to the fire.

The youngster was holding a dead rat with a twig inserted up its backside over the embers of the fire. He held the free end of the stick like a barbecue fork. I watched, mesmerised like the children who had watched me, as he turned the dead animal, drew it to his nose, sniffed it as if to test if it was done, then held it over the charcoals again. He looked at me and smiled shyly. Perhaps he wondered at my stare.

'*Petit déjeuner,*' he managed in French. '*Très bon!*' and he licked his lips.

I smiled back at him, I hoped reassuringly, trying to reinforce the bond of our common humanity. However, our worlds were really too different to connect more over a brief encounter. As I left the lamp, nodded thanks and turned away, I thought my heart would burst.

They were real friendships, real relationships in Kisangani. We connected at so many levels – and I had doubted that. How stupid of me, I thought. I missed Bob and Jimmy and all the faces of the boat. I missed the curious contentment and puzzlement of my life there. But at one level, I still had a voice which said: 'And what would you have done there? Be a farmer?'

On the boat and in Kisangani, I had found complex and rewarding human connections, across cultural, educational and economic divides, and that was what this trip was about. Now, I had left. It was time to finish what I started and go home.

From Lubutu, a small town 239 kilometres from Kisangani through the forest until about 80 kilometres short of Walikale, the next town, there was a surprise – 120 kilometres of four-lane superhighway! The collapsed bridge near Kisangani must have still been preventing trucks coming through from the west, and there was nothing coming from the east either. It seemed very strange to be cycling along such an evidently brand-new piece of extraordinarily high-quality road with just a few other cyclists and an occasional pedestrian.

At tiny Walikale, I stayed for a couple of days with the three priests (two Polish and one elderly Dutch) at a Catholic mission. They gave me a warm welcome, lunch of some cheese, potatoes and coffee with milk – all rare treats – and a chance to sleep through the afternoon. Over dinner, they expressed dismay at the road.

'You will have only one more day's cycling on tarmac,' said Father Mietek, one of the Polish priests. A German company had been building the road for five years, but EU loan funding had stopped and now they were pulling out. 'When the road starts going into the mountains it deteriorates,' continued Father Mietek. 'The road is closed because it is too muddy to pass.' That was why no vehicles were coming from the east, I thought. And towards Kisangani, there was still the problem of the collapsed bridge. Why hadn't the Germans spent five years modestly improving the entire length of the Bukavu to Kisangani road rather than improving such a short stretch to superhighway status? This was bilateral 'aid': EU-subsidised loan funding created a debt for the Zairean people, but created an income and jobs for EU companies. There was no incentive to the donors or contractors to minimise the job. Zaire continued to astonish, but it was not only Zaireans who had *le système*.

'Do you think Zaire is going backwards?' I asked Father François after dinner. He was a seventy-year-old Dutchman who had been in Zaire since 1948. He had told me that he had not spoken English for many years, but each morning and evening he listened to the BBC World Service – 'I do not listen to the Dutch service because they always talk about the weather!'

'That it is going backwards is very clear,' he answered in his precise English. 'At the level economic it is going backwards, in education, in health, in everything.'

'I get very worn down by all the misery,' I said. In the villages *en route* from Kisangani I was hearing how rising prices made so many goods unaffordable. On the road, one woman asked me for soap. I had seen soap sold by the quarter bar in village markets in an effort to make it affordable, but it was still expensive. I knew the small pleasure afforded by my end-of-day bucket shower and the feel of being clean – my toiletries bag now was only my plastic scoop cup, toothbrush, toothpaste and soap (soap was one of life's true essentials) – but I felt very sorry for her and gave her mine. Some village markets were bare – I could not even buy sugar – and I was told that they had been raided by elephant poachers who lived in the forest. Instead of buying, I gave away some anti-malarial tablets, ointment and T-shirts. There was hunger, even malnutrition, surprising in such lush forest but apparently caused because mothers lacked education on proper nourishment for their children. I met university and high-school graduates who had returned to a subsistence life in their village because there were no jobs and they could not afford to live in the cities. However, wherever I stayed, folk were all touchingly optimistic that things would improve once Mobutu went. 'Are you optimistic that things will improve?' I asked Father François.

'If you do not have optimism in Zaire,' he said, 'you have nothing.'

Soon after Walikale, the road started climbing, and I left the dense, humid rainforest behind. The worst muddy stretch of 36 kilometres through the mountains was only passable for cyclists. As I pushed the bike through mud, fortunately not as slippery or extensive as in Cameroon, I encountered cyclists coming from Bukavu. The Lake Kivu valley was very fertile, and the fathers had told me that, during colonial times, a lot of food was produced there, brought to Kisangani and sent downriver to supply Kinshasa. Even now, the trading route was important. As trucks could not get through, the bicycles were being used as packhorses. I have never seen such heavily laden pushbikes – and with their loads, they were only capable of being pushed!

Fortunately, the old narrow bitumen recommenced at Hombo, a small town about 110 kilometres after Walikale, but I was slowing. The road seemed to go up for several days, and although I was getting stronger, it was very tiring. The nights were becoming very cold and food was hard to find. I subsisted on fried manioc, grilled corn and sweetened coffee.

'*Ça donne la force!*' grinned Zaireans – it gives strength. They were referring to manioc and I learnt the truth of that. One piece of fried manioc guaranteed another 20 kilometres of energetic pushing or peddling!

One evening near dusk, I arrived near the summit of a steep mountain road – it had taken five hours to push the bicycle 21 kilometres! I was at the entrance to the Kahuzi-Biega National Park, a sanctuary for gorillas and other animals. I decided to cycle the 18 kilometres through the park to the far gate before nightfall, leaving myself just one day's cycle ride down the Lake Kivu valley to Bukavu by the side of the lake. It was a glorious ride through a misty world of mountain forest, laced with moss and thick clumps of bamboo. Along the way, I encountered many baboons and monkeys with a white stripe on their nose, but fortunately – given their size – no gorillas! At the barrier on the far side, I was invited to put my tent up with the park guides and guards. They even lent me a warm sleeping bag, which was great! I had been suffering at night as I still had no jumper and only a silk sleeping sheet.

Around a campfire, they talked about the gorillas and tried to convince me to come with them the next day.

'Usually, it only takes one or two hours to find a family group,' said Hervé, the most sociable and talkative of the men. 'Of course, some days we do not find them at all!' They had four family groups that they tracked each day, and took people to see groups that had been nearby.

It would cost US$120. At first, I baulked.

'Yes, it is a lot,' said Hervé. 'It would be good if all the money came to the park, but it does not.' About 75 per cent was meant to go to the government and 25 per cent to the park's management. Probably *le système* saw some money going astray. However, some money made it, as the guards were neatly uniformed, had rifles, seemed well trained and knowledgeable about their jobs and had sleeping bags!

I slept on it – but their tales of seeing a 200-kilogram silverback, the dominant male in any group, and the rest of a gorilla family, were tempting. In the morning I decided to go.

We were a party of four – one guide, Lambert, two armed guards, Jacques and Thomas, and myself. Then, just before we set off around 8 a.m., two visitors arrived. They were two Swedish doctors from the Pentacostal church hospital near Bukavu. Apparently, they had spent a day walking through the forest looking for gorillas a while back and had not found them. Now, they were back for a second try and joined our party.

What a day! It was very tiring traipsing through the bamboo forests on steep, slippery tracks tangled with *liane* and prickly plants and then sloshing through reed-filled swamp. We spent several hours following one trail, only having to turn back because of elephant.

'They are the most dangerous!' whispered Lambert, clearly fearful.

As we continued into the afternoon, my legs turned to jelly. They were exhausted from days spent cycling or pushing up mountain roads and now I was using different muscles. Unlike everyone else, I was also in cycling shoes, not walking boots, and therefore the most clumsy. Adventurous cyclist falls over in safari park! How embarrassing!

Just as we were near giving up, after six hours of walking in the forest, we found a family group of gorillas. They were extraordinary animals to see (especially just a few metres away) as they grazed on bamboo shoots amongst the trees and thick undergrowth. There were several younger males munching away and smaller females and youngsters playing in trees, but the huge male silverback was not keen on us getting too close. We stood taking photos and as long as we stayed at the right distance – around 5 metres – he just sat munching shoots. Occasionally, he got a gleam in his small, highly intelligent brown eyes that seemed to say, let's terrorise these folk. He seemed to especially distrust or dislike the Swedish males. A few times when they stepped forward to take a photo, he made a rush toward them, beat the ground, then sat back on his haunches and beat his chest. He made a fearsome noise and if pushed to it, he might have attacked. However, his body language seemed to say, leave me alone – I want to eat in peace, and I could not blame him.

We stayed, observing, for about an hour, then had to leave. We had a long way to go back.

One of the worst aspects of that long day was hunger. I know Lambert and the two guards persevered longer to find the gorillas because the Swedes were having a second go, and because for me there would be no second chance. Yet the three Zaireans and myself had had no food. There were no biscuit stalls or sandwich bars to stock up with a picnic. We had breakfasted together on strong, sweetened tea, but after that nothing.

The Swedes had day packs of food and cigarettes. At every rest stop they disappeared behind a tree. We heard the rustling of paper, munching sounds, and saw the wafts of smoke from their cigarettes. Yet they never offered to share any of it with any of us. Their furtiveness was laughable.

The generosity of Africans was thrown into sharp contrast. Even in the poorest villages I was offered hospitality and food. And I was offered the one lamp in the remotest village of all.

Again, I wondered how I could have questioned the friendships I had on the boat and in Kisangani. It was now two weeks since I left, and I found I was still missing my life there – and especially the people – with the same kind of intensity with which I initially missed people from my life in London.

Zaire was like nowhere else – it was truly a bizarre world of its own with disconcerting rules of its own. Yet everywhere in the world, people could be kind. And everywhere, like the two Swedes (and me?), people could be very peculiar indeed.

PART THREE

Crossed and Baffled

'I have lost a great deal of happiness, I know, by these wanderings (in Africa). It is as if I had been born to exile; but it is God's doing ... I am away from the perpetual hurry of civilisation, and I think I see far and clear into what is to come; and then I seem to understand why I was led away, here and there, and crossed and baffled over and over again, to wear out my years and strength.'

– DAVID LIVINGSTONE, quoted in
Fawn M. Brodie's *The Devil Drives*

Seventeen

Road to Hell

Bukavu, Zaire – Bujumbura, Burundi

It was only 34 kilometres from the Kahuzi-Biega National Park down the mountain side to Bukavu on the shores of Lake Kivu; how the world changed in that short distance. I swept down broad curves into a soft, green, cultivated land where the roads were paved and well maintained, where there were frequent trucks, bush taxis and even sedans. Roadside stalls and markets were filled with fruits and vegetables. After two weeks of frugality, tomatoes, pineapples, cucumbers, potatoes and tamarillos seemed exotic, a sign of fertility and wealth. People were plentiful, too. They looked prosperous and well fed, and walked with a brisk stride – to and from church in their Sunday best outfits, to and from markets.

The entire scene felt less wild, more domesticated, than further west in the forests and mountains I had come through during the past two weeks. I had been wearing all my clothes at night to keep warm, so there had been no chance to wash them – and it had been too cold to tempt me to wash my hair for several days. My Akubra was battered and holed, the panniers were faded and carried a permanent coating of dust and mud, the bike needed a wash – generally Ibn and I looked grubby and worn. I felt like a misplaced forest warrior against these almost suburban Sunday scenes.

Finally, at one curve, a long finger of Lake Kivu glistened into view! Then, Bukavu, too! The collection of shimmering buildings seemed like an incredible civilisation, nestled at the southern end of the lake. On the other side of the lake, another steep, green mountain side rose, backed by further layers of high, misty, green hills – Rwanda. I paused and took in the magnificent scenery.

Wow! I had crossed the mountains and reached Lake Kivu. It was one of a series of lakes – the Great Lakes region of Africa, lure to European explorers in their search for the source of the Nile – that ran north and south through this fertile, volcanic region of East Africa. Yes, East Africa! I had broken free from the equatorial forests of Central Africa, and from now on, the scenery would become drier, until finally, I would reach plains and savannah in Tanzania, familiar territory to me from previous travels.

I did not pause long, as I was keen to make Bukavu, have a day's rest, then

leave Zaire. Father François at Walikale had told me, 'One can observe Zaire, but one can never understand Zaire.' For now, I was tired of being in a world I could only observe. I wanted to escape the distorted reality of this bewildering country and get to countries I could understand.

(In retrospect, these were rather ironic sentiments: I was headed to Rwanda. It was six weeks before the outbreak of the Rwandan civil war.)

My stay in Rwanda was to be brief – a short day's ride through it to Burundi. I planned to cross the border at Bukavu into the Rwandan town of Cyangugu, travel down a road marked in red on my Michelin – that is to say, a good one – cross the border into Burundi and arrive in Cibitoke, the first small place marked, by nightfall. The map was not clear about the distance to my planned destination – I thought about 50 kilometres inside Rwanda and another 30 or 40 to Cibitoke – nor was it clear about the nature of the terrain. I was aware of a tense political situation and had heard there had been fighting in Kigali, the capital, away to the north and far off my route. The alternative route to Burundi, inside Zaire, was unpaved. Between bad roads and bad politics, the choice was easy. Surely, I thought, a brief flit through this troubled country could not be too eventful. I was in for some surprises.

The first thing I noticed on entering Rwanda was the hostility in the eyes of people I passed. Their stares were unblinking, creating a nervousness in me that I thought I'd lost long ago. In fact, their stares seemed filled with unleashed aggression, much stronger than I'd previously encountered on the road – it made me feel very unwelcome. I pedalled straight through.

The road climbed on broad, sweeping curves through land that looked like a patchwork of market gardens, cultivated in tiny terraced fields of tea – a scene reminiscent of the paddy fields of Asia. Also reminiscent of Asia was the sheer number of people, even more than had been on the Bukavu side. I encountered them in villages, in fields and walking along the road edges. The land seemed fertile but how did they all eke a living from such small plots?

In fact, Rwanda and its southern twin, Burundi, were fertile in both crops and people. The population in Rwanda was over seven million, in Burundi about six million. Each country was roughly half the size of England, a little bigger than Wales, but there was little industry and the land was among the most densely populated and intensely farmed in the world. Both countries had a temperate, humid climate and mountainous terrain. Rwanda was known as the 'land of one thousand hills' – which accounted for the field terracing and also for even higher practical population densities – nearly four hundred per square arable kilometre. No wonder the place looked like a market garden – these people weren't farmers, they were gardeners!

As I cycled, I noticed very obvious differences in people – the tall, thin, lighter-skinned folk with long noses and high brows, the classic Tutsi body type, and the shorter, stockier, darker-skinned folk with broader noses, the classic Hutu body type. There were many who did not fit these neat descriptions – mixed ancestry and intermarriage were common – but that this was a country inhabited by people of very different ethnic stock was an easy conclusion.

In fact, there were three groups of people in Rwanda, the third being the Twa, a pygmy race, who represented just 1 per cent of the population. However, the proportions of Hutu to Tutsi was extremely important for understanding Rwanda and Burundi's histories and future prospects. The Hutu vastly outnumbered the Tutsi – in Rwanda, by approximately ten to one, in Burundi, by approximately six to one. There seemed some anthropological dispute, but it was generally believed that the Hutu were a farming tribe of Bantu origins who, from the ninth century, migrated northwards and gradually overran the Twa pygmies who had previously controlled these mountainous regions. In turn, from the fifteenth century, the Tutsi, a pastoralist and nomadic tribe of Nilotic origins, migrated from the north.

No matter the ethnic body type of the individual, as I cycled through southern Rwanda, I consistently saw hostility – directed against me. People's eyes seemed to throw daggers. Children chased me and threw stones at me. Right, I thought, if I'm not welcome, let's get out of here fast!

Directly south was Lake Tanganyika. Bujumbura, the capital of Burundi, on the north-eastern banks of the lake about 160 kilometres south from Bukavu, had been my planned destination for tomorrow, but to get there, I now realised I had to climb out of the Lake Kivu watershed, cross the mountains, then descend into the Lake Tanganyika watershed. The distance might be short, but the day would be long.

I was struggling up a hill around midday, surrounded on either side by mud-brick and straw-roofed huts clinging to the steep slopes. People were in their compounds, but given their lack of warmth I was not taking much notice. Rather, I was looking at my cycle computer's record of my speed (a pathetic 6 kilometres per hour) when I became aware there was someone in the middle of the road, standing in my path.

I looked up to see a tall, thin man, wearing nothing but a dirty loincloth, just metres ahead. He was staring wild-eyed at me, then rapidly ran forward and grabbed hold of my handlebar bag to stop my ascent. He started babbling, his words were a tangle of French and the local language, but I knew he wanted money. Alarmed, I yelled loudly for help and tried to turn the bike, thinking my best chance was to flee downhill, but he was too strong and held the bike firmly in place. Suddenly he found the fruit knife that I kept, perhaps foolishly, in the front pocket of my handlebar bag. He grabbed it and waved it menacingly, then yelled, coherent at last, 'You whites have everything! We blacks have nothing!'

Simultaneously, men and women villagers rushed to the road. Several men grabbed the man and disarmed him. One of my rescuers, a young man in a holey red T-shirt gave me back my knife and reassured me.

'Do not worry,' he said. 'He is only a fool.'

I stood for a while holding my bicycle, letting the shaking subside. All this way and this was the first time I had been attacked. It was alarming how quickly a bad situation could emerge. Travelling alertly and with a smile had always stood me in good stead – but today there had been few smiles. I said thank you to the young man, but around me was a silent, morose crowd. I moved on.

As I crossed my last mountain pass, I swiftly descended (recklessly now, using speed to evade the ever-present, stone-throwing children) to the border.

'You have come from Bukavu today?' On the Rwanda side, officials had been taciturn, but at the Burundi post the guard was more talkative. 'You are lucky – they have closed the border to Zaire now.'

'Why?' I questioned.

'This morning, an opposition leader was pulled from his car in Cyangugu – and lynched!' This morning, in Cyangugu? It must have happened just after I passed through. 'It was retaliation,' continued the guard, 'because yesterday a government minister was murdered in Kigali.' He paused and looked reflective.

'Ah, things are tense in Rwanda,' he said.

Suddenly, I had an image of the frightened, persecuted eyes of Fatimata and Ibrahim in Mali. Belatedly, I realised that I had not been seeing hostility in the eyes of Rwandans today. Just as I had at first misjudged the Tuaregs as sly looking, I had misjudged the people I had passed. I had been in a very unhappy country, taut from rumour and terrible occurrences. What I had been seeing was fear.

*

At the time of my journey, I knew some of the background to the ethnic tensions and the history of the massacres and reprisal killings in Rwanda and Burundi. As subsequent events unfolded, I learnt more about the social, political and economic ingredients leading to this dreadful tragedy. They are complex and compelling and, certainly in hindsight, deliver a sense of walking along a road with an inevitable destination of hell.[1]

Before the arrival of Europeans, Hutu and Tutsi had lived side by side on the *musozi* (hills) for centuries. For each of his wives, each man had a separate compound – a *rugo* – and each *musozi* was covered with dozens of *rugo*. The societies of the highly developed Rwandan and Burundian kingdoms were tightly controlled and organised. A king – *mwami* – was at the top of the hierarchy and was treated as a divine being, but economic, social and political control was administered by the three chiefs of each *musozi* – an agricultural land chief, a pastoral land chief and a chief of men. Most chiefs were Tutsi, and the Tutsi developed myths and rituals to justify the class distinction between themselves as cattle-owning rulers and Hutu as cultivating subjects. However, some agricultural land chiefs were Hutu and there was no evidence of any fighting or massacres between Hutu and Tutsi in pre-colonial times – instead, they came together to fight invaders or to capture more land.

From the outset, Europeans noticed the ethnic distinctiveness and immediately stereotyped the two groups. Without any foundation (other than Tutsi's own mythology), Europeans perceived the Tutsi as superior beings, too fine to be 'negroes', with origins as far flung as Ethiopia and Egypt.

Unfortunately, as Gérard Prunier assesses, the stereotyping drove systems, behaviours and attitudes.

First, the Belgians, who took colonial control of Rwanda and Burundi from the Germans after World War I until independence in 1962, established a system giving the Tutsi access to education and positions of power and authority. For instance, the three-chief system of the *musozi* was coagulated into one chief, always a Tutsi; also Hutu rarely had access to secondary or tertiary education, other than for seminary training. Second, and perhaps most tragically, the system and messages of sixty years of colonial power powerfully affected the self-images and attitudes of the Hutu and Tutsi themselves – giving the Hutu dangerously resentful inferiority complexes and the Tutsi insensitive, inflated egos.

The time bomb created by these legacies of Belgian colonialism first exploded in Rwanda in 1959, when, following the death of the *mwami*, a Tutsi clan grabbed power and murdered Hutu leaders. The Hutu turned on their

---

[1]A primary source I have used to enlarge my understanding of the history leading to the genocide and of subsequent events has been Gérard Prunier's excellent book *The Rwanda Crisis – History of A Genocide* (Hurst & Company, 1997). Prunier is a journalist and Africa scholar whose work I would recommend to anyone interested in further reading about this tragic situation.

oppressors and as many as 100,000 Tutsi were massacred. By 1964, over 300,000 Tutsi were living in exile in surrounding countries, including Burundi, Uganda, Tanzania and Zaire. Independence came in 1962 under a government led by a moderate Hutu, Gregoire Kayibanda. During the sixties and seventies, exiled Tutsi mounted guerrilla raids into Rwanda, which provoked further bloodshed and reprisal killings of Tutsi. In 1972, the butchering in Burundi of more than 200,000 Burundian Hutu by Burundian Tutsi, led, in Rwanda, to both a Hutu uprising, and the ousting of Kayibanda in an army coup d'état led by Major General Juvenal Habyarimana, a Hutu.

After thirty years, many Tutsi counted themselves as nationals of their new homes and had made new lives for themselves. However, large numbers – and especially the young exiles born outside Rwanda – idealised their homeland, ignored its overpopulation, were blind to their own ethnic stereotyping, and dreamed of and planned for their return.

Thus, in the early nineties, 5000 Tutsi rebels belonging to the Rwandan Patriotic Front (RPF) – the political and militant arm of exiled Tutsi – invaded Rwanda from Ugandan bases. They were well trained and armed, funded by exiled Tutsi from all over the world, and supported by Ugandan troops.

During the 1991 RPF attack on Kigali, France, Belgium and Zaire flew in troops to aid Habyarimana. The invasion was repulsed but again led to reprisal Tutsi killings. Fighting continued. Later in 1991, Habyarimana agreed to introduce a multi-party constitution, reneged, then faced another RPF invasion and was forced to negotiate. The 1993 Arusha peace accord provided for a transitional government with RPF representation. Exiled Tutsi – returnees, as they were called – started coming back.

Extremist Hutus could not accept the deal, and the plot for a final solution was put in place.

On the night of 6 April 1994, President Habyarimana's plane, returning from Tanzania, was shot down, allegedly by rocket attacks orchestrated by the Hutu extremists, and the president, along with Burundi's President Ntaryamira and others, was killed. Within hours, Tutsi and moderate Hutu named on death lists were being executed. Within days, the illiterate, impoverished Hutu villagers, indoctrinated, used to accepting tight social control and desperate for land, were incited over radio and by local leaders, to take up any arms and kill their 'aggressive Tutsi neighbours'. They, and the rampaging extremist Hutu militia, the Interahamwe, did.

The stories from the genocide were truly awful: of Jean Kambamba, the prime minister of Rwanda (now the first person ever to be sentenced for the crime of genocide) being asked by local officials in a Rwandan town to intervene to save the lives of dozens of Tutsi children hiding in a local hospital but doing nothing.[1] Of the Hutu teacher who was forced to watch his heavily

---

[1]*International Herald Tribune*, London, 5–6 September 1998, p 6.

pregnant Tutsi wife be disembowelled, then have the foetus pushed in his face, the killers shouting, 'Here! Eat your bastard!' Of the 40,000 bodies that floated down the Kagera River to pollute Lake Victoria. Of the mutilations – breasts and penises chopped off. Of the UN operation mobilised to evacuate only foreign nationals. Followed to the letter, this led to Tutsi on lorries heading for the airport being offloaded at militia roadblocks and slaughtered in front of watching French or Belgian soldiers, and to a Russian woman being forced to abandon her Tutsi husband.

Within six weeks, at least 500,000 Tutsi and an unknown number of moderate Hutu were murdered by extremist Hutu, and more than 100,000 other Hutu were dead, murdered in simultaneous massacres carried out by the RPF. Three months later, without foreign intervention (except for the French government's patrolling of a safe zone in the south-west), the RPF gained control and Major General Paul Kagame became president. Two million Hutu refugees were in exile, another 1.2 million were in the French safe zone.

I appeared on the border just as all these events were beginning to unfold. The time bomb had started to tick.

That evening near dusk, I was still cycling to Cibitoke. People along the way had informed me there was a motel there.

'It is a very nice motel, *madame*,' said a young boy who I had stopped to ask. He volunteered, 'It costs 1500 Franc Burundian,' – then about US$7.50.

That was actually a lot compared to what I had paid elsewhere, so on a value-for-money basis, I started looking forward to a shower with running water. I was weary after crossing two mountain passes and, being fairly tense, a real shower, something I had not had since leaving Kinshasa, would be a very special treat. Maybe there would even be a bed with proper sheets, I mused, prematurely.

Finally, after a few encounters with surly and arrogant Tutsi military at checkpoints, I made Cibitoke, a modest, quiet town, and found the modern-looking brick motel set back from the road. I left Ibn on the verandah, rolled off my sweaty gloves and walked into the bar.

Oops. The entire bar hushed and drunken, bloodshot eyes turned to look at my entry. It was filled with Tutsi military in dark-blue uniforms and blue berets, their guns slung over shoulders, lying on small tables, standing against walls. Drunken soldiers are never great companions, but this army had a particularly brutal reputation.

Burundi represented the flipside of Rwanda's horror. Despite very similar demographics, the Hutu majority remained violently suppressed in Burundi by the minority Tutsi. Since 1966 when the monarchy was overthrown and a Tutsi military government seized power, attempts by majority Hutu to overthrow Tutsi rule were met by ethnic massacre. Perhaps the worst was the killing in 1972 of any Hutu who had formal education, wealth or a government job. There was no international coverage.

In June 1993, Melchior Ndadaye, a Hutu, was elected president, but in October 1993, the Tutsi-controlled army led a coup and murdered him. In subsequent months, between 50,000 and 100,000 people, primarily Hutu, were killed. Finally, the government regained control and Cyprien Ntaryamira, another Hutu, became president. However, the Tutsi-led army continues to attack Hutu communities, and the situation gets little attention from the world's media.

I had heard the stories and felt myself become more alert. There were a few salacious calls of '*Ça va?*'. I felt myself bristle. I was not going to take any nonsense from people I did not respect.

'Can I see a room, please?' I asked the barman, the only man in civvies. He stood under the 'Bar/Reception' sign. Before acknowledging my presence, he served several drinks and then several more before agreeing to show me a room.

After another delay while he hunted for the key, he took me out the back to a separate block and unlocked the room. The floor and walls were dirty, the handbasin was filthy, the bedlinen had clearly been recently used ... and then, when I turned the faucet, there was no water. Disappointing, but when I asked for a bucket of water ...

'There is *no* water, *madame*.'

What?! Even in the villages, there were always wells or pumps for water.

'The pipe is cut, *madame*.'

And the price for this luxury? He had to consult the proprietor – but when he came back the response was not good.

'2000 francs, *madame*.' Nearly US$10.

Well, I demanded to see the proprietor. The price was clearly inflated, it was the most expensive room for who knows how long – and for filth and no water.

I was led to the presence of the army captain, a middle-aged, thin-faced, hard-eyed Tutsi who was drinking beer at a table in the bar. Oops again.

I was already angry, but when he arrogantly told me *that* was the price, I felt fury envelop me.

A one-sided argument ensued as I let him know that I knew he was over-charging me and that the hotel and the room were in a disgraceful state. I was not going to be subdued by this thug. In fact, I enjoyed having him as a target for my anger.

He did not respond, just watched superciliously.

Stupidly, I continued. I let him know my views on Burundi, on Tutsi murderers, and on ...

I was overwrought and the bar was silent.

Finally, the captain spoke.

'It is the politics – we have no money.'

'Oh,' I said sarcastically. 'And how did you become the proprietor of this motel?' Shut up, Pamela, I told myself. Do you want to get shot?

Finally, I had penetrated his patience. Evilly, he told me I could stay some-where else. His quiet, sinister manner clearly said I would not be safe if I left. At least for US$10, I would have a locked door to sleep behind. At last, I took my own advice and shut up, paid, took the key and let the captain have a final piece of my mind.

'If this is your asset, why don't you look after it? You could wash some walls instead of drinking beer and shooting people!' Then, I rushed with my bike to my room, locked the door and did not venture out until daybreak.

I knew I had been childish and foolish, and I wondered where the anger came from. I felt he got the overspill of my accumulated fear of the day.

The cries of the man who attacked me at knife-point during my few hours in Rwanda have stayed with me. Perhaps he was not such a fool.

Later, I heard that Cibitoke had been the scene of a recent massacre of Hutu by the Tutsi military. It was still a war zone, where houses were torched and deserted, fields were abandoned. The local Hutu lived in total fear of the military, or had fled as refugees to neighbouring Zaire. The military had taken over the motel and were using it as their base.

I was pleased I had abused the captain.

Then, I had another worrying thought. My furious reaction was over trivi-alities. How could people who had suffered massacres of loved ones, real abuses and tragedies, on either side, ever forgive and live side by side again?

From Cibitoke, it was only a day's cycle ride to Bujumbura, the small, airy capital of Burundi that sat on the north-eastern banks of Lake Tanganyika, facing the far shores of Zaire. It was a pleasant city to look at, and offered an agreeable lifestyle for the elite, but I found no comfort about the country's future.

I located Shell and met the *directeur général*, who arranged for me to stay at a hotel and introduced me, mainly socially, over the weekend, to some locals and expatriates. Unsurprisingly, politics was the main subject of discussion; however, few people expressed a point of view about the current atrocities or proposed a path for the future – mainly, they discussed how the situation affected their leisured lifestyles.

After a morning of windsurfing on Lake Tanganyika and volleyball on the beach, Matthuis, the good-looking, playboy son of a wealthy German indus-trialist, took me out in his speedboat to look at hippos. 'The Tutsi are scared again,' he said. 'After the killings in the seventies there's now a new genera-tion of educated Hutu who want power. But only Tutsi are in the military and that's the big problem.' Then, he continued, 'We can't go to our home in the hills anymore – there is no water or electricity and it's too dangerous. And we keep the boat ready all the time – if trouble flares, we can flee to Zaire.'

Later, at a barbecue lunch by the lake, I chatted with Christine, a young

Belgian woman, wearing designer shorts, T-shirt, sunglasses and bright-red lipstick. 'I work for Catholic Relief Services,' she said. 'I organise the delivery of food to refugee camps in the north – I'm only in Buju on the weekend.' She didn't look like an aid worker, and I expressed my surprise. 'Oh, I came to Burundi on a holiday but I liked the sun and lifestyle, so I had to find something to do,' she said. 'It is very good here.' I was even more stunned. What about the ongoing killings and instability? 'Oh,' she sighed, '*c'est un peu pénible*,' – it's a little tiresome.

Meanwhile, the Hutu seemed invisible in the elite circles in which I mixed during my short stay – administrative and business power and wealth were still with the Tutsi, yet these civic leaders seemed unprepared to take responsibility for the massacres. Always 'they' did it – 'they' being Hutu militia or Tutsi military. Clementine, a Tutsi secretary, told me about the murder the previous year of President Ndadaye.

'He was extreme and the Hutu wanted power. They say they are the majority, so it is time, well, maybe ...' She sounded unconvinced. 'They say they found a plan for the Hutu to kill the Tutsi, even the babies. They have weapons and machetes.' The Tutsi army had no weapons? 'Well, of course, they should not have killed him.' She spoke without a trace of conviction.

On my last night in Bujumbura, the peace was shattered by gunfire. Before I left the next morning, I heard two different accounts about the fighting and killing in a Hutu suburb.

The Tutsi version: 'The Hutu want to kill the Tutsi. A gang of Hutu jumped a military truck and this caused the fighting.'

The Hutu version: 'We are the majority – 86 per cent of the population. It is time we had control. They [the Tutsi] are scared, so the military came into Hutu areas just to make problems and then, there is trouble.'

With all the conflicting rumours, with all the bad blood, with all the ethnic stereotyping, how could a stable and peaceful future – for both Burundi and Rwanda, for Hutu and for Tutsi – be achieved?

(In 1998, Rwanda's President Major General Paul Kagame, still with the help of Uganda, invaded the country I knew as Zaire, now the Democratic Republic of Congo. For a long time, the RPF hid their involvement. At the time of writing, the rebels hold Kisangani, Bukavu and eastern Congo. Invasion of another country to rout extremist Hutu rebels and to get access to its land and mineral wealth seems to be the Rwandan Tutsi solution – though, given Kabila's determination to take the land back, it is still unlikely to bring them stability or peace.)

Out of Bujumbura, on my way southwards to Tanzania, I met a Hutu, a worldly, educated man, at Resha, a beautiful but deserted tourist resort on the edge of Lake Tanganyika. After a lively and thoughtful political discussion, my friend concluded, 'I believe there must be separate Hutu and Tutsi states,' he said solemnly. 'I don't think we can live together anymore.'

Was that the only solution?

Like the expats in Bujumbura, I had no answers and thought mainly about evading the clutches of this menacing situation. I cycled fast, avoided further contact with supercilious and aggressive military, and headed for the border. I never imagined, then, how the presidents' date with destiny would affect me.

Eighteen

The Road Home

Kigoma, Tanzania – Dar Es Salaam, Tanzania

Fortunately, it did not take long to cross the border and reach Kigoma from Burundi – just a brief ride inland, over the mountains to Manyovu on the border with Tanzania, my seventeenth and last country on this journey, then a day's ride south-east back to the shores of Lake Tanganyika. I was pleased to be away from the killing fields.

Kigoma was a quiet, dusty town, set back from the lake, but near enough to find lovely outlooks. I stayed there for several days, needing time to regain composure. I erected my tent in the grounds of a lake-side hotel. A real hotel, not run by military but by a friendly Indian family, with electricity and water! I treated myself to a couple of nights in a plain room with a bed, fresh sheets, a fan and a running-water shower – bliss! Then, conscious of my evaporating budget, I took the cheaper option of camping in the unkempt garden by the shore.

Each evening, I sat on a plastic chair in the long-grassed beer garden, drink in hand, gazing westwards out over the silver, lapping water of the lake waiting for the inevitable sunset spectacle. As the quality of light changed, the mist seemed to rise on the faraway shores – the lake was 50 kilometres wide. Suddenly, Zaire would emerge silhouetted against the white, glowing sky. Mountains, marked at 1700 metres on my Michelin, were mere low, dark waves on the horizon. In my mind's eye, I could see the tangle of forest nurturing the intense lives existing within its dark canopy.

I was nostalgic for Zaire and my life there. Had I thought Zaire was surreal and emotionally tortuous? It was far harder to live with and feel other people's fear and hatred.

As dusk fell, a spectacular lightning show commenced. Soaring cumulonimbus clouds loomed sombrely above those Zairean forests, backlit by sudden flashes of lightning. There was no musical accompaniment, no trombone rumble and bass roar of thunder – the show was too distant. It was mesmerising.

I felt my spirit soar back to Zaire and come down in a forest clearing. It was dusk. Women had come back from the fields, and were setting the cooking fires, flickering glows playing across scattered compounds. Children walked back from the spring, buckets filled with water on their heads. The thump of manioc being pounded echoed against the tangled green walls of the forest. It got darker and there was the buzz of conversation and laughter. Another day had been survived. Muscles ached and bodies were stretched. Women worried about their children. There were many sighs. I was the observer, the stranger in their midsts.

It was very fanciful. I doubted that I would have had such an active imagination seventeen months ago – or felt so kindly to strangers, to the forest.

Yet, more fancifully still, I felt the silent spectacle behind the clouds was sent by the spirits. They had been protecting me, but now, I was venturing outside their safekeeping.

Of course, this was probably just a projection of my own feelings. I was turning my back on the forests and on the African life I knew. I was going home.

At Kigoma railway station, there was a sign which read 'Dar Es Salaam – 780 miles'. 1200 kilometres. My bicycle computer showed over 13,000 kilometres – what remained was a mere bagatelle.

A lot of the time, my thoughts were about what would happen after the journey, outside Africa: what next, what has the journey meant to me, will William and I survive, did I want us to survive? He had sent a letter to Bujumbura suggesting he join me for a leg of the journey here in Tanzania, making it sound like I was on an outing. It had depressed me to realise how little he related to what I had experienced (maybe just as well, given Bob!) – and how I no longer wanted him to be part of my journey.

What work would I do, how could I spend more time with my family back in Australia, how could I repay villagers for their kindnesses? I also thought a lot about being clean again – permanently, rather than transiently at the end of day after a bucket shower. I wanted new clothes – a tight skirt to show off my muscular, brown legs and a sexy shirt instead of shorts and T-shirts, sandals instead of cycling shoes, and no Akubra. For months I had had no scents in soaps or

toiletries, and I wanted perfume and smelly moisturisers and shampoos and conditioners. I wanted red nail polish for my toenails again.

Well, cool it, I told myself, echoing the spirits. You have more than 1200 kilometres and a month of village life to go.

In fact, I had soon another incentive for getting to the coast quickly.

At Kigoma, I got a call through to Mr Pereira, the general manager in Dar Es Salaam.

'Your parents are arriving next week,' he told me. Oops. They had been planning to come to meet me when I arrived, and had asked for an ETA, which I had sent in a letter from Kisangani. I guess I had been optimistic. Now, they would be waiting in Dar at least two or three weeks.

At least that long – I still needed to check whether my planned route was feasible! In London, I had seen that the road to the coast swept northwards through the Serengeti Game Reserve. I figured bicycles and lions did not mix, and had come up with a plan to follow the shorter route along the railway line from Kigoma through Tabora to Dodoma before rejoining the road to Dar Es Salaam. It was good in theory, but there was no track indicated next to the Central Line, as it was called. Even when I bought a detailed map of Tanzania in the Kigoma market, there was no track marked next to the line until Urambo, near Tabora and at least 400 kilometres from Kigoma.

It took two visits to Kigoma railway station to get a meeting with Stationmaster Massare, but it was worth it. He was a round-headed man, with beaming eyes, a Moslem who habitually wore a fez. With some trepidation, I told him of my plan and asked about a cycling track.

'Oh, yes!' he replied enthusiastically. 'As a young man, I cycled the line!' Stationmaster Massare was great. He loved his railway – a true railway man – and wanted me to know aspects of every part of the route. He told me to come back next day and he would have drawn me up a guide. I returned and he handed me a neat sheet of paper with every station and their distances from Kigoma marked. However, my eyes immediately leapt to his annotations: at various points he had marked 'Beware of wild animals.'

Maybe the adventures were not over yet.

It was March 11 when I finally left Kigoma, along the railway line, with an enthusiastic and cheery farewell from Stationmaster Massare.

'I hope you have a safe journey and a safe reunion with your parents,' he said as he grasped my hand in a traditional handshake: handgrip, thumbgrip, handgrip.

Then, he thrust 1000 Tanzanian shillings, about US$2, at me.

'To buy things on your journey,' he said. He was very kind.

The last leg had begun. Initially, there were many pedestrians and I tinkled my newly acquired bell to clear a passage. Initially, also, there were shunt lines, and I had to pause, heave the bike over the track, then continue. Hard work, but it would soon be over. Or so I told myself.

That day, my track dwindled in and out of existence. When it was there, it was very narrow and littered with rocks and tumbled chippings. In parts, it was very muddy. About every kilometre, there was a culvert and the track stopped. I was obliged to haul Ibn and his load over a hill of chippings, over the line, bump down the sleepers, then reverse the process having passed the culvert. The sun was beating down, and I was not nearly as cheerful as I had been that morning. Then, too, the track eroded into a narrow gully, so that rocky protrusions caught at the panniers, pedals and ankles. Ouch! Worse still, the gully sometimes opened into a sharp drop. If I tumbled, I would either land on chippings or fall into the tall grass only to be impaled on a hidden rusting rail!

'*Poly, poly,*' I said to myself in the meagre Swahili that I had picked up. It meant slowly, slowly, and in fact, for most of the day, I walked. And pushed, heaved and bumped my way forward.

Towards the end of the day, I came across a railgang. They spoke little English – Swahili, the national language, which bound this country across tribal groups, was a proud inheritance from the days of 'The Teacher', Julius Nyerere, their first president, who had stayed in power until 1985. In my teens, I had heard of Nyerere and admired his campaign for the right of Africans to manage their affairs in an African way and for the unswerving way in which he stuck to his beliefs. One of the strong-looking, shirtless members of the gang suggested I take the road to Kalenge, rather than follow the track. He used the magic words, 'for cars' as he pointed to a nearby gravel road. I had seen it but had not known where it went. Then, he used a daunting word and pointed along the line: 'chippings'. No problem. I took the road!

The last 8 kilometres were beautiful: the road climbed through gorgeous, egg-shaped hills covered in grass that shone bright in the late evening light. The beauty seemed a good reward for a hard day – I had covered under 50 kilometres from Kigoma, and less as the crow flies.

In Kalenge, I asked for the 'chairman', rather than the 'chief'. In the *ujamaa* (socialist) villages, the leader was the chairman of the CCM – Chama Cha Mapinduzi (Party of the Revolution). This was another legacy of Julius Nyerere. Nyerere became president of Tanganyika in 1961 and of Tanzania, after merger of the mainland with the island of Zanzibar off the coast, in 1963. The country had been neglected by the British who had favoured investment in nearby Kenya and Uganda, and Nyerere wished to foster his country's growth under a socialist model. In 1967, the Arusha Declaration announced that collective agricultural villages, known as *ujamaa* villages and based on the Chinese collective farming model, were to be formed. This meant forced resettlement of villagers and a code of self-help, tool-sharing and obligatory work on commonly held land. In his speech at Arusha, Nyerere implored men in the villages and people in the towns to work harder. 'The truth is that in the villages the women work very hard. At times they work for 12 or 14 hours a day ... The energies of the millions of men in the villages and thousands of women in the towns, which are at present wasted in gossip, dancing and drinking, are a great treasure which could contribute more towards the development of our country than anything we could get from the rich nations.' In many of his views he'd been proved ahead of his time, but his appeals to people's better natures didn't work. Nor did collectivisation: it was a disaster for agricultural output, made worse because of a lack of western aid to the socialist regime. However, this and other policies did seem to break tribal allegiances, and of all countries in Africa I had visited, Tanzanians had the strongest sense of national identity and pride.

'There are more chippings on the line ahead to Uvinza,' said the elderly chairman after he showed me I could stay in the *ujamaa* village's truck yard. 'The line has recently been re-ballasted.' Great. The good news was the road continued to Uvinza, tomorrow's destination. Then, before wishing me goodnight, the chairman added, 'Watch out for lions.'

The next day was uneventful, except that the way was through thick scrub and I saw pug marks in the sand.

'Yes, that would be *simba*,' – lion, said the stationmaster at Uvinza, who let me camp at the station overnight, 'but do not worry. It is the wet season. The grass is long and food is plentiful. The lions will not come for you – you would be too tough! Ho, ho!'

Ho, ho, indeed. These stationmasters of the Central Line were *very* droll.

Then, he added, as an afterthought, 'Watch out for lions on the route to Malagarasi tomorrow.'

Why couldn't Africa ever be easy?

The next morning, I stopped for breakfast at a nearby *chai* (tea) stall. In Tanzania, breakfast was always sweetened tea and chapati – the influence of Indian traders was strong.

'Aren't you worried about lions?' asked the young girl who served me.

Well, I hadn't been.

Before leaving along the rail track to Malagarasi – the road had stopped – I placed my fruit knife in the front pocket of my handlebar bag. I had kept it buried in a rear pannier after the attack in Rwanda, but now I figured I needed it strategically available!

Soon, I was alone on the track, which ran through green scrubland scattered with rocky outcrops. I tried to watch for lions, but the way was still strewn with chippings. While my concentration was on the track, a baboon family slouched across the line. Startling and spooky! But it wasn't long before I had no time to worry about imaginary foes – I was being attacked by real animals, those I hated and feared the most (after dogs) – tsetse flies! One of the reasons the British did not invest much in Tanzania was because the tsetse flies carried sleeping sickness, killing their cattle and undermining the ranching industry. An interesting fact, but not something I thought hard about while under attack!

God. It was awful. The bastards were everywhere, biting me incessantly. Despite sweltering heat, I pulled out more clothes for protection. I wore socks, long trousers, two T-shirts, my Gortex rain jacket, and wrapped my scarf Tuareg-style around my head, leaving only my eyes showing. I even attached a leafy branch I tore from a tree through my hairband to act like a swishing pony tail against my back and coated any visible skin and thin clothing layers with mosquito repellent. All had limited efficacy.

I was expiring of heat exhaustion and still being bitten. The bastards got inside the scarf and buzzed near my ear, driving me mad with anticipation of the next bite. They bit my hands and my bum, and even managed to get inside the rain jacket. I was totally distracted: if a lion had attacked, I'd have barely noticed!

Near midday, I arrived at a railway siding.

'*Karibu*,' – welcome. Some children, who had been playing in the sand, now obviously found me quite amusing.

'*Karibu*,' said their father, coming out from the building. I looked like some maniacal Lawrence of Arabia-type figure, yet the man accepted my presence. Tanzanians, I thought, were a sanguine lot. Little rattled them. After a calming carbohydrate snack – Pancake *à la* Pamela, made with chapati, orange juice and sugar – I continued on my way.

The afternoon was even hotter, the fly attacks even more intense – and after another couple of hours enduring this hell, my calm totally deserted me. Seeing a railgang camp – they occurred infrequently, about every 15 kilometres – I pedalled frantically over toward the iron huts. A few young women, wives of the railgang, were seated under the meagre shade of a skinny thorn tree.

Getting near, out of range of the bush and dreadful flies, I let Ibn fall, stripped off my outer clothing, jumped up and down to rid myself of the skin twitches caused by the bites, and shrieked in distress.

The girls screamed, leapt up and ran for their huts!

So much for sanguine Tanzanians.

However, they soon realised I was harmless, if half mad from the tormenting flies, and they invited me to sit in the shade with them and share their lunch. Some things were truly the same throughout Africa. Anna, the eldest and spunkiest, and the other girls, spoke Swahili; I spoke English – yet we had a good time. I wondered at our connection. Why hadn't I been able to use sign language and smiles so effectively with the women at the beginning of my journey? I remembered how I used to think of women as ephemeral ghosts floating through the background of my village life. I must have changed quite a bit since then, I thought. But how had I changed? And into what? It was hard to see transitions in an ongoing life.

Calmed again, I set off around 4 p.m. for Malagarasi, now about 20 kilometres away. I was joined by a couple of boys, friendly lads on Chinese bicycles who also spoke no English.

'Malagarasi?' the elder of the boys, a lanky youth with doleful eyes, about fifteen, asked.

'Malagarasi,' I nodded, then asked, 'Malagarasi?'

'Malagarasi,' replied the boy.

Common destination established, we pushed and heaved together for the next two hours. In the cool of late afternoon, there were fewer tsetse flies and the way seemed less threatening and tormenting with company, even silent company. Again, I realised the change in my attitude from way back in Senegal and Guinea. Once, wouldn't I have jumped at their arrival and been irritated by their company? I laughed at my past attitude. The last couple of kilometres were very beautiful. It was just on sunset and the orange glow shimmered over the wide, low swamp flats that stretched to the horizon on either side of the track. The setting sun backlit the majestic dark-grey and white clouds. We could see Malagarasi railway siding in the distance on the far side of a swampy lake, but our progress was slow. On the rail bridge over the lake, there was no provision for pedestrians or cyclists, so we had to balance our bicycles on the steel girders and, carefully, push our way forward. Fortunately, there were no trains.

In Malagarasi, Stationmaster Matthuis, a Moslem like Stationmaster Massare in Kigoma, welcomed me. He knew Massare and greeted me like a long lost friend.

'Please, put your tent up here,' he said. His suggested place by the station smelt rather high so, instead, I chose a breezy spot on the concrete foundations of a now demolished railway building. It was Very Fine. Until about 10 p.m. Then, as I lay in my tent, a wild storm struck, sweeping in across the swamp flats and I discovered my breezy spot was directly in the way of the strong winds. I brought my panniers inside the tent to help weigh me down, then lay spread-eagled and wide-eyed, wondering if I was about to lift off.

Around 2 a.m., the train from Dar Es Salaam pulled in. I was pleased to see it because it meant there was less chance of being run down by a late train tomorrow! (The timetable indicated trains in both directions should pass this section of the line during the night – but African timetables were not terribly reliable.) Also, I was hungry. So, I boarded the train, walked along the carriages to find the dining car, and asked the crew for some food. They were surprised to see me, but sold me a couple of hard-boiled eggs and some bread.

'Where did you come from?' asked Peter, a very handsome guard with an enchanting smile who had been having his dinner.

'Malagarasi,' I replied, thinking that not only did I seldom find African men irritating these days, but more worryingly, I was bewitched by their muscles and good looks. Was this a permanent awakening? Would I be running after great physiques in Europe, too? Peter knew none of my inner dismay. He merely looked surprised.

'Where are you going?'

'Malagarasi.'

Peter was confused and did not really believe I was staying in such a small place – until I disembarked and waved him off into the turbulent night. I chuckled, having thoroughly enjoyed his bewilderment.

It was a brief interlude of exhilaration on this long road home.

The next morning dawned bright and clear, and I was hopeful of better conditions. Always the optimist.

Stationmaster Matthuis approached me as I packed up. He was holding a sharp, curved *panga* – a machete – obviously well-used, with animal skin on the handle for a better grip.

'Take this,' he said. 'For *simba*.' Hmm.

'Thank you.' I think.

The track by the line was a little squelchy from the night's rain, but nothing that an old hand from Cameroon's mountains could not handle. Ahead, right across the track, lay a muddy stretch, slightly different from others, a pale grey and deeply marked by human and monkey prints. I cycled in.

And flew over the handlebars, landing in a neat bellyflop in the mud.

Yuk! Picking myself up, I saw that the mud had glued thickly to the wheels and drive mechanism. I tried dislodging it with water from my bottles – but it was like cement. Thick, hard, sticky, immovable. Cement mud. Not sure what to do, I sat on the rail, dazed, took in the mud all over me and Ibn, and sobbed.

So much for exhilaration and optimism. My resilience was clearly slipping.

Suddenly, on this quiet line where I seldom met anybody, an elderly man in Moslem robe and *tarboosh* appeared on a small track that emerged out of the bush nearby. He paused near me.

'*Jambo*,' he said, using the Swahili greeting.

'*Jambo*,' I replied.

He looked gravely at the bicycle, then he looked me up and down. 'Are you going to change your clothes?' he enquired solicitously.

'No,' I replied. He nodded, looked wise, and said nothing else. Then, he ferreted in the bush for some twigs, came back and scraped at the mud on the chain. He saw that a stay on the rear carrier had broken.

'Do you have some string?' I found his calm movements, and silence on all the usual questions, soothing. I brought out some thick linen cotton from my toolkit, and, patiently, he tied the stay back in place. 'This is the track that Livingstone and Burton and Speke used,' he said as he was finishing, and pointed to the walking track he had come from. I nodded, interested in this information, and he continued, 'It was the old slave route.'

Then, as quietly as he had appeared, he left me, slowly picking his way between the tracks toward Malagarasi.

I decided to continue. I tugged the bicycle for about a metre through the mud – and got cement mud all through the chain and gears again.

Slow bloody learner!

I sobbed again, took a couple of aspirin to calm down, then set about finding twigs myself.

That day was not easy. There were long patches of cement mud, and I found I had to lift Ibn onto the track and bump my way along the sleepers every time it appeared. Having left at 8.30 a.m., I covered 22 kilometres and arrived in Nguruka, the next station, at 2.30 p.m. By that time, I was very fragile, wanting to burst into tears at every problem. The essential part of the African experience was at work again – emotional ups and downs. Unfortunately, I was entering a prolonged period of a profound 'down'.

Nguruka station was just a German colonial-style building (the Germans built the Central Line before World War I, when Tanganyika was their colonial possession), and a few scattered huts. The small village each station served was often one or two kilometres away, and I hardly ever made the detour to see them. However, the stationmaster told me there was a government rest house in Nguruka, so I cycled there, gave myself an early day and slept the afternoon away. It should have helped, but in the evening I went for a walk around the tiny market of this remote railway town – and was mobbed by children and brushed on the breast by some filthy old man. Everyone watching laughed, and instead of shouting at him, I became hysterical and ran back to the guesthouse crying.

'Have you been robbed?' asked the gentle manager.

How could I explain why I was so upset? I didn't understand myself and was annoyed by my reaction. Not so long ago I had felt on top of the world. Now it was all too much. Not much of a Real Adventurer today. But I knew that much of it had to do with my exhaustion and was probably the inevitable consequence of finishing such a long, arduous journey – after seventeen and a half months in Africa, I didn't want any more challenges or adventures. I simply wanted to go home – I had endured enough! I buried myself in a book I had bought in Kigoma – a trashy read, but by the light of a kerosene lamp, it took me to another world, outside Africa, where it seemed part of my spirit now wanted to be.

The next day, I was calmer. For a while. For the following stage of the journey between Nguruka and Usinge, the line ran across several kilometres of swamp. It was raised on pylons only about a metre above the shallow water, with no girder to the side, no pathway for a bicycle. I just had to bump over the sleepers and listen for trains. Electric maintenance vehicles approached silently and swiftly and the greatest danger was that one might choose this time to appear. If so, I'd either be squashed meat or swimming like a tadpole. There was no room for two of us on this line.

Then, I found a more immediate problem. Sleepers were missing, forcing me to balance Ibn on one rail and straddle the metre-wide gap in between. When two were missing, I had to balance Ibn on one rail, and use his weight as a counterbalance as I edged forward on the other. I felt like I was playing snakes and ladders with some malevolent spirits, who were starting to think up new obstacles to wear me down.

Well, bugger them! I dug deep and found some of my own spirit. I crossed the swamp.

But the spirits weren't done with me. Next came 30 kilometres of wet sand to abrade Ibn's gear rings and long stretches of tsetse-fly country to grind down my willpower.

Oh, God.

That evening in Kombe station, my tent erected on the platform, I decided I knew hell. It was a long, straight railway line, heat, chippings, culverts, lion pug marks, swamp, sandy track, heavy bike to push and heave and lift and balance, and biting tsetse flies.

Who asked if I ever thought of giving up? Just about everybody. It was one of the standard questions. Next time someone asked, I knew what I'd say: following the Central Line in Tanzania, I thought about it every day, every kilometre, every minute.

In fact, in my head, I had noisy arguments between opposing viewpoints.

Why are you doing this to me? I asked myself in a stroppy voice. Next time you think of doing something like this, *remember* today!

'Stop *moaning*!' I scolded myself.

Then I changed tack and talked to myself in a more conciliatory and soothing tone. Just stay cool a little longer. Think of the adventure – all the monkey tracks, the bird calls, the empty bush. This is where Sir Richard Burton travelled!

Going nuts, I guessed.

It took another couple of days of hell to reach Tabora, a big, sprawling, dusty town. Civilisation. The remoteness of the areas I had been in was clearer back in a place with electricity, cars, shops, chocolate and pineapples.

Ibn and I were both sick.

Ibn's rear derailleur had fallen apart – probably a screw lost bumping down the line. Fortunately, dirt and grease had kept it together until I cleaned it in Tabora. I was not a bad mechanic now, but for this I needed some springs and screws, so I found a *fundy* – mechanic.

The grease-covered *fundy* who worked at the kerbside performed a miracle. Not only did he fix the derailleur, he overhauled the rear hub, stopping a long-standing, annoying rattle.

My illnesses were harder to heal.

I was sick at heart. One evening in Tabora, I sat on my bed, inside the mosquito net, and scrawled manically in my journal.

'I want variety and cleanliness. I want fruit and vegetables, not scratched-plastic-plate cafés with grubby, greasy dishes and horrible, sweet tea. I do not want any more peanuts, bananas and beer as the only treats. I do not want any more dirt and mud, sweat and discomfort, and rain and sand, and gritty, falling-apart shoes and faded shirts. I do not want bucket showers, squat toilets, mosquito bites, dry skin, cracked lips and dirty toenails. I want rock and roll, movies and television, not Zairean music and no electricity, no books and *nothing* Fine!'

My experiences in Tanzania were proving tough, but were being made worse because part of me no longer wanted to be there: the release from this struggle was close enough to taste and after a year and a half and 13,600 kilometres, I was finally allowing myself to admit how emotionally exhausted I was.

I was also physically sick. The two days before Tabora, my body began aching all the time, everywhere – muscles, bones, teeth, fingers, kidneys – even breathing hurt my chest. My eyes watered continuously. Every movement was an effort. I survived on doses of aspirin and sugar to briefly raise the pall of pain. Possibly not surprising after all the lifting and heaving I had done, but even after two days of almost continuous sleep on arrival in Tabora, I still ached and my eyes watered. Given my success with the bicycle *fundy*, I decided to take myself to a body *fundy*, and went to see some Chinese doctors.

I was hoping they would find something wrong – something that was easy to cure.

They found things. In fact, they found a bit of everything – round worms, traces of malaria, eye infection, urinary tract infection, flu – but nothing totally debilitating. I was simply worn out. Much less easy to cure.

By now, the phrase 'I want to go home' was a continuous refrain in my head. Sitting here wouldn't quiet it, so I decided I better get going. I was 450 kilometres from Kigoma, and 900 kilometres from Dar. Earlier, these distances would not have fazed me, but now they seemed too far.

'There are chippings on the track,' said the stationmaster at Tabora. 'You can take a road until Melongwe.' A hundred kilometres closer to Dar. I took the road.

That first day out of Tabora, I only made it 13 kilometres to the small village of Inara. Then, I lay down to die. The previous night I had taken the medicine for worms the doctors had prescribed: eight large pills!

Surprise, surprise – I got sick.

I stopped at a small stall for a Coke, hoping that would cure my nausea, then lay wretchedly in some shade waiting to feel better. Villagers may have thought me odd, but I no longer cared – I was focused entirely on my stomach. Late in the afternoon I vomited (after a rush to ask for a latrine!) and started feeling marginally better, but my limbs were still weak – no good for the sandy route which lay ahead. I was still lying on my back with my hat over my face, thinking I better get up and ask about a place to stay when footsteps approached.

'*Jambo*,' said a woman's voice. '*Jambo*.'

I removed my hat from my face and sat up.

'My name is Esther,' she said. She was an elderly woman, round in body, with a kindly face. She had elephantiasis in her lower legs. Poor thing. Seeing her standing there immediately put my stomach woes in some perspective. 'It is too late now to go further today. You can stay with me.' She was a mind-reader!

We walked slowly back to her compound, a mud hut where she served teas and a back yard enclosed by a brush fence. Chickens pecked in the dry sand and I erected my tent in one corner. The setting and Esther's kindness and generosity were very familiar, and her story of years of hardship and struggle since her husband died leaving her with ten small children to raise was like so many others I'd heard. Maybe that's why I dreamt that night of another woman I'd admired. Dreaming was unusual as, after cycling days, my sleep was generally very deep. Perhaps it was because I had slept so much during the day. Whatever the cause, in the quiet darkness, my mind travelled to Beayop, the tiny village deep in the forests of Equatorial Guinea where I had met Marie Carmen. I could see her very plainly, grilling peanuts, worrying about her children. 'We try, we try – but the children are always ill.' I snapped awake, sure I had heard her voice.

This was my first haunting by the women I had met in the villages. I did not realise how common it was to become.

As I was leaving the next morning, revived in body and spirit by my time with Esther, I spoke with her about how far I had come, how dispirited and exhausted I was, but how determined I was to finish.

'Ah, you are a woman, then,' she said.

Though my struggle, self-imposed and for a limited time, was trivial compared to the ongoing struggle of Esther and the other women I had met, I felt this was a huge compliment.

On leaving Inara, I was told I had to go through Rubaga to get to Kisengi and Melongwe. It was a very quiet bush road, littered with holes, cement mud, and fallen logs that I had to lift Ibn over or crash through the thick bush to pass. There were no signs of villages, crops or humans, though I saw plenty of animal prints: monkey, bird – and lion. As the kilometres mounted, I kept expecting to turn the corner and arrive in Rubaga. Where the hell was it?!

Finally, late in the day, I came across signs of human life – footprints, then cornfields, a few huts, then even a couple of dilapidated buildings from the colonial era. Rubaga?

Two dogs rushed at me, baring their teeth and growling. I leapt off Ibn and put him between myself and these wild beasts. An old pro now ... A few men who had been sprawled under a shady tree roused themselves and came over to me. They were all quite drunk. Wild beasts, too.

'Rubaga?' I asked, after we had finished the greetings.

'Kisengi,' said one of the men who spoke some English. I had missed Rubaga entirely then.

'Where is Rubaga?' I asked.

The men, all shifty looking as well as sozzled, seemed confused. Then, a thin, elderly woman in a ragged *pagne* and T-shirt arrived. She was not drunk and had better English.

'This is Rubaga,' she said, using her hands to point to the bush.

Finally, I realised that rubaga was not a place – it meant 'wild bushland for firewood'.

Well done, I thought wryly.

The woman informed me that the road continued to Tura, another station beyond Melongwe. However, she suggested I leave the road and take a short cut through the fields.

'There are too many *tembo* ahead,' she said. *Tembo* were elephant.

'How far?' I asked about the short cut. It was near dusk and I should be thinking about staying, but I had a bad feeling about this village – probably caused by the drunken men who still stood in a circle leering at me. My attraction for muscular bodies had not totally eradicated my alertness for danger.

'A half hour,' she replied, so I left, using her directions.

After about ten minutes, once I was well clear of Kisengi and human habitation again, I realised I was being followed.

One of the drunks who had greeted me came up behind me on a bike, following closely and ranting in a jumble of Swahili and English. It scared me after my lonely day on bush tracks – and because it was so similar to an occasion in the bush in Sudan many years before, when I'd been followed by a drunk, then attacked. I stopped on the narrow path and let him pass. He did, then immediately slowed his pace, forcing me to pass him. After I'd cycled by, he accelerated and stayed close behind me, shouting more aggressively now. The light was dimming and we were on a narrow, rutted and muddy track passing through high cornfields. What could I do?! My heart was racing and my antennae for danger were raising the alarm. I let him pass, then he slowed, I passed him again – a real cat-and-mouse game. His eyes were staring wildly, the sign of out-of-control aggression I had come to be wary of in men. The fourth time I let him pass, my fear spilt over into anger.

'Now, fuck off!' I yelled.

He understood that English. Oops.

He lurched to a halt in the middle of the track ahead of me, and pulled out the *panga* which had been hanging from his waist. He waved the *panga* menacingly and chopped it through the air. Now, he could speak English.

'This is Tanzania. I am Tanzanian! You are not Tanzanian! You must not say that to a Tanzanian!!'

Oh, shit! I stopped, let him rave and watched him closely for his next move. One part of me was very scared, another part was angry that he had suddenly found my language (it had become irritating to find that some Tanzanians spoke English only when they wanted to), while a third part of me assessed my options: I could not risk a fight, there was no one about to help me; if I turned, he'd see I was scared and chase me. Anyway, I couldn't outpace him. I had to go past, and go past bravely – I reckoned attack was the best policy against a cowardly drunk.

I cycled towards him, shouting a stream of insults.

It worked. He abused me, waved the *panga*, but didn't make a move to grab me.

I breathed again once I was beyond him, and found adrenalin helped me to increase my speed. He followed, continuing his verbal abuse from behind.

I was shaking badly by the time I saw a clearing, a school and another group of men – maybe teachers who spoke English, I thought – sitting under a tree. A safe haven, I hoped. I cycled towards them with the drunk following me, still shouting. I appealed to the men.

'Please, who speaks English? This man threatened me with a *panga*!'

Not one of the men moved, showed any sign of hearing or understanding me. Instead, they spoke in Swahili to the drunk, ignoring me totally.

There would be no help here, I realised.

I was unnerved by this lack of assistance, uncharacteristic of my experiences elsewhere in Africa. Without goodwill and protection from villagers, I was very vulnerable. Or was this just another case of meeting peculiar people everywhere? Knowing I was close to Melongwe, I rode shakily away – briefly watching that the drunk stayed put. The immediate danger was over.

'Wait, wait!' called a male voice from behind. I turned again and saw it was a young, thin man in neat trousers and a white long-sleeved shirt to whom I had appealed in vain. I was not interested in talking to him now. 'Wait! I saw you there with that man. I speak English. I have come to help you.' I slowed to let him catch up but was angry with him for staying silent when I needed him. 'Some Tanzanians are like that – they are uneducated,' he continued. He was by my side now. 'They think you whiteys, er whites, are animals.'

On the boat on the Zaire River, I had felt a little what it was like to be a racial minority – to lose one's identity. Now, this incident, the clear partiality of the men at the school to the drunk's story and now this man's comments made me feel vulnerable – because of my colour.

Maybe the man with the *panga* was just drunk; maybe he followed, abused and threatened me because I was a woman or because I insulted him; maybe, my colour had little to do with it. But it didn't feel that way. In some ways, this contact with the abuse and violence that can accompany racial discrimination was more upsetting than the attack itself – another awakening encounter with the dark side of being a member of a minority.

I let the man show me to Melongwe station, where I met the senior permanent way inspector, Jumaane. He was a gentle, sympathetic man who suggested that, for safety, I sleep inside, not on the platform. For once, I took the advice.

As I left the next morning, following the railway track again, I wondered again at this attack. After the knife incident with the fool in Rwanda, it was the second. Would they come in threes? Why two near the end of the journey? Should I be nervous of some Tanzanians' attitudes to white strangers? Had Nyerere's continual pillorying of the country's colonial past left a legacy of contempt for Europeans? Or was it more personal? Was it to do with me, the vibes I was sending out, that I was travelling when I was too exhausted, when I had less patience? Were my protective spirits sleeping on the job, or had I left them behind in the forests of Zaire?

This futile reflection was interrupted by the arrival of more bloody tsetse flies. Oh, God.

I reckoned the risk from dangerous men was relatively small in Africa, and as long as I was in the right frame of mind, it could be managed. What was far worse was the relentless torture from nature and the elements – and tsetse flies were the worst torture, the *very* worst, that nature could offer.

Today, the elements were not to be outdone.

Soon, it was pouring rain and I was pushing through knee-deep water. Shit.

Then, when the water seeped away, the tsetse flies came back.

After the torture I had to take a day off in Tura, but then the next day it began again. After morning rain, the sun was sweltering and the sky was filled with wonderfully high, white cumulonimbus clouds, so characteristic of the East African savannah. It would have been beautiful if I had not to endure hours of murderous tsetse fly attacks, then long kilometres of cement mud that cattle crossings had turned into deep, sharp, criss-crossing crevices. What few reserves I had disappeared. All my coping mechanisms had stopped.

I threw Ibn to the ground, crouched low with my rain jacket pulled over my head and shouted.

'What do you want from me?' I yelled at the evil spirits I felt were hiding behind the clouds, still testing me by making me relive every obstacle of the journey. 'What have I done to you? Leave me alone!'

Tsetse flies bit at my lips, my back, my nose, my ears.

Then, I began wailing, rocking myself forward and back, forward and back, and inside I was just one silent scream.

The fragility of my psychological state was alarming, yet, registering that self-indulgent screaming got me nowhere, after a few minutes, I picked myself up, tried to numb myself to the ongoing attacks, and little by little, kept going.

It was near sunset when I finally cycled into Kitaraka station. Progress was proving so slow – after five days, I was still less than 200 kilometres from Tabora.

A man approaching me on a bicycle greeted me, 'Welcome to us.'

'Thank you,' I said, smiling wanly back, yet vaguely surprised by how calmly he took my arrival.

'Welcome, Pamela,' called the stationmaster, as I parked my bicycle near his office. How did he know my name? 'Joseph called me on the intercom to tell me to expect you.' Aha! Joseph was the stationmaster at Kazikazi station, where I'd stopped for lunch.

'My name is Georgie,' he told me. 'Joseph and I are the two eldest on the line – Joseph has thirty years of service and I have thirty-one years.' He reminded me of my grandfather and uncles, who were all engineers on the railways in Western Australia – they always counted years of service and were proud railway men.

Georgie invited me to spend the night in one of the worker's cottages near the station, and, after sunset and settling in, I went back to chat with him. I had barely arrived when the bells began to ring.

'It is Joseph,' called Georgie as he left me to answer the intercom. 'The train is in Kazikazi.' Sure enough, when he returned a minute or two later, he told me the train from Kigoma was on its way. He moved off into the dark to change the points and signals. I had seen the train pass many times now and the various crews were getting to know me. I wondered who might be on this one.

Peter, the attractive young guard I had first met in Malagarasi!

The train only stopped long enough to exchange greetings, and for me to get scones, jam and cream (!) from the dining car. Then, the train was gone and Georgie and I were left in silence. We brought chairs out onto the platform and sat watching the full moon, comfortable together.

'Is it true that in Europe women are marrying younger men?' he asked suddenly. Perhaps he saw me chatting enthusiastically with Peter.

'Yes,' I said, 'and it's a good idea, too – to get them young while they are strong!'

'Ah, no!' Georgie pretended to be shocked. 'You could not do that here. Although, if a woman was rich enough …' He told me that he and his wife had ten children and five grandchildren. 'The women these days. They are not good to us,' he lamented, I think mock seriously. 'Before, once you were married, the women were responsible for the digging, the children, drawing the water, the cooking … but now they want us to get the firewood and water.'

'Excellent!' I said. Men everywhere really were something special, but at least somebody was trying to teach this old dog new tricks. 'And what about the cooking?'

'Not the cooking. That is always the women's duty!' I offered him a scone, but he thought that was strange food. 'You should have real food – *foufou*!' he said. 'Perhaps you do need a man to cook for you!'

'Where do I find one?' I cried.

The banter continued, the evening passed rapidly. Georgie was another funny man of the Central Line and with his good humour and ready laughter he helped me to forget my troubles. Like so many folk had done over quiet, healing evenings elsewhere in Africa.

My swings between near madness on the road and oases of calm with kind people along the way continued the next day as I cycled to Manyoni. From there, I joined a road down into the Rift Valley. At least I had finished with the railway line, the chippings on the track and hauling Ibn past culverts. And, thankfully for my sanity, I had seen the last of the tsetse flies. The Rift Valley marked a fault line, where East Africa was being pulled away from the rest of the continent – an interesting phenomenon, a valley with its own climate and vegetation. However, I was only interested in covering kilometres, and the way was still not easy. Long stretches of the road were churned by cement mud, both wet and dry; the heat in the rift was intense. Fortunately, without the added horror of tsetse flies I could keep a lid on my most alarming emotions and just keep going.

That evening, I arrived in Bahi, a small village in the middle of the rift. I could barely push the bike anymore, let alone ride. I saw an old man, stooping, walking slowly, and stopped to ask about a place to stay.

'*Habari?*' he asked – how are you?

'*Choko sana,*' I said tearfully – very tired. 'Is there a guesthouse?' I asked him in my limited Swahili. That evening I was too tired for comparisons of my physical state to his, too tired to compare his years of hardship to my brief encounter with this tough life. My mind knew I was lucky, but body and soul just needed rest.

'*Hapana* guesthouse,' he replied – no guest house. He told me the chairman lived another 4 kilometres away. I could not make it that far.

'*Choko,*' I muttered, then, 'I must stop,' in English. He must have seen my exhaustion, because he pointed to a nearby track.

'Mission,' he said. Mission. Thank you, Lord, spirits, whoever!

The nuns invited me to stay, diffidently, but I was just grateful the day was over. A younger nun, Sister Fides, ushered me to a small, simply furnished but clean room and left me alone. My journal for that night was a scrawl, barely legible. 'Electric light. Clean. Bath. Cold water on tap. Bucket of hot water to have a bath. Dinner provided in my room. No questions. No need to talk. All in my comfy room. Thank you. And just 60 kilometres to Dodoma. "The road is bad," said Sister Fides. Damn. I suppose I will get there tomorrow. Then sealed road. Take it for one more day. Please. Please.'

I did make Dodoma the next day, cycling non-stop like a woman possessed. But even then it took me nearly seven hours to cover the final 70 kilometres of sand, up out of the rift. Dodoma was the capital of Tanzania, purpose built, one of Nyerere's ideas, but attempts to shift the government there from Dar Es Salaam had been half-hearted. The place still had dusty roads and the ambience of a small country town. For me, however, it was return to civilisation and I treated myself to a comfortable hotel. From my room, a heavenly retreat, I telephoned Mr Pereira at Shell in Dar – and heard that my parents, Gwen and Frank, had arrived safely. Now, it was up to me to get there soon – and safely.

Here in Dodoma – unlike in Tabora – I discovered that Ibn was sicker than I was. Wet sand had efficiently ground down the teeth of the gear cogs and the clogging mud had stretched the chain. Not too much of an issue when I had been pushing, but after cleaning Ibn and cycling around town, I realised I only had bottom gear. On every other gear, the chain slipped.

I went to a *fundy*.

'You can get spares in Dar Es Salaam,' he said.

Great.

I had the option of waiting – either for spares from Dar, or for spares to be sent from the UK via DHL – or pressing on. It was an easy decision. On Easter Saturday morning, I telephoned Mr Pereira to confirm my arrival in six days on Thursday afternoon. With just 450 kilometres to Dar, in normal times, even on poor roads, it should have been doable and, despite my drive problems, I simply wasn't willing to make any compromises on time now. Dar Es Salaam, I learnt, meant 'Haven of Peace'. Urgently, I needed to arrive in my haven of peace.

The last road was freshly sealed tarmac with no potholes, and a continuous descent to the coastal plain! A rare treat, one I'd longed for across Africa. It should have been a wonderful, easy, fast way home. However, shortly after setting out, I discovered that despite my legs spinning like tops to get drive from the lowest gear, my efforts could only deliver a maximum of 15 kilometres per hour. With a new drive mechanism, I'd be averaging twice that. It was a nightmare. And to make my self-imposed appointment in Dar Es Salaam, I rapidly calculated that I'd have to cycle seven to eight long hours each day.

Shit, I thought and sighed. Then, gritting my teeth, I decided that through sheer will I would make it. Nothing would stop me now.

Had I forgotten everything I'd learned?

Of course, the spirits were going to make sure I remembered – and regretted

– not travelling more slowly, at a pace more in tune with Africa and myself.

The first three days to Morogoro, the major town along the route to Dar, were tests of endurance. The road passed through wide plains of grassland known as the Masai Steppe – home to the ranging cattle of the Masai tribe – and I cycled with a strong wind in my face and my legs still spinning furiously. Feeling unable to cope with any more of my own distress, I shut down my emotions and focused on cycling the long hours necessary to cover my planned daily distances. Until the third day from Dodoma, I resisted changing the worn rear tyre that was giving me problems – it was the tyre that had taken me across Zaire. However, this was no time for sentiment. I had a timetable to adhere to. I left it at the roadside with other litter.

It was funny to think how back in Koundara market near the beginning of this journey, I'd been so scathing about litter. Now, I not only thought there were more important issues in life here in Africa, I knew that a worn tyre would have numerous uses for someone – it wouldn't remain litter for long.

On the fourth day, after Morogoro, a bustling, large city, the road became busier and the scenery hillier, but it still consistently went down. Little about the scenery, the people or the greetings and waves from passing cars flickered into my attention – my mind was on mounting kilometres. I kept pedalling on, and on, and on – even as thunder clouds mounted and blocked the sun – and on – even as the storm hit and lightning cracked around me and the road became a flooding river of water – and on: I was determined to make Chalinze that night, my penultimate night.

A storekeeper called me from the rainswept road. 'Stop! Stop!' he cried grabbing my attention. 'A cyclist was killed in a storm like this a few days ago!'

Finally, my single-bloody-mindedness to keep going was tempered by prudence. Heeding his warning, I stopped for the day with him at Ubenazomozi, about 20 kilometres short of Chalinze, watched the ongoing lashings of rain and flashes of lightning from his store, but I was not a talkative guest. I felt thwarted, paced up and down like a caged animal and, under my breath, swore at the evil spirits for sending me yet another obstacle.

On the fifth day, Wednesday, I passed Chalinze and headed for Kibaha for the night, a town about 45 kilometres outside Dar. I wanted to make Kibaha to ensure I still arrived in Dar at noon on Thursday.

It wasn't a good day.

As I arrived on the flatter coastal plain, the scenery began to be dominated by palm trees, rather than scrub and the air was heavy with humidity – and my own foreboding. I felt engaged in a battle with the spirits: my objective, to make Dar safely; theirs, to stop me.

Ho, ho. Stop being so dramatic, I thought. You've come all this way. It'll be okay now. But all through the day, as I was passed by more speeding vehicles, stared at by glum adults and pestered by aggressive children on bicycles,

I felt something was building up to happen. Was it just another thunderstorm?

Around 5 p.m., I arrived in Malenzi – a tiny truck stop, busy at this hour with vehicles and people waiting for lifts. At any other time on the journey, being body sore and tired, I would have been ready to stop. From a man waiting for a bush taxi, I discovered that it was 20 kilometres to Kibaha. I had misgivings about continuing – it was getting too close to dusk to still be cycling – but it was feasible. Nothing would stop me. No, nothing.

I kept going and, after covering another 10 kilometres, passed through a small village.

'*Jambo!*' I called to some children. The palm trees and huts looked pretty in the late-afternoon sunlight. Within the hour, I'd be in Kibaha, probably just before nightfall.

'*Jambo!*' they called back to me.

Out of the village, cars and trucks passed in bursts – sometimes a lone vehicle or a group of five or six, then I was alone on the quiet road for several minutes. There was an uphill stretch – the vehicles whizzed by rapidly, but I was moving very, very slowly.

Suddenly, everything I'd ever dreaded erupted.

There was motion around me. One man cut me off, another prevented me turning back down the hill.

'Money! Give us some money!' grunted one of the raggedly dressed men in English.

I was dumbfounded, shocked – but as in the previous attack, while scared, my mind started quickly evaluating options. I could hear a vehicle toiling up the other side of the hill – possible help! I must stall them, I thought.

'You're drunk,' I said, noticing their staring eyes, wanting to say anything except yes or no.

The truck came into view, an army truck, laden with armed soldiers. I leapt into action, adrenalin rushing. I dropped Ibn and sprinted toward the truck.

'Help! Stop! Help!!' I yelled, waving my arms. The brave soldiers did not even slow down.

Moments later, my screams died and I was left on an empty road with two men – who were now impatient and angry. One grabbed at Ibn and, to my horror, started running down the hill, pushing him and all my belongings away. My fear evaporated; my mind was stunned.

Sixty kilometres to Dar. Was this how my journey would end? As everyone had said it would? In theft? In death? In …?

The other man pushed me backwards into the scrub and I fell down. He punched me in the face, very hard. I was dazed and his arms pinned me to the ground. His weight felt like granite, there was nothing I could do. He was drunk and unpredictable. I stopped screaming, but had a hold of his T-shirt. It ripped in my hands. He pulled back a clenched fist close to my face.

'Do you want more?' he growled.

I shook my head and let go of his shirt; I was passive to my fate, a wounded, shocked zebra in the jaws of the lion.

He went to hit me again, but stopped in mid-blow, leapt to his feet and ran back to the road. Perhaps he was fearful of his mate making away with the loot. I struggled to my feet and stumbled to the road.

They were both still visible, running back down the hill pushing Ibn.

'I'm 60 kilometres from Dar,' I thought again. 'This can't be happening ...'

A group of vehicles rushed passed and I screamed hysterically at them, but nobody stopped. Then, I jumped in front of a four-wheel-drive coming up the hill. The driver would have to run me down or stop. He stopped. It was a narrow, busy road at this hour, cars started banking up behind him, and I saw a truck going down the hill also put his brakes on. Villagers came rushing onto the road, emerging from the bush.

I ran down the hill, and saw Ibn sprawled on the road and I ran to him. The bandits had gone but they had cut off the handlebar bag. I slumped by Ibn and sobbed. I might have lost some valuables but at least I had my best friend.

Suddenly, there was a scream, louder than mine, and two men came out of the bush, one supporting the other who was holding his bloody head – and my handlebar bag. I thought the injured man was one of the bandits and I rushed toward him and grabbed my bag. Rifling through the contents, I found my passport, my camera, my sunglasses and my moneybelt were missing. Foolishly, in these last humid, tired days, I had stopped wearing my moneybelt.

The man with the bleeding head was led away, and people were gathered all around me. The road was chaos now, villagers everywhere, cars and trucks blocking both directions. People pulled at me, trying to stop me as I started walking into the bush to see if the bandits had dropped anything. I stumbled through the grass, then suddenly spied my sunglasses, then my camera, then my passport, then my moneybelt. The bandits had gained nothing. In fear, they had dropped it all.

I staggered back to the road – I was in a dazed shock – and overheard a conversation amongst some Europeans about the injured man.

'It was a *panga*. They hit him on the back of a head with a *panga* when he tackled them.'

I blinked, taking this in.

'Wasn't he a bandit?' I asked, interrupting their conversation.

'No,' one of the Europeans said, 'he was in a truck.'

He had been in the truck I had seen brake when I was screaming for help. He had run from the truck, followed the bandits into the bush, tackled them and been struck. I looked at Ibn – my *panga* from the stationmaster at Malagarasi was missing.

Wildly, I left the Europeans and hunted for the injured man, someone I badly wanted to thank and help. But he had already gone. His partner had bundled him into their truck and driven off in their original direction – away from Dar – but hopefully toward the nearest hospital. (Sadly, even from Dar, I was unable to trace him.)

Then, a village woman handed me the digging stick I had carted from Ghana. It was the digging stick given to me by Lydia and the women of Bawku which I had kept, even through ruthless shedding of extra weight, as my own protective *juju*. It must have fallen off in the struggle. Finally, I began to feel safe again. I hugged the woman, and now sobbed on her shoulder – for my safety, for all the women and men like her who had helped me, for the suffering and struggle of us all, for who knows what.

She took my emotion stoically.

It was now nearly dark, and the road was still blocked. The group of Europeans wanted to take me to Dar; I let them take Ibn and me to Kibaha. A 10-kilometre gap in cycling was the price for staying sane.

That night in the hotel where I was deposited, I got the shakes, wondering at my near miss. I had to reach Dar and get out of the clutches of these malevolent spirits.

The next morning was Thursday 7 April, 1994, eighteen months since I had set out from Dakar, and as the hotel had a telephone, I rang Mr Pereira at Shell, to tell him about the attack and my ETA into Dar.

'Stay where you are!' he exclaimed. 'Don't you know what has happened?'

'No.'

'Last night, the plane carrying the president of Rwanda and president of Burundi was shot down near Kigali,' he said. 'They were killed – and our president has announced a day of mourning.' The presidents had been flying home after being in Dar Es Salaam engaged in talks about the growing ethnic violence in their countries.

The bad spirits had not only sought to stop me that night, they had started an evil process for Central Africa: the Rwandan civil war.

'We can have no publicity for your arrival,' continued Mr Pereira. 'Not even the media are allowed to work today.' Despite my determined cycling to escape Rwanda's and Burundi's menacing situations, their bloody destiny would still affect me, as so many in Africa. 'Please, stay another day at Kibaha.' But I could not wait for Africa, not even for one day. I had to know I was safe, that it was over. I cycled for Dar.

During those last kilometres, I felt numb. I entered the outskirts of Dar and saw houses and billboards and petrol stations and shops ... but found it hard to assimilate my feelings. There was joy – soon I would see my people, soon I would have finished what I had started, soon I would be safe – but there was painful sadness too: what had my struggle meant? What could I do for Marie Carmen, for all those people who had helped me fulfil my dream? I already felt helpless, too privileged.

As I got closer, just a handful of kilometres to go, the introspection disappeared, the weight in my muscles lifted. I stopped for a cold drink, to wipe my face, and even bought a few balloons, blew them up and tied them to Ibn so he could look festive. Now, I was shaking with excitement.

Dar was a familiar city from previous visits, so I could conjure my arrival in my mind. My official finish was to be at the Hotel Kilimanjaro, near the palm-fringed waterfront of Dar's peaceful harbour. I could imagine the smells and sounds of smoking, rattling vehicles along the harbour road, the bustle of the shell market and the hustle of the street vendors. Dhows – graceful Arab boats with white lateen sails – would be drifting alongside modern cargo ships and rusty tugs on the blue waters of the Indian Ocean – the ocean on which I'd grown up, my ocean. Yes, I was coming home.

Mr Pereira met me on the outskirts of the city and he seemed as thrilled to see me as I felt to see him. Then, in a car, he led me to the hotel.

My parents were waiting and my heart was bursting with anticipation. To have people I loved waiting for me was the best finish. I turned into the drive of the hotel and there was my mother, looking just the same as ever, trim in trousers and shirt, smiling madly, camera looped around her wrist, waiting with open arms. I did not punch the air like some triumphant athlete – that was not how I felt. I just reached out and hugged my mum.

'Don't think up anything else like this again, please,' she said, and I nodded, quite happy to make such a promise. (For the moment.) Then, I turned to my father.

'You've got fat,' he said. Forthright but contented, as ever.

Thanks, Dad. I gave him a hug. So nice to be back in the warm bosom of one's family!

I cast around the small crowd for William. Despite my doubts about our relationship, I had hoped he would be there. Not that he had said anything, but … It turned out he had been in Dar until the previous day – he had planned to meet me as another surprise – but then he could wait no longer. Work demanded he go back to London. The spirits did not seem to want us to be together. I hid my disappointment and turned back to the people who *were* there.

The intoxicating exhilaration of the moment took over. It was so extraordinary! I felt intensely alive, with so much energy – the grin would not be wiped off my face!

I grinned and grinned, even when Mr Pereira announced that I would have to 'arrive' again tomorrow for the cameras, and for an official welcome by the minister of tourism and sport! I hated donning my dirty clothes again, and the rains and blocked drains of Dar's streets meant even in the short cycle ride from the hotel I was drenched and splashed with mud, so I looked the part! I still grinned when I had to 'arrive' a third time for a film crew, and 'arrive' again for the newspapers. I even continued grinning when I saw the headline for my efforts – 'Austrian Pedals For Women's Cause'.

So what? These were small trials. In eighteen months, I had travelled through seventeen countries, by boat for 1750 kilometres, by bicycle for 14,527 kilometres. I had crossed Africa, alone – with the help of many, many village and city friends. And I was back, safe, with my folks who knew me. My father had brought me a can of asparagus spears and my mother had brought me new undies, a bra, clothes, sandals, mascara and perfume. And she had red nail polish for my toenails. What more could any woman want?

Epilogue

After Words

'You're not dead!' cried one of my Australian friends, when I telephoned from the safety of London.

'I'll tell you now,' said an English friend, 'I didn't think you were going to survive!'

'I was very worried about you.' A Canadian friend. 'I had imagined you raped or hacked to death or worse.'

What pessimists! I'm glad I didn't know their certainty about my fate *before* I left!

But then, in Tanzania, I had begun to truly doubt my safety and had been craving to be back in a place where I did not have to live off my wits, nor use my antennae to constantly judge people and situations, nor prepare strategies in my head for dealing with possibly tricky situations. (Not that my highly sophisticated strategy of yelling for help from passing vehicles had worked all that well!)

Now, back in London, I still felt incredibly exhilarated about life and over-whelmed by my own accomplishment – after realising a dream, what do you do next? I was full of energy, I could not stop talking, talking, talking, and I was happy to let days pass having fun. I let down my guard. I was home and I was safe, wasn't I?

One disappointment during these halcyon days was that William and I weren't doing that well. He didn't seem too interested in my journey, he just wanted things to get back to the way they were. Meanwhile, I was starting to realise my past life in London was just that – past. Soon after getting back, I started mixing with a new crowd of cycling and adventure-traveller friends; moreover, I had no money nor inclination to resume my previous City lifestyle. Clearly, I would need to get some freelance consulting work to survive, but that would be temporary. After that, I didn't know. Maybe William would be part of my new life, maybe not – I needed time.

I wasn't given it.

One Sunday morning, six weeks after returning from Africa, I was cycling on Ibn along Streatham High Street in south London, returning from a swim at a nearby pool. Suddenly, a red car sped out from a side street, cutting me off, forcing me to swerve to avoid being hit.

'Fuck off!' I yelled in fright, and shook my fist.

I should have eradicated those unlucky words from my 'under stress' vocabulary.

The car came back into the lane in front of me and braked hard, making me hit the rear bumper. A young white woman leapt out. She had the mad, drugged, wide eyes I had feared in African men. Swearing and spitting, she ran at me and began punching me in the shoulders. I was frozen, unprepared for an assault in London. My passivity seemed to feed her rage. Then, as I shook myself into action and went to cycle away, she pushed me into the main passing lane.

There was a break in traffic. I was lucky – for the moment.

How dare she?! As I picked myself up, I was so angry. Now, I wanted to shout at her! Count to ten, I told myself. Be calm. This is one weird, unpredictable woman.

'I'm sorry,' I said quietly, before intending to cycle on. 'I don't think you should be driving – you're either very drunk or on drugs.'

Wrong thing to say, Pamela. Not your best judgement.

The woman was enraged. She raised the mobile phone she'd been carrying – an early model, shaped and weighted like a brick – and struck me across my face! My left cheek split open, cut through to the bone. She drove off.

I was left, shocked, my face wound dripping thick pools of blood on the road.

'Don't worry, dear!' called a woman's voice. I looked up dully, and saw an elderly woman on a balcony. 'I have her number plate – and I've called Scotland Yard.'

I had encountered a modern disease of the urban jungle: road rage.

Fortunately, with the witness's supporting testimony, the woman was convicted and sentenced to one month's imprisonment. However, during the summer before the trial, as my face healed, but with a deep scar, I became increasingly isolated in my flat. My relationship with William did not survive further strain. My buoyancy and confidence evaporated and I started suffering panic attacks. I had cycled across Africa, and now I was afraid to walk in London's streets!

I had gone from the very high of my life into the lowest of pits.

A consultant physician at the London School of Tropical Medicine said it all: I went there to be checked out for tropical diseases and he was impressed that, after eighteen months in village Africa, I had nothing wrong with me (not even any worms – so those dreadful pills worked). But when he heard of the assault, he exclaimed, 'You shouldn't cycle in the wilds of south London!'

London's threatening jungle was too frightening for me and, once more, I decided it was time to 'go home'. This time, to Australia.

Had evil spirits followed me back from East Africa? Or, as Françoise, my friend from those days in Guinea after the dog bite, might have wondered: was it a good spirit who made this woman hit me? Was it saving me from an evil spirit waiting to do something worse?

Who knows? Back again in Europe, the stories of spirits didn't seem as compelling as they did on lonely African roads. Or did they?

However, I was, and still am, haunted by the spirits of those people I met. Faces rise unbidden in my mind and I wonder how they are. I worry about Bob and his posting in war-torn eastern Congo. I have heard Marie Carmen in Equatorial Guinea has been seriously ill and is paralysed from malaria. It still seems too cruel that our lives could be so different.

The haunting memories of these people led to this book. Their gifts to me of friendship, generous hospitality and security contrasted sharply with the explosion of stories in the news – about the killing in Rwanda and, more recently, the war in Congo. While stories about irresponsible big men and the terrible consequences of their actions have long been the focus of international media coverage of Africa (and thus have shaped many westerners' ideas about the continent), my explorations into contemporary Africa demonstrated the far richer and more complex reality of most Africans' lives. It made the villagers' gifts – and the story of that 'other' Africa: the hard-working, unheard women – seem an important story to tell.

The greeting I learnt in Cameroon – '*Aysha!*' – I recognise your struggle – is one I remember. It sums up well how I feel about the villagers whose lives I shared briefly. Both men and women taught me a lot about myself, and through my own struggle and suffering, I learned just a little what their lives are really like. I respect them. With this book, to them all – but particularly to the women – I say, '*Aysha!*'

And what about me? Did I change?

I still like clean toilets and appreciate showers with strong, running water. I still find men by turns infuriating, lazy, humorous and sexy creatures. But I don't cycle in London anymore and I use purple nail polish on my toe nails instead of red. Does that count?

Changes are hard to spot.

At the outset, I thought *Esprit de Battuta* – my Real African Adventure – was about having the courage to take risks to pursue a dream. During the journey, I thought it was about having the patience and stubbornness to keep at it. After the journey, I think it's about respecting others, learning from them, having fun and just chilling out. So, that's different. While I can still be an obstinate, independent, irascible old so-and-so, I have also become more mellow, happier to let go of control, and to let time and events sort the future out. If I get too uptight, I remember the boat journey on the Zaire River where days just unfolded. But then again, maybe that's just part of getting old.

I had wanted to be a Real Adventurer – was I? My romantic notions of what this meant definitely changed during the journey. For me, the experiences that made me feel a Real Adventurer turned out to be the emotional turbulence of, as Ibrahim the Tuareg put it so well, appreciating the taste of life. And especially, the exhilaration and despair of appreciating the taste of others' lives. The aftermath of this experience has made me understand that my emotional responses and judgements depend on so much: my culture, social background and life experience certainly, but also my physical state and even my mood of the day! As a result, I try (not always easy) to be slower to judge and form opinions, seek to understand others' realities and be more accepting of multiple 'truths'.

I also have a strong sense of priorities and what is worth worrying about. It's amazing how remembering my Tuareg friends, Ibrahim and Fatimata, and their frightened, persecuted eyes, sorts issues and puts daily worries into perspective.

Would I do it again? Would I chuck my career again knowing what the journey delivered? Silly questions, I think. I had to do the journey – it happened because at the time I needed to do it. If I felt an obsession grow again, I would do something like it again. Likewise, the outcome is nothing discrete, I have merely taken a different life path.

And it seems like a bloody meandering one with many bizarre twists and turns!

After two years in Australia, I came back to the UK to seek opportunities to work in Europe and Africa – and ended up working for Shell! Yes, working for the company that had only reluctantly supported me at the outset of the journey, thinking (like everyone else as I now know) that I'd die!

'Hell of a long recruitment process,' said one friend.

Yet, together with the irony, there was also a weird synchronicity. I was being offered a chance to give something back to a company whose people had provided friendship and untold practical assistance, who had expanded my knowledge of urban Africa, and who thereby had helped me realise my goals, tangible and intangible. The position was with a team of people working to change Shell's organisation culture. After the publicity surrounding the breakdown of Shell's relationship with the Ogoni community in Nigeria, one sought-after characteristic of the new culture was for staff members to be more open and responsive in their dealings with local communities. Suddenly, I was being given an opportunity to give something back to village Africa.

Of course, accepting their offer also involved a dilemma. Shell had been criticised for its operations in Africa. Given my caring for the local villagers, how could I work for such a company? I did my own research, to add to the eighteen months I had on the road researching first hand the complexities of life in Africa, and concluded the Nigerian situation had arisen due to fault on all sides, some due to Shell, some due to the corrupt politics of Nigeria. One article in *The Economist* helped me to decide that Shell were sincere in their desire for change.

'Shellman says sorry' was the headline to an article in which Cor Herkströter, then chairman of the Shell Group, apologised for their handling of plans to scuttle the Brent Spar drilling rig in deep water and of the negotiations with the Ogoni people in Nigeria. 'We got it wrong.'

So, I was being offered a job to change Shell, and Shell were saying they wanted to change. I jumped at the opportunity ... and, so far, it is Very Fine – another kind of adventure.

It's funny how this life path seems to have a few unpredictable bends in it.

Similarly, at times during the journey, my two purposes – having a Real African Adventure and helping rural African women – seemed in opposition. Not anymore. Through this book, and by supporting fund-raising for WOMANKIND Worldwide, I hope to give back something to the rural women of Africa I came to admire. Hopefully, amongst others, the women of Bawku in northern Ghana will benefit: Leaye will get her drums and Lydia will get her dam.

Now, I have to work out how to get back to Africa – still one of my obsessions.

I remember the determined words of Lydia: 'If you are after something, you must grab it. Otherwise, you cannot say you are too tired.'

But then, who knows what the spirits have in mind?

Appendix

Distance Log

Date	Stop	Cumulative Distance (km)	Daily Distance (km)	Departure Time	Arrival Time	Cycling Time (hr/min)	Maximum Speed (kmph)
1992							
1/10	Dakar	0					
2/10	Mbour	75.5	75.5	0900	1500	0422	35.0
3/10	Fatick	143.4	67.9	0900	1400	0412	22.2
4/10	Kaolack	189.6	46.2	0800	1100		
5/10	Karang	283.8	94.1	0830	1630	0556	24.8
6/10	Banjul	308.2	25.5	0900	1200	0143	24.0
7–12/10	Banjul	419.2					
13/10	Sibanor	512.6	93.3	0700	1800	0641	27.2
14/10	Tintaba	578.4	65.9	0730	1730	0512	29.1
15/10	Farafenni	631.7	53.2	0930	1600	0402	37.0
16/10	Kaur	673.4	41.8	1100	1530	0339	26.9
17/10	Georgetown	755.5	82.1	1030	1900		24.7
18–20/10	Georgetown						
21/10	Basse-Santa-Su	835.0	79.3	0830	1730	0550	34.0
22–23/10	Basse-Santa-Su						
24/10	Kounkané	893.2	58.2	1100	1700	0414	22.4
25/10	Missara	969.5	76.2	0830	1700	0550	32.0
26/10	Koundara	1028.9	59.4	0830	1730	0544	31.5
27–28/10	Koundara						
29/10	Bensani	1096.6	67.7	0900	1700	0452	30.0
30/10	Kounsitel	1128.1	31.4	0800	1230	0338	29.6
31/10	Bentala	1173.5	45.4	0900	1330	0411	24.8
1/11	Tianguel Bory	1222.5	49.0	1130	1930	0541	33.5
2/11	Horibougou	1251.7	29.1	0800	1700	0443	20.5
3/11	Labé	1296.4	44.7	0800	1600		
4–14/11	Labé	1325.8					
15/11	Pita	1362.5	36.6	1430	1700	0217	47.5
16–17/11	Pita						
18/11	Dalaba	1419.5	57.0	1130	1700	0429	41.5
19–20/11	Dalaba	1430.2					
21/11	Mamou	1486.6	56.4	1300	1530	0339	51.4
22–30/11	Conakry						
30/11	Mamou						
1/12	Timbo	1536.1	49.5	0830	1600	0455	29.6
2/12	Dogomet	1594.4	58.3	0930	1730	0621	27.4
3/12	Dabola	1643.9	48.5	0900	1700		26.2
4/12	Cisséla	1718. 5	74.6	0900	1700	0545	30.5
5/12	Kouroussa	1810.7	92.2	0800	1730	0737	30.5

Date	Stop	Cumulative Distance (km)	Daily Distance (km)	Departure Time	Arrival Time	Cycling Time (hr/min)	Maximum Speed (kmph)
6–7/12	Kouroussa	1814.6					
8/12	Kankan	1900.9	86.3	0730	1630	0704	28.1
9/12	Kankan	1921.5	20.6			0148	19.5
10/12	Kankan	1939.1	17.7			0133	21.3
11/12	Niandakoro	2032.2	93.1	0730	1700	0700	28.4
12/12	Siguiri	2802.0	49.8	0900	1500	0350	22.9
13/12	Doko	2135.2	53.2	0800	1400	0442	29.8
14–15/12	Doko	2168.0					
16/12	Korémale	2201.2	33.2	1400	1600	0243	26.0
17/12	Siby	2280.7	79.5	0800	1730	0714	31.0
18/12	Bamako	2334.2	53.5	0800	1400	0447	25.7
19–28/12	Bamako	2350.9					
29/12	Santiguila	2423.9	72.6	1000	1800		38.0
30/12	Konobougou	2508.2	81.6	0930	1800		24.8
31/12	Ségou	2590.2	83.1	0930	1800		24.8
1993							
1–3/1	Ségou						
4/1	Sansanding	2652.8	62.6	1100	1800		22.1
5/1	Kolongotomo	2699.2	46.4	1100	1830		15.3
6/1	Macina	2741.5	42.0	0930	1600		15.3
7/1	Macina						
8/1	Diafarabé	2790.9	47.9	1230	1830		16.4
9/1	Say	2832.2	41.2	1230	1800		18.3
10/1	Djebbé	2870.7	38.5	1000	1730		21.8
11–14/1	Djenné	2888.4					
15/1	Sofara	2944.6	56.2	1030	1815		18.8
16–21/1	Sevaré	3011.7	67.0	0900	1800		20.2
22–25/1	Niger River						
26/1–4/2	Timbuktu						
5–8/2	Niger River						
9–12/2	Sevaré	3038.7					
13/2	Diallo	3094.1	55.4	1000	1730	0418	24.1
14/2	Bankass	3145.8	51.7	0800	1230	0431	27.8
15/2	Koro	3198.8	53.0	0730	1600	0505	36.5
16/2	Ouahigouya	3300.4	101.6	0730	1830	0749	24.1
17/2	Yako	3378.1	77.1	1030	1830	0545	27.8
18/2	Lay	3457.9	79.8	0800	1800	0633	23.5
19/2	Ougadougou	3492.9	35.0	0700	1300		26.0
20–27/2	Ougadougou	3533.0					
28/2	Bobo-Dioulasso	Train					
1–6/3	Bobo-Dioulasso						
7/3	Ougadougou	Train					
8–12/3	Ougadougou						
13/3	Toéssé	3610.2	77.2	0930	1800	0536	25.7
14/3	Po	3689.2	78.9	0730	1730	0540	27.4
15/3	Bolgatanga	3755.2	66.0	0730	1630	0513	25.0
16–17/3	Bolgatanga						
18/3	Bawku	3850.0	85.2	0700	1900		35.5
19/3–1/4	Bawku	3985.9					
2/4	Garu	4015.7	29.8	0600	0900	0233	18.7
3/4	Nakpandori	4049.4	33.7	0600	1000	0334	24.0

Date	Stop	Cumulative Distance (km)	Daily Distance (km)	Departure Time	Arrival Time	Cycling Time (hr/min)	Maximum Speed (kmph)
4/4	Nakpandori						
5/4	Gushiegu	4144.2	94.8	0630	1800	0707	28.9
6/4	Yendi	4209.3	65.8	0700	1630		
7/4	Bimbilla	4284.9	75.6	0900	1700	0630	24.3
8/4	Salaga	4367.2	82.3	0700	1600	0622	24.8
9/4	Yeji	4401.5	34.3	0630	0930	0238	31.5
10/4	Atebubu	4474.3	72.8	0700	1400	0538	26.2
11/4	Ejura	4537.6	63.3	0700	1400	0526	28.0
12/4	Kumasi	4639.3	101.7	0700	1630	0754	44.0
13/4	Kumasi						
14/4	Accra	Land Rover					
15/4	Kumasi	Bus					
16–19/4	Kumasi	4666.2					
20/4	Obuasi	4732.8	66.6	0700	1500	0533	39.5
21/4	Foso	4823.9	91.1	0800	1700	0643	41.5
22/4	Elmina	4914.5	90.6	0700	1530	0704	41.5
23–24/4	Elmina						
25/5	Apam	5006.0	91.5	0700	1400	0535	45.0
26/4	Winneba	5035.2	29.2	0800	1100	0207	30.5
27–28/4	Winneba						
29/4	Accra	5104.3	69.1	0730	1400	0438	41.0
30/4–8/5	Accra						
9/5	Ada Junction	5199.5	95.3	0800	1500	0609	33.0
10/5	Keta	5293.2	93.6	0900	1730	0631	27.0
11/5	Lomé	5335.7	42.6	0730	1300	0405	19.1
12–15/5	Lomé	5340.1					
16/5	Aneho	5385.2	45.4	0900	1300	0237	32.5
17/5	Grand Popo	5414.2	29.0	0800	1200	0155	22.7
18/5	Cotonou	5512.8	98.4	0730	1900	0704	34.0
19–22/5	Cotonou						
23/5	Grand Popo	Taxi					
24/5–1/6	Grand Popo						
2/6	Cotonou	Taxi					
3/6	Benigbé	5581.4	60.3	1100	1700	0419	40.0
4/6	Ilaro	5646.8	65.4	0830	1730		55.1
5/6	Abeokuta	5714.8	68.0	0830	1500	0507	51.0
6/6	Ibadan	5787.4	72.6	0630	1300	0509	45.5
7/6	Lagos	Car					
8–12/6	Lagos						
13/6	Ibadan	Car					
14/6	Ibadan						
15/6	Iwo	5837.4	50.0	1100	1700	0322	42.0
16/6	Ilesha	5925.6	88.2	0730	1700	0717	42.0
17/6	Akure	6003.2	77.6	0830	1600	0533	49.0
18/6	Ifon	6098.7	95.7	0830	1600	0609	42.5
19/6	Benin City	6191.6	92.8	0730	1600	0634	38.0
20/6	Onitsha	6326.5	134.9	0700	1900	0959	54.0
21/6	Onitsha						
22/6	Owerri	6400.0	73.5	0900	1600	0618	35.0
23/6	Aba	6482.3	82.3	0800	1700	0544	34.0
24/6	Itu	6587.8	105.5	0730	1600	0719	43.0
25/6	Itu						
26/6	Calabar	6665.1	77.3	0930	1530	0553	50.0

Date	Stop	Cumulative Distance (km)	Daily Distance (km)	Departure Time	Arrival Time	Cycling Time (hr/mins)	Maximum Speed (kmph)
27–28/6	Calabar	6685.7					
29/6	Akpat	6790.2	104.5	0900	1630	0610	52.5
30/6	Ikom	6924.0	133.8	0730	1700	0820	55.0
1/7	Eyumojuk	6975.5	51.5	0930	1600	0352	45.5
2/7	Mamfé	7031.4	55.9	0800	1600	0515	26.4
3/7	Mamfé						
4/7	Kendem	7092.4	61.0	0730	1700	0651	27.8
5/7	Tibn	7125.0	32.6	0800	1630	0513	22.2
6/7	Bali	7159.5	34.4	0830	1630	0516	25.8
7/7	Bamenda	7183.9	24.0	1330	1600	0229	30.0
8/7	Bamenda						
9/7	Bamenda Station	7188.7	3.8	1600	1700	0036	32.0
10/7	Bamessing	7216.2	27.5	0700	1900	0454	40.0
11/7	Jakiri	7258.2	42.0	0930	1900	0559	24.4
12/7	Bangourain	7290.7	32.1	1200	1600	0304	27.2
13/7	Foumban	7332.7	41.9	0930	1500	0436	32.0
14–17/7	Foumban	7335.0					
18/7	Bafoussam	7405.1	70.1	0930	1700	0557	55.5
19/7	Bafang	7465.7	60.6	1000	1800	0615	46.5
20/7	Nkongsamba	7525.6	59.9	1000	1730	0538	50.0
21/7	Nyombe	7594.6	69.0	1100	1700	0425	53.5
22/7	Douala	7690.6	96.0	0800	1600	0624	50.0
23/7–2/8	Douala						
3/8	Edea	7761.3	69.9	0845	1500	0433	45.5
4/8	Bounyebel	7854.2	92.8	0930	1800	0645	50.0
5/8	Yaounde	7953.3	99.1	0830	1630	0732	54.5
6–11/8	Yaounde	7957.6					
12/8	Mbalmayo	8006.8	49.2	1030	1500	0315	54.0
13/8	Mbalmayo						
14/8	Mengong	8099.9	93.1	1030	1700	0601	50.0
15/8	Biba	8160.2	60.3	0900	1600		
16/8	Ambam	8235.7	75.5	0930	1700		
17/8	Ebebiyin	8272.8	37.1	1030	1600	0320	33.5
18/8	Beayop	8350.8	78.0	0800	1730	0702	34.5
19/8	Mikomessing	8378.6	27.7	0800	1100	0246	32.0
20/8	Niafang	8445.6	67.0	0830	1500	0505	38.5
21/8	Bata	8520.2	74.6	0830	1430	0528	37.0
22–25/8	Bata	8532.6					
26/8	Malabo						
27/8	Malabo						
28/8	Luba	8589.2	56.6	1300	1700	0344	37.0
29–30/8	Luba	8652.4					
31/8	Boat						
1–2/9	Bata						
3/9	Mbini	8699.3	46.9	1000	1600	0346	33.0
4/9	Mbini						
5/9	Cogo	8791.0	91.7	0800	1630	0647	39.0
6/9	Cocobeach	8792.4	1.4	0830	0900	0018	8.0
7/9	Ntoum	8884.9	92.4	0730	1630	0747	37.0
8/9	Libreville	8928.0	43.2	0800	1100	0232	42.5
9–17/9	Libreville	9059.3					
18/9	Ntoum	9114.8	55.4	1200	1530	0316	49.5
19/9	Kango	9182.7	67.9	1100	1600	0409	39.0

Date	Stop	Cumulative Distance (km)	Daily Distance (km)	Departure Time	Arrival Time	Cycling Time (hr/min)	Maximum Speed (kmph)
20/9	Kango	9187.8	5.1	0830	0930	0024	35.0
21/9	Bifoun	9275.4	87.6	1000	1730	0532	43.5
22./9	Makoke	9316.4	441.0	0930	1200	0307	32.0
23/9	Makoke						
24/9	Lambaréné	9384.0	67.6	0830	1700	0547	44.0
25–27/9	Lambaréné	9404.7					
28/9	Tchad	9467.6	62.9	1300	1700	0439	47.5
29/9	Fougamou	9515.5	47.9	1000	1530	0336	35.5
30/9	Guidouma	9571.0	56.0	1100	1600	0415	22.0
1/10	Mouila	9637.5	66.0	0830	1530	0535	31.0
2/10	Ndendé	9728.0	90.5	1030	1830	0650	34.5
3/10	Moukoro	9768.4	40.5	1300	1700	0314	26.3
4/10	Nyanga	9833.7	65.3	0900	1630		30.0
5/10	Loubetsi	9908.1	74.4	1030	1600	0532	31.0
6/10	Loubetsi						
7/10	Mumanga	9984.3	76.2	0900	1730	0606	23.7
8/10	Dolisie	10059.9	75.6	0730	1700	0654	23.4
9–14/10	Pointe Noire						
15/10	Dolisie						
16/10	Nkayi	10155.9	95.6	0830	1600	0646	35.0
17/10	Bouensa	10229.1	73.2	0900	1630	0549	48.8
18/10	Kinkembo	10300.8	71.8	0900	1600	0621	44.5
19/10	Moundila	10332.2	31.4	0800	1200	0325	29.5
20/10	Kinkala	10401.9	69.7	0900	1800	0642	30.0
21/10	Brazzaville	10488.5	86.6	0830	1630	0613	46.5
22–25/10	Brazzaville	10509.1					
26/10–13/12	Kinshasa	11315.4					
14/12	Matadi	Truck					
15–18/12	Matadi						
19/12	Boma	Car					
20/12	Muanda	Bus					
21/12	Muanda	11346.4	31.0	1030	1600	0250	22.0
22/12	Muanda	11386.2	39.8	1000	1600	0249	50.5
23/12	Muanda	11416.8	30.6	1030	1600	0201	23.1
24–26/12	Muanda	11445.9					
27/12	Matadi						
28/12	Kinshasa	Truck					
29/12–4/1	Kinshasa	11537.1					
1994							
5–9/1	Zaire River						
10/1	Mbandaka	11555.7	19.6				
11–13/1	Zaire River						
14/1	Lisala	11563.0	6.3	arr 0750			
15/1	Zaire River			dep 1100			
16/1	Bumba						
17–18/1	Zaire River						
19/1	Isangi						
20–21/1	Isangi	11614.6					
22/1	Zaire River						
23/1–6/2	Kisangani	11791.8					
7/2	Pene Rukula	11862.9	71.4	1030	1530	0442	50.0
8/2	Batianguma	11943.2	80.3	0830	1630	0550	47.5

Date	Stop	Cumulative Distance (km)	Daily Distance (km)	Departure Time	Arrival Time	Cycling Time (hr/min)	Maximum Speed (kmph)
9/2	Utiandulu	12027.5	83.5	0800	1700	0557	47.5
10/2	Lubutu	12072.9	45.4	0800	1230	0309	46.5
11/2	Ungele	12215.9	84.4	0900	1700	0546	52.5
12/2	Utaweza	12248.3	91.0	0830	1700	0646	48.5
13/2	Walikale	12301.6	53.3	0800	1300	0416	48.0
14/2	Walikale						
15/2	Itebero	12342.6	41.0	1200	1600	0335	33.0
16/2	Hombo	12421.4	78.8	0800	1830	0755	33.0
17/2	Miowe	12465.2	43.8	1030	1600	0413	47.0
18/2	Tshivanga	12504.4	39.2	0730	1800	0722	34.5
19/2	Tshivanga						
20/2	Bukavu	12539.8	35.4	1000	1300	0232	42.0
21/2	Bukavu	12554.0	10.4			0053	31.0
22/2	Cibitoke	12635.5	81.4	0800	1730	0604	52.5
23/2	Bujumbura	12720.8	85.3	0700	1700	0517	56.5
24–28/2	Bujumbura	12745.6					
1/3	Resha	12811.3	65.6	0900	1400	0347	53.5
2/3	Resha	12819.6	8.4			0033	29.0
3/3	Nyanza-Lac	12893.5	73.9	1030	1600	0441	50.0
4/3	Manyovu	12939.4	45.9	0800	1800	0623	52.5
5/3	Kigoma	13012.3	72.9	0830	1830	0714	33.0
6–10/3	Kigoma	13049.5					
11/3	Kalenge	13098.7	49.3	1000	1900	0639	29.4
12/3	Uvinza	13171.7	73.0	0830	1600	0636	25.8
13/3	Malagarasi	13232.7	61.0	0900	1800	0626	17.8
14/3	Nguruka	13257.7	25.0	0930	1430	0258	14.9
15/3	Kombe	13325.3	67.6	1030	1830	0626	22.2
16/3	Urambo	13396.9	71.5	0930	1600	0620	23.0
17/3	Tabora	13496.7	99.8	0900	1930	0828	23.8
18–22/3	Tabora	13551.0					
23/3	Inara	13567.5	16.5	1100	1400	0144	20.6
24/3	Kigwe	13603.2	35.6	0830	1130	0330	29.6
25/3	Melongwe	13682.9	79.7	0830	1900	0746	27.0
26/3	Tura	13732.5	49.6	0830	1600	0535	23.4
27/3	Kitaraka	13797.8	65.3	1030	1830	0601	21.7
28/3	Manyoni	13864.1	66.3	0900	1730	0605	23.6
29/3	Bahi	13940.2	76.9	1000	1900	0632	26.1
30/3	Dodoma	14009.4	69.2	0930	1800	0644	25.6
31/3–1/4	Dodoma	14021.9					
2/4	Naco Ranch	14114.6	92.7	1100	1930	0700	34.5
3/4	Barega	14206.2	91.6	1000	1900	0704	44.5
4/4	Morogoro	14324.0	117.6	0730	1730	0803	49.0
5/4	Ubenzomozi	14384.5	60.5	1200	1600	0323	55.5
6/4	Kibaha	14481.9	97.4	0800	1800	0638	52.5
7/4	Dar Es Salaam	14526.6	44.7	1100	1600	0309	46.0

Bibliography

Adamolekun, Ladipo, *Sékou Touré's Guinea, An Experiment in Nation Building*, London, Methuen, 1976.

'*Au revoir*, Mobutu Sese Seko – or is it *adieu?*' *The Economist*, 10 May 1997, p. 67.

Battuta, Ibn, *Travels in Asia and Africa 1325–1354*, London, Routledge & Kegan Paul, 1984.

Bayliss, Philippa, *An Introduction to Primal Religions*, Edinburgh, T. & T. Clark, 1988.

Brodie, Fawn, *The Devil Drives*, London, Eland, 1986.

Chamberlain, M. E., *The Scramble for Africa*, Harlow, Essex, Longman Group, 1995.

Collins, Robert O., *Western Africa History, Vol. I of African History: Text and Readings*, Princeton, New Jersey, Markus Wiener Publishing, 1990.

Collins, Robert O., *Eastern Africa History, Vol. II of African History: Text and Readings*, Princeton, New Jersey, Markus Wiener Publishing, 1990.

Collins, Robert O., *Central and South African History, Vol. III of African History: Text and Readings*, Princeton, New Jersey, Markus Wiener Publishing, 1990.

Cooper, Christine, and Schaffer, Matt, *Mandinko, The Ethnography of a West African Holy Land*, London, Holt, Rinehart and Winston, 1980.

Crowther, Geoff, *et al*, *Africa on a Shoestring*, 6th edn, London, Lonely Planet, 1992.

Davidson, Basil, *The Story of Africa*, London, Mitchell Beazley, 1984.

'Ex-Rwandan Prime Minister Gets Life Term for Genocide', *International Herald Tribune*, 5–6 September 1998, p. 6.

Haynes, Jeff, *Third World Politics, A Concise Introduction*, Oxford, Blackwell, 1996.

'Heading for an African War', *The Economist*, 5 September 1998, pp. 61–2.

Hudgens, Jim and Trillo, Richard, *West Africa, The Rough Guide*, London, The Rough Guides, 1995.

Imperato, Pascal James, *Mali, A Search for Direction*, Colorado, Westview Press, 1990.

Kingsley, Mary, *Travels in West Africa*, London, Everyman's Library, 1992.

Laye, Camara, *The African Child*, trans. James Kirkup, London, Fontana, 1980.

Manning, Olivia, *The Remarkable Expedition*, London, Weidenfeld & Nicolson, 1985.

Martin, Phyllis M. and O'Meara, Patrick, eds, *Africa*, 3rd edn, Oxford, James Currey, 1995.

Newton, Alex, *Central Africa, A Travel Survival Kit*, London, Lonely Planet, 1996.

Park, Mungo, *Travels Into the Interior of Africa*, London, Eland Books, 1983.

Parrinder, Edward Geoffrey, *West African Religion*, 3rd edn, Peterborough, Epworth Press, 1969.

Prunier, Gérard, *The Rwanda Crisis – History of a Genocide*, London, Hurst & Co., 1997.

'Rebellion Spreads in Congo', *The Economist*, 15 August 1998, p. 47.

Riviére, Claude, *Guinea, The Mobilization of a People*, Ithaca, New York, Cornell University Press, 1977.

Scott, Earl, ed., *Life Before the Drought*, Sydney, Allen & Unwin, 1984.

'Shellman says sorry', *The Economist*, 10 May 1997.

Shillington, Kevin, *History of Africa*, rev. edn, Basingstoke, Macmillan Education, 1995.

'Triumph of the Old Guerrilla Network', *Sunday Times*, 11 May 1997.

'War in the Heart of Africa', *The Economist*, 22 August 1998, p. 44.

Whitaker's Almanack 1998, London, The Stationery Office, 1998.

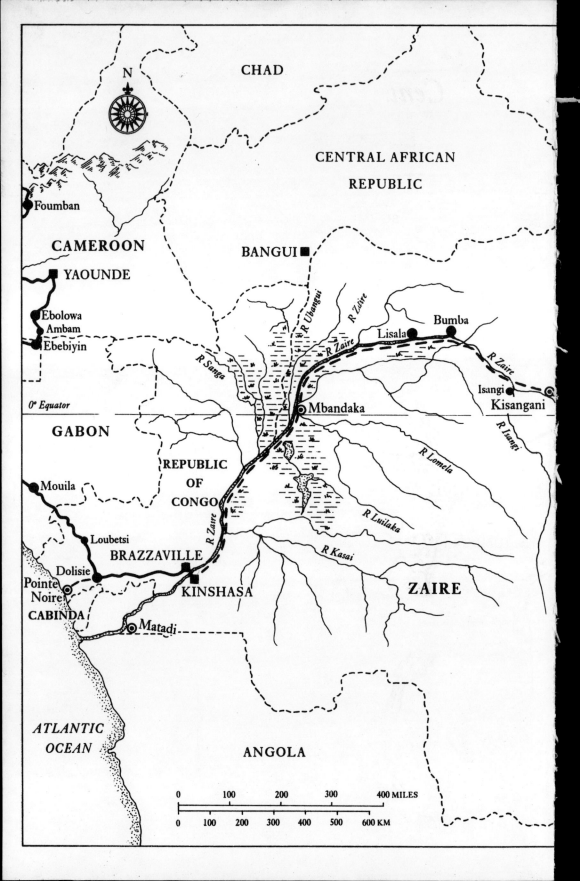